D0090068

THE GAMBLE

John Sides and Lynn Vavreck

THE GAMBLE

Choice and Chance in the 2012 Presidential Election

With a new preface by the authors

PRINCETON UNIVERSITY PRESS

Princeton and Oxford

Copyright © 2013 by Princeton University Press

Published by Princeton University Press, 41 William Street,
Princeton, New Jersey 08540
In the United Kingdom: Princeton University Press, 6 Oxford Street,
Woodstock, Oxfordshire OX20 1TW

press.princeton.edu

All Rights Reserved

Fourth printing and first paperback printing, with a new preface by the authors, 2014

ISBN 978-0-691-15688-0
Paperback ISBN 978-0-691-16363-5

Library of Congress Control Number: 2013942892

British Library Cataloging-in-Publication Data is available

This book has been composed in Minion and Ideal Sans

Printed on acid-free paper. ∞

Printed in the United States of America

10 9 8 7 6

To Serena, Ethan, and Hannah, with gratitude and love.—JMS

This one's for you, Larry—for professional inspiration and personal grounding. And for you, Jeff, for the opposite.—LVL

CONTENTS

FIGURES AND TABLES

PREFACE TO THE PAPERBACK EDITION

The scientific study of presidential elections arguably dates back to a 1948 book called *The People's Choice*. Its authors, Paul Lazarsfeld, Bernard Berelson, and Hazel Gaudet, set out to understand the 1940 presidential race between President Franklin Roosevelt and Wendell Willkie in an unprecedented fashion. Setting up shop in Erie County, Ohio, they interviewed a sample of residents every month from May through November of the election year, thereby tracking the opinions of the same people interviewed at multiple points in time.

What they found was surprising to many. At a time when the rise of fascism and the development of mass media—especially radio—had raised fears about people's susceptibility to propaganda, Lazarsfeld and colleagues found that people's views of the candidates were mostly stable. Very few people switched their support from Roosevelt to Willkie, or vice versa. Campaign propaganda did not seem as powerful as many believed it would be.

But the campaign still mattered, just in more subtle ways. For one, it helped to reinforce the opinions people already had. If you were a Roosevelt supporter, the campaign solidified this choice. The campaign also pushed undecided voters to the candidate that they were already predisposed to support. Undecided voters whose demographic profile made them look like Democrats mostly ended up supporting Roosevelt, and those who looked like Republicans mostly ended up supporting Willkie. Lazarsfeld and colleagues showed that a campaign could be consequential, even in an electorate in which many voters were not up for grabs.

In the years after this book, other scholars began to use social science methods and data to study elections. Lazarsfeld would help author a second book, this one about the 1948 election. Not long afterward, a team of social scientists at the University of Michigan wrote other seminal books about voting behavior and elections—particularly *The American Voter*—as well as articles about individual presidential elections that were published not long after the elections themselves. More recently, there have been notable book-length studies of the tumultuous 2000 presidential election and the historic 2008 election, when the first African-American, Barack Obama, was elected president.

The Gamble fits squarely in this tradition. It is the story of how Republicans nominated Mitt Romney to challenge Barack Obama in 2012, and how Obama ultimately won reelection. We tell this story using similar kinds of tools as these earlier books, including quantitative data and statistical methods. Indeed, one of our central sources of data is a survey not unlike the one in Erie County, Ohio: multiple interviews with the same set of voters over the year before the election. The main difference is whereas that 1940 survey focused on 600 voters in one county, ours includes 45,000 voters across the United States. These tools help us to identify why voters decided as they did and how the campaign affected them along the way. This, in turn, helps explain why Obama won and what implications his reelection has for party competition in future elections.

There is a parallel tradition of campaign narratives written by journalists. In fact, perhaps the canonical book in this tradition—Theodore White's *The Making of the President*—was published not long after the first social scientific accounts appeared, when White documented the 1960 election between Richard Nixon and John F. Kennedy. White would write other installments after the 1964, 1968, and 1972 presidential elections.

Journalists working in this tradition rely on different sources of information than do social scientists. Rather than crunch data, they spend many months on the campaign trail, following the candidates. They conduct interviews with the candidates, their campaign strategists, and sometimes a small number of voters. These books seek to answer a similar question about the election—why did the winner win?—but mainly by focusing on the decisions the candidates made. These books thus paint vivid pictures of the characters in the campaign—their personalities, their strengths and weaknesses, their foibles and eccentricities. These books dwell on dramatic moments. They tell lots of good stories. After the 2012 election, several such books were written, including Dan Balz's *Collision 2012* and Mark Halperin and John Heilemann's *Double Down: Game Change 2012*.

The Gamble differs in key respects from these books. We lack the access to the candidates that journalists can negotiate; and thus we cannot ask the candidates why they did what they did. What we can do, however, is figure out whether their actions made an impact on voters. That is where those 45,000 voters, a few graphs, and the statistics waiting in the appendix become useful.

To take one example, consider a storyline being pushed by Romney after his loss. He blamed his loss on the fact that Obama had given "gifts" to key constituencies. For instance, Obama's signature achievement in his first term, health care reform, mandated insurance coverage of contraceptives. Romney argued that "free contraceptives" helped Obama woo female voters. In *Double Down,* Halperin and Heilemann report Romney's claim, but lacking any means of testing it and any countervailing data from the Obama campaign, they let the claim stand. By contrast, we use our survey data to examine how much the debate over reproductive rights affected voters. Contrary to Romney's claim, we found that the issue of reproductive rights did more to keep male voters from *leaving* Obama than it did to attract women to him. Most women for whom this issue was important had already chosen their candidate before the debate about contraception and the controversies that followed throughout 2012.

To be sure, both kinds of books about an election are valuable. It is important to understand what was going on inside campaign war rooms and what was going on inside the voting booth. Each tradition—social science and journalism—can complement the other. When they diverge, however, we think that science should be privileged, to the extent that it rigorously tests competing claims using carefully collected data. Interestingly, this belief has become prevalent not only among scientists, but also among some journalists and a fair bit of the population. Hard data and scientific approaches increasingly animate the conversation within journalism, perhaps most visibly in outlets like Nate Silver's 538 website (which lived at the *New York Times* during 2012) and the wonkish blogging of Ezra Klein (in 2012 at the *Washington Post*). Campaigns are increasingly scientific themselves—gathering data, running experiments, and constructing statistical models to predict voter turnout and preferences for the candidates. Modern campaign strategy increasingly resembles what Sasha Issenberg provocatively called "The Victory Lab" in his book of the same title. There is every reason to think, then, that the understanding of campaigns and their effects will draw more and more on approaches similar to ours.

Part of *The Gamble*'s contribution draws directly on its social science lineage. In essence, previous studies told us where to look to identify important patterns and the likely impact of the campaign. For example, 70 years after the Erie County study, we find that many of the same patterns still exist. Preferences for Obama or Romney tended to be stable for the vast majority of Americans, and relatively few switched their support from one to the other. At the same time, the campaign helped to reinforce the views of those who appeared to make up their mind early on. And for those who remained undecided, the campaign led them to a predictable choice:

undecided Democrats mostly gravitated to Obama and undecided Republicans to Romney.

We also push in directions less well-explored in the previous literature. One direction concerns presidential primaries, which remain vastly under-studied relative to presidential general elections. Indeed, the last major study of campaign dynamics in presidential primaries—Larry Bartels's *Presidential Primaries*—was published in 1988. The 2012 presidential primary was a propitious one to study, as it featured a highly fluid Republican race with multiple frontrunners. We are able to show that the ups and downs in the polls followed a predictable pattern, driven largely by news coverage. We also show that Mitt Romney—who never experienced any real ups or downs and was often underestimated by commentators—remained the frontrunner by several key measures. Part of our contribution stems from new technologies that automatically gather and analyze news coverage from thousands of media outlets. This allows us to ascertain how much and what kind of attention the media paid to each candidate, and to do so in nearly real time as the campaign unfolded.

Another less-explored direction concerns the general election campaign. Only recently have scholars been able to measure the volume of advertising and field activity with anything approaching precision. In 2012, we marry data on both ads and field mobilization to our survey data and to data on the election results. This allows us to evaluate the impact of various forms of campaigning simultaneously and in comparison to other factors that affect election outcomes, such as the state of the economy.

Three key findings emerge. First, we show that when either Obama or Romney was able to out-advertise the other, the polls could move—but the effects of the ads typically wore off quickly. This contrasts with a piece of conventional wisdom from 2012: that the Obama campaign's decision to air an early advertising blitz in the summer helped defeat Romney. In all likelihood, the effects of the summer ads on vote choice had long worn off by November.

Second, the Obama campaign's field organization appears to have earned Obama votes, and more than Romney's field organization earned him. But the number of votes won was not likely large enough to determine the outcome in crucial battleground states. This again contrasts with the conventional wisdom, which attributed his victory, implicitly or explicitly, to the strategic mastery of the Obama campaign on the ground.

Finally, the kinds of campaign effects that we identify—which certainly appear real—are small compared to the fundamental factors that affect elections. Romney would have needed vast quantities of additional campaign resources—over and above the $1.2 billion he and his allies already had—to offset the advantages Obama had as an incumbent president presiding over a slowly growing economy.

Our account, however, remains necessarily limited. The scientific understanding of an election takes time, and we will be learning more about 2012 for years. For one, 2012 certainly showed that money raised by outside groups is becoming a larger part of the money spent in an election campaign. The question is what impact it has, and whether its impact differs much from money raised by the candidates themselves. For example, during the Republican presidential primary, a few wealthy supporters of Newt Gingrich and Rick Santorum contributed millions of dollars to outside groups supporting them. Did this encourage Gingrich and Santorum to stay in the race longer, even though winning the nomination was always a long shot? Groups supporting Romney also raised a great deal of money during the primary and general election campaigns. How much did this help him? Would it have been preferable to raise more of his own money and rely less on these groups, given that Romney's campaign team could have directly controlled how that money was spent?

The impact of new campaign tools also remains a contested subject. The tools of "The Victory Lab" have led to many innovations, especially in Democratic campaigns. In 2012, the Obama campaign used experiments with its fundraising emails to determine, for example, what kinds of subject lines would generate the most donations. Other innovations of the Obama campaign—such as having its supporters contact targeted voters via Facebook—also received a great deal of press. However, we know little about the impact of many of these innovations. There is no question that campaigns will continue to innovate—in how they deliver advertising to voters, in social media, and in other kinds of tactics and strategies. Measuring effectiveness, however, remains a significant challenge.

On the first page of *The People's Choice*, the authors write: "Every four years, the country stages a large-scale experiment in political propaganda and public opinion." This statement reminds us that, however consequential Barack Obama's victory in 2012 proves to be, this particular election is just one of many that have occurred and will occur. Future elections will likely refine and improve on what we have learned to date.

FOREWORD

Many books are written about presidential elections. Journalists typically write the first accounts after the election. Too often the work of political scientists on this election follows years later, coming out when journalists and politicians are deep into the weeds of the next election. This means that common interpretations of what happened in a particular election and broader analyses of electoral politics outside the academy do not reflect the research done by political scientists because this work comes out too late or is too technical in its presentation.

To some extent blogging has helped bring the views of political scientists to the public earlier. In addition, political campaigns increasingly hire social scientists to conduct analysis while the election is unfolding, but most of that work is proprietary and not publicly available. Finally, prominent journalists, particularly the new breed of wonkier analysts, frequently draw on the work of political scientists to inform their work. But this is all fragmentary and rarely presented in a book that is accessible to the lay public as well as experts.

This book is an effort to bring to the analysis of the 2012 presidential election the insights of first-rate political scientists at a speed that matches the publication of books by journalists while taking advantage of the web to offer first versions of many of the chapters while the election unfolded. By publishing some of the chapters on the web as quickly after events like the primaries and the conventions as possible, the authors and the Press sought to make this analysis part of the current reporting on the election.

We also asked the authors to write in a way that captures the drama of electoral politics for the public. I asked them to tell this as a story with a strong narrative line, a political *telenovela*.

To do this required the authors to give up the traditional process of academic writing with the preparation of papers that are presented to their academic peers at conferences and the writing of peer-reviewed articles, all culminating in a manuscript that itself is reviewed and revised before publication. It required them to jettison as much of the field's technical jargon as possible. It is a bold move for the authors and it is their gamble. Let me be clear that this manuscript was subject to peer review. Indeed we are in debt to the reviewers who agreed to read the manuscript in pieces and understood the audiences inside and outside the academy we wanted to reach. This was supplemented by a kind of crowd-sourcing of the reviewing process, with the authors receiving reactions to the chapters available on the web.

At the same time the Press has taken its own gamble. We made chapters of the book available for free download beginning immediately before the conventions. These chapters stimulated discussion and comments on the ideas the authors put forward as well as on their empirical research on the campaigns and on public opinion. Our hope is that this will highlight the contributions political science can make to our understanding of elections and create better-informed coverage of not only this election but elections in the future. We hope that the free downloads will stimulate interest in the book itself.

Just as the election was a gamble for the parties and the candidates, this book is a gamble for the authors and the Press. It is a gamble that I believe has paid off, but the final verdict is up to you, the readers.

Charles T. Myers,
for Princeton University Press

ACKNOWLEDGMENTS

We are grateful to so many people who, from the very beginning of the project, helped us write this book. We wanted to enter the conversation among journalists about the 2012 election and were delighted to be welcomed into that conversation by so many of them. We thank the political reporters, editors, and commentators who gave us advice, read a chapter of the manuscript, listened to an early presentation of our findings, and/or took our work seriously, in both casual conversation and their work. These include Mark Barabak, Molly Ball, Dan Balz, Jonathan Chait, Jon Cohen, Nate Cohn, Jay Cost, John Dickerson, E. J. Dionne, Ron Elving, Sam Feist, Craig Gilbert, Joshua Green, Chris Hayes, John Hockenberry, Caroline Horn, Sasha Issenberg, Ezra Klein, Steve Kornacki, David Lauter, David Leonhardt, Ryan Lizza, Alec MacGillis, Charles Mahtesian, Scott McLemee, Doyle McManus, Gregory McNamee, Roger McShane, Peter Overby, Guy Raz, Aaron Retica, Benjy Sarlin, Walter Shapiro, Nate Silver, James Surowiecki, Sean Trende, Romesh Vaitlingam, James Warren, Frank Wilkinson, and Jeff Zeleny. We are particularly grateful to Paul Glastris, Ezra Klein, Aaron Retica, and Nate Silver for giving us outlets at the *Washington Monthly*, Wonkblog, Campaign Stops, and 538, respectively, where we could publish initial analyses and essentially crowd-source some of the review process via their readers and commenters. We thank two readers in particular, Patrick Kennedy and David Scocca, who wrote to us of their own accord with useful suggestions. We also thank Kevin Quealy for his help in designing several of the graphs in this book. A handful of political professionals and campaign staff answered our questions and helped us understand the decisions campaigns and candidates make in real time. These include Fred Davis, Alex Gage, Rayid Ghani, Craig Handzlik, Alex Lundry, Keith Nahigian, Brett O'Donnell, and Dan Wagner. We are grateful for their time, trust, and candor.

Many of our colleagues in political science provided valuable feedback on analyses and drafts of chapters: Larry Bartels, Heath Brown, Lara Brown, Kevin Collins, Morris Fiorina, Alan Gerber, Danny Hayes, Marc Hetherington, Seth Hill, Gary Jacobson, Phillip Klinkner, Brendan Nyhan, Michael Tesler, and the anonymous peer reviewers of the manuscript. In particular, Larry Bartels and Danny Hayes went above and beyond the call of duty by reading substantial chunks of the manuscript. And Larry Bartels in particular pushed us to think harder and take more seriously the dynamics at work in the campaign. This book would not be the same without his input and attention. We are also grateful to audiences at places where we presented some of our findings: Vanderbilt University, the University of Maryland, the Russell Sage Foundation, the Washington DC American Politics Workshop, the University of Massachusetts, Washington University–St. Louis, Princeton University, Fordham University, the University of Denver, the University of British Columbia, Iowa State University, the University of Minnesota–Twin Cities, Seton Hall University, Greenberg Quinlan Rosner Research, the National Academy of Sciences, Chapman University, UCLA, the University of California, Berkeley, and Binghamton University. We thank Seth Masket not only for inviting us to the University of Denver but also for collaborating with us in examining the impact of Obama's and Romney's field offices.

Analyzing and writing about the election in real time necessitates high-quality survey data—and a lot of it. We thank Doug Rivers, the Chief Innovations Officer at YouGov, Inc., who partnered with us and through the 2012 Cooperative Campaign Analysis Project provided the survey data that underpin much of the book. He also gave us a platform, the Model Politics blog, to preview findings from the data. We also thank Adam Myers at YouGov for responding to our many questions and requests, week in and week out. We thank Gary Jacobson, Mark Blumenthal of Pollster, Matt Barreto of Latino Decisions, Jay Leve of Survey USA, and Tom Jensen of Public Policy Polling for their help in obtaining other polling data. Paul Hitlin of the Pew Center for Excellence in Journalism and Alex Griswold of General Sentiment provided important data on media content and tone. John Geer of Vanderbilt University teamed with us to purchase a license from The Nielsen Company that allowed us access to advertising data at a daily level. Josh Putnam supplied valuable data on primary delegate counts. Hans Noel and Martin Cohen supplied data on endorsements in previous presidential primaries. This project would not exist without the generosity of all these people. We also thank those who helped us with research assistance: Jessica Burnell, Colm Fox, Jake Haselswerdt, Justine Huetteman, Brian Law, and John Ray. And for their help in producing a video about the book, we thank Sebastian Hernandez, Matt Boatright-Simon, and Meg Sullivan in the UCLA Media Relations office.

The original motivation for this book was to give political science a louder voice in this conversation about the 2012 election. To do that, we knew we had to write and release chapters as the campaign was unfolding and ultimately release the book in its entirety within several months of the election. No university press had ever done such a thing—and, not being political reporters with inside scoop to dish, we suspected that trade presses would not be very interested. Fortunately, Princeton University Press was willing to take a chance. We thank Peter Dougherty, Eric Crahan, Terri O'Prey, Jenn Backer, and Jessica Pellien for their support and patience with us in shepherding, improving, and promoting this project. Most of all, we thank our original editor, Chuck Myers, who recognized this as an opportunity for academic publishing to innovate. He convinced his board to trust him (and us) and came up with a way to provide rigorous peer review despite the accelerated pace of this project. We thank him and Princeton University Press for their confidence, encouragement, and support.

Our deepest gratitude goes to our friends and families who were often the collateral damage *The Gamble* left in its wake. One Saturday afternoon in February, five-year-old Ethan Sides got up from a nap and went looking for a playmate, only to find his sister still sleeping, his mother out running errands, and his father hunkered down, working on this book. After his father put him off repeatedly, Ethan got a piece of paper and a pen, went to his playroom, copied some words from one of the road signs from his train set, and then returned to tape those words to the door of the home office: "DO NOT ENTER." By way of explanation, he added: "So you'll play with me more." Both Ethan and Hannah are hereby promised a lot more Saturday afternoons. That promise extends to all the people close to us who have gotten less of our time than they wanted in the last year and half. Most importantly, Serena Wille and Jeff Lewis, who took on much more than their usual (large) share of household management, child care, and many other tasks, are getting their spouses back. We are grateful for their sacrifices, which enabled us to spend more time writing, analyzing data, traveling, and speaking. Without Serena, much perspective on this project would have been lost. And without Jeff, we would still be organizing data.

Finally, we thank everyone who read the e-chapters and blog posts and then engaged us in discussing this election. We hope our experiment with e-publishing encourages other scholars to consider publicizing their work while it is underway—thereby promoting political science to journalists, politicians, and citizens alike. It strikes us that two winners of the 2012 election were data and science, and we hope that they only grow more prominent in campaign strategy, reporting, and commentary. The scientific study of politics has never been more relevant.

THE GAMBLE

CHAPTER 1

Ante Up

Here is a number: 68. That is how many moments were described as "game-changers" in the 2012 presidential election, according to an exhaustive search by Tim Murphy, a reporter at *Mother Jones* magazine. A few of these allegedly game-changing moments were cited in jest. The writer for the Celebritology blog at the *Washington Post* joked that the troubled actress Lindsay Lohan's endorsement of Mitt Romney could be a game-changer. A few of these moments were plausibly important, like the raid that killed Osama bin Laden. But the rest of the list is comprised largely of blips that failed to transform the race: the attempted recall of Wisconsin governor Scott Walker, Ann Romney's speech at the Republican National Convention, the *Des Moines Register*'s endorsement of Mitt Romney, a video of a Barack Obama speech from 1998, and so on and on. All told, Murphy found that the term "game-changer" had been mentioned almost twenty thousand times in the ten months before the election. It was, according to one reporter, the single worst cliché of the campaign.[1]

The search for "game-changers" may make for grabby headlines, but it does not really help us understand presidential elections in general and the 2012 presidential election in particular. American presidential elections are rarely decided by a single moment that changes everything. Instead, presidential elections depend on national conditions, especially the state of the economy, and the candidates' efforts to mobilize and persuade voters. Both are important. Our goal in this book is to understand what role these factors, including some of the 68 alleged game-changers, played in deciding the

2012 election and what that might teach us about the dynamics of presidential campaigns. In other words, how and why did Obama win again? Our answer turns more on the advantages incumbent presidents have even in slowly growing economies and less on television advertising or field organizations, although we will investigate the effectiveness of both of these, too. Could Romney have won? To do so, he would have needed large advantages in campaign effort that were hard to achieve in a presidential election that pitted two qualified, well-financed candidates against one another. That neither Romney nor Obama had a large and sustained advantage helps explain how the $2.3 billion that they and their allies spent did not move the polls very much. Presidential campaigns do affect people, but because Obama and Romney matched each other almost dollar for dollar, the effects of this campaign were often in equal and opposite directions.

Choice and Chance

We think of an election outcome as having two ingredients: choice and chance. By *choice*, we mean the choices that the media make—in terms of who and what to cover, and how to cover them—and the choices that candidates make, such as their message, when and where to run advertisements, and how much to invest in a field organization. By focusing on choice, we zero in on many of the things that were called game-changers—if not quite all 68. By *chance*, we mean the circumstances in which candidates find themselves and over which they have less control, such as how well the economy is doing, who their opponent is, who endorses them, and the balance of Democrats and Republicans in the electorate. We call these circumstances the "fundamentals" of elections. They are the national conditions that set the stage for the campaign. By studying choice and chance simultaneously, we can compare their impact. We can evaluate how much work the fundamentals do to influence elections alongside the work that candidates do to win votes. This helps us answer such questions as: roughly how much campaigning might be necessary to overcome a disadvantage in the fundamentals?

Our story has three central lessons. First, as political science research has long shown, the fundamentals structure outcomes in advance of the campaign. They provide predictability and stability to how people vote and thus to who wins elections. The fundamentals typically do not make for headlines about "game-changers." But they make a difference. In the Republican primary election, support within the network of party leaders strengthened Romney's campaign and helped him survive a series of challenges from the other candidates. In the general election, people's longstanding identification with a political party was a powerful influence: most people who actually voted knew how they would vote a year before the general election. Moreover, the advantages based on economic fundamentals were hard to dislodge. In 2012, a slowly growing economy was enough to make Obama the favorite, and that advantage was borne out on Election Day.

Second, media coverage and campaign strategies can shift votes, thereby creating volatility in the race. But this happens only when the coverage and campaigning favor one side—such that one candidate dominates the airwaves, for example. In the Republican presidential primary, news coverage and intense campaigning produced instability because lopsided moments occurred often, creating the surges of many different candidates. But in the general election, news coverage and intensive campaigning were accompanied by stability among voters precisely because Obama's and Romney's efforts were so balanced. We liken the general election period to a "dynamic equilibrium," whereby a vigorous and dynamic campaign often produced a stable equilibrium in the polls.

Third, when imbalances during the campaign do occur, their effects are often short-lived. In the primary, the surges of the candidates were sustained by favorable coverage that came after the media's "discovery" of the candidate's potential. But within a few weeks, increased media scrutiny of the surging candidate helped bring about the candidate's decline. In the general election, where the media coverage did not systematically favor either candidate, it was the political advertisements whose effect did not last long. Any advertising advantage that Obama or Romney opened up in the battleground states on a Monday would shift votes in his favor that day. But most of that shift would be gone by Tuesday unless the campaign sustained its advantage. And because both Obama and Romney, combined with their allies, spent roughly a billion dollars each, it was tough for either candidate to dominate the airwaves for long. The Obama and Romney campaigns largely neutralized each other's efforts, leaving Obama, the candidate who benefited most from the underlying fundamentals, the eventual winner.

Our Moneyball Approach to Understanding Political Campaigns

"We're picking up steam," a tired but enthusiastic Romney campaign staffer told Vavreck in September. "The rallies seem really energized. People love him. We're going to win this thing!" According to a top Romney strategist, staff who traveled to battleground-state rallies from the campaign's Boston headquarters came back and said the same thing as Election Day approached. One staff member who attended a rally in Philadelphia said, "That is not what a losing campaign looks like." Yes, it just "felt" like Romney had momentum. But believing in the size of the rallies showed how feelings and gut instinct could lead you astray.

These stories reminded us of *Moneyball: The Art of Winning an Unfair Game*. In this book, Michael Lewis describes how Billy Beane, the now famous general manager of the Oakland Athletics, turned baseball into "moneyball" by eschewing expensive superstar players—which the team could not afford given its small payroll—and building a team of bargain players who had undervalued skills. Beane found these players by using data to identify the specific skills that were most important for winning games and then finding lesser-known players who had those skills. His old-fashioned scouts were skeptics of this approach, rejecting the data for what they "knew" in their gut to be true about players.

Today, virtually every baseball team uses advanced statistical analyses to evaluate players, and moneyball has bled into other areas, including elections. More and more, campaigns are not relying on intuition but on data about what does and does not work to persuade and mobilize voters. The Obama campaign pushed further in this direction than any previous campaign. For example, they sent out different fund-raising emails to random groups of supporters to see which subject lines and messages would generate the most contributions. Before these tests, Obama's staff members sometimes bet on which email would be the most effective. As one later reported—in a telling indictment of relying only on instinct—"We basically found our guts were worthless."[2]

Moneyball may have infiltrated campaigns but unfortunately not a great deal of political commentary. The same bits of folklore are trotted out as if they are fact in election after election. For example, "undecided voters break for the challenger" emerged again in 2012, especially among Romney supporters who believed it meant they were destined to win. One of our major motivations in writing this book was to inject a bit of "moneyball" into our understanding of presidential campaigns—to do for *explanations* of why the winner won what forecasters like the *New York Times*'s Nate Silver or the *Huffington Post*'s (and fellow political scientist) Simon Jackman did to *predict* who would win. Our approach is deeply informed by data and seeks to test the instincts and pet hypotheses of commentators, practitioners, reporters, and academics alike in a rigorous and scientific manner. The best way to know whether Obama won because of his ground game or Romney lost because he was perceived as an out-of-touch plutocrat is to delve into hard numbers on field organization or voters' perceptions of Romney and estimate their effect, while simultaneously accounting for competing explanations. Other books may spell out why the campaigns did what they did, but *The Gamble* demonstrates whether what they did made any difference.

Our approach goes beyond firsthand accounts from campaign insiders. While insiders can provide valuable insight into why decisions were made, their assessments of whether those decisions made any difference may be biased. To be fair, a strategist's job is only to win an election. In the heat of a campaign, they do not have the time to conduct a science experiment to figure out what is working. Nevertheless, after the campaign, insiders often act as if they know exactly what worked and why. If their candidate won, the argument too often goes, then clearly what they did worked. They have an incentive to exaggerate the campaign's impact and the genius of their own strategizing. After all, if people perceive them to be brilliant, it helps ensure they get hired when the next election comes around. We are not suggesting that all campaign consultants do this. But the temptation is always there, and it makes relying on only paid strategists to understand how much the campaign affected voters a bit like relying on doctors who are paid by a drug company to tell us whether its new drug works. The incentives for campaign consultants are all wrong.

By contrast, journalists and commentators—who also opine on why an election turned out as it did—are more likely to provide something campaign operatives often cannot or will not: actual scrutiny of what campaigns did and said, which sometimes sheds light on the true consequences of campaigning, including ones that the operatives would prefer to downplay. But journalists also face conflicting incentives. After all, it will not make the front page to write that nothing important is happening on the campaign trail or that the candidate gave the same speech today that he gave yesterday and the day before that. So at times journalists seem to "root for the story"— suggesting that campaign moments may be, could be, might be critical. Maybe even game-changers. As one writer for a major political publication told us during the campaign, "I generally try to spot potential trends before they become conventional wisdom." Of course, trying to "spot potential trends" can mean pushing a dramatic thesis well before the evidence actually backs it up. Journalistic accounts of campaigns also tend to put journalists themselves in the background. These accounts implicitly suggest that journalists are merely observers of the story of an election rather than characters in that story—even though, as we will show, the tenor of news coverage can profoundly affect the public's views of the candidates, especially during primary elections.

In explaining the 2012 election, we take conventional wisdom and political reporting seriously, investigating many campaign moments to see how they may have moved voters. But we also draw on a rich research tradition in political science and other social sciences that evaluates the effects of presidential campaigns. This research identifies patterns that occur and reoccur over many elections, giving us a sense of what to look for and where to look for it. Indeed, we are but one in a long series of political science studies of individual elections, stretching back to the 1940 presidential race.

We draw on multitudes of data from the 2012 election and previous elections. Historical data on the economy, presidential approval, and presidential election outcomes. Data from hundreds of public polls. Data on the individual opinions of approximately 45,000 voters who were interviewed three times in YouGov polls—once in December 2011, once again between January and Election Day, and once again after the election. Data on campaign news coverage in roughly 11,000 different outlets, including how often they reported on each candidate and how favorable or unfavorable that coverage was. Data on the millions of political advertisements aired, including when they aired, where they aired, and how many were on the air. Data on the location of candidate field offices.

These data enable us to document quantitatively the state of the economy and other fundamentals, the volume and tenor of news coverage, the ad blitzes and ground game in the battleground states, and the shifts (or not) in the polls. These data allow us to arrive at firmer conclusions about why things happened and especially why Obama won. They allow us to adjudicate among alternative explanations. In these data we will find many correlations, but we aim to go beyond these relationships to figure out which correlations are more likely to imply causation. Adjudicating among explanations also means going beyond platitudes like "campaigns matter at the margins" or "in close elections, campaigns can make the difference." We will present much more specific estimates: if Obama aired 1,000 ads in a media market and Romney aired none, how many points did that earn Obama in the polls if nothing else changed? The result is a picture that—whether or not it confirms earlier political science research, folklore, conventional wisdom, or casual punditry—is empirically richer and more robust.

None of this is to suggest that quantitative data can answer every question about the effects of a campaign. Campaigns are not experiments. Often we cannot easily sort out correlation from causation or we simply do not have the exact data we need. Although the Obama campaign was willing to conduct small-scale experiments with fund-raising emails, neither they nor the Romney campaign was conducting large-scale experiments with campaign messages or campaign advertising. Campaigns do not place ads randomly and evaluate whether voters who saw ads voted differently than voters who did not see them. They place ads where they need votes or, more precisely, where they have some chance of gaining votes. Because campaigns are strategic our job is harder and our analyses will come with some uncertainty.

Furthermore, although we can measure a lot of what happened and whether or how it appeared to affect the election's outcome, we cannot know what would have happened if various events had never occurred. Absent a time machine and the ability to rerun an election under different conditions, we cannot observe the counterfactual path that never materialized. But we can make educated guesses about how alternative scenarios might have played out. We can do things like estimate how many more ads Romney would have had to run to beat Obama, how many fewer field offices Obama could have had and still beat Romney, or whether Obama's barrage of advertising about Romney's time at Bain Capital really defined him. In addressing these questions, we can never know for sure what might have been, but data help us evaluate the plausibility of different scenarios.

The Primaries

In primary elections, the candidates are often relatively unfamiliar and voters cannot use their own identification with a political party to choose among the candidates. Because of this, they rely on other information, which is supplied by the news media and the candidates' electioneering. Unlike in general elections, the news media and electioneering are often imbalanced. At different points in time, one candidate may receive much more, and more favorable, news coverage than the others. Some candidates have enough money to run well-funded, professional campaigns, while others are running campaigns on a shoestring budget. As a result, when voters are inundated with information favoring one of the candidates, they often gravitate toward that candidate. In 2012, that happened repeatedly, creating so many ups and downs that the polls seemed almost random. But there was an underlying logic at work.

The surges by candidates like Rick Perry, Herman Cain, Newt Gingrich, and Rick Santorum followed a pattern we call "discovery, scrutiny, and decline." A salient event, like Perry's entry into the race or Cain's victory in the Florida straw poll, drew the media's attention to a candidate they had largely ignored to that point. The "discovery" of this candidate generated a spike in media coverage and a corresponding spike in the candidate's poll numbers. But as a front-runner or at least a strong contender, the candidate soon attracted scrutiny from the news media and his opponents alike. As the tenor of the news coverage became less favorable—revealing, for example, evidence that Cain had sexually harassed women as head of the National Restaurant Association—the candidate's poll numbers began to slip. The result was an often irreversible decline in both news coverage and poll numbers. Looked at this way, the ups and downs in the 2012 primary polls become comprehensible.

Romney, however, did not experience these ups and downs. Underneath the media-driven volatility, the fundamentals of primary elections—in particular, the support of other party leaders—advantaged Romney. For one, although many Republican leaders did not formally endorse any of their party's presidential candidates, Romney had much more support among party leaders than did the other candidates. For another, his campaign was better funded and more professionalized than Gingrich's or Santorum's. For yet another, he was actually the most popular candidate among the largest factions in the party, which tend not to be the most conservative factions. Gingrich and Santorum each won a few primaries and caucuses only in states where the electorate was more conservative and, even then, only when some fortuitous news coverage or extra elbow grease on the campaign trail made them especially visible to voters. But after Gingrich or Santorum won, the reaction among party leaders ranged from deafening silence to outright alarm. In part because of this, Gingrich and Santorum never had enough resources to build a campaign that could compete effectively with Romney's in state after state, and particularly in states where the electorate was not as favorable to them. Campaigning and media coverage alone could not help the other candidates neutralize Romney's advantage.

The General Election

Once the general election campaign began, however, much of the volatility was replaced with stability. In large part, this stemmed from the power of partisanship, one of the fundamentals of presidential elections and American politics generally. In 2012, partisans were very loyal, and the vast majority stuck with their party's candidate throughout the campaign.

A second important fundamental factor was the national economy. The economy structures many things about presidential elections: who decides to run in the first place, what the candidates talk about, and ultimately who wins. Incumbent presidents and parties do better as the economy grows more rapidly in election years. One of the biggest misconceptions of the 2012 election was that the economy unequivocally disadvantaged Obama. True, the economy was not growing robustly and had not escaped the shadow of the 2007–9 recession and financial crisis. But it was growing at a rate that, based on the previous sixty-plus years of presidential elections, was sufficient to predict an Obama victory. It was never going to be a landslide, or even 2008 all over again. Nevertheless, given the economic growth in 2012, Obama was the favorite.

Where, then, does the campaign—the choices of the candidates—fit in if voters are predictably partisan and the economy strongly influences election outcomes? First, we show that the 2012 campaign, like many before it, helped ensure that both partisanship and the economy remained fundamental. During the campaign, partisans became increasingly enthusiastic about the candidate they were already supporting or predisposed to support. Democrats came to like Obama more, and Republicans came to like Romney more. There were moments when some partisans wavered: for Republicans, after the video of Romney's comments about "the 47%" was released; for Democrats, after the first presidential debate, in which Obama was perceived to have performed poorly. But subsequent events brought these wavering partisans back into the fold: for Republicans, the first debate; for Democrats, the later debates. Meanwhile, among voters who were initially undecided, not only partisanship but their views of the economy became more salient as the campaign wore on. Partisanship and the economy tend to make elections predictable, and that tendency often becomes stronger as the campaign rolls along. The campaign in 2012 reinforced the stability in the electorate instead of weakening it.

Second, campaign activity itself—the ads, field organizations, and so on—moved votes. But it was difficult for one candidate to move enough votes to shift the polls or, ultimately, to win the election outright. Although commentators were often looking for the one hard-hitting ad that would somehow stay with voters all the way to the ballot box, we find that most of the effects of ads wore off quickly, within a day. Furthermore, unlike in the Republican primary, where there were big differences in how much money the candidates had raised and thus whether they could afford a robust campaign, Obama, Romney, and their respective allies each spent roughly the same amount of money. Thus it was rare for one side to get a large advantage over the other side. Even when one side had more ads on the air than the other—as Obama did in May and June and Romney did in the week before Election Day—it was impossible to dominate completely. The vigorous efforts of both sides were in large part canceling each other out.

Presidential elections are like a game of tug-of-war. Both sides are pulling very hard. If, for some reason, one side let go—meaning they stopped campaigning—then the other side would soon benefit. But of course the candidates do not let go and that makes it hard to see that their efforts are making a difference. That the polls are not moving may seem to suggest that the two campaigns are ineffective. We argue that it means they are equally effective.

This tug-of-war metaphor also implies something very different than a view of campaigns focused on "game-changers." The continual search for game changers treats a campaign like a boxing match, where the momentum may be shifting back and forth with every punch and the knockout blow could come at any moment. In reality, there are few knockout punches, and most game-changers do not really change the game that much. Even Obama's early attacks on Romney's time at Bain Capital or the 47% video was not as important as some reporting and commentary suggested. We might call these moments "game-samers" instead.

We have titled this book *The Gamble* because it described the election on many levels. A gamble is just a bet on an uncertain outcome, like whether the roulette wheel stops at red or black. As the 2012 campaign got under way, there were at least three bets being made. One was by Democrats, who were betting on an incumbent who, while arguably the favorite, was still facing challenging economic times and a pessimistic public. One was by Republicans, who were betting on which of their many candidates could do something rare: defeat a sitting incumbent president. And one was by voters, who were betting on which candidate would best help the country recover from the worst economic recession in over seventy years.

The title has one more meaning. Although like most academics we typically work slowly, we wanted political science to be part of the conversation about this election as it was happening, not years later. So we have tried to write a scientific book about the election in real time, thinking that it would bring a perspective worth considering. That is our gamble.

CHAPTER 2

The Hand You're Dealt

Thirteen days after he was inaugurated, Barack Obama sat down for an interview with NBC's Matt Lauer. Lauer asked about the Troubled Assets Relief Program (TARP) that had been passed under President George W. Bush and whether its use of federal money to shore up ailing banks and financial institutions would "fix the economy." The following exchange ensued:

> President Obama: Look, I'm at the start of my administration. One nice thing about—the situation I find myself in is that I will be held accountable. You know, I've got four years. And—
>
> Matt Lauer: You're gonna know quickly how people feel—
>
> . . . .
>
> President Obama: That's exactly right. And—and, you know, a year from now I think people—are gonna see that—we're starting to make some progress. But there's still gonna be some pain out there. If I don't have this done in three years, then there's gonna be a one-term proposition.[1]

Obama was right: economic conditions in the country would influence how voters viewed his performance and ultimately whether they supported his reelection. This is why we consider the economy *fundamental*, or foundational, to presidential election outcomes, along with other structural conditions like political partisanship. Why are these things so important? Because, taken together, they correctly predict the winner of most presidential elections in the post–World War II era—even though they are typically measured before the candidate debates, the bulk of television advertising, and much other electioneering. Moreover, many aspects of these fundamentals—such as the state of the economy—will not be affected by the campaign itself. They are beyond the control of the presidential candidates. They are the hand the candidates are dealt.

To illustrate the strong relationship between the fundamentals and presidential election outcomes, we compare economic growth in the year of the presidential election—measured as the change in gross domestic product (GDP) from January to July—and the share of the major-party vote for incumbent parties. Figure 2.1 includes the sixteen presidential elections between 1948 and 2008. The pattern is clear: as GDP increases, incumbent parties do better. In fact, it is hard to beat an incumbent party in a growing economy and even harder to beat the actual incumbent himself, which happened only in 1976 and 1992. Over the last sixty years, objective economic conditions have played a significant role in structuring election outcomes.[2]

A central theme in this book is how much these fundamental factors mattered relative to other factors specific to the presidential campaign, such as the candidates, their messages, television advertisements, debates, gaffes, and so on. Campaign events and strategies certainly can affect who wins or loses

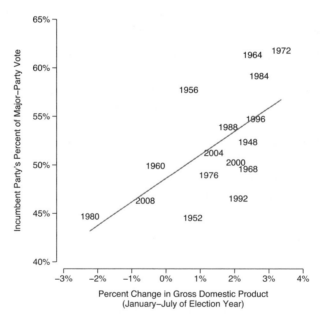

Figure 2.1.
The relationship between economic growth and presidential election outcomes.

a presidential election. But the campaign has to operate in a context that is structured by the fundamentals. This context and the campaign itself deserve attention, and we will give both their due. We begin by highlighting the fundamentals because they help to answer a central question of the election: was Barack Obama the front-runner or the underdog going into 2012?

Our answer centers on the structural conditions surrounding his presidency, especially the 2007–9 recession and financial crisis, the slow economic recovery thereafter, and increasing partisan polarization. We demonstrate that, as 2012 got under way, Obama was arguably more popular than expected based on the economic conditions he faced—especially the deep recession and slow recovery. His unexpected popularity buoyed his chances for reelection because presidential elections are, partly if not primarily, referenda on the incumbent.

But why was Obama more popular than the economy seemed to warrant? Part of the reason is partisan polarization: Democrats held him in especially high regard, something that had not always been true for previous Democratic presidents facing economic headwinds. Another factor was Obama the person. Despite being repeatedly characterized as cerebral and chilly, the majority of Americans saw him as warm, likable, and empathetic—attributes that, as we will see, fewer Americans saw embodied in Mitt Romney. A final factor was the willingness of many Americans, and especially political independents, to blame George W. Bush more than Obama for the state of the economy.

As Obama's first term played out, the question on everyone's mind was whether the halting economic recovery would ultimately doom the president's reelection chances. The fundamentals actually made Obama the favorite. Obama would probably not win as easily as he did in 2008, but 2012 was his election to lose.

The Economy Obama Inherited

The economy that Obama inherited in January 2009 was a wreck. The country was already more than a year into a recession. The unemployment rate had climbed from 5% in December 2007, the start of the recession, to 6.1% in September 2008. At that point, the country was rocked by another calamity: a financial crisis that left banks and investment houses reeling. Banks and brokers had invested heavily in securities backed by home mortgages that many homeowners were ultimately unable to pay. This bet on the housing market seemed smart because housing prices had been rising rapidly, leading to a boom in home construction and ownership. But the housing market proved to contain a "bubble" of overinflated assets that, when popped, threatened the livelihoods of Americans and banks alike. Several financial institutions failed, including Lehman Brothers and Washington Mutual. Others teetered as corporate and political leaders tried to arrange buyouts and mergers that would keep them afloat. At the urging of the Bush administration, Congress passed the Emergency Economic Stabilization Act on October 3, 2008. This legislation allocated $700 billion to TARP, which was to purchase assets such as mortgage-backed securities that banks themselves could no longer convince anyone else to buy.

Despite these measures, the economy continued its slide. In October, November, and December, unemployment increased further, while the Dow Jones Industrial Average lost a fifth of its value.[3] Just after Obama took office, the Bureau of Economic Analysis (BEA) estimated that the country's economic output had plummeted at an annual rate of 3.8% in the fourth quarter of 2008. This initial estimate was woefully incorrect: it had actually fallen by 8.9%, the largest drop in over fifty years.[4] All told, nearly 1.9 million jobs were lost in the last four months of 2008.[5] The recession and financial crisis buoyed Obama's chances as a presidential candidate, but they would cast a long shadow over his first term as president.

Since the 1950s, the University of Michigan has been measuring Americans' evaluations of the economy via its Index of Consumer Sentiment. The index is based on five questions about people's financial circumstances and the country's business conditions and economy. When Obama took office, the index was near its historical low, as Figure 2.2 demonstrates. In the fourth quarter of 2008, 59% of Americans said that they were worse off financially than they were a year before—the most dissatisfaction ever recorded in response to this question.

Upon his inauguration, Obama was in a position somewhat similar to Ronald Reagan's in 1980. Both took office when Americans were pessimistic about the economy and dissatisfied with the incumbent president. In a late November 1980 Gallup poll, only 31% of Americans approved of the job Jimmy Carter was doing. At the same point in time in 2008, only 29% approved of George W. Bush. But Obama's and Reagan's paths quickly diverged. Early in Reagan's first term, there was a sharp, painful recession during which unemployment peaked even higher than it did during the 2007–9 recession. But the 1981–82 recession, in part because it had no accompanying financial crisis to compound its effects, was less severe and was followed by a rapid recovery. By November 1984, unemployment had fallen sharply and consumer sentiment had become more optimistic than at any point since the mid-1960s. These trends were what made the autumn months of 1984 "Morning in America," as

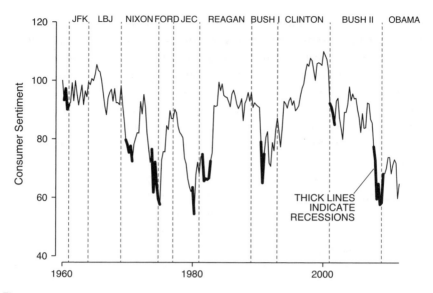

Figure 2.2.
The trend in consumer sentiment, 1960–2011.

Reagan's now famous campaign advertisement claimed.[6] The narrator in that ad went on to say that "more men and women will go to work than ever before in our country's history." Obama could not say the same thing going into 2012.

Digging out of the Recession

During his first term, Obama's primary challenge was to combat the recession and financial crisis he inherited. Once in office, Obama and congressional Democrats moved quickly to pass an economic stimulus package. Some of Obama's economic advisors believed the recession demanded an extraordinary intervention. In a December 2008 memo, Christina Romer, the economist who would become chair of the Council of Economic Advisors, recommended a stimulus of $1.7–1.8 trillion. (By comparison, the stimulus package championed unsuccessfully by Bill Clinton in 1993 was only $19.5 billion, which would have been equal to $29 billion in 2009.)[7] But Larry Summers, the director of the White House National Economic Council, believed that Romer's figure was not politically feasible, even within the administration. Budget Director Peter Orszag believed that a stimulus that large would increase the deficit so much that business confidence would ebb.[8] The plan

Obama ultimately put forward totaled $775 billion, divided among tax cuts, direct payments to state governments, and funding for infrastructure projects. It was crafted to appeal to both Democrats, who would support the outlays for state governments and for infrastructure, and Republicans and conservative Democrats, who would be attracted by tax cuts.

Instead, the stimulus met resistance. This was the first sign of many that Obama's campaign goal of bipartisan cooperation would rarely be realized. After the Senate passed an $827 billion package, House Minority Leader John Boehner said, "Right now, given the concerns that we have over the size of this package and all of the spending in this package, we don't think it's going to work." The initial version that the House passed (an $819 billion package) earned no Republican support. On Twitter, Representative Jeff Flake (R-AZ) called the bill a "Ford Pinto."[9] The stimulus that was ultimately signed into law totaled $787 billion and attracted only three Republican votes, from Senators Susan Collins, Olympia Snowe, and Arlen Specter. The Obama team counted even this as a victory. When he signed the bill, Obama declared, "We have begun the essential work of keeping the American dream alive in our time." And the stimulus apparently helped, increasing economic output and lowering unemployment in each quarter of 2009, 2010, and 2011, according to the Congressional Budget Office (CBO).[10]

But a dramatic economic recovery—like the one that occurred in Reagan's first term—did not occur. Instead, during the first three years of Obama's term, the economy only limped along. Although the financial system was stabilized and the recession was technically over, economic growth was slow. This was in keeping with the general pattern after financial crises. The economists Carmen Reinhart and Kenneth Rogoff have found that after post–World War II financial crises, it has taken four to five years for economic output to return to its previous level.[11] Protracted high unemployment has also been common after financial crises. After Obama's inauguration the unemployment rate was above 8% until well into 2012. Moreover, the unemployed tended to be out of work for long periods—an average of forty weeks by the end of 2011. Before the 2007–9 recession, the highest average had been twenty weeks.

And so Americans remained pessimistic about the economy. In fact, they had never been as pessimistic. Consumer sentiment was lower in the first three years of Obama's term than during every other presidency beginning with Kennedy's, including Carter's. This pessimism was also remarkably stable. Most presidents experience big ups and downs in consumer sentiment, corresponding to economic booms and contractions (see Figure 2.2). Under Obama, consumer sentiment exhibited few notable trends. It became more positive in the first few quarters of 2009 but more negative in the summer of 2011 when the disagreement between Obama and congressional Republicans over whether to lift the debt ceiling sent financial markets into paroxysms and made Americans newly anxious. The range in consumer sentiment was smaller under Obama than it was under nearly every other president. Ordinarily, this lack of volatility might have been comforting, except that optimism was so scarce.

The pessimistic public was also skeptical of, if not downright opposed to, the Obama administration's efforts to revitalize the economy. In a February 2009 Pew Research Center poll, only half thought that the stimulus was a good idea. A little over a year later, in an April 2010 Pew poll, 62% said the stimulus had not "helped prevent a more serious crisis." The public tended to oppose other efforts to stimulate the economy, many of which were deemed "bailouts" for presumably undeserving recipients. The Obama administration's efforts to help General Motors and Chrysler were not popular: only 37% said these efforts were "mostly good" for the economy in an October 2009 poll. The TARP program—a bailout for Wall Street banks, in the minds of many—was also unpopular. In the April 2010 Pew poll, only 42% agreed that "government loans to banks and financial institutions helped prevent a more severe crisis." The unpopularity of TARP should not have been a major political problem for Obama. After all, it was signed into law by President George W. Bush. But only about one-third of the public knew this. Almost half believed it was passed under Obama and the rest did not know. By 2012, opinions about the loans to auto companies had improved, but attitudes toward TARP and the stimulus had not.[12]

The Obama administration did not receive much more support for its other domestic policy accomplishments, even though the first two years of Obama's term were remarkably productive. Not only were the stimulus and the support for ailing auto companies enacted but so were reform to student loans, new rules on financial institutions, and, most important, a landmark health care reform bill, the Patient Protection and Affordable Care Act (ACA). Health care reform had been a longstanding priority of the Democratic Party, and in June 2012 the major parts of the ACA were upheld by a 5–4 vote in the Supreme Court. Although it did not go far enough for some, the ACA nevertheless made fundamental changes to the health care system. Among other things, it prevented insurance companies from denying coverage to people with preexisting medical conditions. It also would eventually establish a financial penalty if people did not purchase health insurance. This "individual mandate" was intended to serve two purposes. First, it would help ensure the viability of insurance markets by preventing healthy people from waiting until they were sick to purchase insurance. Second, it would help achieve the goal of universal, or nearly universal, health coverage. To help ensure that lower-income Americans would be able to afford coverage, the ACA expanded Medicaid, the federal health insurance program for the poor.

But opinion about health care reform was similar to opinion about the stimulus. The public was again roughly evenly divided and polarized along partisan lines. About a year after the ACA's passage, a March 2011 Kaiser Family Foundation poll found that 42% of Americans supported the law but 46% opposed it.[13] The majority of Democrats supported it, but very few Republicans did. At the same time, the public also did not know a great deal about the legislation. For example, an August 2011 Kaiser Family Foundation poll found that only 58% knew that the ACA provided subsidies to help low-income Americans purchase health insurance—down from 75% in April 2010, just after the bill passed.[14]

Opposition to the Obama administration's legislative priorities— particularly the stimulus, "bailouts," and the ACA—was crystallized most visibly in the Tea Party. The Tea Party was not a formal political party but a loosely associated set of groups and voters. People who affiliated with the Tea Party were not a monolith in terms of their political attitudes, but they did share a hostility to what they perceived as an unprecedented expansion of government power under Obama. This was why they aligned themselves with the colonists who resisted the rule of King George III at the famous Boston Tea Party.

The 2010 Elections: The Republicans Resurgent

Opposition to the stimulus, ACA, and other administration efforts made these accomplishments political liabilities for the Obama administration. Nowhere was this more evident than in the 2010 midterm elections. Democratic congressional candidates were already facing an uphill battle. Thanks to their gains in the 2006 and 2008 midterms, they had to defend House seats in many swing districts and in some districts that leaned Republican. The weak economy and a relatively unpopular president—Obama was polling in the mid-40s in the fall of 2010—made Republican gains even more likely. But their 63-seat gain, the largest shift since 1948, exceeded the predictions of most analysts.

Why did the Democrats lose so badly? Tea Party activism appeared influential: Republican House candidates did better in districts where there were more Tea Party activists.[15] Support for health care reform seemed to be another reason. In competitive districts, Democratic incumbents who supported the ACA lost about 6 points of vote share relative to Democratic incumbents who opposed the ACA. According to a team of political scientists, this may have cost the Democrats as many as 25 seats.[16] Overall, the 2010 election was not only a referendum on the economy, it was to some extent a repudiation of Obama's legislative accomplishments.[17]

With the House of Representatives in Republican hands and the Democratic majority in the Senate well below the 60 votes needed to overcome Republican filibusters, the Obama administration was in a difficult position. It had initially assumed that Congress might pass another stimulus bill if a robust economic recovery did not happen. This was impossible after the 2010 elections. Even measures that had been routine in earlier times, such as a vote to increase the debt ceiling so that the government could continue to borrow and spend, provoked considerable debate, in part because newly elected Republican members, many of them affiliated with the Tea Party, favored cuts to government spending. Smaller measures that could have stimulated the economy, such as an extension of the payroll tax cut, necessitated protracted and sometimes acrimonious negotiations. The GOP's resistance was, from an electoral perspective, quite logical. Obama was not the only one who knew that his reelection hinged on economic growth and, as Senate Minority Leader Mitch McConnell said in October 2010, "The single most important thing we want to achieve is for President Obama to be a one-term president."[18] Republicans had little reason to vote for new and ambitious initiatives to stimulate the economy. Obama was thus left with relatively few policy levers that would allow him to fulfill the goal he described to Matt Lauer and "have this done in three years." The GOP wanted him out in four.

At the end of 2011, this is where Obama stood. He was presiding over an economy that was growing, but not fast enough to create very many jobs. He was a disappointment to many Democratic leaders, activists, and other groups on the left. Democratic members of Congress felt ignored or even snubbed. Some Democrats lamented the compromises that were part of the administration's achievements, such as the failure of the ACA to include a government insurance program, the "public option." Others lamented slow progress on gay marriage, mortgage relief, and immigration reform. Still others thought Obama had thrown in his lot too much with banks and financial institutions rather than ordinary Americans. This latter sentiment was articulated most visibly by the Occupy Wall Street (OWS) movement in the fall of 2011. Its goal was to draw attention to economic inequality and argue that large corporations had too much influence in American politics. OWS activists and sympathizers held sit-ins and rallies first in New York and then in many cities in the United States and abroad. Finally, as ever, Obama continued to face staunch opposition from Republicans on Capitol Hill.

This potted history implies that Obama's reelection effort was in trouble—at least based on "the fundamentals" alone. Writing in late December 2011, *Salon*'s Steve Kornacki noted that economic forecasts provided a "sobering reality check" for the White House.[19] But Obama's precarious position belied this striking fact: he was relatively popular—and ironically he owed this, at least in part, to something he campaigned against in 2008: partisan polarization.

The Unexpectedly Popular President

Presidential popularity hinges on several factors. One is the state of the economy. Another is salient events like scandals and wars. There is also, for many presidents, an inexorable decline in popularity. The longer a president is in office, the less popular he is.

Obama's first three years saw no big shifts in the economy, as we have noted, and relatively few dramatic events, such as big scandals. Accordingly, Obama's approval rating—the percentage of people who approved of the job he was doing—had few sharp dips or jumps, as Figure 2.3 demonstrates. The killing of Osama bin Laden produced a modest 5-point bump in May 2011. At two other points there were somewhat steeper decreases in approval: from

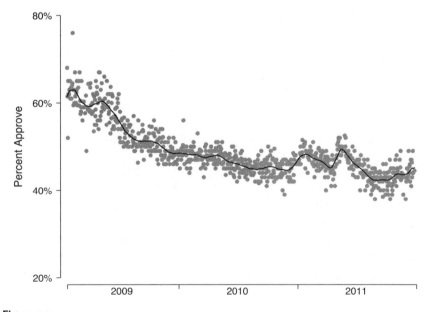

Figure 2.3.
The trend in approval of Obama, 2009–11.
The points represent individual polls, which are located based on the midpoint of the dates the poll was in the field. The line is a smoothed average.

early May through August 2009, and in June and July 2011. Both appeared connected to economic uncertainty, including increases in unemployment in 2009 and the difficult debt ceiling negotiations in mid-2011. However, it is not easy to isolate the causes of these trends, and they are arguably subordinate to the larger pattern: Obama's approval rating was remarkably stable during this period. Most other presidents have experienced greater peaks and valleys in their approval ratings in their first terms.[20] Obama's approval rating looked much like one might expect given the chronic economic challenges he faced: initial popularity in the "honeymoon" after he was inaugurated, which was then gradually eroded by Americans' persistent pessimism about the economy and the overall direction of the country.

But this pessimism never eroded Obama's approval as much as it arguably might have or perhaps should have. How can we know? One way is to predict what Obama's approval would have been based on how the economy and other factors have historically affected approval ratings and then determine whether Obama's actual approval matched, exceeded, or fell short of the prediction. To do so, we used sixty years of quarterly data on presidential approval, which contain polls from 1948 to 2008, and constructed a statistical model of approval that included these factors: three economic indicators (the unemployment rate, the change in GDP since the previous quarter, and the change in inflation since the previous quarter); the presence of events such as war that might push approval up or down; the presence of divided government; and the length of time in office. (The appendix to this chapter describes the model in greater detail.) We used this model to predict Obama's approval in 2009–11. The question we can then answer is this: Was Obama more or less popular during his first three years in office than we would expect given how the economy and other circumstances have previously affected presidential approval?

Figure 2.4 depicts the difference between expected and actual approval of Obama. On average, Obama was about 3 points more popular than expected from 2009 through the first quarter of 2012. The drop in Obama's approval rating in the third quarter of 2011 brought it more in line with expectations, but in the first quarter of 2012 it was once again 4 points above expectations.[21] This feat is something that few presidents have accomplished. Only one president, Kennedy, consistently "beat" the prediction in his first term to an extent greater than Obama did.[22]

Obama's higher-than-expected approval rating might have been especially surprising for two reasons. Indeed, even if his approval had been equivalent to expectations, it might still have been surprising. For one, the economy was not in a garden-variety recession but a deep and prolonged slump. The economic measures we drew on captured some of its characteristics—such as high unemployment—but not all, such as the rise in long-term employment. One

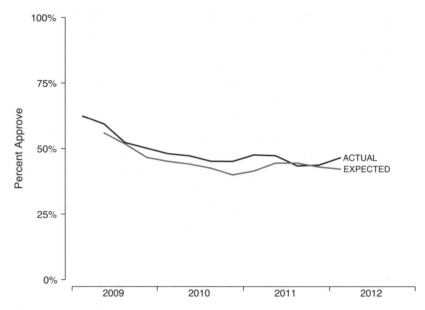

Figure 2.4.
Actual vs. expected presidential approval for Obama.
The figure presents actual quarterly approval alongside the expected approval that
was predicted from a statistical model.

could easily expect that our model would have overestimated Obama's support because it did not take into account what made this recession and recovery unique—or, to use Reinhart and Rogoff's title, why "this time is different."

Second, Obama's race may also depress his approval rating. Studies of the 2008 election have demonstrated that Americans' views of blacks were associated with their views of Obama, and racial prejudice may have cost Obama about 3 points of the vote.[23] Our model did not account for race—indeed the predictions were based on results from white presidents only. We might then expect that the model would have overestimated Obama's popularity by failing to account for the "penalty" of his race. Some evidence confirms this expectation. Using an April 2012 YouGov poll, we predicted Obama's approval rating using a standard measure of attitudes toward blacks, called "racial resentment" by scholars, along with several other factors, including respondents' identification with a political party or as independent and their self-reported ideology on the liberal-conservative scale. Unsurprisingly, those who expressed more resentment of blacks were more likely to disapprove of Obama. To gauge the overall effect of attitudes toward blacks, we assumed a world in which every person had a neutral opinion of blacks—that is, we shifted those with favorable or unfavorable views of blacks to neutrality—and then predicted a "new" approval rating for Obama based on the same set of factors. In this hypothetical scenario, Obama's approval would have increased by almost 4 points overall. (Further details are in the appendix to this chapter.)

We do not want to overstate the results of this simulation, which isolated arguably implausible shifts in attitudes toward blacks and assumed nothing else would have changed. As such, the 4-point estimate is not a sacrosanct number. However, this evidence and the evidence from the 2008 election suggest that negative attitudes toward blacks depress Obama's approval rating more than positive attitudes toward blacks increase it. This makes it even more surprising that Obama outperformed expectations.

The Paradox of Obama's Popularity

Why, then, might Obama's approval have been higher than expected? One culprit was partisan polarization. During the past forty years, the coalitions of the two parties have changed, rendering them more internally homogeneous in terms of ideology and more ideologically distinct from each other.[24] This is certainly true among politicians. In place of conservative Southern Democrats, there are now many more Republicans. And moderate and liberal Republicans—in the Northeast, for example—have become similarly endangered. As a consequence, Republicans and Democrats in the public, although not as polarized as politicians in Washington, are nevertheless more ideologically homogeneous and more polarized on some issues.[25]

In particular, over the past thirty years, and especially during the Clinton and George W. Bush administrations, Democrats and Republicans became far more polarized in their views of the president.[26] This has been true for Obama as well. In the first year of his presidency, an average of 88% of Democrats approved of him but only 23% of Republicans did.[27] This 65-point gap was the largest of any president during his first year in office—perhaps no surprise given the divisions between Democratic and Republican politicians. Evaluations of Obama became only more polarized thereafter. There was a stark disjuncture between how Obama campaigned in 2008—to lead "America" rather than "red America" or "blue America"—and how powerfully the larger forces of partisan polarization shaped the public's views of him. Obama was no more a "uniter" than George W. Bush had been.

But here was the irony: the very forces of partisan polarization that Obama deplored may have buoyed his approval rating. This is most clear if we compare Obama's actual approval rating among Democrats, independents,

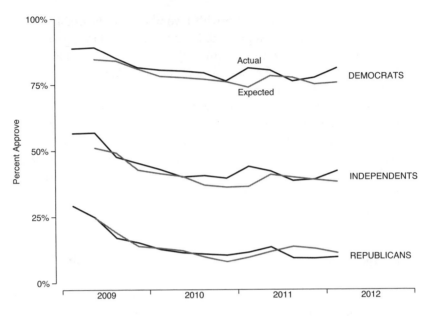

Figure 2.5.
Actual vs. expected presidential approval for Obama among Democrats, independents, and Republicans.

and Republicans to predictions of what his approval rating would have been in each group based on the same data and factors we examined in the previous section. As Figure 2.5 illustrates, Obama's approval rating tended to exceed expectations among Democrats and independents but not among Republicans. In the first quarter of 2012, Obama's approval was 5.5 points higher than expected among Democrats, 4 points higher than expected among independents, but 1.5 points lower than expected among Republicans. This illustrates just how much more polarized are opinions of the president now than they were in the past.

Although commentators have often been quick to compare Obama to Carter, one key difference between them is how much more Democrats have supported Obama than they did Carter.[28] When Carter's approval was at its nadir in the fall of 1979, barely one-third of Democrats approved of the job he was doing, compared to about 20% of Republicans. Even Bill Clinton, now seemingly beloved by Democrats, was less popular among Democrats—63% of whom approved of him in June 1993—than was Obama in his first term. In fact, averaging over each Democratic president's first three years in office, Obama was more popular with Democratic voters than every one of them except John F. Kennedy—and even Kennedy's average approval among

Democrats was only 4 points higher than Obama's. Obama was actually as popular among Democrats during these years as was Reagan among Republicans in 1981–83. These facts fly in the face of frequent fears (or hopes) during Obama's first term that he was "losing the base" or otherwise alienating key Democratic constituencies. For example, a front-page *New York Times* story on September 17, 2011, was titled "In Poll, Support for Obama Slips among Base." Although Obama may have lost support among some Democratic or liberal activists who disagreed with him on various issues, he remained popular among Democrats in the public. And equally important, given the approaching election, the same pattern existed among independents.

The Blame Game

But party polarization and Democratic loyalty could not explain why independents supported Obama more than expected. This leads us to a second factor: the willingness of many Americans to blame the country's economic problems on Obama's predecessor, George W. Bush, during whose tenure the recession and financial crisis began.

There is historical precedent for incumbent presidents' dodging some of the blame.[29] In fact, at least two other presidents, Reagan and George W. Bush, benefited from this. In Reagan's case, he inherited a weak economy, one that was in a recession for the first half of 1980. Soon after he took office, in July 1981, the country entered another, more painful seventeen-month recession that was unmatched until 2007. Thus there was perhaps reason for Americans to blame either Carter or Reagan or both. In an October 1982 *Washington Post*/ABC News poll, roughly equal numbers did: 47% blamed Carter "a great deal" or "a fair amount" for the country's economic conditions, and 44% blamed Reagan. But because Democrats and Republicans tend to view questions of blame through a partisan lens, it is more instructive to examine the views of independents with no leaning toward either party. Among them, Reagan had the advantage: 45% blamed Carter, but only 38% blamed Reagan.

The same was true for Bush. From March through November 2001, the country also experienced a recession. Because the recession came so early in Bush's first term, and because the economic slowdown had begun late in Clinton's second term, there was again debate about whom to blame. Two different polls—by the *Washington Post* in February 2002 and by Princeton Survey Research Associates (PSRA) in May 2003—showed that, in fact, Clinton was blamed more than Bush. In the *Post* poll, 78% of independents thought that the economy was "not so good" or "poor." Among this subset of independents with a negative view of the economy, 69% believed Clinton deserved "a great deal" or "a fair amount" of blame, but only 48% believed this of Bush. Similarly, among the minority who thought the economy was doing well, more credited Bush than Clinton. In the PSRA poll, 30% of independents thought Clinton deserved "most" or "a lot" of blame while 22% thought Bush did.

But for Reagan and Bush, their ability to escape some of the blame for weak economies was not really necessary for them to win reelection. The economy was growing healthily in the first two quarters of 1984 and 2004, as Figure 2.1 demonstrates. For Obama, such a growth rate was not at all assured, and so escaping some of the blame could provide him a crucial edge amid a slowly growing economy.

Obama's ability to escape some of the blame was first evident in a series of Gallup polls between July 2009 and September 2011 and a January 2012 *Washington Post* poll.[30] We confirmed this finding in an April 2012 YouGov poll. When asked how much blame Obama and Bush each deserved for "the poor economic conditions of the past few years," 56% of respondents gave Bush a great deal or a lot of the blame, while only 41% gave Obama that much blame. A similar gap existed among independents with no leaning toward a political party: 58% blamed Bush, but only 42% blamed Obama. Altogether, 47% of respondents blamed Bush more than Obama, 21% blamed them equally, and 32% blamed Obama more than Bush.

At that point, Obama was winning the blame game. Did this explain why his approval rating was higher than expected? Here is one way to address this question. We calculated the difference between how much blame voters assigned to Obama and Bush, which served as a measure of Obama's blame advantage or disadvantage relative to Bush. Using that measure—as well as other relevant factors, including ideology, sex, race, and income—we predicted how much political independents approved of Obama. We then "erased" any blame advantage for either Bush or Obama, which assumed a world in which every independent blamed Bush and Obama equally. What would have happened in this world, holding everything else the same? Obama's job approval would have declined by about 9 points.

To be sure, this exercise is purely hypothetical. We cannot conclude from it that voters' opinions about blame were the definitive reason why Obama seemed to be more popular than he should have been. Life is not a laboratory, and we cannot replay Obama's first three years and have voters blame him less or more than they did in reality. Nevertheless, Obama's lead in the blame game may have helped him retain popularity—especially among independents—even as the country failed to spring back strongly from the recession he inherited.

The Likability Factor

A final reason why Obama may have been relatively popular at this point in his term was his personal likability. That so many voters liked Obama might have seemed surprising, given how often political observers disagreed. *New York Times* columnist Maureen Dowd described Obama thusly: "No Drama Obama is reticent about displays of emotion. The Spock in him needs to exert mental and emotional control. That is why he stubbornly insists on staying aloof and setting his own deliberate pace for responding—whether it's in a debate or after a debacle."[31] Similar ideas had been circulating for a while, such as when commentators homed in on Obama's alleged inability to "connect" with voters.[32] *Atlantic Monthly* writer James Fallows followed up on this in a long article on Obama's first term. He quoted Walter Mondale calling Obama "aloof" and "someone with long experience in the executive branch" saying that "President Obama's extra-high intellectual capacity is simply not matched by his emotional capacity."[33]

Perhaps such impressions are accurate, at least if one has firsthand contact with the president. But during Obama's first term the vast majority of Americans appeared to disagree. Polls showed that Obama was perceived as warm and empathetic—impressions that changed very little even as his approval rating declined. In a January 2012 Pew poll, 71% said Obama was "warm and friendly" rather than "cold and aloof." He was viewed favorably on related dimensions as well, such as "good communicator" and "cares about people like me." That such large percentages of Americans felt this way suggested that Obama's likability stemmed not only from Democrats' party loyalty but from positive impressions among independents and even some Republicans. For example, over half of Republicans and two-thirds of independents said that Obama was warm and friendly. Although pundits often blamed Obama's struggles on his personality, most Americans did not see him as cold or aloof—and this feeling may have buoyed their evaluation of his job performance as well.

Obama at the Beginning of the Election Year

Where did the twists and turns of Obama's first three years leave him as he geared up for a second presidential campaign? Was he the presumptive front-runner or an underdog? An initial answer to these questions can be derived from the fundamental factors that help structure presidential election outcomes. The historical relationship between these fundamentals and presidential elections, combined with plausible estimates of these fundamentals in 2012, provided a sense of Obama's chances of winning. Many of those indicators suggested he was indeed the front-runner.

Forecasting Models

Forecasting presidential elections has become something of a cottage industry among a handful of academics, mostly political scientists and a few economists. A typical forecasting model relies on a few factors, maybe three or four, that predate most of the general election campaign—factors such as presidential approval ratings or the rate of economic growth early in the election year. Ideally, a forecasting model does three things: it draws from plausible theories about how voters make decisions in elections; it is parsimonious (that is, it attempts to predict elections with a few big factors rather than lots of factors that each explain only the idiosyncrasies of one election); and it is accurate.

Because forecasting models do not always live up to these ideals, they have attracted their fair share of criticism. Some critics are incredulous that a model would rely on so few factors, none of which may measure campaign activities such as advertising. Is the implication, critics ask, that the campaign does not matter? Others question whether any forecasting model can generate a reliable prediction because these models are typically based on elections since 1948 or 1952—at most fifteen or sixteen including the 2008 election. Still others point out instances where the models were inaccurate—or even predicted the wrong winner in Dewey-defeats-Truman fashion. If these models are sometimes wrong, critics say, how valuable can they really be?

We think that forecasting models can tell us something useful, provided that they are constructed and interpreted in the right way, because they are based on a defensible theory about how a crucial subset of voters makes up its mind: by evaluating the "performance" of the incumbent president and his party. This is why forecasting models typically include factors like presidential approval, which directly measures views of the incumbent, and economic growth, for which the incumbent is often credited in good times or blamed in bad times (fairly or unfairly). These models also provide a baseline against which to measure how well the incumbent is doing—a baseline that is more than just an impressionistic rendering. For example, in August 2008, *New York Times* columnist David Brooks wondered why Obama was not already winning in a landslide and then opined that voters were "slow to trust" Obama because he was a "sojourner" whose "journey" made it hard to understand "the roots and values in which he is ineluctably embedded."* But at that point in time, most models did not predict a landslide. On average, they predicted that Obama would win with about 52% of the major-party vote—hardly a landslide and, incidentally, about what he did win.[†]

Finally, the forecasting models, taken together, typically correctly predict the winner, even if they do not always predict the exact margin of victory very well. Of the predictions made by various forecasters for the 1992–2008 elections, 85% of them correctly identified the winner—even though most forecasts were made two months or more before the election and even though few of these forecasts incorporated polls from the campaign itself or even took account of who the actual candidates were.[‡] Thinking about the models this way reflects a "forest, not the trees" approach. Any one model will always make errors. And although some forecasters are historically more accurate than others, no one has a special forecasting sauce that makes his or her model the best. So even if the forecasting models predict a range of possible outcomes—from a narrow victory to a landslide—the direction that these forecasts point almost always identifies the winner. Looked at this way, the models will rarely lead us wildly astray.

[*]David Brooks, "Where's the Landslide?" *New York Times*, August 5, 2008, http://www.nytimes.com/2008/08/05/opinion/05brooks.html?_r=1.

[†]Nate Silver tabulated sixteen different predictions from forecasting models in 2008. On average, McCain was predicted to win 48.3% of the major-party vote in these models. Silver, "Models Based on 'Fundamentals' Have Failed at Predicting Presidential Elections," FiveThirtyEight/*New York Times*, March 26, 2012, http://fivethirtyeight.blogs.nytimes.com/2012/03/26/models-based-on-fundamentals-have-failed-at-predicting-presidential-elections/#more-29633.

[‡]John Sides, "In Defense of Presidential Forecasting Models," FiveThirtyEight/*New York Times*, March 29, 2012, http://fivethirtyeight.blogs.nytimes.com/2012/03/29/in-defense-of-presidential-forecasting-models/.

Our forecasting model examined sixteen different presidential elections (1948–2008) and took account of three factors: the president's approval rating, whether his party had been in power for only one term or more than one term, and the health of the economy.[34] The approval rating was from June of the election year. Of course, the trend in approval after June can be a good indicator of what will happen in November. Relying on the incumbent's approval rating on the eve of the election would undoubtedly be a very good predictor, but it would be hard to call that a forecast. Similarly, the length of time the incumbent party has occupied the White House reflects an important historical pattern: the incumbent party's candidate has been more likely to lose when the party has held the White House for longer. After a while it seems as if voters simply think it is "time for a change."[35]

To capture the effect of economic growth on presidential election outcomes, the key is to measure change in roughly the year before the election. Change in the economy has mattered more than the absolute level of any economic indicator. This is why, for example, Reagan could declare that it was "Morning in America" during the 1984 campaign even though the unemployment rate that fall was above 7%. More important was how much unemployment had declined in the period leading up to that election. The reason to focus on the year before the election is that voters have historically been somewhat myopic.[36] Voters have tended to "see" recent economic trends more clearly than those of even a year or two earlier. Thus the economic trend over a president's entire term has been less consequential than what has happened in the year before the election. This was why Reagan could be reelected so easily after a painful recession earlier in his first term.

We incorporated three different economic indicators, measuring changes in each between the start of the first quarter of the election year and the end of the second quarter (January to July). This period captured the recent economic changes that would be at least somewhat visible to voters via news coverage and the like. The first indicator was changes in GDP, an omnibus measure of the country's economic output. The second was changes in the unemployment rate, which typically features in news coverage and certainly did in 2012. The third was changes in incomes, as measured by real disposable income per capita (RDI). These economic indicators have tended to trend together, but when they have not, it has been important. For example, in 2000 economic growth as measured by GDP exceeded growth as measured by RDI. This may have helped explain why the incumbent party's candidate, Al Gore, only barely won the popular vote—and, of course, lost the Electoral College.[37] In Obama's case, the same was true: modest economic growth as measured by GDP was accompanied by a slower decline in the unemployment rate and little change in disposable income. This is why our model included all three factors.[38]

At the end of 2011, Obama's approval rating and the rate of economic growth suggested a narrow reelection assuming that his approval rating as of December 2011 would not change and that economic growth in the first half of 2012 would be equal to growth in the first half of 2011. His expected vote share was just under 52%.[39] This number was lower than a similar prediction for seven of the other incumbent presidents at this point in their first term—including Eisenhower (1955), Johnson (1963), Nixon (1971), Carter (1979), Reagan (1983), Clinton (1995), and George W. Bush (2003). According to the model, only George H. W. Bush was expected to have a lower vote share, based on conditions in 1991 (when the country was still recovering from a recession). Historically speaking, Obama's chances were on the low side, although he was still favored.

But more important for Obama was whether and how economic conditions and approval would change in 2012—and what a forecast using 2012 data revealed about his chances. The accuracy of the forecasting models for elections from 1948 to 2008 improves greatly when election-year conditions are used rather than conditions from the previous year.[40]

To produce a forecast using election-year data, we needed to make some assumptions about how the economy would change in the first half of 2012. Assume for the moment that these were to be the election-year economic conditions: growth in GDP of 1.2% between January and July, a decline in the unemployment rate of 0.1 points in that period, and an increase in disposable income of 0.3%.[41] These numbers were roughly in line with economic conditions in 2012: modest GDP growth, a small decrease in unemployment, and a small increase in disposable income. (In chapter 7, we will revisit this forecast in light of actual economic conditions.) Given these numbers and an approval rating of 46%, Obama was expected to do better than we predicted using the actual 2011 numbers, garnering 52.9% of the major-party vote. Part of the reason this forecast favored Obama was his better-than-expected approval rating. We showed in the previous section that, as of the first quarter of 2012, he was about 4 points more popular than expected based on the economy and other factors. Given our forecasting model, this increased popularity translated into about an additional point of vote share.

To many observers writing in late 2011, the idea that Obama would win 52.9% of the major-party vote seemed unlikely. Regardless of what the models predicted, people thought 2012 would be different. Perhaps the extraordinary pain brought by the 2007–9 recession meant that modest improvement in the economy would not be enough. Or perhaps Obama's better-than-expected popularity would not last. At some point, wouldn't the economy finally "catch up" to him, especially when he had an opponent pointing to the unemployment rate every day and, perhaps eventually, convincing voters to blame Obama for how bad things were? Or perhaps conditions in 2012 would take a turn for the worse—a prospect that seemed entirely possible at the time given ongoing economic turbulence in Europe. All of these possibilities were real. Our forecast simply showed what history could tell us: presidents in their first term who were presiding over even modest improvement in the economy have been likely to win.

Sometimes even modest faith in forecasting models is deemed "economic determinism" by commentators who presume that these models, and even the whole of political science research on elections, imply that elections are only about the economy and campaigns themselves are irrelevant. That is not our view, nor in fact is it most political scientists' view. What made the 2012 election more dramatic was uncertainty about whether and how the economy would change, which in turn made Obama's reelection uncertain. Thus, far from suggesting that the campaign would not matter, the fundamentals in 2012 predicted a close enough election that the campaign could certainly matter and possibly consign Obama to that one-term proposition.

CHAPTER 3

Random, or Romney?

During the Republican presidential primary, someone keeping up with the news might have concluded that Mitt Romney was doomed from the start. He was hopelessly out of step with his party and the Tea Party movement, having converted only recently to party orthodoxy on abortion and same-sex marriage and having championed reform to the Massachusetts health care system that became the literal model for "Obamacare." He even endorsed TARP and a government stimulus in response to the 2008 recession and financial crisis. Conservative blogger Erick Erickson said that if Romney were to win the nomination, "conservatism dies."[1] Moreover, Romney's Mormonism made him alien to the evangelical wing of the party. In February 2012, evangelical leader Reverend Franklin Graham asserted that Mormons were not Christians, a stance supported by the majority of white evangelical Christians, according to a Pew Center poll.[2] On top of that, there was Romney's reputation as bland and robotic. Conservative *Washington Post* columnist Charles Krauthammer said that Romney was "not the kind of guy who sends a thrill up your leg," and the *National Review*'s Jonah Goldberg described Romney as "the most boring guy."[3]

Conventional wisdom in 2011 was that Republicans had not warmed to Romney as a politician or a person. The lack of support for Romney led to speculation about a brokered party convention: for example, "Republicans might have to resort to a doomsday scenario and launch a frantic search for a 2012 savior at their nominating convention."[4] To be sure, there was no reason to rush Romney onto the throne and crown him the nominee. Republican leaders and voters were notably unenthused about all of their party's candidates for president. In that context, the Republican primary—with its many different front-runners—seemed like pure chaos.

This lack of enthusiasm and apparent chaos led many to misunderstand the Republican primary's dynamics. To some commentators, the primary seemed like random commotion. To others, it seemed like a search for "anybody but Romney." Neither was true. There was in fact a logic to the seeming randomness. A wide-open field meant that there were many undecided voters whose views could be shaped by news coverage. And the long campaign before the Iowa caucus gave the news media many moments—debates, straw polls, and the like—that changed the focus of their coverage. Frequently the candidate who performed well or said or did something newsworthy became prominent in media coverage, and often for the first time. The ensuing spike in news coverage helped that candidate rise in the polls. However, this boomlet proved temporary once the candidate faced the inevitable questions and criticism that a front-runner experiences. We describe this dynamic as a process of *discovery*, *scrutiny*, and *decline*.

This process explains the experiences of most Republican candidates with a notable exception: Mitt Romney. Romney was never "discovered" in 2011 because he had already been discovered during his 2008 presidential campaign. He had been through this process, whereas the other candidates had not. Familiarity with Romney was evident in public opinion polls: months before the Iowa caucus, most people could rate Romney favorably or unfavorably, whereas large numbers could not rate many of his competitors.[5] Thus Romney never experienced a sharp spike in positive news coverage and a corresponding increase in the polls. The absence of this dynamic for Romney made him seem disliked by the party, which looked as if it were searching for anybody but Romney.

The truth, however, was different. Much like presidential general elections, presidential primaries have their own fundamentals, and by the end of 2011 Romney led in every category: attention from the news media, money raised, support in pre-primary polls, and endorsements by party leaders. He was popular with Republican voters, even conservatives, and—despite much commentary to the contrary—he was perceived by Republican voters as ideologically close to them. In fact, Republican voters, regardless of which candidate they supported, were not really ideologically divided.

Although the period leading up to the Iowa caucus did not produce a dominant front-runner, by the eve of the caucus Romney had significant advantages. His lead portended his ultimate success.

The Spirit of 2010 and the Dispirit of 2012

On November 3, 2010, the Republican Party was excited and for good reason. The party had just won an historic victory in the midterm election. Even President Obama referred to it as a "shellacking" for the Democrats. And with unemployment at nearly 10% and the president's approval rating at 45%, Republicans seemed on the cusp of achieving what Mitch McConnell had declared to be their primary goal all along: to deny Obama a second term.

Not quite one year later, in the fall of 2011, Republicans found themselves in a very different place. The energy of the Tea Party movement and the Republican Party's conservative wing, which was so important in the 2010 election, had arguably become a liability. In Congress, conservative Republicans opposed the compromise House Speaker John Boehner sought with President Obama on the crucial issue of whether to raise the debt ceiling. The standoff took the country to the edge of default and resulted in the loss of a AAA credit rating for the United States.

Republicans shouldered most of the blame for this debacle. In an August 2011 *New York Times*/CBS News poll, 72% of Americans disapproved of the way Republicans in Congress handled the crisis, while only 47% disapproved of the way President Obama handled it. Opinions of the Tea Party movement and Speaker Boehner soured; one week after the downgrade, only 20% of Americans had a favorable impression of the Tea Party and nearly half thought the movement had too much influence over the Republican Party.[6] At this point, the nominating process for the 2012 presidential election was about to begin in earnest. Even though the unemployment rate was only a little lower and President Obama was not any more popular, much of the enthusiasm of 2010 had dissipated. The Republican Party was less popular than the president, and the Tea Party movement was coming under fire even from within the party.

Adding to the party's challenges were its presidential candidates. To be sure, there was no shortage of them: Minnesota congresswoman Michele Bachmann, businessman Herman Cain, former Speaker of the House Newt Gingrich, former Utah governor and ambassador to China Jon Huntsman, former New Mexico governor Gary Johnson, Texas congressman Ron Paul, former Minnesota governor Tim Pawlenty, Texas governor Rick Perry, former Louisiana governor Buddy Roemer, former Massachusetts governor and 2008 presidential candidate Mitt Romney, and former Pennsylvania senator Rick Santorum were all in the race at some point. Real estate mogul Donald Trump also flirted with the possibility of running.

The problem, however, was that these candidates apparently were not good enough. The phrase "weak field" was thrown around a lot. This was not an insult lobbed by Democrats. Charles Krauthammer said it.[7] Even Rush

Limbaugh joined the chorus.[8] But the field was not wholly unimpressive. In any other year, five current or former governors, two members of the House, a former senator, and a former Speaker of the House would not seem all that weak. Commentators were more adept at simply declaring the field "weak" than at explaining why. After all, the résumés of the 2008 Republican field— three former or current senators, four former or current governors, three members of Congress, and the former mayor of New York City—seemed pretty similar. Krauthammer had called the 2008 candidates a "fine field."[9]

However subjectively "weak field" is defined, it is clear that in 2012 the field failed to excite many within the party. This would seem to have left the door open for other candidates to enter the race. So why did former Alaska governor and 2008 vice-presidential candidate Sarah Palin, New Jersey governor Chris Christie, Indiana governor Mitch Daniels, and South Dakota senator John Thune, among others, decide not to run? Of course, it is not easy to explain the potentially idiosyncratic decisions of possible candidates, but based on systematic studies of both presidential and congressional elections, there are two factors that may have operated in this Republican primary.

First, as the political scientists Gary Jacobson and Samuel Kernell have shown, candidates for office, especially ones with strong credentials and qualifications, are choosy about when they run.[10] They are "strategic candidates," seeking out election years in which the playing field is tilted toward their party or even toward them in particular. In 2012, it was far too early to count Barack Obama out, despite the striking defeat the Democratic Party had suffered in 2010. The advantages he retained may have dissuaded some candidates from challenging him.

For one, incumbent presidents are hard to beat. Since 1900, there have been only five elections in which the incumbent ran for reelection and lost versus fourteen where he ran for reelection and won.[11] Moreover, although the economic recovery after the 2008–9 recession had not been rapid, the economy was growing in 2011 when candidates needed to decide whether to run. As of the spring of 2011, when potential candidates probably needed to make a firm decision (if not yet a public one), economic forecasters were predicting growth rates of 2.7% in 2011 and 3.0% in 2012.[12] As we showed in chapter 2, incumbent presidents running amid this level of economic growth are likely to win. There is no reason to think that potential Republican candidates were running their own election forecasting models, but their intuitions and conversations with advisors may have led them to the same conclusion that our model implied: better wait until 2016 (if then). And even if other factors may have seemed favorable to the Republican Party at that point in time—such as the relatively high unemployment rate or Obama's middling popularity—it may have been a worse bet to challenge Obama under those conditions than to assume he would win and then wait until the end of his second term—at which point, the historical pattern shows, the party controlling the White House often switches.

A second factor affecting whether potential candidates decide to run for office is efforts by party leaders to recruit them or perhaps discourage them. In presidential primaries, party leaders shape the nomination process, even in an era where voters, via primaries and caucuses, more directly determine which candidate wins the nomination. The efforts of party leaders are particularly important during the "invisible primary" that takes place before the caucuses and primaries are held. As an important recent study of presidential primaries argues, the invisible primary consists of conversations and negotiations among party leaders and potential or confirmed candidates.[13] It is "invisible" because these conversations are not always known to the broader public or even to reporters and other professional observers of politics. To the extent that these conversations reflect differences of opinion within the party, it is probably in the party's best interest to keep them invisible, lest all the party's dirty laundry get aired.

Thus it is difficult to say with certainty that party leaders discouraged candidates from running. But there is evidence that they may have. Consider Sarah Palin. She was as close to a bona fide rock star as the Republican Party had. In the run-up to 2010, she had aligned herself with the Tea Party movement and had seen that decision borne out in the Republican takeover of the House and the election of many Tea Party–affiliated candidates. Why did she not run? One possible reason is that Republican leaders did not want her to. In August 2011, the *Huffington Post* conducted a poll with 151 local party leaders in the key early primary states of Iowa, New Hampshire, and South Carolina.[14] The poll was not a representative sample, but its results were suggestive nonetheless. Fully 81% of these leaders said that Palin should not run. Although the majority said they agreed with her on issues, these leaders were evenly split on whether she would "make a good president" and tended to doubt that she could beat Barack Obama (only 37% said she could). One leader said, "I love and admire Sarah Palin. I would vote for her for president should she get the nomination, but I do not believe she is electable as president." Of course, these poll results come with many caveats. Perhaps other party leaders—particularly national party leaders—felt differently. Perhaps Palin did not even care what these or any party leaders thought. But the fact that such opinions existed within the Republican Party may have affected Palin—because she either heard them explicitly or saw the proverbial writing on the wall. The need to campaign for voter support in multiple states means that candidates need the help of party leaders at every level of office.[15] Few party leaders appeared interested in helping Palin.

Of course, the Republicans who chose not to run could have had other motives for doing so, and certainly there was much speculation about these motives. We would only note that their decision not to run was consistent with what a strategic candidate might have thought in 2011 and may have reflected the views of other leaders within the party. A talented and relatively young Republican leader could easily have looked at the fundamentals in the summer of 2011 and decided to wait until 2016. Given that the incumbent party often loses the presidency after two terms in office, the chances of beating the Democrats probably would be better.

The Endorsements Trickle

Given the field they had, the Republican Party then faced the same challenge that parties have faced ever since winning primaries and caucuses became the way in which presidential candidates win delegates to the party conventions: finding a way to consolidate support behind a single candidate, ideally *before* the primaries even take place. This is the chief goal of the invisible primary, one that parties often execute quite well but sometimes struggle with, as they did in 2012. This struggle was probably the best evidence that the Republican presidential field was weak, even by the standards of those within the party.

Because the conversations and negotiations that go on among party leaders are generally private, we must rely on public statements by these leaders to signal whom they support in the nomination race—if anyone. Endorsements by party leaders are the most visible part of the invisible primary. When a party leader endorses a candidate, his or her statement is typically trumpeted by that candidate and then reported in the news media. It is a potentially costly decision by any leader, especially in this Republican primary, when there was real disagreement among party leaders about which candidate to support. Backing the wrong horse, as it were, can become controversial.[16] Endorsements that occur during the invisible primary send a particularly strong signal; after all, anyone can wait until late in primary season and endorse the eventual nominee. Jumping on that candidate's bandwagon is easy at that point. It is riskier to endorse a candidate before the caucuses and primaries even begin.

Endorsements are a misunderstood aspect of primary elections. It is sometimes argued that endorsements do not matter at all. After John McCain and Bob Dole endorsed Mitt Romney, Jon Huntsman said, "You can get all the Doles and McCains in the world as Romney probably will, but in the end, nobody cares."[17] Others argue that endorsements of specific individuals are somehow key—for example, both George H. W. Bush and Jeb Bush garnered headlines when they endorsed Romney in March.

Neither of these perspectives is correct. Endorsements do appear to matter in presidential nominations but not because of what a handful of high-profile politicians decide to do. In the 1980–2004 primaries, a candidate's share of endorsements during the invisible primary was associated with how many delegates that candidate won in the party convention months later—even after taking into account other things that might have affected delegate share, such as fund-raising, media attention, and victories in early caucuses or primaries.[18] Why endorsements matter in this way is still unclear, but they are certainly a prominent and important signal about candidates' standing within the party and ultimately whether a candidate can be the party's standard-bearer.

The number and pace of endorsements through 2011 demonstrated just how different this nomination process was than many others, as well as how seemingly unenthusiastic Republican leaders were about all of the candidates. In Figure 3.1, we show the percentage of Republican governors, senators, and members of the U.S. House of Representatives who endorsed any Republican candidate for president. We include only endorsements before the Iowa caucus and break down the results by each quarter of the year before the election year.[19]

What stands out about 2012 was not only the small percentage of these officeholders who endorsed but the slow pace at which the endorsements accumulated. Clearly 2012 was not like 2000, when a large number of Republican leaders endorsed George W. Bush—many doing so even early in 1999. The pattern in 2012 also differed from that in other years, such as 1988 or 1996, when there were fewer leaders converging on a single candidate such as Bush. In fact, the pace of endorsements in 2012 was even slower than it was in 2008—another year in which Republican leaders struggled to coalesce around a single candidate. It might be surprising to some—given the status that Ronald Reagan has come to have within his party—but 2012 looked more like 1980 than any other Republican presidential primary. It is worth exploring that comparison for insights into why the pace in 2012 was so slow.

In any election year, party leaders are looking for a nominee who meets two criteria. First, the person has to be at least acceptable to various factions within the party. "Acceptable" is the key word, as no single candidate is likely to be the first choice of every faction. Political parties are diverse coalitions of interests, and not every group will favor the same nominee. Many groups may end up compromising. Second, that person needs to be perceived as electable. Although there are always conflicts within any party over how to prioritize ideological fealty versus electability—and, indeed, over how much those two qualities are really in tension—electability remains a crucial consideration. Compromising one's principles is never fun, but it usually hurts even more to lose an election. So party leaders make judgments about how well any candidate is likely to fare against the opposition in the general election.

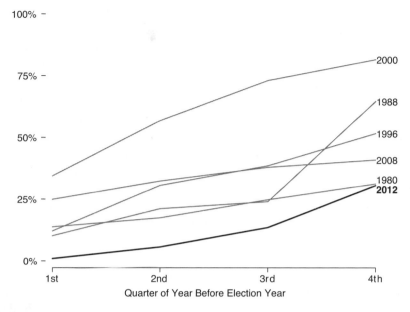

Figure 3.1.

Percent of Republican governors, senators, and House members endorsing a Republican candidate for the presidential nomination.

In both 1980 and 2012, it was hard for the Republican Party to find a candidate who met both criteria. Ronald Reagan, by dint of his many years of work for the party, had built up a substantial base of support among conservatives. But he was not necessarily "acceptable" to moderates within the party, even as he reached out to them in various ways. Moderate Republican leaders shopped around, considering Gerald Ford, George H. W. Bush, and Tennessee senator Howard Baker. Ultimately it was Bush who campaigned the hardest and became the leading moderate candidate—famously calling Reagan's economic plan "voodoo economics"—but there remained concerns about whether he could win the general election. Bush had previously served two terms in the House but had lost two U.S. Senate races and had never held any other elective office, serving instead as chair of the Republican National Committee and director of the Central Intelligence Agency, among other positions. In short, his "record as a vote-getter was weak."[20]

In 2012 something similar occurred. Although there were far more Republican candidates than in 2008, Republican leaders could not find a candidate who was both broadly acceptable within the party and viewed as electable. In particular, it was difficult for leaders to find a candidate who would be acceptable to conservative leaders within the party, including those affiliated with the Tea Party, who were arguably an even larger part of the Republican coalition than they were in 1980. But the candidates with solid conservative credentials were not seen as electable.

Consider, for example, the contrasting views that party leaders had of Sarah Palin. As we have noted, Republican leaders said that they tended to agree with Palin on issues: 37% said that the phrase "takes stands on issues that you agree with" described her "very well." Fewer, however, said this of Romney (27%).[21] But whereas the majority of leaders did not consider Palin electable, the vast majority thought Romney was. The same contrast emerges when comparing views of Michele Bachmann and Romney.[22] Bachmann's challenges in convincing the party of her electability were illustrated by this comment about her from a Republican operative: "They'll give you $13 million to go throw rocks at Nancy Pelosi. They won't give you $13 million if they don't think you're ready to be president of the United States."[23] To be sure, most leaders did not say that they disagreed outright with Romney—a fact that we will return to—but clearly they were less than enthusiastic, as the earlier quotes from prominent conservative pundits illustrate. In the early going, there was only one candidate who met both criteria, at least according to these surveys: Rick Perry. As of early September, he was perceived both as taking the right stand on issues and as someone who could beat Obama.[24] His standing, however, would soon plummet quickly.

The upshot, then, was that many Republican Party leaders adopted a "wait-and-see" approach, sitting on the sidelines rather than signaling their support for any one candidate. This left the race wide open, setting the stage for the multiple front-runners that emerged and the volatile polls that puzzled many observers throughout the primaries.

"Downright Inexplicable"?

On February 21, 2012, Patrick Ruffini, a Republican political consultant, tweeted a picture of the Republican primary polling trends, with their many ups and downs, and wrote, "My two year old could draw a chart that makes more sense than this."[25] Ruffini was not alone. Political reporting and commentary on the GOP primary often saw it as incomprehensible. Former Bush strategist Karl Rove called it "the most unpredictable, rapidly shifting, and often downright inexplicable primary race I've ever witnessed."[26] A Bloomberg article suggested that voters were "shredding the rulebook."[27] The New York Times's David Carr perhaps put it most starkly, in a blog post titled "Who's Leading the Republican Presidential Race? Mr. Random, of Course":

> The dynamism and unpredictability of the race might be assigned to some weakness in Mr. Romney's appeal, or the collective fickleness

of the Republican electorate, but we also need to acknowledge that when it comes to this race, William Goldman's observation about Hollywood—"Nobody knows anything"—applies to the business of politics as well.[28]

The volatility in the polls had its roots in the lack of enthusiasm among party leaders, which was mirrored in Republican voters. In a May 2011 Pew Research Center poll, only a quarter of Republican registered voters called the 2012 field "excellent" or "good"—demonstrating less enthusiasm than they did in both 2007 and 1995.[29] Unsurprisingly, then, many voters had not made a firm decision about whom to support by the fall of 2011. This is hardly unusual in presidential primaries because many of the candidates are not national figures and are unknown to many voters, who may not be paying much attention to the presidential primary to begin with. Voters are thus prone to change their minds during primary campaigns or to make up their minds quite late. In 2011 and 2012, they did both, as the many different front-runners would suggest.

But volatility did not make the 2012 Republican primary incomprehensible. Contra Carr, we can and do "know something." Voters may have seemed fickle, in that some were changing their minds, but they were not doing so randomly. Polls do not move for no reason, and voters are not simply rolling the dice. Polls move in response to new information about the candidates. In 2011 and continuing into 2012, news media coverage was a key source of that information—something that studies of public opinion and elections have routinely found to be true.[30] By charting news coverage and how it responded to events in the campaign, the volatility of the GOP primary polls becomes far more explicable.

The Anatomy of Media Boomlets: Discovery, Scrutiny, and Decline

How did media coverage and voters' dependence on the media for information help explain why, in 2011 and 2012, several candidates surged to become the front-runner, but only briefly? The answer begins with the news media's well-documented focus on the "horse race" of the campaign.[31] Horse-race coverage is about which candidate is ahead or behind or getting ahead or falling behind, which means focusing on metrics like polls and fund-raising and on the strategies that candidates are using. During the 2012 primary campaign, the Pew Center's Project for Excellence in Journalism (PEJ) estimated that nearly two-thirds of news coverage (64%) was framed around horse-race topics.[32]

Although the news media are frequently blamed for horse-race coverage, some blame may rest with news consumers as well. In one study by political scientists Shanto Iyengar, Helmut Norpoth, and Kyu Hahn, voters were sent

CD-ROMs containing news coverage of the 2000 presidential campaign organized by various topics, including strategy and the horse race, candidate biography, and candidate issue positions.[33] As voters navigated this coverage, their reading behavior was recorded. What kinds of stories were read most frequently? Horse-race coverage. This is perhaps unsurprising. Not many people would pass up "New Poll Shows Race Tightening" for "Candidates Release Plans for Entitlement Reform."

The challenge for reporters is that the campaign may not produce newsworthy events or moments every day. Candidates give the same speeches over and over. (Indeed, we heard Romney give virtually the same speech twice in twelve hours on the night before and morning of the Iowa caucus. In the press gallery, reporters were mostly hunched over their Blackberries, ignoring the speech for no doubt the umpteenth time.) Thus reporters may seek out any moment that seems novel or interesting.

One distinctive thing about contemporary presidential primaries, and 2012 in particular, is just how many more potential "moments" there are. In previous years, candidates could count on a spike in news attention when they won more votes than expected in primaries and caucuses. Now such moments include nonbinding "straw polls" and candidate debates—of which there were twenty-seven in 2011–12, far more than in any previous presidential primary.[34] Performance in primaries, straw polls, and debates cannot be established objectively. Instead, reporters and commentators use their own judgment, which is why performing better than their expectations can be so important. (Their judgment may also correspond to how most people, in and out of journalism, would view a particular event, so the fact that news coverage entails subjective decisions does not imply any nefarious media conspiracy.)

The ultimate goal for the news media is to generate a compelling narrative—one that not only draws on the skill and knowledge that reporters feel they have acquired as professional observers of politics but also engages consumers of the news, who are naturally interested in strategy, polls, and other elements of the horse race. This goal is readily acknowledged by reporters. Here, for example, is the *Washington Post*'s Dana Milbank, from a cheeky, but not entirely tongue-in-cheek, paean to Newt Gingrich that was published on January 31, 2012:

> You're the only thing saving us from a long spring of despair, the only person who can, by extending the presidential race, drive up our audience and bring us the revenues we so desperately need. You give us exactly what political journalists crave. Sure, some of us are ideologically biased, but we are far more biased in favor of conflict—and that's why we're all in the tank for you.[35]

We argue that in the Republican presidential primary, as in past primaries, media coverage tended to follow a three-part sequence: discovery, scrutiny, and decline. This sequence described coverage of the 2012 GOP candidates—with one crucial exception: Romney. It also implied the pattern in the polling data: temporary "boomlets" for each of a series of candidates other than Romney.

Discovery

The process of discovery began when a candidate who had previously attracted little news coverage did or said something that reporters and commentators judged to be novel, important, and therefore newsworthy. As a consequence, news coverage of that candidate increased sharply.

Teasing out the subsequent relationship between news coverage and polls can be tricky. If voters do not change their minds absent widely disseminated information, then a surge in news coverage should precede a surge in polls. However, an increase in the polls can also drive further news coverage because candidates who are surging in the polls will attract more attention from the press, thus creating a self-reinforcing cycle between news coverage and poll numbers.[36] We show that both things happened. As best as we can tell from the available 2012 data, the initial increase in news coverage typically preceded the surge in the polls. The news media, responding to events in the campaign, tended to initiate any cycle of discovery, scrutiny, and decline. At the same time, polls and news coverage reinforced each other, as good poll numbers became a rationale for additional coverage. Demonstrating whether reinforcement occurred required some statistical modeling, the details of which we report in the appendix to this chapter.

We focus on news coverage because we think that it, and not the original event that catalyzed the increase in coverage, is what moves polls. These events would not be known to most voters except through news coverage. Few voters witnessed them firsthand. Even the audiences for the nationally televised primary debates were typically small—between three and seven million people. These events were not routinely the subject of campaign advertising either. Moreover, similar kinds of events—straw polls, say—had very different impacts depending on how much news coverage they generated. Finally, in many cases the meaning of events was not obvious. Because there was no readily available standard by which voters interpreted a candidate's performance in a debate or a primary, the media "framed" these events and supplied an interpretation, as they do with many kinds of political events.[37] Their interpretations, expressed in the volume and tone of news coverage, affected whether and how voters respond.

Why would news coverage have this effect on voters in the first place? Why would it push voters toward the candidate who was suddenly prominent in that coverage? The possible answers to this question have been spelled out by political scientist Larry Bartels in his book on presidential primaries.[38] It could happen because voters take cues from others: the more a candidate is discussed in the news, the more voters understand that candidate's positions and chances of winning. It could happen because voters want to be on the winning team. The primary horse race—even, Bartels notes, actual horse races like the Kentucky Derby—may be more fun if spectators have a favorite. It could happen because voters behave strategically—believing that the candidate who is being discussed in the news media is likely to win and then gravitating to that candidate, even if that person is not their first choice, to avoid "wasting" their vote. It could also be simpler than this: voters may tell pollsters they support whichever candidate whose name they can most readily recall, without any other motivation for supporting that candidate. News coverage helps make a candidate's name more accessible in a voter's mind and more likely to be remembered when the pollster calls. We cannot necessarily determine which of these processes was at work, but they all could help explain why a sudden burst of news coverage for an otherwise unfamiliar candidate increased that candidate's poll numbers.[39]

Scrutiny

The news coverage that accompanied the discovery phrase was very often positive. When a candidate turned in an "unexpectedly" strong performance in a straw poll, debate, primary, or caucus, that was framed as suggesting the candidate's strength and potential viability. In short, news coverage created a positive buzz.

But this did not last very long. Once a candidate seemed "serious" enough to pay attention to, that candidate was then subjected to increased scrutiny from both opponents and the news media. As Bartels put it in his study: "unknown candidates who broke out of the pack received very favorable coverage until they showed signs of becoming front-runners; then they were scrutinized much more carefully."[40] Huma Khan of ABC News described the same phenomenon when she wrote this about Newt Gingrich in mid-November 2011: "It remains to be seen whether Gingrich's campaign can sustain his popularity. He's already coming under increased public scrutiny with the recent rise in polls."[41]

This scrutiny took place regardless of what the candidates had done either in the past or in the campaign to that point. It reflected two things: opposing candidates' need to stop the surging candidate from solidifying his or her lead and journalistic norms about vetting candidates. The candidate's opponents began to focus on the front-runner and supplied reporters—on or off the record—with unflattering tidbits from their own research into the candidate.[42] Reporters delved into the candidate's personal history, issue positions, and performance in office and typically discovered a checkered past, controversial statements, and more than a few people willing to go on the record and be critical of the candidate.[43] At times, the candidate him- or herself lent a hand, even unwittingly. He or she said or did things that opposing candidates and reporters judged to be provocative, problematic, or simply mistaken. These "gaffes" only invited further scrutiny. And so the fortunes of the candidate began to turn. Although news coverage of the candidate was still peaking, the tone of that coverage became more negative.

The coverage then conveyed a different story about the horse race. Having heard enough of the candidate's foibles and flaws, voters began to drift away, moving to support a different candidate or declaring themselves undecided. Perhaps the candidate's poll numbers remained higher than they were before the candidate was first "discovered," but they no longer suggested a surge of any significant duration.

Decline

Having devoted some time to writing about a particular candidate, the media had a natural incentive to move on and find a storyline that was novel and more exciting. Unless the candidate did something else that was considered newsworthy, his or her news coverage began to decline, which in turn further drove down the candidate's poll numbers. Then as soon as a different candidate did something judged to be newsworthy, a new cycle of discovery and scrutiny began again.

As we will see, the volatility in 2012 corresponded to this pattern of discovery, scrutiny, and decline. To be sure, understanding this pattern would not have helped us predict beforehand which candidates would surge and when they could surge, but it does help make those surges explicable after the fact. This pattern also shows that the many surges in the 2012 presidential primary were hardly the result of voters chasing after that week's "Mr. Random." Instead they reflected the incentives of the news media to generate novel stories about the campaign and investigate candidates' backgrounds, the incentives of the other candidates to attack anyone who became a front-runner, and the reliance of uncommitted voters on news coverage.

The Rise and Fall of Perry, Cain, and Gingrich

"Texas Gov. Perry Joining Republican Race for President." That was the headline in the *Washington Post* on August 12, the day before Perry formally announced his entry into the race. Within two weeks, CBS News's headline was "Rick Perry Surges to Front in Latest GOP Poll."[44] But by December, his political epitaphs were everywhere: Perry was "languishing in the single digits in most opinion polls" after a "series of gaffes and missteps."[45] In the fall of 2011, a similar fate befell two other Republican candidates: Herman Cain and Newt

Gingrich.[46] Each candidate's story illustrates how, early on, actions judged to be newsworthy drove coverage, with the polls following suit. But soon the tone of that coverage shifted—aided and abetted by their opponents and even by Perry, Cain, and Gingrich themselves—and with it the fortunes of these candidates. Neither Perry nor Cain could recover. Gingrich, as we will see in the next chapter, could do so only briefly.

To chart the media-driven boomlets of these candidates, we rely on two kinds of data. One is simply national polls from the summer and fall of 2011. The other is extensive data on news coverage gathered by the company General Sentiment. General Sentiment has developed computer programs that collect and categorize media coverage from about eleven thousand print, broadcast, and cable news outlets, including national, state, and local media.* Their data provide not only an estimate of how often any particular topic is discussed, such as one of the presidential candidates, but also the tone or "sentiment" of that discussion. Tone refers to how negative or positive that discussion is—as judged by comparing the words in the news to a dictionary of words that are known to have largely positive or negative connotations. For example, if one were monitoring coverage of a company, news coverage that described the company as profitable would be judged as more positive than coverage describing a company as bankrupt. To do all of this via computer programs always raises the risk that the computer will misunderstand the meaning of a particular article, although advances in sentiment analysis have improved the accuracy of computer coding significantly. But computers can code far more content far more quickly than humans, making it sensible to trade off some degree of accuracy for timely and comprehensive data. To help ensure that our conclusions are on firm ground, we rely on a similar set of media data produced by the Pew Center's Project for Excellence in Journalism (PEJ), which also measured the candidates' share of news coverage as well as its tone. See the appendix to this chapter for further details.

*Some further detail and references are here: http://www.cs.sunysb.edu/~skiena/lydia/p1229-bautin.pdf.

Rick Perry was, on paper, a strong candidate—a governor of a large state who had solid conservative credentials and the ability to raise real money. In fact, he outraised all the other Republican candidates in the third quarter of 2011—pulling in $17 million, compared to $14 million for Romney. In July and early August 2011, he attracted episodic news attention, according to data displayed in Figure 3.2. The gray line on this figure includes the mentions of Perry as a percent of mentions of the eight major Republican candidates

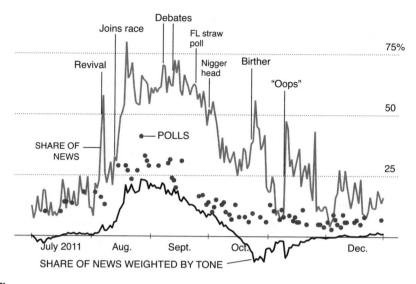

Figure 3.2.

Trends in Rick Perry's news coverage and poll standing.

The gray line represents Perry's share of mentions of the major Republican candidates. The black line represents the share of mentions, weighted by the tone of the coverage. When the black line is above 0, the coverage is net positive; when it is below 0, the coverage is net negative. The gray dots capture Perry's standing in individual national polls among Republicans, dated to the middle of each poll's time in the field and averaging together any polls on overlapping days. The data span the period from July 1 to December 31, 2011.

(Bachmann, Cain, Gingrich, Huntsman, Paul, Perry, Santorum, and Romney). This coverage spiked temporarily when he hosted a religious revival meeting in Texas. But the real boomlet began when Perry entered the race.[47] His poll numbers followed this increase in stories. The three national polls in early August—each poll is displayed as a dot in Figure 3.2—put his standing at 16%, on average. In the first poll taken after his announcement, a one-day Rasmussen poll on August 15, Perry stood at 29%. Other polls in August and early September would put his standing between 24 and 33 points (with the exception of an outlying 41% figure in a Zogby Internet poll). This put him at the front of the pack.

The scrutiny began only four days after his entry into the race. Initially Perry received headlines like these from the *New York Times*:

"Money No Obstacle as Perry Joins GOP Race" (August 13, 2011)
"Shaking Up Republican Field, Perry Officially Enters Race for President" (August 14, 2011)
"A Confident Perry Lingers to Make Friends at the Fair" (August 16, 2011)

"Obama Presses His Case in Crucial Iowa, But Perry Is Close on His
   Heels" (August 17, 2011)

Each of these headlines suggested that Perry was running strongly in the horse
race, which helps explain why the tone of his coverage was positive, on balance.
This is what the black line in Figure 3.2, which weights Perry's share of coverage
by the tone of that coverage, indicates. But things began to change on August
17 with this headline: "Perry Stands by Remarks on Fed Policy and Treason."
While campaigning in Iowa, Perry had said this about the Federal Reserve's
efforts to stimulate the economy and keep interest rates low: "Printing more
money to play politics at this particular time in American history is almost
treacherous—or treasonous in my opinion." Then, referring to Federal Reserve
chair Ben Bernanke, Perry added, "I don't know what y'all would do to him in
Iowa, but we would treat him pretty ugly down in Texas." Reporting on Perry's
comments, Jeff Zeleny and Jackie Calmes of the *New York Times* wrote:

> The comments came at the end of a freewheeling and unscripted day
> of introducing himself to voters and highlighted Mr. Perry's penchant
> for provocative, hard-edged campaigning of the sort that speaks to
> certain conservatives even as it raises hackles elsewhere. A video of
> the remarks quickly circulated, prompting a round of recriminations
> not just from Democrats but from some Republicans—a reminder of
> the old tensions between Mr. Perry and top advisers to former Pres-
> ident George W. Bush.[48]

The article went on to quote criticisms of Perry from Republican strategist
Karl Rove and former Obama economic advisor Lawrence Summers. Reporters also began picking over Perry's November 2010 book, *Fed Up!*, particularly his comments that Social Security was a "Ponzi scheme"—"fraudulent
systems designed to take in a lot of money at the front and pay out none in
the end." This led Perry's spokespersons to walk back his stance, producing
headlines such as "Rick Perry Tiptoes Away from Social Security Stance."[49]
Despite this scrutiny, however, news coverage of Perry was generally positive
in tone in the month after his announcement.[50]

   The real turn in Perry's news coverage came after the candidate debates
on September 7 and 12. In the first debate, Perry again repeated his criticisms
of Social Security, calling it a "monstrous lie," and took heat from opposing
candidates for his economic record as Texas governor and for requiring young
girls to be vaccinated against the human papilloma virus. In the September 12
debate, Perry was again attacked for calling Social Security a Ponzi scheme—a
characterization he did not back away from. In the week after the September
12 debate, the coverage of Perry began to turn negative.[51] Perry's poll numbers

also began to slip. In the five polls conducted between August 27 and September 6, he had averaged 32%. In the four polls conducted partly or entirely in the week after the September 12 debate, Perry's averaged 25%. This was a harbinger of things to come.

On Saturday, September 24, the last day of the Florida Republican Party's "Presidential 5" conference in Orlando, 2,657 attendees cast their votes in the Republican straw poll. The poll itself had no formal significance, like most straw polls during primary season. Its results would not elect any delegates to the national convention. But as a marker of the horse race, it was irresistible. This was unfortunate for Perry. He finished second overall, with 15% of the vote, to Herman Cain, who won 37%. At that point, Cain had been largely ignored by the news media (see Figure 3.3) and was stalled in the single digits in most polls. Cain had held no elective office, having instead built a career as a lobbyist (as the head of the National Restaurant Association) and businessman (most notably as head of Godfather's Pizza). Few expected him to seriously compete for the nomination.

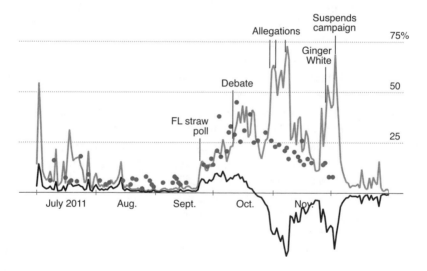

Figure 3.3.
Trends in Herman Cain's news coverage and poll standing.
The gray line represents Cain's share of mentions of the major Republican candidates. The black line represents the share of mentions, weighted by the tone of the coverage. When the black line is above 0, the coverage is net positive; when it is below 0, the coverage is net negative. The gray dots capture Cain's standing in individual national polls among Republicans, dated to the middle of each poll's time in the field and averaging together any polls on overlapping days. The data span the period from July 1 to December 31, 2011.

But his victory in this one straw poll catalyzed a round of media attention, largely at Perry's expense. "Cain Upsets Perry at Florida Straw Poll," declared *USA Today*.[52] "Cain Upsets Perry in Florida Republican Straw Poll," declared Reuters.[53] "Herman Cain Upsets Gov. Rick Perry to Win Florida GOP Straw Poll," declared Fox News.[54] This framing of the straw poll demonstrates how news coverage supplied an interpretation of the event. Not only did news outlets devote attention to this informal and nonbinding poll, they framed Cain's win as a win *over* Perry, even though Cain bested the other Republican candidates, including Romney, by an even larger margin.

Within ten days Cain's share of news coverage increased from essentially nothing to 20%. Meanwhile, Perry's fell. The tone of Cain's coverage was favorable on average. Meanwhile, Perry's coverage continued to become more negative.[55] In part, this was because of a new story about a hunting ranch his family owned in West Texas, which had been known by the name Niggerhead.[56] Perry's poll numbers began to slip further. In the five polls between September 24, the day of the straw poll, and October 3, he averaged 15 points. By the middle of October, many polls put him back in the single digits. Nothing Perry did would turn this around. He made news on two other occasions— once for making comments that suggested doubt as to whether Obama was born in the United States (denoted "Birther" in Figure 3.2) and once for declaring in a November 9 debate that he would eliminate three cabinet departments as president and then forgetting the name of the third one. His rueful comment—"oops"—was by that point merely the capstone on his decline.

Meanwhile, Cain's rise continued. His share of news coverage spiked again after the October 11 candidate debate, in which he emphasized his "9-9-9" tax plan, which would have replaced the existing federal tax code with three 9% taxes (on income, business transactions, and sales). His poll numbers showed a similar pattern. In the weeks between the Florida straw poll and the October 11 debate, his share in the polls increased—averaging 21 points during this period. In the week after the debate, his polling average climbed to 31 points. In some polls at this time, he was the leading candidate overall.

But the scrutiny was coming. The 9-9-9 plan had already attracted criticism from the other candidates; in the October 11 debate, Romney said, "simple answers are always very helpful but oftentimes inadequate."[57] Tax experts were even less favorable. One *Washington Post* story began, "The '9-9-9' plan that has helped propel businessman Herman Cain to the front of the GOP presidential field would stick many poor and middle-class people with a hefty tax increase while cutting taxes for those at the top, tax analysts say."[58] By the third week of October, Cain's coverage, although still quite voluminous, had become more negative than positive. At the end of October, his poll average was about 27%, or 4 points lower than it was after the debate.

His fortunes would change dramatically at that point. On October 31, *Politico* reported that two women had accused Herman Cain of sexual harassment and received financial settlements from the National Restaurant Association during his tenure as president from 1996 to 1999.[59] On November 3, a third woman came forward to accuse Cain of sexual harassment. On November 7, another woman, Sharon Bialek, accused Cain of actual sexual assault. Amid these allegations, news coverage of Cain spiked dramatically. At its peak almost 75% of all mentions of the Republican candidates were mentions of Cain.

These allegations brought further scrutiny of Cain's behavior and the vague and evasive answers he and his spokespersons gave to questions about the allegations. News coverage of Cain became much more negative and his poll numbers continued to drop. In the week after Bialek came forward, Cain's poll numbers averaged 19%. By the end of November, the "decline" phase was well under way. His share of news coverage had plummeted and his poll numbers had slipped further, to about 15%. Cain was then hit with a fourth allegation, this one from a woman named Ginger White who claimed that she and Cain had carried on a thirteen-year affair that had ended only just before he began his presidential campaign. His news coverage spiked again, and his poll numbers fell even further. He was back to single digits in the two national polls right before he suspended his campaign on December 3.

As Cain's fortunes were waning, an unlikely candidate came to the fore: Newt Gingrich. Six months before this point, in June 2011, Gingrich's chief advisors had quit en masse, asserting that he was not interested in running a vigorous campaign—an assertion that, fairly or not, seemed to be confirmed by the fact that Gingrich had just returned from a two-week cruise in the Greek Isles. Gingrich also faced criticism within the Republican Party for his claim that Representative Paul Ryan's plan to restructure Medicare amounted to "right-wing engineering." He later apologized.[60] In July, as Figure 3.4 illustrates, Gingrich made news for attacking a senior member of his party—he criticized Senate Majority Leader Mitch McConnell's proposed compromise during the debt ceiling negotiations—and for his accumulated campaign debts. He then received little news coverage for the summer and most of the fall, while continuing to poll only in the single digits.

But during the month of October, Gingrich's poll numbers began to increase slowly. In the first half of October, he averaged between 7 and 8 points in national polls. In the second half of October, he averaged almost 11 points. This increase was not accompanied by any real increase in news coverage.[61] It could have been driven by his performance in the September and October debates. Although the audiences for these debates were a fraction even of likely Republican voters, they could have been responsible for a small shift in the

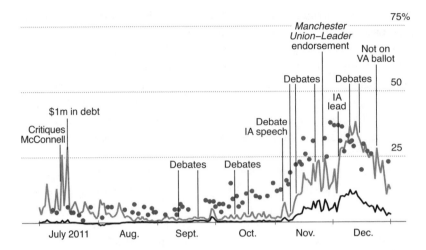

Figure 3.4.
Trends in Newt Gingrich's news coverage and poll standing.
The gray line represents Gingrich's share of mentions of the major Republican candidates. The black line represents the share of mentions, weighted by the tone of the coverage. When the black line is above 0, the coverage is net positive; when it is below 0, the coverage is net negative. The gray dots capture Gingrich's standing in individual national polls among Republicans, dated to the middle of each poll's time in the field and averaging together any polls on overlapping days.

polls. News coverage during this time suggested that Gingrich was a consistently strong debater. For example, in an October 29 article, the *Washington Post*'s Karen Tumulty wrote:

> [T]here are signs that Republicans are giving Gingrich another look. Fundraising has picked up after his strong debate performances and amid the continued frostiness that many activist Republicans feel toward presumed front-runner Mitt Romney, the former Massachusetts governor.

The article goes on to note that Gingrich had raised $1 million in October, which was more than he had raised in all of July, August, and September. Tumulty noted that Gingrich had seen a "modest uptick" in his poll numbers—citing a 3-point increase in *New York Times*/CBS News polls—but that does not appear to have motivated her piece.[62]

Gingrich's surge began to take shape in November. He received a bump in news attention after his November 5 speech at the Ronald Reagan dinner, a fund-raiser for the Iowa Republican Party. The *New York Times*'s Richard Oppel Jr. said that Gingrich "appeared to help his chances" at the dinner. Gingrich was the focal point of this article, even though four other candidates spoke.[63] The article concluded by quoting an Iowa Republican who said that Gingrich "hit a home run tonight." A *Washington Post* article from that same day emphasized the friendly "debate" between Gingrich and Cain that took place after the speech.[64] Although the article noted Gingrich's somewhat higher poll numbers—citing his 12% standing in a new *Washington Post*/ABC News poll—it focused more on his performance in the debate:

> On stage Saturday, Gingrich seized the opportunity to show off his mastery of policy matters. He spoke with ease about the intricacies of health policy, saying the nation's health system should be less bureaucratic and more consumer-friendly.

After the November 9 candidate debate, Gingrich received more and increasingly favorable news coverage.[65] A CBS News poll conducted during and after the November 9 debate put his standing at 15%, which led the *New York Times*'s Trip Gabriel to write that Gingrich was "running near the front of a fractured pack," a fact that Gabriel also credited to his debate performance, although, given the audiences for the debates, it was more likely due to the news coverage complimenting his debate performances.[66] The rest of November followed the now familiar pattern, as Gingrich's share of the news and poll standing increased in tandem.

Even as Gingrich's ascent continued, there were the predictable rumblings. In mid-November the *Post*'s Tumulty wrote, "But whether he will become an actual threat to Romney, or just another fleeting phenom, will depend largely on two things: Gingrich's ability to keep in check the impulses that have been his undoing in the past, and how well he deals with the criticism and scrutiny that go with being a real contender."[67] Tumulty went on to quote the unfavorable view of a "Republican former House colleague" ("The worst in Newt comes out when he is doing well"), to note Gingrich's self-described "controversial" proposals, and to describe his "political baggage," such as his three marriages. Both Gingrich's rivals and news reporters began to dwell on the consulting fees he received from Freddie Mac, the government housing agency that Gingrich himself had criticized for its alleged role in the housing bubble and subsequent financial crisis. In the November 22 debate, Gingrich's endorsement of a path for citizenship for some illegal immigrants led reporters to note that this "could put him at odds with some conservatives in his party."[68]

But the real turning point seemed to come in December when Romney began to attack Gingrich in earnest, mostly on the issues that had been discussed in the previous weeks. A series of *New York Times* and *Washington Post* headlines captured the shift in tone that augured Gingrich's decline.[69] Initially those stories portrayed Gingrich as the front-runner and Romney as back on his heels.

December 5: "In Gingrich, Romney Team Sees Threat"
December 6: "In Iowa, Gingrich Is Gaining Favor, New Poll Shows"

Then as the attacks from both Democrats and Romney increased:

December 7: "New Romney Ad Turns Up Heat on Gingrich"
December 8: "Romney Supporters Slam Gingrich's Leadership Skills,
    Vanity"
December 12: "Mitt Romney Steps Up Attacks on Newt Gingrich"

Some of these attacks on Gingrich came from Republican Party leaders, including former Missouri senator James Talent, former New Hampshire governor John Sununu, and former House member Christopher Shays. Talent said that Gingrich "was not a reliable and trustworthy leader." Sununu said that Gingrich "is more concerned about Newt Gingrich than he is about conservative principle." Shays said, "Newt is an entrepreneur more than he's a manager." Their comments provided a somewhat uncommon glimpse into the conversations ongoing during the invisible primary. They also pointed to an important weakness for Gingrich—one that would be evident in coming months: there was real and sincere opposition to his candidacy within the party, and some leaders were willing to criticize him publicly in order to prevent him from becoming the party's nominee.

As Gingrich came under fire, news stories began to suggest that he was in trouble and that perhaps his campaign was not up to the task of responding. On December 17 the *Washington Post*'s Dan Balz referred to Gingrich's "time of testing" and the "twin problems" that he confronted: "answering his rivals' attacks, which are raining down on the former House speaker," and "how to rapidly build a campaign infrastructure large and sturdy enough to sustain a viable presidential candidacy."[70] This latter point suggests how, despite increases in fund-raising, news attention, and poll standing, Gingrich could still be judged as lacking by other measures of the horse race—in this case, the sophistication of his campaign operation.[71] The consequence of these attacks and news coverage of them was evident in Gingrich's poll standing in December. Gallup polls showed his rapid decline: from 37% in the first week of December to 31% in the second week to 26% in the third week to 23% in the final week. He only faded further as the Iowa caucus approached—although, unlike any of the candidates who had surged earlier in 2011, Gingrich was not quite finished yet.

Anybody but Romney?

By the end of the fall, Republican voters were more enthusiastic about the field than they were six months earlier but less enthusiastic than in past election years. In a November 2011 Pew Research Center poll, almost half of Republican respondents said that the Republican candidates were, as a group, "excellent" or "good."[72] This was low by historical standards: 56% of Republicans had said that of the GOP field in November 2007, and 67% of Democrats had similarly favorable feelings toward the Democratic field at that time. The front-running candidates also elicited less enthusiasm than did their 2008 counterparts. Relatively few Republicans said they would vote "enthusiastically" for Romney, Santorum, or Gingrich in November 2012 if one of them were the nominee.[73] More said that would be voting "mainly against Obama" or would not vote at all. This lack of enthusiasm was especially evident when comparing 2011 to 2010. Before the 2010 election, more Republicans than Democrats said they were more enthusiastic about voting compared to previous elections—a reversal of the pattern in 2006 and 2008. But by late 2011, the parties were much closer to parity.[74] Although voters' stated enthusiasm months before an election may not have predicted whether they ultimately decided to vote, the trends in partisan differences demonstrated how much harder it was for Republicans to get behind a Republican presidential candidate than simply to oppose the Democratic president.

The still unsettled nature of the race was, in the minds of many, a repudiation of Mitt Romney. Early on, quite a few political analysts considered him the front-runner. In April 2010, for example, Mark Halperin said that Romney was "now the front-runner for 2012 and presumably will hold on to that status for the foreseeable future."[75] But throughout the fall Romney was almost always in second place behind whichever candidate was the flavor of the month. On the eve of the Iowa caucus, Romney's poll numbers were in the mid- to high 20s, essentially tied with the fading Gingrich. Romney, who had achieved so much in other aspects of his life, seemed doomed to fail again as a presidential candidate.

In a long piece in *New York* magazine, Frank Rich summed up the conventional explanation for Romney's failure to consolidate support. He is worth quoting at length. Rich began by articulating the "standard analysis of the race," in which Romney's "unyielding 25 percent average in the polls" will ultimately be sufficient for him to prove "Beltway handicappers" correct:

> Eventually primary voters will exhaust all conceivable alternatives. . . . Then they will come home to the 25 percent leader of the pack, because that's what well-mannered Republicans always do.

But then Rich rejoined:

> But this narrative is built on a patently illogical assumption: that a 25 percent minority is the trunk wagging the Republican elephant. What makes anyone seriously assume that the 75 percent will

accommodate itself to that etiolated 25 percent rather than force the reverse? That lopsided majority of the GOP is so angry at the status quo that it has been driven to embrace, however fleetingly, some of the most manifestly unqualified, not to mention flakiest, presidential contenders in American history. The 75 percent is determined to take a walk on the wild side. This is less about rejecting Mitt—who's just too bland a figure to inspire much extreme emotion con or pro— than it is about fervently wanting something else.[76]

This enraged 75% was, to Rich, the "Molotov Party." Thinking of the Republican primary in this way, however, failed to appreciate Romney's strength at this point. Moreover, although it was certainly true that the majority of Republicans were "angry at the status quo," if by status quo one means "Barack Obama," Republican voters' attitudes about their party's presidential candidates were not those of a restive Molotov majority, fervently wanting anybody but Romney.

Part of the reason that Romney was not the consistent front-runner during the fall had to do with how the media covered him. The pattern of discovery, scrutiny, and decline did not apply, as Figure 3.5 shows. Having run

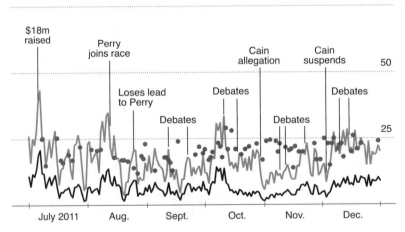

Figure 3.5.
Trends in Mitt Romney's news coverage and poll standing.
The gray line represents Romney's share of mentions of the major Republican candidates. The black line represents the share of mentions, weighted by the tone of the coverage. When the black line is above 0, the coverage is net positive; when it is below 0, the coverage is net negative. The gray dots capture Romney's standing in individual national polls among Republicans, dated to the middle of each poll's time in the field and averaging together any polls on overlapping days.

in 2008, Romney was much more of a known quantity. There was less to "discover" about him. In fact, some of the biggest shifts in Romney's share of news coverage did not have anything to do with what he did or said. These shifts came about largely because of trends in coverage of Perry and Cain. As Perry's share of news coverage increased after he joined the race, Romney's decreased. Romney's share also decreased when Cain was accused of sexual harassment and then increased when he dropped out of the race. In short, news coverage of Romney was far more constant: he never dominated the news but he never disappeared. His poll numbers followed a similar pattern, fluctuating relatively little during these six months, especially compared to the larger ups and downs for Cain, Perry, and Gingrich.

But much like the proverbial tortoise racing against the hare, Romney emerged from the fall as the clear leader in endorsements, fund-raising, media attention, and polls. We summarize all of those data in Figure 3.6. Although, as we have noted, relatively few Republican Party leaders endorsed any candidate, Romney won the vast majority of those endorsements. In fact, he garnered more endorsements from sitting governors, senators, and House members than he did before the Iowa caucus in 2008, when both John

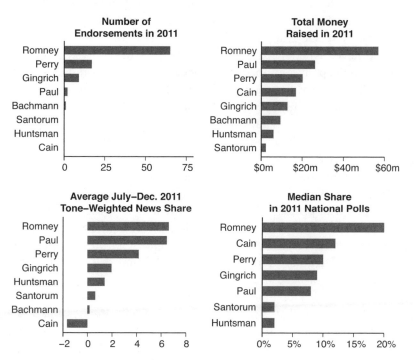

Figure 3.6.
Republican candidate endorsements, fund-raising, news coverage, and polling in 2011.

McCain and Rudy Giuliani earned nearly as many endorsements as he did. It is also important that none of the other candidates could accumulate many, if any, endorsements. Perry, Cain, and Gingrich benefited from media attention but ultimately could not win significant support among party leaders. Their support was, in some sense, not only temporary but superficial. To the extent that pre-Iowa endorsements tell us who the nominee is likely to be—and typically they do—Romney was that candidate.

Romney also raised more money during 2011 than any other candidate and had far more cash on hand at the end of the year—almost $20 million, or about $16 million more than his nearest competitor (Paul). He had consistently received more positive media coverage than any other candidate, besting Paul only slightly but certainly besting Perry, Cain, and Gingrich, despite their boomlets. And although he had not consistently led in the polls, especially in the fall of 2011, his polling median was larger than that of any other candidate. Moreover, at the end of 2011, he was once again in the lead. In the last national poll of the year, fielded December 31 through January 2 by YouGov, 30% of Republican primary voters supported Romney, giving him a 13-point lead over his nearest opponent (Gingrich).

This leads to one of the ironies of this invisible primary period. Because Romney was relatively well-known, he never received the spikes in coverage that Perry, Cain, and Gingrich did. Because of that, he never "surged" in the polls and never experienced the reinforcing cycle of positive news coverage and gains in the polls. This made him appear to be a weak candidate, unloved by many in the party. But this also concealed the underlying structure of the race, which tilted in his favor. Even if Romney was never the heavy favorite, he was the clear front-runner.

The notion of a Molotov Party wanting "anybody but Romney" also suggested a party cleaved by ideology, with the moderate minority supporting Romney and the conservative majority opposing him. But that was not how the Republican Party looked at the end of 2011. In December, two-thirds of likely Republican primary voters viewed Romney favorably, more than had a favorable view of any of the other candidates (see Figure 3.7). Romney was also better known and/or better liked than some other previous presidential candidates. A December 1991 *Time*/CNN poll found that 72% of registered Democrats did not have an opinion of Bill Clinton and only 17% had a favorable opinion. A December 2004 *Newsweek* poll found that only 44% of registered Democrats had a favorable opinion of John Kerry, while 22% had an unfavorable opinion and 34% were unsure. A December 2007 Gallup poll found that 68% of registered Republicans had a favorable view of John Mc-Cain—a number roughly equal to Romney's. In fact, at this point in 2011, views of many Republican candidates were favorable on balance, suggesting

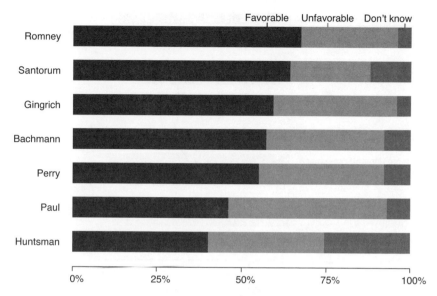

Figure 3.7.

Views of GOP presidential candidates by likely Republican primary voters (December 2011).

Data are from a YouGov survey. *N* = 14,051.

that however unenthusiastic Republicans were about "the field," a majority of them liked most of the candidates in that field.

Moreover, none of the cleavages in this Molotov Party was all that evident, at least when it came to views of Romney. As we show in Figure 3.8, Romney was viewed positively by likely Republican primary voters regardless of whether they were conservatives or moderates, pro-life or pro-choice, relatively wealthy or not, or Tea Party members or not. In fact, Romney was viewed *more favorably* among the very constituencies that were supposed to want anyone but him. For example, about 74% of conservative Republican primary voters had a favorable view of him, compared to 62% of liberals and moderates. Even if some in the party were not enthusiastic about Romney, they were not, as Rich was careful to note, rejecting him.

Why would moderate and conservative Republican voters have such similar views of a candidate allegedly anathema to conservatism? One reason was that they did not see Romney as all that liberal. In a YouGov poll conducted right before the Iowa caucus, Republican primary voters were asked to place themselves and several of the Republican candidates on a liberal-conservative scale. On average, respondents placed both themselves and all of the candidates on the conservative side of the spectrum (see Figure 3.9).[77]

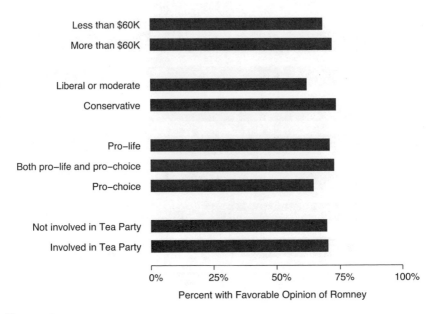

Figure 3.8.
Views of Romney by different groups of likely Republican primary voters (December 2011).
Data are from a YouGov survey.

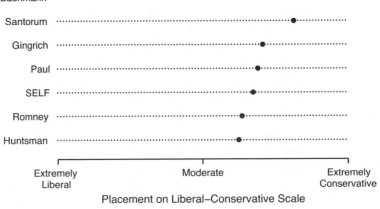

Figure 3.9.
Ideological placements of GOP presidential candidates and themselves by likely Republican primary voters.
Data are from a YouGov survey conducted December 31, 2011–January 2, 2012. *N* = 281.

Although Romney was placed slightly to the left of the average Republican primary voter, the difference was minimal. Romney was only slightly further away from this average voter than was Gingrich and actually closer than was Bachmann or Santorum. This did not mean that all Republican voters were ideologically closer to Romney than anyone else. On average, Huntsman was perceived by moderate Republican voters as closer to them than was Romney. And conservative Republican voters considered Gingrich, Paul, Santorum, and Bachmann to be closer to them than Romney. But despite Romney's record as Massachusetts governor and despite vocal opposition from some conservative opinion leaders, Republican voters did not see Romney as a closet liberal. He was shaping up as a candidate who could prove acceptable to a range of factions within the party.

One last finding suggests the Republican Party was not nearly so restive as Molotov cocktail analogies would suggest. If conservatives and moderate Republicans were really warring camps—and if the volatility in the fall were the result of conservatives seeking "anybody but Romney"—you might expect that by December 2011 supporters of the various candidates would be ideologically divided. To see if this was true, we created measures of social and economic conservatism based on attitudes toward various salient issues, including taxation of the wealthy, health care, abortion, and gay rights.[78] Drawing on a large December 2011 YouGov survey, we mapped the location of the average supporter of each of the Republican candidates (see Figure 3.10). All of these respondents identified as likely Republican primary voters. For comparison, we also mapped the average Democrat, Republican, and independent, as well as those who supported Obama in a head-to-head race with Romney.

In fact Republican primary voters, regardless of whom they supported, were ideologically similar. The only exception was supporters of Huntsman, who were too small a group to be consequential anyway. To be sure, the supporters of the candidates were not identical. Supporters of Bachmann, Gingrich, Perry, or Santorum were more socially conservative than Romney supporters. Those who supported Gingrich, Perry, or Santorum were more economically conservative. But these differences were not large. For example, if we imagine social conservatism as a 100-point scale ranging from liberal to conservative, Santorum supporters were 16 points more socially conservative than Romney supporters. Similarly, Gingrich supporters were only 9 points more conservative than Romney supporters on economic issues. Contrast that to the gaps between Obama and Romney supporters: 36 points on social issues and 48 points on economic issues.

Why were supporters of the various Republican candidates so ideologically similar? Possibly because Republican voters were not choosing on

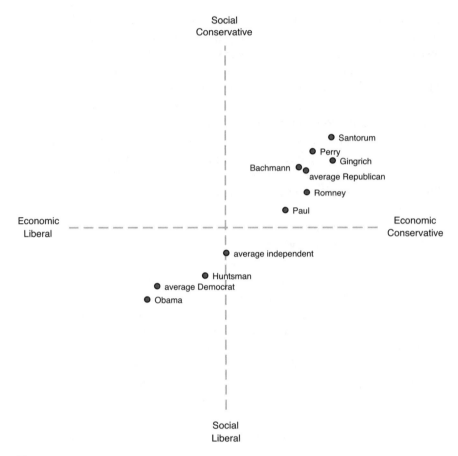

Figure 3.10.
Ideological location of supporters of each Republican candidate and Obama.
The graph maps the ideological location of the average supporter of each Republican candidate. All of these supporters also identified themselves as likely Republican
primary voters. The graph also maps the ideological location of the average Republican,
Democrat, and independent, as well as those who supported Obama in a two-way race
against Romney. The economic scale includes attitudes toward government-provided
universal health care, increasing taxes for the wealthy, and government regulation of
business. The social scale includes two measures of attitudes toward abortion as well as
attitudes toward gay marriage. Source: December YouGov poll. The number of respondents in the poll is 44,998. The number of likely Republican primary voters is 14,415.

ideological grounds. For example, Bachmann was arguably much more conservative on social issues than were her supporters, who may not have known
or cared. If voters did not have ideology foremost in mind, this would undercut
the characterization of the Republican Party as ideologically divided—with
restive factions of moderates and conservatives, evangelicals and Chamber

of Commerce types, "well-mannered" Republicans and "Molotov" Republicans who struggled to agree on a nominee. The lack of meaningful ideological rifts also suggests that lengthy discussions of which candidate would appeal to which faction were beside the point: there was not that much daylight among the factions.

The various candidates' supporters may have looked similar because the candidates were, too. Ramesh Ponnuru could almost have been summarizing our results when he wrote this on December 2, 2011, on the website of the *National Review*.

> The Republican party now features a remarkable degree of programmatic consensus. The entire field wants to cut corporate tax rates, convert Medicaid into block grants, and (the asterisk candidacy of Gary Johnson aside) protect unborn human life. Even Jon Huntsman, the candidate positioned farthest left in the field, favors these policies. None of them enjoyed such uniform support in previous primaries, and some of them had none.
>
> When the candidates differ, it is typically on issues that are unlikely to matter during the next presidency. Representative Bachmann may, unlike some of the others, wish to abolish the EPA, but no conceivable Congress within the next eight years will grant her wish.
>
> The narrowness of the candidates' differences on pertinent issues militates in favor of picking the one who can best implement the sensible agenda they largely share.[79]

Ponnuru's view was not shared by every Republican, but the title of his article, "Romney's the One," was a much more accurate description of the race in December 2011 than was "Anybody but Romney." Many signs did suggest that Romney would be "the one." He was ahead of his rivals, and sometimes far ahead, on the most important metrics of the horse race. He was well-liked overall and, contrary to much conventional wisdom, perceived as moderately conservative—certainly well within the party's "programmatic consensus." But the first serious tests of the race were yet to come.

CHAPTER 4

All In

The Pizza Ranch in Altoona, Iowa, sits amid a long series of strip malls. When we arrived at 5 PM on January 2, 2012, the eve of the Iowa caucus, Rick Santorum was due to appear in an hour. Carl Cameron of Fox News was the first person we encountered—deeply tanned with pancake makeup, talking seriously into his microphone. The second person was a man selling Santorum buttons, three for $10. We bought some. We grabbed a table in the back, ordered a pizza, and waited for Santorum to arrive.

A second, smaller dining room had been set aside for his remarks. Over its doorway was a sign indigenous to the Pizza Ranch: "Faith, Family, Friends." The sign had no apparent relation to Santorum's "Faith, Family, and Freedom Tour," but the similarity probably helped explain why Santorum chose this Pizza Ranch, and many others across Iowa, for campaign events. The restaurant had a ranch-y decor: rusted tractor seats and farm tools, pictures of John Wayne, and wood paneling on some of the walls. Incongruously, the rustic vibe was interrupted by the world's most sophisticated soda fountain, with a touch-screen, twenty different Coca-Cola products, and the ability to dispense shots of lime, orange, vanilla, cherry, and cherry vanilla. Initially it looked like a thin crowd. But soon people started to arrive, including seniors and—not surprising, given the possibility of a pizza dinner—families with children of all ages.

At 6:03 PM Santorum's pickup truck pulled up, someone opened the door and yelled, "Ladies and gentlemen, the next president of the United States!" and Santorum walked in wearing his usual button-down shirt and V-neck sweater vest. By now the Pizza Ranch was standing room only, and the energy inside seemed perfectly in tune with Santorum's late surge in the polls. After making his prepared remarks in the adjacent room, he came into the main dining area and spoke to the rest of us. Seemingly unprepared for the crowd, Santorum had no amplification other than a megaphone, which made his voice tinny and hard to hear. He stood on a small platform only about four inches tall. Lights hanging down from the ceiling blocked many people's views of Santorum's face. After he was done complimenting Iowans for their thoughtful dedication to the task of picking presidents, the crowd chanted, "We pick Rick!" He worked the perimeter of the room, signing photos and books and posing for pictures with kids. When he finished, he hopped in his pickup truck and drove away.

Later that night we made our way to a Romney rally in a large commercial warehouse in Clive, Iowa. The middle of the warehouse floor had been cleared for the event. Private security and local police were abundant. Whereas Santorum had a four-inch riser, Romney had a stage built for the candidate and his surrogates. Whereas Santorum simply got out of his pickup and hustled in the front door of the Pizza Ranch, Romney's entourage rolled up to the back of the warehouse where the candidate waited for the right moment to make his entrance. After speeches by his sons and South Dakota senator John Thune, Romney, hidden from the crowd, appeared on a nine-inch riser that led from the back door to center stage. As Romney walked forward, shaking hands along the rope-line, he appeared just a bit taller than everyone he passed. Every camera got the shot of Romney standing above a crowd of people reaching to touch him. Someone had thought about this entrance.

And someone who understood the media had thought about the rest of the room. There was a banner behind the stage reading "Believe in America" with American and Iowan flags flanking it; professional lighting to ensure high-quality photographs and video; and a dedicated press area with risers for the TV cameras and tall ladders for photographers wanting crowd shots. There was also loud music to generate enthusiasm during the long wait for Romney's arrival (Van Halen's "Right Here, Right Now," Tom Cochrane's "Life Is a Highway," the obligatory Toby Keith); blue Romney T-shirts everywhere; homemade signs ("Iowa Picks Corn and Presidents"); and Romney staffers moving through the crowd handing out business cards in case anyone needed a ride to the caucus the next night. There were two separate microphone checks before Romney showed up. Needless to say, no megaphones were necessary.[1]

The contrast between these two events tells us much about the Republican primary and how Romney became the party's nominee. Santorum's rally came right before he would win a narrow victory in the Iowa caucus, the first of several primary and caucus victories. His success, and Newt Gingrich's brief resurgence a few weeks later, showed again how campaign events could lead the news media to pay sudden attention to a candidate, thereby generating a spike in the candidate's poll numbers. But as before, these boomlets proved to be temporary—illustrating the process of "discovery, scrutiny, and decline" that we discussed in the last chapter—and did not derail Romney's ride to the nomination. To be sure, Romney's ride was not perfectly smooth. It looked less like the quickly accelerating momentum so often visible in presidential primaries and more like "slow-mentum." But however slow, it was steady. Neither Gingrich nor Santorum, much like Rick Perry and Herman Cain in the fall, could muster a significant challenge to Romney.

Santorum and Gingrich's successes depended on two factors. First, they needed a state with demographics favorable to them—that is, a Republican electorate tilted more toward strong conservatives and evangelicals. These groups were not adamantly opposed to Romney, but they were often more likely to support another candidate as their first choice. Figure 4.1 shows this fact: the more of a state's primary voters who identified as "very conservative" or as born again or evangelical, the fewer of them who voted for Romney in

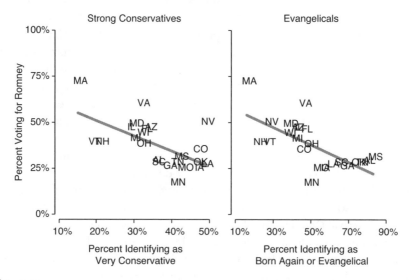

Figure 4.1.

Primary voter demographics and support for Mitt Romney.

Each graph displays Romney's share of the vote in various primaries or caucuses and the percentage of voters who identified as "very conservative" or as evangelical or born again. Data are from the 2012 primary exit polls, except in Colorado, Minnesota, and Missouri, where the data are from pre-election surveys conducted by Public Policy Polling.

the primary.[2] Second, Santorum and Gingrich needed voters to hear about them; favorable demographics were not enough. People who might have been predisposed to support either of them still needed to learn enough about them to believe that they were the right choice. So Gingrich's and Santorum's successes also depended on either a burst of favorable national news coverage—"discovery," as we have called it—or the ability to campaign effectively enough on their own to reach voters via ads, local news coverage of their campaign appearances, and the like.

But Gingrich and Santorum faced two problems: the sequence of state primaries and caucuses, and Romney's campaign itself. Although a few states gave Gingrich or Santorum surges, the sequence of states made it hard for either of them to generate much momentum. Primaries in states with demographics favorable to them were interspersed with primaries in states with demographics favorable to Romney. Even as dramatic or unexpected victories by Gingrich or Santorum generated news coverage for them, a Romney victory soon followed.

Moreover, neither Gingrich nor Santorum could run effective enough campaigns to build sufficient support in the states with less favorable demographics. One reason is that they could not match Romney's support among party leaders and donors. In fact, party leaders often reacted to their boomlets with concern, while Romney continued to receive more leaders' endorsements. Romney's support within the party helped contribute to his financial advantage. This gave him a second advantage: a more professionalized campaign operation. Despite occasional infusions of cash to Gingrich's and Santorum's campaigns, mainly to affiliated super-PACs, and despite a few states where Santorum arguably out-campaigned Romney at the retail level, neither Gingrich nor Santorum could compete effectively with Romney either on the airwaves or on the ground. The rallies we attended in Iowa were microcosms of this fact: Romney's rally may have lacked the ramshackle charm of Santorum's, but it showcased not only his financial advantage but also his campaign's diligence and professionalism. This matters more than symbolically; a better-run campaign delivers a candidate's message and mobilizes voters more effectively.

Finally, Romney developed a broader base of support within the party. This was a surprising accomplishment for a man who, as we saw in the previous chapter, faced an alleged majority of the party wanting "Anybody but Romney." Even among Republican voters whose first choice was a candidate other than Romney, Romney was often their second choice. Commentators frequently assumed that Republican voters would behave ideologically. If a hardcore conservative favored Gingrich, and Gingrich stumbled, then, the story went, this conservative voter would fall back on another of the more

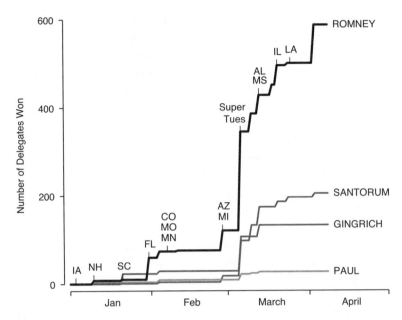

Figure 4.2.
Delegates won up until Santorum's exit from race.
The graph does not include the 332 delegates who were not bound by state primaries or caucuses to vote for a candidate. Data courtesy of Josh Putnam of Frontloading Headquarters.

conservative candidates, like Santorum. But this was not how all Republican voters reasoned. Many who were ideologically closer to another candidate supported Romney, at least in part because they believed he would defeat Obama.

Romney's broad appeal did not mean he was going to win every state. But, crucially, he still won delegates even in these less hospitable states. Figure 4.2 shows this pattern of delegate accumulation up until Santorum's exit from the race, at which point Romney became the de facto nominee. Over time, Romney's share of the delegates increased steadily—a fact that was rarely dramatic enough to drive news coverage but was the ultimate confirmation of his viability and even inevitability. By April, the party had made its bet: it was all in on Romney.

From Des Moines to Manchester

In the fall of 2011—well into December, in fact—Rick Santorum was not a candidate on many people's radar. He had solid credentials as a social conservative

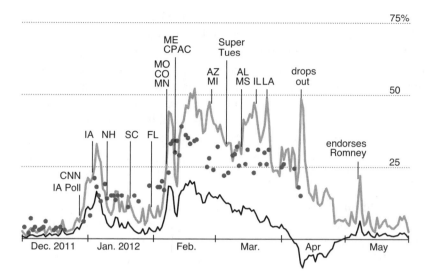

Figure 4.3.
Trends in Rick Santorum's news coverage and poll standing.
The gray line represents Santorum's share of mentions of the major Republican candidates. The black line represents the share of mentions, weighted by the tone of the coverage. When the black line is above 0, the coverage is net positive; when it is below 0, the coverage is net negative. The gray dots capture Santorum's standing in individual national polls among Republicans, dated to the middle of each poll's time in the field and averaging together any polls on overlapping days. The data span the period December 1, 2011–May 31, 2012.

but had gained little traction in the race. As Figure 4.3 illustrates, he garnered little news coverage in the first weeks of December, much as he had in the months before. In national polls he was in the single digits. Santorum was even languishing in polls in Iowa, where he had virtually taken up residence in order to campaign around the state, working under the (ultimately correct) assumption that Republican caucusgoers, 57% of whom identified as evangelicals in 2012, were a receptive constituency.

But in late December, Santorum finally began to gain ground. In a December 21–27 CNN/*Time* poll of Iowa Republicans, 16% supported him—a fraction two or three times greater than in earlier polls. This one poll was all it took for the news media to "discover" Santorum. His share of the news coverage increased sharply after the poll results became public, as the news stories took note of the poll.[3] For example, the *New York Times* headline on December 28 was "News Is Good for Santorum and Bad for Gingrich in New Polls."[4] Several other polls that were fielded around the same time as the CNN poll were not as favorable to Santorum, but taken together, these polls suggest that he was doing significantly better in the days around Christmas.[5]

Why would Santorum suddenly surge in Iowa after these many months of campaigning? As we argued in the previous chapter, voters do not change their minds for no reason or without some new information. In the week leading up to these polls, several things took place that could have benefited Santorum. First, a super-PAC working on his behalf—the Red White and Blue Fund—began airing ads in Iowa. It bought a small amount of advertising time the week of December 12–18 and a much larger amount in the two following weeks. These ads could have been seen by respondents to the polls showing Santorum's surge.

In addition, on December 20, Santorum was endorsed by Bob Vander Plaats and Chuck Hurley, prominent social conservatives affiliated with an organization called the Family Leader. The endorsement was not only reported in local Iowa media but accompanied by robocalls to Iowa voters that began on December 22 and were paid for by the Family Leader's super-PAC, Leaders for Families.[6] Perhaps it was no coincidence, then, that the CNN poll showed Santorum surging especially among conservative Christians. In an early December CNN poll, 7% of those identifying as "born again" supported Santorum, but in the later poll 22% did. The increase among those who did not identify as born again (from 4% to 10%) was smaller. To be sure, there is only circumstantial evidence that these advertisements or endorsements mattered, but the timing seems right.

Amid this spate of positive advertisements and favorable news coverage, Santorum continued to notch gains in the polls and then outperformed his polling numbers and ultimately won by a very narrow margin over Romney— although this was evident only after a recount. On the night of the caucus Romney came out on top. Essentially it was a tie, but it still amounted to an extraordinary come-from-behind victory for Santorum. It doomed the candidacy of Michele Bachmann, who had also courted social conservatives and campaigned extensively in Iowa. She suspended her campaign the next day.

Romney's second-place showing was important, however. He was never expected to do very well in Iowa, at least compared to states such as New Hampshire or Michigan where the primary electorate was more moderate and where Romney had certain home-state advantages. An early December headline—written when Gingrich was surging in Iowa and nationally—said "Romney Faces Uphill Battle in Wooing Iowa Voters."[7] Commentators were also quick to point out that Romney did not campaign in Iowa as Iowans were said to expect: by visiting the state frequently. All told, Romney held only 39 events in Iowa before the caucus, according to data gathered by the *Des Moines Register*.[8] Santorum held 314. In November, ABC News reported on the "ill will" created by Romney's decision to skip a series of events one particular weekend.[9]

But appearances—or, in this case, a lack of appearances—were deceiving. Beginning a year before the 2008 campaign, the Romney team had built a list of supporters and volunteers that they then turned to in 2011. They also used information from their extensive database of voter characteristics to target new potential supporters. They then contacted both old and new supporters via phone calls from individual volunteers and via "tele-townhalls" (large-scale conference calls) with Romney that sometimes attracted thousands of listeners. Other candidates used these forms of contact as well, but not as ably. Romney's ability to target, contact, and mobilize supporters meant that he did not need to campaign extensively *in* Iowa or establish a traditional field operation with multiple offices and other visible manifestations of the "ground game." But the Romney campaign was nevertheless active and apparently effective.[10] Essentially tying Santorum in unfriendly territory was a significant accomplishment. Had Romney done much worse, it is possible he would have had a tougher road ahead in New Hampshire.

In the wake of Iowa, Santorum experienced what typically happens after a candidate beats expectations in the Iowa caucus: a burst of favorable news coverage.[11] This was, in some sense, a continuation of the "discovery" of Santorum that began with his surge in the Iowa polls. Santorum's poll numbers increased both nationwide and in New Hampshire, whose primary was a week after the Iowa caucus.

His surge proved short-lived. Santorum quickly entered a scrutiny phase, wherein news coverage of him subsided and became less favorable, as Figure 4.3 demonstrates. Indeed, on January 5, only two days after the Iowa caucus, a *New York Times* blog post implicitly noted that the scrutiny had begun: "Following Rick Santorum's sudden rise to prominence in the race for the Republican presidential nomination, new attention has been paid to his views on foreign policy issues."[12] The article then discussed his view that the West Bank was "part of Israel" and called it an "extreme stance." The following day, another *New York Times* post referred to Santorum's "spunk" but also the "rough edges and lack of polish that go along with a presidential campaign that was for months conducted largely out of the public eye." The article discussed a "testy exchange" Santorum had with college students over the issue of gay marriage.[13]

The same lack of polish was evident when we saw Santorum a week later at Mary Ann's Restaurant in Derry, New Hampshire. There were certainly more reporters awaiting him there than at the Altoona Pizza Ranch. If Santorum could beat expectations in New Hampshire, his momentum might build, making this week critical to his campaign. And yet he pulled up to the restaurant in the same pickup truck, with the same megaphone, and this time had to give his stump speech three times—once outside the front door—to accommodate everyone who could not fit inside the restaurant. The student-council feel of Santorum's campaign, however pleasing in its authenticity, fed into the ongoing scrutiny.

The New Hampshire contest ultimately proved less dramatic than the one in Iowa and some later primaries. Although the race tightened in the closing days, thanks in part to increasing support not only for Santorum but for Jon Huntsman, it was always Romney's race to win. New Hampshire was arguably Romney's home field, and not just because he had been the governor of neighboring Massachusetts and had a house on Lake Winnipesaukee. The electorate in New Hampshire was tilted more in Romney's favor, with many fewer strong conservatives and evangelicals (see Figure 4.1). Thus Romney never trailed in the New Hampshire polls, and his share of the vote was almost exactly what the last pre-election polls predicted.

A "Vulture" and a Newt

The coverage of Romney's New Hampshire victory suggested he was ascendant. A front-page story in the *New York Times* began, "Mitt Romney swept to victory in the New Hampshire primary on Tuesday, turning back a ferocious assault from rivals who sought to disqualify him in the eyes of conservatives, in a contest that failed to anoint a strong opponent to slow his march to the Republican nomination."[14] Only eleven days later the front page of the *New York Times* read very differently: "For Mitt Romney the South Carolina primary was not just a defeat, though it was most emphatically that. It was also where his campaign confronted the prospect it had most hoped to avoid: a dominant, surging and energized rival."[15] The rival, of course, was Newt Gingrich.

What happened in this short period to arrest Romney's momentum after his near victory in Iowa and his victory in New Hampshire, the combination of which had given him his largest lead in some national polls?[16] And how was it that Gingrich, whose campaign had endured setback after setback, became Romney's "energized rival"? Three factors were at work. First, renewed attacks on Romney's tenure as the head of Bain Capital by Gingrich and others catalyzed a spate of negative news coverage. Second, the South Carolina electorate was favorably disposed to prefer a candidate like Gingrich to Romney (nearly two-thirds of primary voters would identify as evangelicals). Third, and fortuitously, Gingrich enjoyed a second episode of "discovery," thanks to his performance in the debates preceding the South Carolina primary. The resulting news coverage made him salient to South Carolina voters.

Immediately before but especially after the New Hampshire primary, Romney finally experienced what the front-running candidates before him— Perry, Cain, and Gingrich—had also experienced: scrutiny. Now that he was gaining in the polls, his opponents attacked him more aggressively and the media paid notice. The news coverage that Romney received after his New Hampshire victory was some of the most negative of the entire primary campaign. This is illustrated in Figure 4.4, where the measure of news coverage that is weighted by its tone declines during this period of time.[17] The tone of news coverage has been smoothed in these figures to iron out daily bumps and wiggles that might not be significant. But in the original unsmoothed estimates, the decline in tone was even starker. From January 12, two days

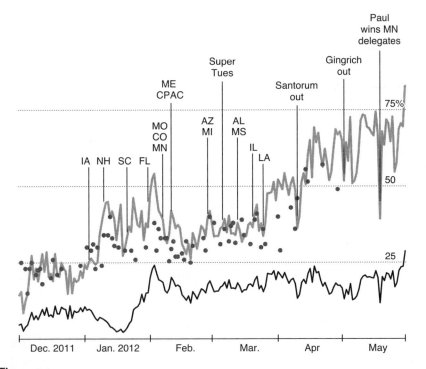

Figure 4.4.

Trends in Mitt Romney's news coverage and poll standing.

The gray line represents Romney's share of mentions of the major Republican candidates. The black line represents the share of mentions, weighted by the tone of the coverage. When the black line is above 0, the coverage is net positive; when it is below 0, the coverage is net negative. The gray dots capture Romney's standing in individual national polls among Republicans, dated to the middle of each poll's time in the field and averaging together any polls on overlapping days. The data span the period December 1, 2011–May 31, 2012.

after the New Hampshire primary, until January 18, coverage of Romney was, on average, negative every single day—dragging down the smoothed trend line in Figure 4.4.

The attacks from Romney's rivals centered on his experience as the head of Bain Capital. They began right before the New Hampshire primary when the main super-PAC supporting Gingrich, Winning Our Future, announced that it was planning to release a twenty-eight-minute documentary criticizing Romney's record at Bain and then bought almost $1 million worth of advertising time in South Carolina to air these criticisms.[18] The documentary featured interviews with people who had lost jobs at companies that Bain Capital had bought and later sold. To the news media, Gingrich himself described Romney's activities this way: "They apparently looted the companies, left people unemployed and walked off with millions of dollars."[19] Rick Perry chimed in, too, referring to Bain as "vulture capitalists."[20] These attacks succeeded in driving news coverage: the number of combined mentions of Romney and Bain Capital increased from a negligible 145 on January 1 to over 5,600 on January 10, the day of the New Hampshire primary. The number would spike to over 10,000 mentions on January 13. The tone of this coverage was generally negative.

All of this left Romney "scrambling to avoid a prolonged and nasty battle over his business record before it [did] lasting damage"—to sample from news accounts that illustrated just how quickly the tenor of coverage changed after New Hampshire.[21] Romney did so by mobilizing surrogates like Nikki Haley, the governor of South Carolina, who defended Romney's record. Other Republicans expressed some concern that this line of attack represented a broadside on private enterprise itself.[22] Romney could also take heart that voters did not necessarily have an opinion about his tenure at Bain. In a YouGov poll from January 21–24, 47% were not sure whether Romney mostly created or eliminated jobs during his time there. Moreover, among Republicans, opinions ran in Romney's favor: 50% believed that he created jobs and only 14% said he eliminated jobs (the rest were not sure).[23]

Nevertheless, Romney's share in national polls of Republican voters declined during this time by an estimated 8 points.[24] National polls of the entire electorate also showed that views of him became more unfavorable. In the two polls taken immediately after the New Hampshire primary, more people had favorable than unfavorable views of Romney. By the eve of the South Carolina primary, three straight polls showed the opposite. For example, in a January 13–16 Public Policy Polling survey, 53% expressed an unfavorable view of Romney while only 35% expressed a favorable view.[25]

As Romney's momentum stalled, Gingrich once again surged. He did so largely because of his performance in two candidate debates held between the New Hampshire and South Carolina primaries—one in Myrtle Beach on

January 16 and one in Charleston on January 19. In the first debate, Gingrich drew attention for challenging debate moderator Juan Williams, who questioned previous statements Gingrich had made that Barack Obama was the "food stamp president" and that poor children would learn valuable lessons from working as janitors.[26] Gingrich's pointed response—among other things, he said, "And if that makes liberals unhappy, I'm going to continue to find ways to help poor people learn how to get a job"—earned him a standing ovation from the debate audience. In the second debate, Gingrich was asked by moderator John King about the claim by Gingrich's ex-wife Marianne that he had asked her for an open marriage. Gingrich denied the claim and decried "the destructive, vicious, negative nature" of the media.[27]

Figure 4.5 shows just how the two debates catalyzed the news media's attention to Gingrich. The day after the first South Carolina debate, Gingrich's share of coverage spiked from 7% to 16%, and then to 27% after the second debate.[28] Gingrich's national poll numbers increased in the wake of this news

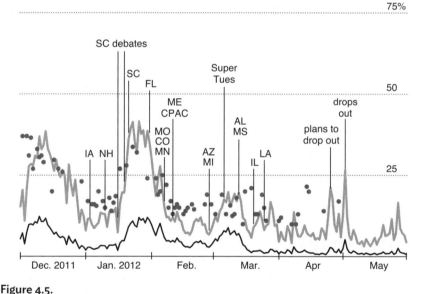

Figure 4.5.
Trends in Newt Gingrich's news coverage and poll standing.
The gray line represents Gingrich's share of mentions of the major Republican candidates. The black line represents the share of mentions, weighted by the tone of the coverage. When the black line is above 0, the coverage is net positive; when it is below 0, the coverage is net negative. The gray dots capture Gingrich's standing in individual national polls among Republicans, dated to the middle of each poll's time in the field and averaging together any polls on overlapping days. The data span the period December 1, 2011–May 31, 2012.

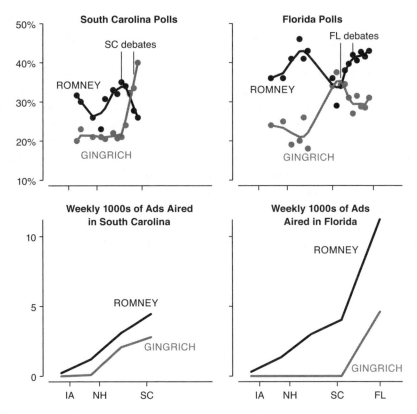

Figure 4.6.
Trends in South Carolina and Florida polls and political advertising.
The top row displays the individual South Carolina and Florida polls for Romney and Gingrich, with a smoothed trend line. The bottom row displays the weekly number of ads aired by Romney, Gingrich, and their affiliated super-PACs during this time period. The horizontal axes are marked with the dates of the primaries and caucuses.

coverage. In four polls conducted between the New Hampshire primary and the first South Carolina debate, Gingrich averaged 16%. In the four polls that were either in the field when the first debate occurred or conducted after that debate, Gingrich averaged 23%.[29]

What did all this mean in South Carolina? The polls in South Carolina suggested that Gingrich began to surge after the two debates and news coverage thereof (see Figure 4.6).[30] Romney's share in the polls dropped dramatically during this time. Furthermore, this post-debate news coverage appeared to blunt Romney's advantage in televised political advertising. His campaign and affiliated super-PAC, Restore Our Future, aired about four thousand more ads than Gingrich did during the three weeks before the South Carolina primary—and in fact increased their advertising edge in the week before the primary.[31] But this was not sufficient to halt Gingrich's surge. To gauge the impact of Romney's advertising advantage, we examined the volume of pro- and anti-Gingrich advertising in each of the South Carolina media markets. The majority of the anti-Gingrich ads were sponsored by the pro-Romney super-PAC Restore Our Future, with most of the rest sponsored by Ron Paul and his affiliated super-PAC. In a few markets there was near parity between pro- and anti-Gingrich ads, but in most markets, ads attacking Gingrich were more numerous. This imbalance in ads did not appear to matter: Gingrich surged by essentially the same amount in all of these markets, no matter what the balance of ads was.[32] (The appendix to this chapter supplies more detail.)

On the night of the primary, Gingrich was understandably ebullient. He said, "We don't have the kind of money that at least one of the candidates has. But we do have ideas, and we do have people and we proved here in South Carolina that people power with the right ideas beats big money."[33] But Gingrich was about to face even bigger money, and a real lack of people power, further south in the Sunshine State. Florida's primary was only eleven days away.

Sunshine for Romney

After the South Carolina primary, Romney needed to turn things around quickly. His next opportunity to do so came two days later at the Republican debate in Tampa, Florida, on January 23. Before the debate took place, Romney released his 2010 and 2011 tax returns—the first returns he had released during the campaign. His failure to release them had been the subject of repeated news stories and attacks from his Republican opponents. At one point before the South Carolina primary, Gingrich said, "If you're a South Carolinian, you say, 'Wait a second, why don't you want me to know about it? Why are you going to wait until after I've voted?'"[34] Romney's tax return showed that he paid a relatively low tax rate—just under 15%, or $6.2 million on $45 million in income—but he did not shy away from defending this fact. At the debate he said, "I pay all the taxes that are legally required and not a dollar more." Ultimately, releasing these returns was enough to shift attention away from the subject.[35]

Having retained the counsel of veteran Republican debate coach Brett O'Donnell, Romney came out swinging at Gingrich in the debate—"a far different demeanor than he displayed during two lackluster debates last week," wrote Dan Balz and Rosalind Helderman in the *Washington Post*. Gingrich, meanwhile, "was far more subdued."[36] In the next debate, on January 26, Romney was judged similarly. Balz and Amy Gardner wrote that Romney "stepped up at a critical time" while Gingrich "did not have the kind of dominating performance" that he did in the South Carolina debates.[37] Romney was again aided by prominent Republicans, most notably former House majority leader Tom DeLay and former Senate majority leader and presidential candidate Bob Dole. DeLay called Gingrich "erratic" and "undisciplined."[38] Dole issued a statement that said, in part, "Hardly anyone who served with Newt in Congress has endorsed him and that fact speaks for itself."[39] Just as in December, Gingrich could not translate his boomlets of media coverage and poll numbers into support among party leaders.

For Romney, these debates appeared to shift the tenor of news coverage about him, portending a similar pattern that would benefit him after the first general election debate in October. Although the volume and tone of Gingrich's coverage changed little between the South Carolina and Florida primaries (see Figure 4.5)—despite the attacks of Romney, Dole, and others—coverage of Romney became much more positive over these eleven days (see Figure 4.4).[40] This positive shift in news about Romney began before the polls in Florida started to shift in his direction, suggesting that it was driven more by events like the debates than the polls themselves.[41]

Romney had other advantages in Florida. One was the electorate, which was less tilted toward evangelicals than it was in South Carolina. Another was his superior campaign. It was better funded, better organized, and arguably more effective. This is readily evident in the volume of television advertising aired by both him and Gingrich (see Figure 4.6). Although Gingrich was somewhat able to keep pace in South Carolina, thanks to an infusion of cash to his super-PAC from casino magnate Sheldon Adelson, it was difficult for him to be in two places at once. Only in the week before the Florida primary, and after another infusion from Adelson, was Gingrich able to go up on the air. All told, Romney dominated the airwaves in Florida much more than in South Carolina. In South Carolina, his ads and those of his super-PAC aired almost twice as much as Gingrich's. In Florida, they aired over four times as often. In the week prior to the Florida primary, Gingrich closed the gap but still languished farther behind Romney than he did in South Carolina.[42]

Did Romney's advertising advantage help him in Florida, above and beyond the possible benefits of more positive news coverage? Some evidence suggests that the ads mattered. Two Survey USA Florida polls—one taken on January 8, right before the New Hampshire primary, and one taken on January 27–29, right before the Florida primary—showed a 14-point increase in the percent rating Gingrich unfavorably. But Gingrich's favorable rating did not drop by the same amount in every media market. It dropped in rough proportion to the balance of anti-Gingrich ads and pro-Gingrich ads. The more Romney's attacks outnumbered Gingrich's positive ads, the more

Floridians came to dislike Gingrich. In fact, if we assume, hypothetically, that Gingrich had been able to match the ads attacking him with an equal amount of promotional advertising, his drop in favorability would have disappeared.[43] (Again, more details are in the appendix to this chapter.)

The main limitation of this analysis, however, is that there might have been factors other than anti-Gingrich advertising that drove these trends. Perhaps Romney ran his attack ads in markets where support for Gingrich was already weakening. If so, his ads piggybacked on a trend rather than caused that trend. But one other piece of analysis did suggest that anti-Gingrich advertising could have mattered. In early December 2011, the political communications firm Evolving Strategies conducted a randomized experiment in which people were shown no political ads, an ad promoting Gingrich and an ad attacking him, or ads promoting and attacking Romney.[44] The ads about Romney had no effect, but the two ads focused on Gingrich did. Most important, the effect of the ad attacking Gingrich outweighed the effect of the ad promoting him: people who saw both ads were about 15 points less likely to prefer Gingrich as their first choice compared to someone who saw no ads. To be sure, this experiment was conducted almost two months before the Florida primary and did not involve the precise ads Romney and Restore Our Future aired in Florida. It also cannot explain by itself why the anti-Gingrich ads aired in Florida appeared more effective than those aired in South Carolina. But it suggested that Gingrich was vulnerable to the kinds of attacks he experienced in Florida.

Romney's advantage extended beyond advertising to field operations. As was true in Iowa, Romney had a ground game that no other candidate could match. Knowing that a significant fraction of voters would vote early—ultimately about 38% did—Romney's team obtained lists of voters who had requested an absentee ballot and identified voters their statistical models predicted were likely supporters.[45] The campaign then followed up with these voters via phone and mail to make sure they sent in their ballot. Ultimately Romney did much better than Gingrich among those who voted early—something that suggests, although it cannot determine, that his campaign's tactics helped.[46]

Meanwhile, Gingrich's campaign organization had no well-developed infrastructure of field offices and volunteers. As late as January 23, the *Washington Post* reported that Winning Our Future had to step in and try to create this infrastructure.[47] In Florida it was too little, too late. Gingrich did not have a field office in central Florida until January 13, only about two weeks before the primary. Like Romney's campaign, his campaign also obtained lists of voters who had requested absentee ballots, but the Gingrich campaign did not update its lists as diligently, meaning that volunteers were sometimes talking to Floridians who had already mailed in their ballot.[48]

Perhaps the Gingrich campaign organization would have been strengthened had Republican Party leaders stepped forward to endorse him, thereby generating additional donations or helping him bring onboard a larger group of seasoned campaign professionals. But this did not happen. In fact, Republican Party leaders were mostly leery of Gingrich's success, just as they had been during the first Gingrich surge in December 2011. According to one news report, which cited "leading Republican figures,"

> They said that if Mr. Gingrich won Florida, they anticipated further efforts to pressure leading Republicans, including former governors like Jeb Bush of Florida and Haley Barbour of Mississippi, as well as officials who passed up presidential runs this year, like Gov. Mitch Daniels of Indiana, to help build a firewall around Mr. Romney.
>
> They predicted intensifying criticism of Mr. Gingrich's record and style, both through the Romney campaign and among conservative commentators who think having Mr. Gingrich as the nominee would sink the party's chances of winning the White House.[49]

If there was ever "fear and loathing on the campaign trail," Gingrich seemed to cause it.

Just as it is hard to know how much the Romney campaign's professionalism helped him, it is hard to know how much the Gingrich campaign's amateurism hurt Gingrich. Nevertheless, Gingrich was not able to counteract this movement toward Romney. On election night in Florida, after Romney had trounced him by almost 15 points, Gingrich claimed to be "putting together a people's campaign"—just as he had suggested after South Carolina.[50] At this point, however, people were mostly leaving his campaign. Gingrich's high-water mark in the campaign had passed, and his poll numbers would never recover.

The Santorum Surge

Romney seemed to be cruising after his Florida comeback. Four days later he won the Nevada caucuses handily, besting the runner-up, Gingrich, by almost 30 points. The following day, the *Washington Post*'s Aaron Blake summed up the status of the race by saying that Romney had "confirmed his status as the prohibitive front-runner," while Gingrich had "fallen quickly" and Santorum "couldn't pick up the pieces" after Gingrich's collapse. Blake went on to express amazement that Santorum had chosen to focus on Colorado and Missouri rather than Nevada, concluding that "the payoff is pretty minimal for Santorum even if it works out."[51]

Well, it did work out. On February 7, Santorum won the Colorado and Minnesota caucuses as well as the nonbinding Missouri primary. Santorum beat Romney by almost 6 points in Colorado and by almost 30 points in both Minnesota and Missouri. In Minnesota, Romney actually came in third behind Santorum and Paul. It was, said the *Huffington Post*'s Jon Ward, "a very bad night for Romney."[52] He did far worse in these states than he did in 2008, when he won Colorado and Minnesota. Santorum, by contrast, "stunned the political world."[53] Was the outcome that surprising? Not entirely. Late polling showed Santorum in the lead in both Colorado and Minnesota.[54] Perhaps the best signal of Romney's impending losses was his own behavior: he began to attack Santorum and worked to lower expectations about his performance in these states.[55]

How did Santorum do it? Certainly the electorate in these states was more favorable to Santorum. As Figure 4.1 demonstrates, these states' likely voters had larger concentrations of evangelicals. Pre-election polls also confirmed that evangelicals were more likely to support Santorum than Romney. For example, Santorum led Romney 37–27% among self-identified Colorado evangelicals, who were 45% of the poll's sample, but trailed 18–46% among non-evangelicals.[56] Moreover, turnout, especially in the caucuses, was low, and therefore caucusgoers and primary voters in these states may have been disproportionately activist conservatives who preferred Santorum to Romney. In the Colorado pre-election poll, Santorum led Romney among those who identified as "very conservative" but trailed him among those who identified as "somewhat conservative" or "moderate." Such statistics support the explanation offered by the *Washington Post*'s Dan Balz: "the lack of enthusiasm for his [Romney's] candidacy among conservatives."[57]

With so little pre-election polling and no exit polls in these three states, we cannot definitively establish how much their electorates were tilted toward evangelicals or any other constituency favorable to Santorum. But even if we assume that there was such a tilt, it alone was not sufficient to explain Santorum's success. After all, Santorum had received relatively little national media coverage since the New Hampshire primary, and he received very little immediately before the Colorado, Minnesota, and Missouri contests. These three states may have had a larger-than-average share of *potential* Santorum voters, but that could not explain why they became *actual* Santorum voters.

Certainly part of the answer was that Gingrich's star fell so rapidly after Florida. This was evident in his lackluster fund-raising.[58] It was also evident in his share of news coverage (see Figure 4.5). When Gingrich was surging, as he was going into South Carolina, he—and not Santorum—was the first choice of groups like evangelicals and strong conservatives. He won both groups in

South Carolina, according to the exit poll. But with Gingrich firmly in the "decline" phase, this created something of a vacuum that Santorum could fill.

Santorum filled it by outhustling the other candidates in these states, despite his seat-of-the-pants campaign. He did so in part with a little outside help and in part with the shoe-leather campaigning that even an underfunded campaign can do (much as he did in Iowa). And with the other candidates doing far less to contest these states, the information his campaigning produced—via advertisements, voter contact, rallies, and local news—likely helped him persuade and mobilize voters. Santorum's campaign benefited from the support of a super-PAC, the Red White and Blue Fund (RWBF), largely funded by wealthy businessmen William Doré and Foster Friess.[59] Thanks to their support, RWBF actually aired more ads in Missouri and Minnesota than did any other candidate or affiliated super-PAC. In the three weeks before the two caucuses and the primary, RWBF aired 121 ads in Missouri (no other candidate aired any) and 193 ads in Minnesota (Romney's super-PAC aired 150 and Paul aired 125).[60] In Colorado, where Romney did advertise and Santorum did not, RWBF organized a phone bank to mobilize Santorum voters.[61]

Santorum also did quite a bit of work himself. In the seven days before these primaries—from January 31 to February 6—Santorum held nine events in Colorado, twelve in Minnesota, and two in Missouri.[62] He held more events in each state than did Gingrich, Paul, and Romney combined. Gingrich appeared only once in Minnesota and once in Colorado, virtually guaranteeing—or perhaps acknowledging—that he would not rebound from his defeat in Florida by winning in one of these states. Romney appeared only once in Minnesota, twice in Colorado, and not at all in Missouri.

Santorum's campaigning did not much affect his national news coverage (see Figure 4.3), but it did appear to affect his local news coverage. We tabulated the number of mentions that Romney and Santorum received during this seven-day period in both the national news media and the local news media in each state. Overall, Romney received about five times as many mentions as Santorum in the national news—as one might expect given that Romney was the front-runner and Santorum mostly an afterthought. But in Colorado, Minnesota, and Missouri, Romney received roughly three times as many mentions. On the day before the caucuses and primary were held, Romney received only twice as many mentions. To generate even half as much local media attention as Romney was arguably an accomplishment for Santorum, a candidate who was polling in the single digits nationally and all but written off by many commentators.

In the wake of his trifecta, Santorum was "discovered" again, this time earning a far greater amount of media attention than he did after the Iowa caucus. This spike reflected how important it is for candidates not only to succeed but to succeed relative to the expectations of reporters and commentators. Santorum was expected to do well in Iowa, based on pre-election polling, but far fewer predicted his victories in these other three states. The day after the primary, he received 44% of the mentions of the Republican candidates. Except for a brief dip on the day when Romney won the Maine caucus and Ron Paul won the straw poll at the Conservative Political Action Conference, Santorum received this level of attention for the rest of February. Santorum's poll numbers increased as well. Prior to these primary victories, Santorum had been polling around 14%—down from 20% right after the Iowa caucus. After these primary victories, his poll numbers shot up 20 points, putting him even with or ahead of Romney in most polls. The increase in his poll numbers was particularly pronounced among social conservatives.[63]

But Santorum's challenges soon emerged, and they were very similar to Gingrich's. Most important, he needed to win delegates. For all the attention his victories in Colorado, Minnesota, and Missouri received, they netted him exactly zero delegates (see Figure 4.2). Missouri's primary was simply a "beauty contest" with no bearing on delegate allocation. The Colorado and Minnesota caucuses—like the Iowa caucus—amounted to straw polls. They informed the selection of delegates to later state party conventions, where the actual delegates were chosen, but there was no one-to-one relationship between the candidates' share of votes in the caucuses and their share of the delegates chosen at these conventions. In this sense, Aaron Blake was absolutely correct: there was not much payoff to Santorum's victories in terms of delegates.[64]

What Santorum did get was, potentially, the momentum needed to win primaries with delegates up for grabs. But the next primaries, held three weeks later, were on less favorable terrain: Arizona and Michigan. In both states, the number of evangelicals and self-identified strong conservatives was lower than in Colorado, Minnesota, Missouri, and Iowa. To compete effectively there, he would need a continued burst of positive news coverage, an effective retail campaign, or both.

He got neither of these things. The tenor of news coverage remained more positive than negative, but it became less positive as the Arizona and Michigan primaries approached.[65] This was once again due to the inevitable scrutiny that a front-runner receives. Not three days after his victories in Colorado, Minnesota, and Missouri, Santorum earned critical news attention for appearing to suggest that women were not equipped to serve in combat because of their "emotions." He then clarified his statement, saying that he meant the emotions of men, who would have a "natural instinct" to protect women.[66] About a week later, he was described as "defending" his remarks that Obama subscribed to a "phony theology" and that government-run schools were "anachronistic."[67] Although not all media stories about Santorum featured such controversies, they nevertheless signaled that, as the *New York Times*'s Michael Shear put it, Santorum was "under more scrutiny for his background and positions."[68]

Few within the Republican Party rallied to Santorum's side. Only one Republican member of Congress, Representative Robert Aderholt, endorsed him the wake of his victories in Colorado, Minnesota, and Missouri. Other leaders were either silent or outright fearful of a Santorum nomination. Republican governors were described as "looking on with apprehension to an autumn of defending Rick Santorum's views."[69] One conservative columnist, the *New York Times*'s Ross Douthat, said that a Santorum candidacy in the general election "would almost certainly be a debacle."[70] A lack of party support did not help Santorum overcome another obstacle: his perennially underfunded and seat-of-the-pants campaign. It was difficult even to discern who worked on or advised Santorum's "MacGyver model" of a campaign.[71] The lack of campaign professionals was something Santorum claimed as a virtue, saying that he refused to hire a pollster or field specialist because he was already in touch with Americans. But his campaign was reaching its limit operationally once again. At this point, Santorum did not have the luxury of setting up shop in Iowa for months on end or of campaigning under the radar in states like Minnesota and Missouri that Romney and the other candidates were not contesting. As the new front-runner, Santorum would be challenged all the time and everywhere. He could not keep up.

In Michigan, Santorum (and his affiliated super-PAC) at least made it competitive—airing just over 5,700 ads to Romney's nearly 6,700. This was in an apparent attempt to defeat Romney on his home turf, where his father, George, had been governor and where the polls were essentially tied. The Santorum camp was pleased simply to make Romney spend money in what might have been a safe state. "No matter what the results are, we've won. This is Romney's home state," said Santorum advisor John Brabender.[72] But in Arizona, where Restore Our Future aired over 1,000 ads in roughly the month before the primary, the majority of which attacked Santorum, Santorum aired no ads. In the Super Tuesday states, Santorum was also buried. Romney or Restore Our Future aired over 12,600 ads in Georgia, Idaho, Ohio, Oklahoma, and Tennessee. Santorum aired none and his affiliated super-PAC aired only about 760. Put another way, in these states Romney aired about seventeen ads for every one of Santorum's. The same was true after Super Tuesday: Romney's spending in Alabama and Mississippi vastly exceeded that of Santorum and Gingrich.[73]

To be sure, Romney's spending did not guarantee him victories. He did win in Michigan and Arizona, but on Super Tuesday Gingrich won more votes in his home state of Georgia, while Santorum won more votes in North

Dakota, Oklahoma, and Tennessee. Santorum also won more votes than Romney in Alabama and Mississippi. But Romney's spending, combined with the sequence of states, meant that he was rarely competing at any significant disadvantage for long. On Super Tuesday he won the most votes in Alaska, Idaho, Massachusetts, Ohio, Vermont, and Virginia—states where the electorates were less tilted toward constituencies that tended to prefer Gingrich or Santorum (see Figure 4.1).[74] Immediately after Alabama and Mississippi, the race moved to Illinois, which was much more favorable terrain for Romney.

Santorum's inability to halt Romney's path to the nomination was illustrated most clearly in how the news covered him (see Figure 4.3). After coverage of Santorum spiked in mid-February, it became largely dependent on his successes in primaries and caucuses. When Romney won, Santorum's share of coverage dropped—for example, as it did after the Arizona and Michigan primaries and again after Super Tuesday. When Santorum won, as he did in Alabama, Mississippi, and Louisiana, his share of coverage went up. The same was not true for Romney (Figure 4.4), whose share of coverage remained largely static whether he won or lost. Even more telling is the tone of the news coverage, which is captured in the black line in these figures. Beginning in the middle of February and continuing through his exit from the race, news coverage of Santorum grew less and less favorable, no matter whether he won or lost.

Santorum's poll numbers also dropped somewhat from their peak after the Colorado, Missouri, and Minnesota contests—leveling off at roughly 27% throughout March, which was about 5–6 points behind Romney. This stasis worked to Santorum's disadvantage. For one, just as we found in the previous chapter, his poll numbers and news coverage were mutually self-reinforcing. (See the appendix to this chapter.) Initially his successes in primaries and caucuses drove news coverage, which in turn drove polls. But over time, his polls both reflected and influenced news coverage—and without a sustained lead in the polls, it was likely that his news coverage would become less favorable, as it did.

Ultimately, whatever Santorum's strengths among certain elements of the Republican Party, he could not effectively unify the party. Santorum himself seemed to realize this. Right before the Illinois primary, Santorum suggested that he would not win except by the most divisive means: a brokered convention where, he declared, "The convention will nominate a conservative. They will not nominate the establishment moderate candidate from Massachusetts."[75] Others in the party did not want the fight to go that far and started endorsing Romney—as did Marco Rubio and Paul Ryan at the end of March—and suggesting that Santorum should give up. "Santorum Ignores Pressure to Bow Out to Romney," was the *New York Times* headline on March 25, citing the sentiments of former governors Jeb Bush and Haley Barbour as well as

Senators Jim DeMint and Lindsey Graham, who were apparently not swayed by Santorum's victory in the Louisiana primary the day before.[76] A week later, Santorum was not being covered even on Fox News, which suggested that Fox implicitly believed Romney would be the nominee.[77] Faced not only with this pressure but with the hospitalization of his daughter on April 6 as well as polls that suggested he might even lose the primary in his home state of Pennsylvania, Santorum suspended his campaign on April 10.[78] About a month later he endorsed Romney, just as Gingrich, who finally dropped out on April 25, had done.

Nobody but Romney

How Romney clinched the nomination was not just a story about the struggles of his opponents or about his own campaign coffers. It was a story about how Republican voters perceived him and why many of them supported him—enough, at least, to ensure that he was well ahead in the delegate count by the time Santorum dropped out and Romney became the de facto nominee. One piece of conventional wisdom, the "Anybody but Romney" story, suggested that Romney had important, if not fatal, shortcomings as a candidate. Romney had, the story went, a ceiling of support within the party—perhaps no more than 25%—because he was ideologically out of step with the majority of his party, especially with crucial constituencies like Tea Party supporters and evangelicals who were not convinced by his evolution from a moderate Massachusetts governor to a conservative presidential candidate. But this story was, by and large, a fiction.[79]

The simple fact that at points during the campaign majorities of Republicans chose to vote for a candidate other than Romney was sometimes taken as an indication of these voters' "deep dissatisfaction" with Romney.[80] But polling data suggested otherwise. Figure 4.7 depicts the fraction of likely Republican primary voters that had favorable views of Gingrich, Santorum, and Romney from February through April. (The remainder had either unfavorable views or no opinion.) On balance, Republican voters had favorable views of all of these candidates, although somewhat less favorable views of Gingrich. Most important, their views of Romney were similar to their views of Santorum and even slightly more favorable by early April, when Santorum dropped out.[81] In short, most Republican voters liked Romney.

This was true even among supposedly hostile wings of the party. As we showed in the previous chapter, in December 2011 the groups believed to be least friendly to Romney actually viewed him as favorably as—if not more favorably than—the groups that were in his corner did. The same was true in

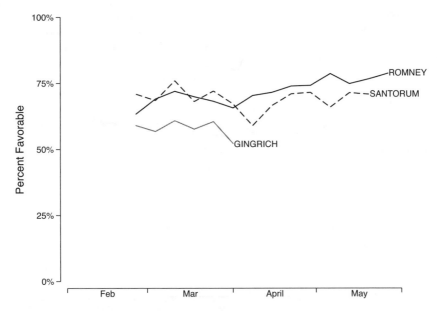

Figure 4.7.
Views of Gingrich, Romney, and Santorum among likely Republican primary voters.
Data are from February–May YouGov polls (*N* = 7,034).

2012. For example, 75% of those who identified as Tea Party members had a favorable view of Romney, compared to 67% of nonmembers.[82] Seventy percent of those who identified as "born again" had a favorable view of Romney, as did 72% of those who did not identify as born again. Even though groups like born-again Christians were often less likely to vote for Romney than for other candidates, they did not like him any less. Similarly positive sentiments toward Romney were evident among supporters of the other candidates. Romney was viewed favorably by 62% of Gingrich supporters and 65% of Santorum supporters. Indeed, he was more popular among his opponent's supporters in 2012 than in 2008. In a January 2008 Pew poll, for example, only 57% of John McCain's supporters and 50% of Mike Huckabee's supporters had a favorable view of Romney.[83] Whatever antagonisms may have existed among Gingrich, Romney, and Santorum themselves did not fully carry over to their followers. Most Republicans liked all of the major Republican candidates, period.

Romney's history as a moderate—thought to be troubling to an increasingly conservative party—also proved to be surmountable. Republican voters did not appear to believe the candidates were all that ideologically dissimilar.

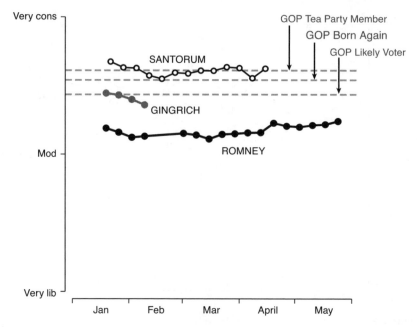

Figure 4.8.
Republican voters' perceptions of the ideologies of Gingrich, Romney, and Santorum. The graph presents where Republican likely voters located Gingrich, Romney, and Santorum on the liberal-conservative spectrum—specifically, a 5-point scale ranging from "very conservative" to "very liberal." The dashed lines represent the position of the average Republican likely voter, Tea Party member, and born-again Christian as of December 2011. All data are from YouGov polls.

This was true before the Iowa caucus, as we also documented in the previous chapter, and it continued to be true throughout the winter and spring. Figure 4.8 shows where Republican voters placed Gingrich, Romney, and Santorum from January until May, when Romney captured enough delegates to win the nomination.[84] For comparison's sake, the figure also includes the ideological location of the average Republican voter as well as Republicans who identified as a Tea Party member or as being born again.

Throughout the primaries, Romney was generally perceived as more moderate than the average Republican voter, while Gingrich was perceived as very similar to and Santorum as more conservative than this voter. This is a different position than Romney was in during the 2008 presidential primary. In that race, YouGov polling showed that likely Republican primary voters perceived Romney as more conservative—and therefore ideologically closer to the average Republican primary voter—than Rudy Giuliani, John

McCain, and even Mike Huckabee.[85] Romney was also endorsed or highly praised by a variety of conservative figures and news outlets in 2008, including Rush Limbaugh and the *National Review*.[86] Obviously, compared to the 2012 Republican field, Romney was seen in a different light. But in absolute terms, Romney was not that much further from the average voter than was Santorum: on the 5-point scale that respondents used to locate the candidate, Romney was about 0.97 points from the average Republican voter and Santorum about 0.85 points from this voter. The difference of 0.12 is only about 2% of the length of the scale. But Romney was perceived as further from the average Republican who was born again or a Tea Party member. Both of these groups were closest to Santorum. And that fact may have best illustrated the challenge facing Romney: how to win despite being seen as more moderate than high-profile constituencies within the Republican Party.

This challenge proved to be less significant than it appeared at first glance. Despite common portrayals of the Republican Party as dominated by Tea Party members, evangelicals, pro-life activists, and the like, these groups are actually *minorities* within the party. That is to say, more Republicans do not identify as Tea Party members than do identify as members. Thus the groups least likely to have supported Romney were also relatively small in number, while the groups more likely to support Romney were larger in number.

Figure 4.9 depicts this fact. The figure plots the percentage of various groups that supported Romney or that supported Santorum as well as each group's share of Republican primary voters. The data are from YouGov polls conducted between January and early April, right before Santorum dropped out. The groups that seemed most problematic for Romney are less numerous: only 18% of Republican primary voters described themselves as "very conservative"; 23% of Republican primary voters said that abortion should always be illegal; 33% said that they were Tea Party members; and 34% said they were born again. Much more common was to identify as moderate or conservative, to believe that abortion should be legal in some or all cases, and not to identify as a Tea Party member or as born again.

Thus the nature of Romney's appeal within the party actually worked to his advantage. He did better with these larger, less conservative groups— precisely those that could supply him the most votes. By contrast, Santorum's appeal was stronger in these smaller groups that, despite their visibility in news coverage, could not deliver enough votes. Although they dominated certain states, which candidates like Santorum and Gingrich sometimes won, they were not numerous enough in the party as a whole to constitute a winning coalition themselves. An irony of the GOP nominating process was this: although Romney was often described as out of step with the mainstream of

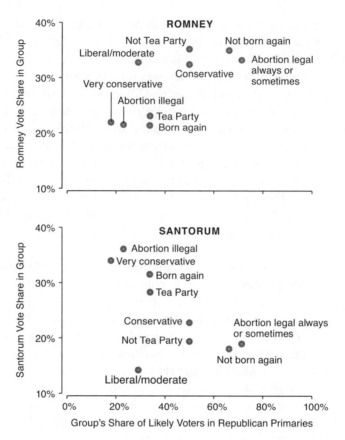

Figure 4.9.
Romney and Santorum support among groups of Republican primary voters.
Source: YouGov polls conducted from January through April 7–10, right before
Santorum dropped out of the race. The groups depicted in the graph are not mutually
exclusive.

the party, he was actually the preferred candidate of the mainstream of the
party. Santorum's appeal was far more niche.

Romney's candidacy was buoyed not only by the scarcity of true ideo-
logues in the Republican Party but by the fact that so many Republican voters
did not choose a candidate on strict ideological grounds. The conservative
commentator Ann Coulter was one. She gave a speech to the Conservative
Political Action Conference in which she backed Romney, saying, "You can
call him square, and that seems to be what a lot of right-wingers don't like
about him. . . . I think we have had enough of hip. Hip has nearly wrecked
the country. Let's try square for a while."[87] Among the Republican electorate,

this same tendency was evident in several ways. First, many people who supported Romney were actually ideologically closer to either Gingrich or Santorum. Across all of the YouGov polling between January and Santorum's exit from the race, only about half of Romney's supporters were ideologically closest to him.

Second, many people who supported a candidate other than Romney considered Romney their second choice. In other words, people who supported one of the "more conservative" candidates—like Bachmann, Gingrich, Perry, or Santorum—did not automatically default to another of these candidates.[88] We have a unique way to demonstrate this. The YouGov polling data from January onward were actually preceded by early interviews with these same people, which were conducted in December 2011 before the primaries even began. That is to say, YouGov interviewed a large sample of about 44,000 people in December and then peeled off different groups of 1,000 people each week beginning in January and interviewed them again. We can thus look at who voters supported when they were first interviewed in December and then when they were reinterviewed in 2012.

Consider the supporters of three candidates who dropped out early in the primary season: Bachmann, Huntsman, and Perry. When these supporters were reinterviewed in January, February, March, or early April, Romney had won over of 23% of Huntsman supporters, 16% of Bachmann supporters, and 20% of Perry supporters. Although most of these voters were not supporting Romney—Perry and Bachmann supporters were most likely to end up supporting Santorum—that Romney could win over any of them showed that people's decisions were not purely about ideology.[89]

If it was not ideology, what was buoying Romney's support? One possible explanation is electability: on balance, Republican primary voters were more likely to believe that he could beat Barack Obama than that Gingrich or Santorum could beat Obama. Figure 4.10 depicts the trends over time. On average, about 75% of Republican primary voters believed Romney could beat Obama, and this did not vary much over time. But Republicans were less confident in Gingrich: initially 53% believed he could beat Obama, and this declined to 47% by the end of March. They were also less confident in Santorum. Right before he dropped out of the race, only 50% believed he could beat Obama. Overall, 36% of Republican voters believed that only Romney could beat Obama, whereas 7% believed that only Santorum, Gingrich, or both could beat Obama.

Voters' perceptions of electability were also strongly correlated with their vote preferences—arguably more so than was their ideological proximity to the candidates. To demonstrate this, we divided Republican voters into six groups—broken down first by whether they were ideologically closest to

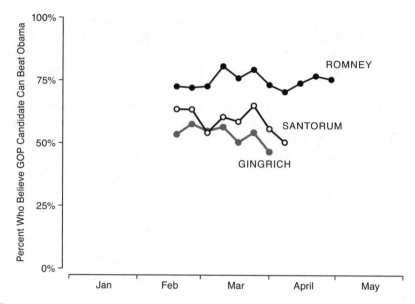

Figure 4.10.
Perceptions of the Republican candidates' electability.
The graph presents the percentage of Republican primary voters who believed Gingrich, Santorum, or Romney could beat Barack Obama in the general election. Data from YouGov polls.

Romney or to Gingrich or Santorum, and then by whether they believed that Romney could not beat Obama, that Romney and Gingrich and/or Santorum could beat Obama, or that only Romney could beat Obama. Figure 4.11 depicts Romney's share of the vote among each group.

For those who believed that Romney was going to lose, it did not much matter whether Romney was their closest ideological kin: few of these voters supported him. Among those who thought that only Romney could beat Obama, the majority supported Romney no matter whether they perceived him to be ideologically closest. Ideological proximity only expanded Romney's advantage among these voters (from 60% to 79%). But in this middle group—those who believed that Romney but also Gingrich and/or Santorum could beat Obama—proximity mattered. This made sense. If you believed that Santorum could beat Obama, and you also believed that Santorum reflected your beliefs more than Romney did, then you should have voted for Santorum. Thus Romney did relatively poorly with this group (19%) but much better among those who believed he was ideologically closest to them (51%). All told, Republican voters appeared to gravitate more to the candidate they thought could win in November than to the candidate whose ideology most closely matched theirs.

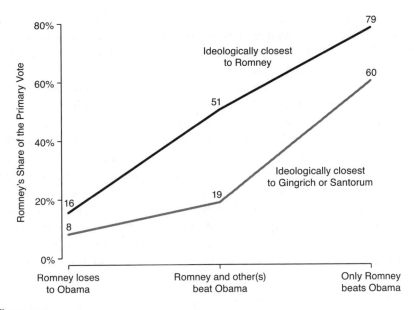

Figure 4.11.
Electability, ideology, and the Romney vote.
The graph presents the percentage of Republican primary voters who supported Romney, broken down by whether they were ideologically closest to him and whether they believed he, Gingrich, and/or Santorum could beat Barack Obama. Data from YouGov polls from January through early April (before Santorum's exit).

This was potentially important for Romney. Romney's coalition was evenly divided, as we have noted, between voters who were ideologically closest to him and those who were not. But in this latter group, nearly all believed he could beat Obama and half believed that only Romney could accomplish this. Romney's supporters appeared driven by a mix of sincerity and expediency.

One last piece of evidence suggests just how important expediency could have been, especially with a substantial number of Republican voters not yet settled on a candidate. One problem in determining whether perceptions of electability influenced how Republican voters chose a candidate is that cause and effect is not clear. Did voters decide who was electable and then pick that candidate? Or did they choose a candidate for other reasons and then, naturally, decide that this candidate was electable?[90] One way to adjudicate between these questions is via a randomized experiment. In a YouGov poll conducted right before the Iowa caucus, Republican likely voters were first asked which candidate they supported in the primary.[91] Then they were randomly given information about who was likely to win the primary (based on the betting market Intrade), information about how well each candidate would do against Obama (based on current polling), or both pieces of information. At this point, Romney was favored to win the nomination and was the candidate polling best against Obama. Finally, respondents were asked again which candidate they supported.

As expected, people responded strongly to this information. After seeing that Romney was favored to beat the other Republican candidates and win the nomination, support for him increased by 20 points.[92] After seeing that Romney was the Republican most likely to beat Barack Obama, support for him increased by 9 points. These results show how information about the candidates' viability in the primary and electability in the general election could have affected voters' choices. These results also dovetail with campaign events in March and April. In a two-week span at the end of March and beginning of April, the percentage of Republican voters who believed Santorum could beat Obama dropped 15 points (see Figure 4.10). During this same period, Romney gained 7 points in YouGov polls. Soon thereafter, Santorum dropped out, and Romney was on his way to the nomination.

The Standard-Bearer

At the Santorum event in Altoona, Iowa, we were approached by a man selling a book he had written. It was a retelling of *The Cat in the Hat*, starring Barack Obama as "The New Democrat." The illustrations resembled the Seussian originals, although the verses differed slightly. To wit:

> I'll make friends with our enemies.
> They'll do us no harm. . . .
> If they see we are weak
> We must therefore disarm!

We asked the author, Loren Spivack, who he was supporting in the Republican primary. He said either Santorum or Perry ("definitely one of the Ricks"). Then we asked if he would vote for Romney if Romney were the nominee. He paused a moment, shrugged, and said, "Yeah."

Mr. Spivack encapsulates some key aspects of the Republican primary. He was, like many Republican voters, not quite settled on a candidate. There was in his tone a certain lack of enthusiasm about the field—in contrast to his enthusiastic opposition to Barack Obama. Indeed, even in early March, two months after the Iowa caucus, Republican voters were not as enthusiastic about voting for Gingrich, Romney, or Santorum as they were about voting for John McCain in 2008.[93] But Spivack was willing to support Romney, even if Romney was not his first choice. Commentators sometimes mistook this constellation of attitudes for outright opposition to Romney and believed it evidence that, in an increasingly conservative party, a "Massachusetts moderate" could never break through.

But many in the party felt otherwise, including elected officials, donors, activists, and voters. This was why so many more leaders endorsed Romney than the other candidates and why Romney was able to collect so much more in campaign contributions. Indeed, it would have been unprecedented in modern presidential primaries for a candidate to win the nomination with as little support from the party as Gingrich and Santorum had. Their surges, however dramatic, were the equivalent of sugar highs. Gingrich and Santorum never received the nourishment to sustain their candidacies over the long haul—and nourishment is precisely what party leaders and donors provide. This enabled Romney to use his war chest to help defeat them.

Moreover, Santorum's and Gingrich's weaknesses belied the possibility that one of them could have beaten Romney if the field had been winnowed sooner—leaving Romney face-to-face against a single more conservative candidate—or if Gingrich and Santorum had banded together to form a "unity ticket," as apparently they discussed doing before the Michigan primary.[94] (The effort foundered because the two camps could not agree who would be the presidential candidate and who the vice-presidential candidate.) Although we should always be careful drawing conclusions from any hypothetical alternative history, it does seem as though Gingrich and Santorum would have faced many of the same problems even in this two-man race.

For example, without Gingrich in the race, Santorum might have won South Carolina but which other states thereafter? Santorum still would have faced a better-organized Romney campaign in Florida—the same challenge he faced later in 2012. Moreover, the things that made party leaders leery about Gingrich or Santorum from the outset—in Gingrich's case, his checkered personal history and reputation within the party; in Santorum's, his strongly conservative positions on social issues; in both of their cases, their chances of beating Obama—would not have changed in either hypothetical scenario. And these possible flaws would have been revealed in news coverage, and perhaps even more so, given the greater scrutiny either would have received in a two-man race with Romney. Nor is it clear that a Gingrich-Santorum unity ticket could have defeated Romney. Indeed, the "unity ticket" would have presented the Republican Party the chance to nominate not one but two people who had few endorsements from party leaders, an underpopulated funding network, and—at the time of the "unity ticket" negotiations—few delegates pledged to support them.

But could Gingrich or Santorum, or Gingrich-Santorum or Santorum-Gingrich, have won a few primaries, maybe even in Michigan, generated momentum, and then used this support in the electorate essentially to force party leaders into supporting them? Recent presidential nominations have shown that this is difficult.[95] Nominees have not won purely on grassroots support alone. Moreover, given Romney's lead in delegates and the effort and dollars that party leaders and donors had sunk into his campaign, even a Romney weakened by a loss in his home state of Michigan may have been preferable, certainly to the "unity ticket" of Gingrich and Santorum and likely to any other potential nominee, whom the party would have had to rush to the campaign trail very quickly.

Romney's victory also demonstrated that, contra stereotypes like the "Molotov Party," many Republicans—leaders and voters alike—are not arch-conservatives seeking ideological orthodoxy at all costs.[96] We have shown that groups like evangelicals and Tea Party members, while important to the Republican Party, do not comprise the majority of Republican voters—even if they seem like the face of the party on the evening news. Many in the GOP—about 30%—were ideologically closest to Romney to begin with. And many others were pragmatists who wanted to win in November even if that meant supporting a candidate (Romney) who was not ideologically closest to them. Romney's victory undercuts the claim that this Molotov GOP was "determined to take a walk on the wild side."[97] Indeed, moderates and pragmatists in the Republican Party have tended to prevail in presidential primaries. Since Reagan's nomination in 1980, every competitive Republican presidential primary has featured the triumph of a relative moderate over at least one if not more conservative candidates.

On May 29, when Mitt Romney won the number of delegates needed to clinch the nomination, it felt like an anti-climax. The talk of "Anybody but Romney," the "Santorum surge," the brokered convention—it was all a distant memory. Romney had not won every primary, losing a total of 13. This was more than Bob Dole lost (6) and more than George W. Bush lost in 2000 (7). But it was fewer than Bill Clinton in 1992 (18), John McCain in 2008 (18), and Barack Obama (21). Moreover, the apparent "slowness" of Romney's path to the nomination was mainly due to a rules change, not to Romney per se. Between 2008 and 2012, the Republican Party had actually elongated the primary calendar, moving Super Tuesday about a month later. Once this fact is taken into account, Romney actually earned delegates at about the same rate as did John McCain in 2008.[98] Ultimately presidential nominees do not need to win all the primaries or win them in quick succession.

The day he clinched the nomination Romney said, "Our party has come together with the goal of putting the failures of the last three and a half years behind us. I have no illusions about the difficulties of the task before us."[99] He was talking about the difficulties of making America economically prosperous. But, as it turned out, he could have been talking about the campaign to come.

CHAPTER 5

High Rollers

On April 9, 2012, Jann Wenner and Eric Bates, the publisher and editor of *Rolling Stone* magazine, interviewed Barack Obama. It was, they could not help but note, the "longest and most substantive interview the president had granted in over a year." Before the interview began, Wenner and Bates gave Obama a gift. Obama knew immediately what it was. The last time Wenner had interviewed him, Obama had commented on his flashy socks. This time Wenner came prepared, giving Obama two pairs, one "salmon with pink squares" and one with "black and pink stripes." Obama liked them—"These are nice"—but then seemed to hesitate. "These may be second-term socks," he said.[1]

Soon after this interview, Obama's chances of wearing those socks seemed to be decreasing. On May 4, the Bureau of Labor Statistics reported the monthly jobs numbers. The *New York Times*'s headline referred to an "ebb in jobs growth" and the leading paragraph noted, "The nation's employers are creating jobs at less than half the pace they were when this year began." Although the unemployment rate ticked downward, from 8.2 to 8.1%, this was only because so many Americans had essentially dropped out of the labor force and stopped looking for work. In sum, the report was "disappointing" and unemployed workers were "pretty discouraged."[2]

A month later, the news got even worse. The initial jobs report for May found that even fewer jobs had been created than in April, and the unemployment rate increased slightly, back to 8.2%. CBS News called the report "rotten," and the *Huffington Post* quoted an economist saying, "This is horrible."[3]

Obama acknowledged the challenges the country faced but promised improvement: "We will come back stronger. We do have better days ahead." Meanwhile, Mitt Romney pounced, calling the jobs report "devastating news for American workers and American families" and saying "the Obama economy is crushing America's middle class."[4] With the economy wobbly and the presidential campaign beginning in earnest, the summer of 2012 seemed like it could provide a real turning point in the race—perhaps even vaulting Romney into the lead.

This was not to be. Obama had the lead as Romney clinched the nomination, and Obama would retain that lead as the party conventions were set to begin in late August. In many respects, his lead was predictable. Even with the wobbly economy, Obama was still forecast to win. The lead he retained throughout the summer was one he should have had based on economic conditions alone. Moreover, many voters were reliably partisan and did not appear to change their minds during this time. Partisanship rendered them immune from the events that captivated political observers during the summer of 2012, such as Obama's advertising blitz and the string of "gaffes" committed by Obama and Romney. A small number of potentially persuadable voters may have responded to these events, but our data suggest that for most voters—more than 90%—their initial choice seemed like the right one.

The stability was also a direct consequence of the campaign itself. Stability is typically a *feature* of the competitive environment of presidential campaigns. Unlike candidates in many down-ballot races, the major-party presidential nominees are usually evenly matched. They tend to have roughly equivalent resources: lots of money, professional campaign organizations, and so on. In short, they are good at competing, most of the time, and this means their efforts neutralize each other, even though thousands of advertisements are being aired and tens of thousands of doors are being knocked on. In a tug-of-war, the flag in the middle of the rope does not move if both sides pull with equal force—even though both sides are pulling hard.

This is much different than the dynamic we described in the Republican presidential primary. There the candidates were not evenly matched. Some were well connected, well funded, and well prepared. Others were running campaigns out of their pickup trucks. Because voters were not familiar with many of them, new information gleaned from news coverage or electioneering could have a powerful effect—thus the cycle of discovery, scrutiny, and decline that we documented for Perry, Cain, Gingrich, and Santorum. In the general election, the effects of news coverage, campaign ads, and the like were much harder to see. Although the efforts of the candidates may have produced small shifts in the polls, in general the candidates were so evenly matched that their efforts canceled one another out.

A presidential general election campaign typically resembles a concept from the sciences called a "dynamic equilibrium." In a dynamic equilibrium, things are happening, sometimes vigorously or rapidly, but they produce opposing reactions that are roughly the same size or magnitude and that occur at roughly the same rates. Thus, the entire "system"—populated by candidates, media, and voters—appears stable, or at a "steady state," to use more scientific nomenclature, even though it is not static. Reams of news coverage and vigorous campaigning coincide with stable polls.

But the equilibrium can be thrown out of balance. If one candidate were not as good a campaigner, or adopted a poor strategy, or inexplicably decided to sit out the campaign, the polls would likely move toward the other candidate—just as the stronger team in a tug-of-war can move the flag tied to the rope. Lopsided campaigns can produce larger campaign effects. It is just that lopsided campaigns have been relatively rare in recent presidential general elections. This makes uncovering the effects of presidential campaigns challenging. Stability may actually be the result of two highly effective campaigns, not two dismally ineffective campaigns.

The summer of 2012 was interesting precisely because it seemed like it might disrupt the campaign's equilibrium. Both candidates made big bets. Romney's choice of Paul Ryan as a running mate seemed to signal a shift in Romney's message from Obama's handling of the economy to a debate about the size of government and the national debt. The Obama campaign bought a lot of advertising unusually early in the general election campaign, attacking Romney even before he officially had the nomination.

But neither of these gambits amounted to much—at least in terms of votes. Over the summer months, Obama and Romney fought hard, but largely fought to a draw. Voters were ambivalent enough about issues surrounding the economy and the size of government that neither candidate could clearly win the argument. Moreover, Obama's early advertising advantage produced at best a short-lived boost. And though both candidates had good and bad news cycles—thanks in part to their assorted gaffes—these also proved temporary. News coverage of both candidates was actually quite balanced.

The summer of 2012 left Obama, the favorite, with a slim lead—one that was predictable but not entirely comfortable. He was probably right not to wear those socks. Meanwhile, Romney was hoping for a comeback that did not come.

The "Mathematically Impossible" Favorite

Since 1948, incumbent presidents running in growing economies have typically won elections, and those running in declining economies have typically lost. As we showed in chapter 2, even modest economic growth in an election year has been sufficient, as voters tend to weight recent trends most heavily. At the end of 2011, growth in 2012 was forecasted to be large enough to make Obama the favorite. One survey suggested that GDP would grow at a rate of 2.4% in 2012. Based on the historical relationship between election-year growth in GDP and presidential election outcomes, this growth rate would have predicted a 2- to 3-point Obama victory.[5]

The problem for Obama in the summer of 2012 was that this forecasted growth rate had not come to pass. Indeed, even when this forecast came out, it was already more pessimistic than the forecast before it (which predicted 2.6% growth). Actual economic growth would bear out this pessimism. In the first quarter of 2012, GDP grew at an annualized rate of 2.0%. In the second quarter, it grew at an annualized rate of 1.3%.[6] Combined with the stagnant unemployment rate, the economic picture was darkening at precisely the wrong time for Obama.

Obama's situation resembled that of previous Democratic incumbents. Democratic presidents seeking reelection have typically experienced lower rates of economic growth in their election year than in other years. For Republican incumbents, the opposite has been true: in election years, economic growth has increased at a faster rate than in other years. In other words, presidents of both parties have presided over economic growth, on average, but that growth has not occurred at the right time to maximize Democrats' electoral advantage. Because voters weight election-year growth more heavily, this asymmetry has paid dividends for Republican presidential candidates, giving them 3 to 4 points more of the vote, on average.[7]

But even with the slowing economy, was Obama the underdog? Looking at isolated indicators, it was easy to believe he was. For example, growth in personal income was sluggish and, taken alone, forecast an Obama defeat.[8] Moreover, consumer sentiment in the first half of 2012 plateaued as the economic news worsened. Had it continued on its previous trajectory, Obama's chances would have looked good. Instead, consumer sentiment looked more like it did during George H. W. Bush's first term than it did at the same point in the first terms of incumbents who, unlike Bush, were reelected.[9]

But other indicators did not tell this same story. Perhaps the most important of these was the inflation rate, which remained at historical lows. Analysts who surveyed a large set of economic indicators concluded that Obama was still the favorite, despite the slowdown in growth in early 2012. For example, political scientists Robert Erikson and Christopher Wlezien examined the Conference Board's Leading Economic Index, which is comprised of ten different economic measures. Based on analysis of presidential elections from 1952 to 2008, the index suggested Obama was the favorite. Figure 5.1 shows

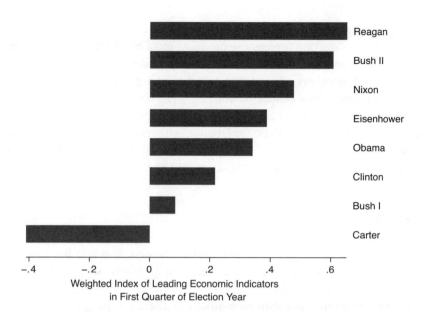

Figure 5.1.
Index of economic indicators for incumbent presidents.
The figure depicts the value of the Conference Board's Leading Economic Index,
summed across these incumbents' first term until the first quarter of the election year
for these incumbents. The index is weighted so that recent quarters count more heavily.

why this was possible. For each elected incumbent president who was running
for reelection, the figure presents the summed value of this economic index
from inauguration through the first quarter of the reelection year, weighted so
that more recent quarters count more heavily. The value of this index under
Obama was higher than it was under the two incumbents who lost, Jimmy
Carter and George H. W. Bush, and under Clinton in 1996, when he won.[10]

It was very difficult for some commentators to believe that an economy
slowly recovering from a painful recession and financial crisis still favored the
incumbent. In May, *New York Times* columnist David Brooks wrote, "Why is
Obama even close? If you look at the fundamentals, the president should be
getting crushed right now."[11] Election analyst Charlie Cook expressed a similar
sentiment in August: "Incumbents generally don't get reelected with numbers
like we are seeing today."[12] In September, *Politico*'s Jonathan Martin wrote: "If
it was true that winning elections is mostly a matter of numbers—as some
political scientists and campaign operatives like to argue—Barack Obama's
reelection as president should be close to a mathematical impossibility."[13] Although it was true that certain economic indicators looked less favorable for

Obama, a broader survey of indicators revealed the opposite. Moreover, a review of various election forecasting models—most of which used some combination of factors like economic indicators, presidential approval, and early trial heat poll numbers—found that, taken together, these models predicted that Obama had a 60% chance of winning.[14] The election was far from a lock for Obama, but he was more likely to win than to lose. And even if this assessment seemed overly optimistic for Obama, 2012 was still not a year in which he should have been "crushed" or in which his reelection was an "impossibility." If history were any guide, Obama was still likely to win.

Predictably Partisan

As the summer campaign got under way in earnest, it might have seemed as if Obama and Romney were in a similar, and unfortunate, position: suddenly unpopular within their own party. Reports suggested that the two parties were struggling—not with each other but internally. In Carl Cannon and Tom Bevan's summary of the Republican primary, they wrote, "True, Mitt Romney ended up winning the nomination. But he did so with a split Republican base."[15] Meanwhile, Obama was said to face a "a growing rebellion on the left as he courts independent voters and Republicans with his vision for reducing the nation's debt by cutting government spending and restraining the costs of federal health insurance programs."[16] Fights within political parties are often a tempting story for the news media, since intraparty squabbles are more unusual than fights between the political parties. *New York Times* columnist Gail Collins described one or both of the allegedly fractious parties as "rabid guinea pigs in a thunderstorm," "a herd of rabid otters," and "rabid squirrels" in 2009 and 2010.[17]

But presidential campaigns tend to pull each party *together*, not drive them to internal collapse, belying the many stories about these fractured, divided, rebellious parties—to say nothing of stories that suggest the possible obsolescence of political parties themselves.[18] In presidential elections, partisanship reigns, and predictably so.

Among Americans, political partisanship is on the rise. This may seem counterintuitive on its face. Time and time again we are told that political independents are the "the vast middle ground" or the "the fast-growing swath of voters."[19] But this misses a crucial fact: most independents actually identify with a party, at least to some extent. When you ask survey respondents who identify as "independent" if they lean toward the Democratic or Republican Party, most in fact do. In 2008, only about 11% of Americans were true or "pure" independents, according to the canonical data in the American

National Election Study (ANES), and this number was smaller among actual voters, since independents are less likely than partisans to vote.[20] In fact, the fraction of pure independents has declined over time; it was 18% at its high point in 1974.

Identification with a political party, even if nudging is required to reveal it, is not only pervasive but consequential and increasingly so. Despite all of the ink spilled about fractured parties, in contemporary presidential elections the vast majority—typically near 90%—of partisans vote for their party's candidate when there is no serious third-party candidate (and loyalty is still high when there is such a candidate). A similar rate of loyalty is evident even among independents who lean toward a party. They look much more like true partisans in terms of their voting behavior than they do pure independents. For example, in 2008, "pure independents" who reported voting in the presidential election split 51%–41% for Obama, with the remainder voting for another candidate. The vast majority of Democrats (90%) voted for Obama, and so did 90% of independents who leaned Democratic. Similarly, the vast majority (92%) of Republicans voted for John McCain, as did 78% of independents who leaned Republican. Independent "leaners" are certainly not identical to partisans in every respect, but they tend to act like loyal partisans in presidential elections.

These patterns are not unique to 2008. Party loyalty has increased generally. As the Democratic and Republican parties have taken ever more distinct positions on issues, partisans have better sorted themselves ideologically—with liberals increasingly identifying as Democrats and conservatives as Republicans.[21] There is less and less reason for partisans to stray from the fold.

Even if they were tempted to stray, the campaign itself helps prevent that. Strengthening people's natural partisan predispositions is one of the most consistent effects of presidential campaigns. Democrats or Republicans who initially feel a bit uncertain or unenthusiastic about their party's nominee will end up dedicated supporters. Scholars have documented this for a long time. One of the earliest studies of presidential elections, which followed voters during the 1940 campaign, found this: "Knowing a few of their personal characteristics, we can tell with fair certainty how they will finally vote: they join the fold to which they belong. What the campaign does is to activate their political predispositions."[22]

This is why a presidential nominee who emerges from a hotly contested primary can so readily consolidate support within the party. It may also explain why divisive primaries have not appeared to hurt the presidential nominee in the general election.[23] The hotly contested 2008 primaries are a good example. In states where the primary was very competitive, Obama actually did a little bit better in the general election. One possible reason was that competitive primaries forced Obama to build up his campaign organization and actually made it stronger for the general election.[24] Ultimately, despite the protracted battle between Obama and Hillary Clinton, supporters of Clinton or any of the other Democratic candidates tended to vote and to vote for Obama at high rates.[25]

What was remarkable about the 2012 election was just how quickly partisans gravitated to their party's candidate. Democrats and Republicans were predictably partisan even before the general election campaign got under way—in fact, even before Romney sewed up in the nomination. Only days after Santorum dropped out, the very first Gallup tracking poll found that 90% of Republicans supported Romney in a head-to-head race with Obama, while 90% of Democrats supported Obama. Large majorities of both parties also said that they definitely planned to vote in November.[26] This was true even though about a third of Republicans said they would have preferred another candidate to Romney.[27] The divisive Republican primary did not make for hard feelings. In fact, it was not long before reporters on the ground were writing about the "newfound enthusiasm" for Romney among Republicans.[28] The campaign was rallying partisans as usual.

The predictable partisanship of most American voters had one other important manifestation: it solidified their vote intentions, making preferences stable over time. This also was no surprise: studies of presidential elections have repeatedly found that most voters know who they plan to vote for early on and do not change their minds during the campaign. In 1940, for example, the presidential campaign "served the important purpose of preserving prior decisions instead of initiating new decisions."[29] In 1980 the same thing was true: "changes in political attitudes did take place during the presidential campaign, but the magnitude of these changes was not large enough to alter many individuals' vote predictions."[30]

This was also the norm in 2012. In December 2011, the polling firm YouGov asked 45,000 Americans who they would vote for if the presidential election pitted Romney against Obama. Among all respondents, 45% chose or were leaning toward Obama and 41% chose or were leaning toward Romney. About 4% chose another candidate and 10% were not sure. (Among respondents who were registered voters, Obama led by a similar margin, and fewer, 6%, were unsure.) How many of these voters stuck with their initial choice into 2012? Every week, when YouGov reinterviewed a different set of 1,000 of the initial 45,000 people, an impressive number of them stuck with their initial choice.

Consider the people who were reinterviewed in April, at the same time that Gallup found such high rates of loyalty among Democrats and Republicans. As Table 5.1 shows, even though four months (and essentially the entire Republican primary) had elapsed, 92% of those who supported Romney in

Table 5.1.

The Stability of Vote Intentions from December 2011 to April 2012.

December vote intention	April vote intention				
	Obama	Romney	Other candidate	Not sure	Total
Obama	96%	2%	1%	1%	45%
Romney	4%	92%	2%	2%	41%
Other candidate	10%	40%	44%	6%	5%
Not sure	26%	26%	8%	40%	9%

Note: Data consist of YouGov poll respondents who were interviewed at two points in time: December 2011 and April 2012. Percentages are within each group of December respondents and should be read across the rows.
$N = 3,594$

December still supported him in April. Similarly, 96% of Obama's supporters stuck with him. Few voters switched their votes between interviews: 4% of Romney's initial supporters defected to Obama, and 2% of Obama's voters left him for Romney. Similarly, 2% of Romney's and 1% of Obama's supporters moved into the undecided category. Most everyone appeared to know who they were going to vote for long before Mitt Romney even became the Republican nominee. This kind of stability would ultimately constrain what Obama and Romney could hope to accomplish during the campaign that followed. The basic features of the election were in place: a slowly growing economy and a high degree of partisan loyalty. If things stayed the same, not very many voters were up for grabs.

The Misunderstood Undecided Voter

But what about the voters who were up for grabs? These voters, the proverbial "undecided voters," are sought after by political campaigns but often mocked by pundits and commentators. The 2012 election was no exception. The Republican pollster Jan van Lohuizen called undecided voters "cave dwellers."[31] MSNBC's Chris Matthews unleashed this diatribe:

> People say, "this election's hard for me to decide." You'd have to be a bonehead not to be able to decide between these two guys. It is so easy. . . . People are still scratching their heads trying to decide what's—well, gee, just don't vote. Don't bother if you have to think at this point. What's your problem?[32]

Saturday Night Live aired a parody in which serious-looking "undecided voters" asked "meaningful" questions: "When is the election?" "What are the names of the two people running? And be specific." "Who is the president right now? Is he or she running?" "Can women vote?" Actually investigating the prevalence of such stereotypes is hard. In a survey of 1,000 people during a typical presidential campaign, there will be only a few dozen undecided voters—too few for statistical analysis. But by combining ten different YouGov surveys from May through July—a combined sample of 10,000 respondents—we took an unusually nuanced look at 592 respondents who declared themselves undecided.[33]

As with most great comedy, the *Saturday Night Live* skit contained a kernel of truth. Compared to voters who stated a preference for a candidate, undecided voters in the summer of 2012 were indeed less attentive to politics. Only a quarter of undecided voters said they were very interested in politics compared to 60% of "decided" voters. They were also less informed about the political world. Only 38% could correctly identify Speaker of the House John Boehner as a member of the U.S. House of Representatives, whereas 63% of decided voters could do this. Undecided voters did no better than guessing when asked whether the Republican Party or Democratic Party was more conservative, whereas 80% of decided voters knew it was the former. Undecided voters were also, and unsurprisingly, less likely to vote: 30% of them reported that they rarely make it to the polls, compared to 8% of those who had a candidate preference. That said, undecided voters were hardly the ignoramuses presented on *Saturday Night Live*. They may have followed politics less closely, but that did not mean they knew nothing about it.

Moreover, most of these undecided voters had political identities and opinions about political issues. Despite the common stereotype that undecided voters are independents who do not affiliate with a political party, only about 30% of them were independent and an additional 7% were not sure of their party identification. The remaining 63% identified with or leaned toward either the Democratic or Republican Party.

In fact, what most distinguished these undecided voters was not that they were independents but that they were disgruntled partisans. A more academic description of them is "cross-pressured"—that is, having political opinions that were in some tension with each other. That cross-pressured voters exist, and are often less interested in elections, has been well-known to scholars for more than sixty years.[34] In 2012, cross-pressures were evident in various ways.

Undecided Democrats were unenthusiastic about Barack Obama—something relatively rare given the increasing partisan polarization in attitudes toward the presidents that we have described. Whereas 79% of decided Democrats approved of Obama, only 17% of undecided Democrats did. As one undecided voter who had supported Obama in 2008 put it, "he has not lived up to the 'hope and change' he professed. . . . He seems stuck."[35] Undecided Democrats tended to disapprove of the president's performance on a range of issues—from the economy to the deficit to health care—and also expressed less favorable attitudes about the president's personality.

Undecided Republicans were similarly uninspired by Romney. The majority, 64%, believed that he "says what he thinks people want to hear," while only 8% believed he "says what he believes." (Decided Republicans were more evenly divided between these alternatives.) In fact, undecided Republicans had a less favorable view of Romney in the summer of 2012 than they did in December 2011. Undecided Republicans were cross-pressured in another sense: their policy views were more at odds with those of their party. They were twice as likely as decided Republicans to support gay marriage but half as likely to favor repealing the Affordable Care Act.

The prevalence of cross-pressured partisans among undecided voters raised an interesting possibility: that they could be lured to the other side. In fact, presidential campaigns can make defection among cross-pressured voters more likely.[36] At the same time, campaigns can also herd undecided partisans back into the fold. In 2012, little about the undecided Democrats and Republicans suggested that they were all that enthralled with the other guy: most undecided Democrats did not like Romney and most undecided Republicans did not like Obama. Ultimately, these undecided voters could have provided a significant boon if they broke for one candidate, and the candidates were crafting messages with this very much in mind.

Jobs, Jobs, Jobs

"4.3 million new jobs," declared an ad for Obama. "President Romney's leadership puts jobs first," said an ad of Romney's. As the general election campaign got under way, there was no doubt what issue was foremost on voters' minds and in the messages of both candidates. In a May *Washington Post/ABC News* poll, 52% said that the economy and jobs were the "single most important issue" in their choice for president. No other issue attracted more than single digits. In 2012, Romney's and Obama's campaign teams took a look at the most salient issue—the state of the nation's economy—and came up with the same answer: "the economy is on our side." They both could not be right.

A candidate's message is the argument for his or her election boiled down to a few sentences or even a few words. These messages are often developed well before the general election begins in earnest. They can be modified or recalibrated but are replaced wholesale with caution. The candidate changing his or her message is usually the candidate who is losing, and a new message is taken as further proof of the challenges this candidate faces.

Candidates design their messages around the context in which they find themselves—the hand they are dealt, as we called it in chapter 2. There are personal constraints. For example, an older candidate who has served in government for a long time cannot easily present him- or herself as a candidate of "new ideas." He or she may be instead, as was Hillary Clinton in 2008, the candidate of "experience." There are constraints that come from the issues that are salient to voters. As in 2012, candidates tend to emphasize the issues most important to voters, which means that opposing candidates are often discussing many of the same things.[37] To do otherwise risks appearing inattentive or uncaring.

In a typical presidential campaign, the economy tends to benefit one party: the incumbent's party when the economy is good and the challenger's party when the economy is poor. The candidate who benefits from the state of the nation's economy should emphasize the economy as a campaign issue. This candidate can take credit for good times, as Ronald Reagan did in 1984 when he called it "Morning in America," or blame the incumbent party for bad times, as Barack Obama blamed George W. Bush in 2008. In *The Message Matters*, Lynn Vavreck calls this type of candidate a "clarifying" candidate—one who must clarify which party is responsible for the economy in order to win.[38] Specifically, a clarifying candidate should take credit for the growing economy or blame the opponent for a shrinking economy. Not doing so can be a mistake. Al Gore's 2000 campaign shows what can happen when clarifying candidates fail to attach themselves to the incumbent party's strong economic record.

Candidates disadvantaged by the economy—the "insurgent" candidates in Vavreck's framework—have a different, and arguably harder, task. They must shift the focus of the election to an issue other than the economy. Specifically, they must find an issue on which their position is more popular than their opponent's *and* on which the opponent is committed to an unpopular position. Insurgent issues are often difficult for candidates to find. One reason for this is that their opponents sometimes can and do wriggle out of their previous position on the issue and simply adopt the same position as the insurgent candidate—effectively neutralizing the issue. The clarifying candidate must be truly stuck with his unpopular position for the insurgent issue to win votes.

Amid the weak economy in 1980, the incumbent Jimmy Carter was the insurgent candidate and chose to attack Reagan on nuclear weapons and arms control, suggesting that electing Reagan would only increase the likelihood of nuclear war. But Reagan, who was not irrevocably linked to the view Carter accused him of, simply took the same position as Carter, declaring his support for reducing the number of nuclear weapons and thereby neutralizing Carter's attack.[39] In fact, in presidential elections from 1952 to 2008, only four insurgent candidates have won: Kennedy, Nixon, Carter, and George W. Bush. For example, Kennedy did so by shifting the discussion to the New Frontier and to a Cold War competition with the Soviets over everything from nuclear missiles—the "missile gap" that Kennedy highlighted—to space exploration. Because there was no easy way to disprove the existence of the missile gap, it was difficult for Nixon, as a member of the administration who allegedly presided over this gap, to claim otherwise.

What made 2012 unusual was that, at the outset of the general election campaign, *both* candidates behaved like clarifying candidates—something that has happened in just one other postwar election (1992). To measure the prevalence of different issues in Romney's and Obama's campaign messages, we drew on campaign advertising data collected by the Campaign Media Analysis Group (CMAG). Figure 5.2 reports the percentage of the ads aired between May and July 2012 that mentioned various issues.[40] During this time, Obama and allied Democratic groups aired the majority of ads (179,463 and 19,781, respectively), although Romney, the Republican National Committee (RNC), and allied Republican groups aired nearly as many (166,399 combined). These numbers are important to keep in mind when comparing the percentages in Figure 5.2, especially since Democratic groups aired relatively few ads.

That both Romney and Obama acted like clarifying candidates is evident in how much of their summer advertising mentioned jobs: 82% of ad airings for both candidates. This far outstripped any other theme, although both candidates devoted attention to the budget, government spending, and taxes, too. Obama's advertising also mentioned several other issues, including Romney's tenure at Bain Capital, while Romney focused on a smaller set of issues, including energy and health care. But clearly the economy dominated each candidate's advertising. As Figure 5.2 shows, the economy also figured prominently in the ads aired by the RNC and by the outside groups on both sides. The economy was also the dominant issue in news coverage.[41]

But Obama and Romney framed their economic appeals very differently. The Obama campaign focused on the extent to which the economy had improved. One ad reminded voters that since Obama's inauguration there had been "26 straight months of private sector growth" and "4.25 million jobs created."[42] An animated graphic showed job losses throughout 2008—colored in Republican red—and then job gains soon after Obama took office, which of course were colored Democrat blue. The ad's tagline was, "Do we really want to change course now?" In another ad, Obama took a similar tack. He first reminded viewers of what he confronted when he took office: "We're still fighting our way back from the worst economic crisis since the Great Depression."

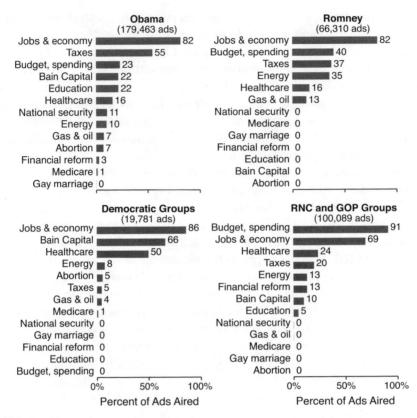

Figure 5.2.
Issues mentioned in Obama and Romney advertising, May–July 2012.
The figure depicts the estimated percentage of Obama and Romney ad airings in
May–July 2012 that mentioned each of these issues. Data from the Campaign Media
Analysis Group.

While acknowledging that "we're still not creating [jobs] as fast as we want,"
he then cited the "4.3 million new jobs" that had been created, promoted his
own plan for creating more jobs, and criticized Congress for failing to act on
it.[43] The Obama campaign's message was simple: even if times were not great,
they were at least getting better, and because of the incumbent.

Romney's economic message committed him to jobs as well: "President Romney's leadership puts jobs first," said one early ad titled "A Better
Day."[44] The difference, of course, was how Romney portrayed the health of
the economy under Obama. After the May jobs report showed unemployment ticking up, Obama suggested at a June 8 press conference that the real
issue was job losses in state and local government while "the private sector is

doing fine." Romney pounced. One ad consisted almost entirely of newscasters like Diane Sawyer reacting with concern to the jobs report, juxtaposed with Obama's "private sector" comment.[45] The tagline then read, "Has there ever been a president so out of touch with the middle class?" followed by a link to the webpage www.obamaisntworking.com. Another ad pivoted off Obama's comment with testimonials from "middle-class workers" describing the challenges they were facing: layoffs, long-term unemployment, bankruptcy, no health care, a slashed pension. One man said, "Sometimes I feel like a failure." Romney's message was the opposite of Obama's: the economy was still terrible, Obama was to blame, and only Romney could bring about that "better day."

Within Romney's messaging there were also hints of an insurgent campaign theme. The focus on the budget—present in 40% of Romney's ads during May–July—shifted the subject from the economy to government spending and the size of the federal deficit. In other ads, Romney touted his own record of balancing the budget as Massachusetts governor and criticized Obama for his "broken promise" to rein in government spending and the deficit.[46] Instead, Romney argued, Obama created a "debt and spending inferno."[47] This message was often linked to Romney's broader message on the economy: In "A Better Day" the voiceover says, "From Day 1, President Romney focuses on the economy and the deficit." Romney made the argument that the debt and government spending hurt the economy—for example, by requiring the United States to borrow more money from China, which Romney warned was taking away American jobs as firms relocated their operations to China where labor was cheaper.[48] To Romney, smaller government—embodied in the "Cut the spending" banner that hung at his early campaign appearances—was an economic stimulus plan in its own right. This message set up a different kind of comparison to Obama, moving beyond just the employment numbers to implicate Obama's domestic policymaking. But this message was still subordinate to Romney's broader critique of Obama's economic record.

Navigating Public Ambivalence about the Economy

Romney and Obama could not both win the argument about the state of the nation's economy even if they thought they could. What were the promises and pitfalls that lay ahead as each centered his campaign on the economy? Why did they both think this was a winning strategy? Answering these questions means understanding the public's ambivalence about the economy and issues related to it. Americans' "on the one hand, but on the other hand" mentality presented opportunities and challenges for both Obama and Romney.

As we have argued, the objective economy favored Obama. But public views of the economy did not depend wholly on statistics, and Obama faced a public concerned about the economy and his stewardship of it. That gave Romney an opening he could exploit. But Romney also faced a public that was not ready to embrace him as the alternative to Obama.

Americans' concern about the economy was very evident in the summer of 2012. In a mid-May YouGov poll, respondents were asked about the condition of the economy both in the recent past and at that moment. When asked what the condition of the economy had been in 2008, most said that it had been "fairly bad" (36%) or "very bad" (49%). When asked about the economy "these days," 42% said fairly bad and 28% said very bad—a positive trend, but one that still left 70% of the country dissatisfied with the economy. When asked directly about the trend in the economy, Americans did not seem optimistic. Among respondents in the May, June, and July YouGov surveys, 37% said the economy was getting worse and 36% said it was the same.[49] Only 21% said that it was getting better, and the remainder was not sure. These assessments had barely changed from when these same respondents were interviewed in December 2011. At this point, the public's pessimism seemed persistent.

Naturally these assessments were also colored by partisanship: only 17% of Democrats said that the economy was getting worse, compared to 60% of Republicans. But independents who did not lean toward either party were closer to Republicans: 43% said the economy was getting worse. Undecided voters also tilted toward pessimism. The plurality (45%) thought that the economy was the same, but many more said that it was getting worse (34%) than it was getting better (6%).

Given this pessimism, it is not surprising that voters tended to disapprove of Obama's stewardship of the economy. Only 36% approved of Obama—and even fewer among independents (24%) and undecided voters (18%). The intensity of opinion was not in Obama's favor either: independents and undecided voters were more likely to "strongly" disapprove than only "somewhat" disapprove.

There was one silver lining for Obama: people tended to blame the state of the economy less on him than on his predecessor, George W. Bush. In mid-April, as we reported in chapter 2, 43% of Americans said that Obama deserved a great deal or a lot of the blame, while 51% said this of George W. Bush. The same was true in May and June, according to other polls by the *Washington Post* and Gallup.[50] But in a late July YouGov poll, Obama's advantage waned: 46% blamed Obama and 48% blamed Bush. Independents and undecided voters still blamed Bush more, but the trend was not good news for Obama. His message about the economy—essentially, "it's getting better, so leave me in charge"—confronted a skeptical public. It is not hard to see how Romney thought this was a plausible weakness to exploit.

However, Romney's decision to focus on the economy was, in another sense, questionable. Objective economic conditions were not in his favor, and the four previous presidential candidates who focused on the economy despite this disadvantage lost: George McGovern, George H. W. Bush in 1992, Bob Dole, and John McCain.[51] The Romney campaign's point of historical reference, however, seemed to be Jimmy Carter in 1980.[52] They apparently believed that although Obama led now, Romney would come from behind at the end, as they believed Reagan had. This was a mistaken view of the 1980 race; Reagan actually led for much of the fall.[53] Moreover, as we have argued, economic conditions in early 2012 were much better than they had been in early 1980. Obama was also far more popular than Carter.

Another challenge for Romney was this: even if voters were pessimistic about the economy and frustrated with Obama's stewardship of the economy, they were not yet ready to embrace Romney as an alternative. For one, Americans were somewhat uncertain as to how a President Romney would affect the economy and, among those who had an opinion, were no more confident in him than in Obama. In early June, a YouGov poll asked respondents how the economy would be affected if Obama or Romney were elected president. In Obama's case, 30% thought that the economy would get better and 39% thought it would get worse. The remainder thought it would stay the same (15%) or did not know (16%). By contrast, 27% did not know how the economy would do under Romney. Among those who had an opinion, Romney was no more favored than Obama: 25% thought the economy would get better and 33% thought it would get worse. The pattern was similar among undecided voters.

Second, Americans were not convinced that Romney understood the challenges they faced. In a mid-June YouGov poll, 44% said that Obama understood "the current economic situation facing most Americans" either very or somewhat well, while 48% said he understood it not too well or not well at all. By contrast, fewer Americans (37%) believed that Romney understood what Americans were facing while 49% believed he did not. The difference, of course, was that twice as many Americans were not sure about Romney (14%) as about Obama (7%).

Even more fundamentally, Americans tended to believe that Romney was less likely to "care about" them than Obama was. They also saw Romney as more concerned about wealthier Americans than about the middle class and poor. Romney's challenges in this domain began well before the general election was really under way. Right after the Iowa caucuses, in a January 7–10 YouGov poll, we asked respondents how well the following phrases described Obama and Romney: "is personally wealthy," "cares about people like me," "cares about the poor," "cares about the middle class," and "cares about the wealthy."[54] Respondents could answer very well, somewhat well, not very well, or not at all well.

Even in this poll, conducted at the outset of Gingrich's and Perry's attacks on Romney's time at Bain Capital, Romney's disadvantages were evident. The disadvantage was not so much about personal wealth: the vast majority of respondents thought that "personally wealthy" described Romney (89%) and Obama (84%) very well or somewhat well, although many more said "very well" in reference to Romney than Obama. More people described Obama as caring about the poor (62% said somewhat or very well versus 38% for Romney), the middle class (56% versus 49%), and "people like me" (51% versus 42%). But more, 84%, described Romney as caring about the wealthy. Only 58% said that of Obama. Among true political independents, who lack the party loyalties that shape such responses, there were similar gaps in views of Obama and Romney.

Romney faced an additional disadvantage: how these attitudes were structured. The more voters thought "personally wealthy" described Romney, the more they thought that "cares about the wealthy" described him. But people's belief that Obama was personally wealthy did not translate as strongly into the belief that he cared about the wealthy.[55] A similar contrast arose with regard to caring about the wealthy versus other groups. Voters who believed that Romney cared about the wealthy were less likely to think that he cared about "people like me," the poor, or the middle class. But voters who believed that Obama cared about the wealthy were actually *more* likely to think that he cared about these other groups.[56] Romney's empathy gap was not just about which candidate was perceived to care more for average Americans, it was also about whether caring about the wealthy meant caring less about everyone else.

Some of Romney's disadvantage was endemic to the Republican Party, which has traditionally been seen as aligned with wealthy interests. In 1953, a Gallup poll asked respondents, "When you think of a people who are Democrats, what type of person comes to mind?" About 38% selected words like "working class," "middle class," and "common people" while only 1% selected words like "rich" or "wealthy." The opposite was true when asked about Republicans: 31% picked words like "wealthy" and "business executive" while only 6% chose "working class" and its kindred. Over forty years later, in a 1997 poll, the same findings reoccurred.[57] In 2012 these same stereotypes were again in evidence. When asked which party would be "better for" different groups, majorities or pluralities of respondents said that the Democrats would be better for the poor and middle class, while the majority said that the Republicans would be better for Wall Street.[58] Perhaps because of these images of the Republican Party, Republican presidential candidates have often faced an "empathy gap." Voters have been more willing to say that the Democratic candidate "cares about people like me" than to say this of the Republican candidate in every presidential election from 1980 to 2008.[59]

So Romney's situation was nothing new or even unusual. But it was not inevitable that the Republican Party and Romney would face an empathy gap. Rick Santorum showed that it was possible for a Republican candidate to be perceived as in touch with the middle class. In a February poll, voters perceived Santorum as more similar to Obama than Romney. For example, 49% said that Santorum cared about "people like me," while 51% said that of Obama but only 35% said that of Romney.[60]

Of course, the point is not that Republicans should have nominated Santorum instead of Romney. There was no reason to think that Romney's "empathy gap" would inevitably be fatal. Republican presidential candidates have routinely won without closing this gap.[61] But the question was whether Romney could be one of those winners, especially when the Obama campaign would soon seek to magnify this image of Romney as a rich guy who cared more about the wealthy than the middle class. For while the Romney campaign believed that voters' shrinking incomes were Obama's pressure point, Obama believed that Romney's income was his.

"What about Your Gaffes?"

Although political candidates try to have a disciplined message, unscripted moments happen. And when they do, commentators take note. "Here's an unpopular opinion," wrote the *Washington Post*'s Chris Cillizza on June 10. "Political gaffes matter."[62] He was writing right after Obama suggested the "private sector was doing fine." Political gaffes often fascinate reporters and commentators. Most days on the campaign are repetitive, as candidates deliver the same speech in a different town. But once in a while something happens that is unexpected and, from the candidate's point of view, undesired. These blunders almost always make the news, since they may be the only interesting thing that has happened on the campaign trail in a long time.

But do blunders matter to voters? Often not so much, and this election was no exception. The summer of 2012 saw a series of gaffes that received ample attention by the press and seemed likely to shape the race in critical ways, as voters might use them to make inferences about the candidates' competence, empathy, and readiness to lead. But as it turned out, the gaffes in May, June, and July were largely non-events. Sometimes "unpopular opinions" are unpopular for a reason.

After Obama's "private sector" comment, the summer provided several other opportunities to test Cillizza's proposition. On July 13, Obama spoke his famous phrase "you didn't build that" in a campaign speech in Roanoke:

> There are a lot of wealthy, successful Americans who agree with me—because they want to give something back. They know they didn't—look, if you've been successful, you didn't get there on your own. You didn't get there on your own. I'm always struck by people who think, well, it must be because I was just so smart. There are a lot of smart people out there. It must be because I worked harder than everybody else. Let me tell you something—there are a whole bunch of hard-working people out there.
>
> If you were successful, somebody along the line gave you some help. There was a great teacher somewhere in your life. Somebody helped to create this unbelievable American system that we have that allowed you to thrive. Somebody invested in roads and bridges. If you've got a business—*you didn't build that*. Somebody else made that happen. The Internet didn't get invented on its own. Government research created the Internet so that all the companies could make money off the Internet.
>
> The point is, is that when we succeed, we succeed because of our individual initiative, but also because we do things together. There are some things, just like fighting fires, we don't do on our own. I mean, imagine if everybody had their own fire service. That would be a hard way to organize fighting fires.[63]

Obama was apparently making the case for the positive role of government in people's lives. But Republicans accused the president of disrespecting small business owners and entrepreneurs. It was, said Romney in an e-mail solicitation, "a slap in the face to the American dream."[64]

The tables were soon turned, however. In late July, Romney took a well-publicized trip to Britain, Israel, and Poland to demonstrate his foreign policy expertise. In London, just days before it would host the Olympic Games, Romney insulted the mayor by saying he had concerns over the city's preparedness, provoking a British tabloid to call him "Mitt the Twit."[65] In Israel, Romney insulted Palestinians by suggesting that "cultural differences" explained why Israel was more economically prosperous than Palestinian areas. In Poland, a Romney staffer barked "kiss my ass" at a member of the traveling press who shouted, "What about your gaffes?" to Romney at the Tomb of the Unknown Soldier. A CNN headline summed up the week: "Was Romney's trip 'a great success' or gaffe-filled disaster?"[66] No candidate wants that to be the question asked after a trip abroad.

Gaffes are supposed to matter because the twenty-four-hour news cycle and the opposing side's eagerness to publicize gaffes make it nearly impossible for voters to avoid hearing about them. This was what Cillizza argued about Obama's "private sector" comment: "Is there anyone paying even passing attention to politics who hasn't seen the Obama clip five times at this point—which, by the way, is less than 96 hours after he said it? Answer: no."[67]

The actual answer was yes. To be sure, gaffes can generate some news coverage, and that coverage may not be favorable. In Figure 5.3, we present the daily volume of news coverage of Romney and Obama for May through August. (We presented similar figures for the Republican primary candidates in chapters 3 and 4.) This includes the number of "mentions" of each (the gray line) as well as the volume weighted by the coverage's tone (the black line). The graph is scaled so that the vertical axis could accommodate the spikes in news coverage that would come in the fall. This helps put the volume of coverage in the summer in perspective.

The question is whether any of these gaffes generated a spike in news coverage, visible in the gray line, and unfavorable coverage to boot, in which case the black line should dip below zero, where negative coverage outweighs positive coverage.

Neither of Obama's gaffes produced much in the way of a spike in coverage or unfavorable coverage. The trend in Obama's news coverage was driven more by a natural periodicity—coverage tended to drop off on Saturday—punctuated by spikes when he endorsed same-sex marriage and when the Supreme Court upheld the Affordable Care Act, a.k.a. "Obamacare." For the most part, coverage of Obama in May and June was positive, except in early May when he traveled to Afghanistan and on May 20 and June 1, when first Newark mayor Cory Booker and then Bill Clinton contradicted the Obama campaign's attacks on Romney's experience at Bain Capital.[68] The dip in the favorability of Obama's coverage came in July, about three days after his "you didn't build that" remark. This was driven in part by a Romney effort to push back against Obama's attacks on his time at Bain Capital. Romney seized on Obama's remark and argued that Obama wanted Americans to be "ashamed of success."[69] However, Obama's remark was not the only reason for this less favorable news coverage, since Romney also accused him of rewarding supporters with federal grants and loan guarantees.

For most of the spring and early summer, coverage of Romney resembled coverage of Obama, rising and falling each week with the occasional spike around a notable event, such as a well-received speech Romney gave at Liberty

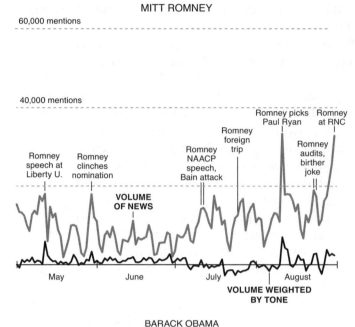

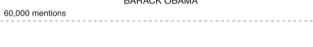

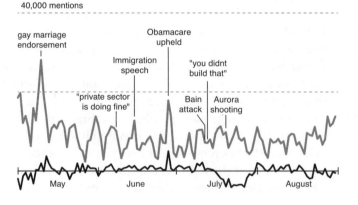

Figure 5.3.

Trends in Romney's and Obama's news coverage.

The gray line represents the volume of mentions of each candidate. The black line represents the volume of mentions, weighted by the tone of the coverage. When the black line is above 0, the coverage is net positive; when it is below 0, the coverage is net negative. The data span the period from May 1 to August 31, 2012.

University and his receiving enough delegates to clinch the nomination in late May.[70] But in July, news coverage of Romney was more negative than positive most every day. Although Romney was already experiencing unfavorable coverage leading into his trip abroad, the trip did not help. Coverage of Romney was negative every single day he was traveling.

However, this coverage did not necessarily penetrate quite as far as Cillizza believed. It is always easy for anyone who follows politics professionally—such as journalists and political scientists—to assume that everyone else does likewise. But many ordinary Americans, if not most of them, have better things to do than stay glued to cable news, and they may be oblivious to whatever the chattering classes are chattering about.

To illustrate, take Obama's "private sector is doing fine" comment. In a June 16–18 YouGov poll—about a week after the press conference—we asked this question:

> In a press conference last week, President Obama was asked about the state of the economy. How did he describe economic growth in the private sector?
> • The private sector is doing fine.
> • The private sector is struggling.
> • The private sector is mostly the same as it was.
> • I didn't hear what he said.

In total, 47% of respondents gave the correct answer. Nine percent said "struggling" and 4% said "mostly the same." About 39% said that they had not heard. More than half of Americans had not heard or did not know what Obama had said.

This leads to an even more important point: the people who are likely to have heard about a presidential candidate's gaffe are the least likely to change their minds. People who are interested in politics enough to follow the news also tend to have stronger opinions about politics—ones they are reluctant to change. This is why undecided voters in this June poll were much less likely to know about Obama's comment. And this is why the voters who did know about Obama's comment expressed a preference for Obama or Romney that was no different than the one they expressed when they were originally interviewed in December 2011.[71] Politically engaged people have stable preferences in presidential elections that cannot be easily shifted by gaffes.[72]

The same stability was evident in the national polls throughout the summer. Figure 5.4 depicts Obama's and Romney's standing in the polls, with demarcations for these gaffes and Romney's selection of Paul Ryan as his running mate. We drew on polling averages developed by Stanford University

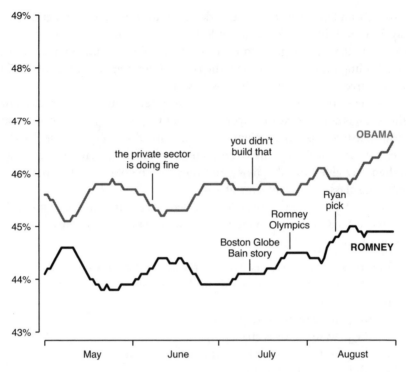

Figure 5.4.
Poll standing of Obama and Romney in spring and summer of 2012.
The figure presents averages from state and national polls developed and presented
by the *Huffington Post*'s Pollster site.

political scientist Simon Jackman for the *Huffington Post*'s Pollster site.[73] These averages not only helped separate true movement in the polls from random fluctuations due to sampling error, but they also took into account the systematic tendency for some polling firms to be a bit more "pro-Democratic" or "pro-Republican" than other firms.[74] This tendency, sometimes called a "house effect," usually has to do with idiosyncrasies in a polling house's methodology, not a deliberate attempt to favor one party.

There was little evidence of a notable shift after any of these gaffes. Apples-to-apples comparisons of individual pollsters showed the same thing. The Gallup poll conducted mostly the week before Obama's "you didn't build that" comment had Obama up 2 points. The Gallup poll conducted the week after had Obama up 1 point—a statistically insignificant shift. Rasmussen's polling and the RAND American Life Panel also suggested little to no movement. YouGov polls actually suggested a small change in Obama's favor. The same stability was evident before and after Romney's foreign trip.[75]

Voters who were potentially persuadable were somewhat more sensitive to these events, but not in a way that produced a consistent trend in favor of either candidate. We considered voters as "potentially persuadable" if, when first interviewed in December 2011, they said that they were undecided or supported some other candidate besides Romney and Obama. This was about 20% of respondents. We have already described the attitudes of undecided voters and why this made them up for grabs. The same was true of those supporting a third-party candidate, since typically many of these voters end up supporting a major-party candidate. Although by the summer, some of these voters may have chosen Obama or Romney, their initial uncertainty in December 2011 suggests that those choices were not necessarily set in stone. Examining the opinions of these voters when they were interviewed again in the summer suggests whether these gaffes pushed susceptible voters either way. In particular, we investigate whether they changed their vote intention as well as whether they viewed Obama or Romney more favorably.[76]

At two moments in particular—Obama's private sector comment and Romney's foreign trip—there were small but temporary shifts in persuadable voters' attitudes about the candidates but very little shift in vote intentions. After Obama's "you didn't build that" line, views of Obama and Romney shifted a little bit in Romney's favor. For the sake of easy interpretation, imagine candidate favorability as a 100-point scale ranging from very favorable views of Romney and very unfavorable views of Obama at one end to very unfavorable views of Romney and very favorable views of Obama at the other end. Between the surveys conducted just before and after Obama's speech, the views of these persuadable voters shifted in Romney's favor about 4 points on this 100-point scale. However, among this group, actual vote intentions shifted little across these two weeks. Across the two surveys bracketing much of Romney's foreign trip, there was an even smaller shift in candidate favorability—about 2½ points in Obama's favor—but virtually no shift in vote intentions.[77]

Ultimately, gaffes did not move the large majority of "decided" voters and moved only this minority of persuadable voters a little. Why? Part of the reason is that these gaffes did not put either candidate at a significant disadvantage in news coverage. Even Romney's trip, which did generate negative coverage of him, took place when coverage of Obama was equally if not more negative. This balance in news coverage is another feature of the tug-of-war or dynamic equilibrium in presidential general elections. Because news coverage was balanced in the summer and because the polls themselves were stable, there was little reason to expect either one to move the other. To provide some statistical confirmation of this, we examined the relationship between polls and news coverage for May through August—looking in particular to see whether one candidate's advantage in news coverage (depicted in Figure

5.3) translated into gains in the polls for the electorate as a whole (depicted in Figure 5.4). We found no such relationship (see the appendix to this chapter). Any ups and downs in the news coverage, including after these gaffes, did not appear to change minds.

This finding is different than the process of discovery, scrutiny, and decline in the Republican presidential primary—but predictably so. In the primary, we often found evidence of a relationship between news and polls, particularly for surging candidates like Rick Santorum. But in the general election the dynamics were much different. The two candidates were more familiar to voters and reporters alike. So Obama and Romney did not surge from obscurity to prominence in news coverage the way that several Republican presidential hopefuls did. They had long ago been "discovered," and coverage was never going to decline until after Election Day. The general election campaign was really just an extended period of scrutiny. Unlike in the primary, voters in the general election could also rely on their own party affiliation to form opinions about the candidates. This in turn made the opinions of most voters stable and thus the horse-race polls as well.

Obama's Gamble: The Bain Attacks

Romney's personal wealth and experience in private equity had been a fixture of the campaign even before the summer of 2012. Romney himself made various off-the-cuff remarks that highlighted his personal wealth: offering to bet Rick Perry $10,000 in a fall 2011 debate, noting that he had good friends who owned NFL and NASCAR teams, mentioning that his wife owned not one but "a couple of" Cadillacs, and so on. That Romney took so long to release his tax returns, and then released only two years of returns, was taken by his critics as suggesting he had something to hide. Romney's tax returns and time at Bain Capital were the subject of attacks from Newt Gingrich and Rick Perry in the primary, as we discussed in chapter 4. Now the Obama team would renew this line of attack.

The Obama campaign and its affiliated super-PAC, Priorities USA Action, sought to "define" Romney in much the same way as had Gingrich and Perry: as a wealthy person who had little in common with ordinary Americans and as a businessman more concerned about profit than people. This argument was the corollary of Obama's positive message on the economy: take one of Romney's apparent strengths—his business experience—and turn it into a liability.

The attacks on Romney were two-pronged. The Obama campaign focused on how Bain Capital had allegedly engaged in outsourcing—sending American jobs to countries like China and India in order to boost the bottom line of the companies it acquired and to line Romney's own pockets with the profits. Six different ads made this argument, citing a *Washington Post* story as evidence.[78] In perhaps the most notable ad, "Firms," a recording of Romney singing "America the Beautiful" played as a series of headlines was interspersed with images of empty factories. The headlines proclaimed that Romney had outsourced jobs to India and had millions in a Swiss bank account and in tax havens in the Bahamas and the Cayman Islands. The ad's tagline was "Romney's not the solution. He's the problem." Fact-checkers would later conclude that this argument was, at best, half true, but nevertheless commentators said that this ad "might be the most devastating TV ad of the campaign so far."[79]

The second prong of these attacks, from Priorities USA Action, presented workers who had lost their jobs because Bain Capital had bought and then shuttered the businesses that employed them. Several workers were from a steel company that had closed several years after being purchased by Bain Capital.[80] One worker, Donnie Box, said that Bain Capital "shut down entire livelihoods."[81] Another, Joe Soptic, recounted how he lost his health care, which he believed delayed the diagnosis of his wife's fatal cancer. Soptic said, "I do not think Mitt Romney realizes what he's done to anyone, and furthermore I do not think Mitt Romney is concerned."[82] In another ad, Mike Earnest, who was laid off from a paper plant, recounted how workers at the plant had built a temporary stage, from which company officials informed them that the plant was closing. Earnest said, "It turns out that when we built that stage, it was like building my own coffin, and it just made me sick."[83] These ads questioned two things. One was Romney's skill as an economic steward. After alleging that, under Romney, Bain Capital had bought companies from which workers were subsequently laid off, one ad asked skeptically: "Now he says his business experience would make him a good president?"[84] The other was Romney's ability to understand the middle class. Donnie Box suggested a fundamental estrangement between people like him and people like Romney: "They don't live in this neighborhood. They don't live in this part of the world."[85] Perhaps most succinct was the tagline in these ads: "If Romney wins, the middle class loses."

As we showed in Figure 5.2, ads referring to Bain Capital constituted about a quarter of Obama's advertising during the summer and about two-thirds of Priorities USA's. But the decision to advertise early, and to emphasize Bain Capital, becomes more evident if we examine advertising volume over time. Figure 5.5 presents the number of ads aired between January and August 2012 by Obama, Priorities USA Action, and the combination of Romney, the Republican Party, and various GOP-aligned groups. We scaled the vertical axis to anticipate the large increase in advertising that would come in September and October and dwarf these early ad buys.

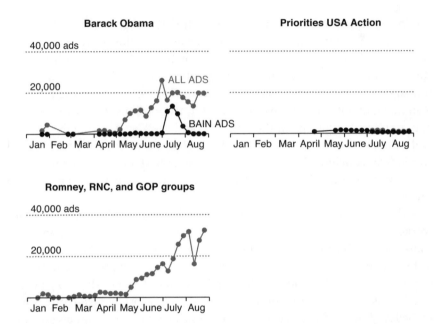

Figure 5.5.

Volume of television advertising in early 2012.

The figure depicts the estimated weekly number of ads aired by Obama, Priorities USA Action, and Republicans from the week ending January 15, 2012, to the week ending August 26, 2012. Data from the Campaign Media Analysis Group.

The spike in Obama's advertising in May and June is readily evident. During these months, Obama alone was airing more ads than Romney, the RNC, and the GOP groups combined. This was the push that Obama's team intended, but it was not about Bain. The Bain Capital ads appeared in July, and during that month they constituted a substantial fraction of Obama's advertising (38%). By contrast, the Priorities USA ads were aired much less frequently. This is perhaps unsurprising given Obama's well-documented reticence to embrace super-PACs as a vehicle for electioneering and the concomitant challenges Priorities USA faced when fund-raising.[86] In this period, Priorities USA aired a very small fraction of the total advertising on Obama's behalf and less than half of the advertising about Bain Capital in particular. One final and important thing to note is that the Democratic advertising edge disappeared by the third week of July. The Republicans out-advertised the Democrats for the rest of July and most of August.

Of course, television ads are also intended to reach viewers indirectly: by generating coverage in the news media—or what political professionals often call "earned media." So it may have mattered less how often the Bain ads aired

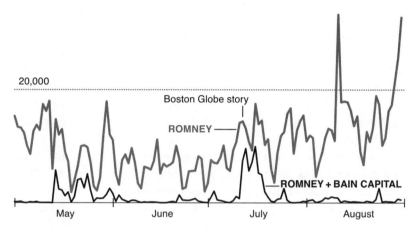

40,000 mentions

20,000

Boston Globe story

ROMNEY ———

ROMNEY + BAIN CAPITAL

May   June   July   August

Figure 5.6.
Trends in news coverage of Mitt Romney and Bain Capital.
The gray line represents the volume of mentions of Romney. The black line represents the volume of mentions of Romney and Bain Capital combined. The data span the period from May 1 to August 31, 2012.

and more how much news they generated. Figure 5.6 displays not only the number of mentions of Mitt Romney in the news media (the same quantity presented in Figure 5.3) but the number of mentions of "Mitt Romney" and "Bain Capital" combined, which captures stories that focused on Romney's career at Bain. As it turned out, Bain Capital was in the news for a very brief time and not entirely for reasons having to do with the ads themselves.

Despite an advertising push that began in June, coverage of Romney and Bain Capital spiked only for about one week in July—from July 12 to July 20 (which was, perhaps not coincidentally, the day of the mass shooting in Aurora, Colorado). The initial catalyst for this spike was not a new ad but a widely discussed July 12 story in the *Boston Globe* detailing how Bain Capital had listed Romney as CEO on government documents three years beyond the date Romney had given as the conclusion of his employment at Bain.[87] This potentially extended Romney's control from 1999 to 2002, encompassing a period during which, the Obama campaign alleged, Bain Capital had engaged in specific instances of outsourcing or shutting down businesses. The Obama campaign then suggested that misrepresenting Romney's role might constitute a felony, outraging the Romney camp.[88] Rounding out the day was the release of a new Romney ad criticizing Obama's outsourcing attacks as false.[89]

Coverage of Romney and Bain Capital increased on that day and even more on July 13, when approximately 50% of the mentions of Romney had to do with Bain Capital.

Coverage declined somewhat on July 14—in part due to the usual Saturday lull—which was when the Obama campaign released the "Firms" ad and Obama and Romney continued to joust over the Bain attacks.[90] It picked up again on July 15 and 16 before tapering off. Several *New York Times* headlines convey the steady pace of stories: "Romney Ad Faults Tone of Obama Campaign's Attacks," "When Did Romney Step Back from Bain? It's Complicated, Filings Suggest," and "After Weekend of Attacks, Romney Campaign Shields Itself with Polls."

There is no question that this week of news coverage was generally unfavorable to Romney. As Figure 5.3 showed, the coverage was net negative for Romney during most of this period, improving only at the very end before dropping off on July 20.[91] Moreover, news coverage of Romney and Bain was more negative than coverage of Romney overall. Coverage of Obama also became more negative. During July 17–19, coverage of Obama was even more negative than Romney's. This was when Romney began a counteroffensive that included attacks on Obama for his "you didn't build that" comment and for alleged cronyism. Then Bain Capital receded from the news.

This episode illustrates the challenges of focusing on Romney's experience at Bain Capital. Clearly the *Boston Globe* story plus the Obama campaign's attacks generated negative press for Romney initially. But as Romney struck back, both candidates had to deal with negative press—not because the press itself was critical but because it was covering what the candidates were saying, and what they were saying was largely critical of each other. Obama could not escape attacks any more than Romney could. Thus the Romney campaign, even as it seemed to be back on its heels, helped neutralize the Bain attacks, at least in terms of the tenor of news coverage.

Perhaps, however, all of these attacks and counterattacks did not neutralize each other. Perhaps the attacks on Romney's record at Bain Capital were more effective. If that were true, public opinion should have moved in Obama's favor. But it did not. As Figure 5.4 shows, if anything, Romney's standing in the polls *increased* in July, narrowing Obama's lead. Among the potentially persuadable voters we discussed earlier, there was also no clear shift against Romney during this time: indeed he received more support from those voters at the end of July than at the beginning.

Other measures of what voters thought about the candidates showed few trends. For example, at the beginning of May, the percentage of voters with a favorable view of Romney was 40% in YouGov polling. This briefly increased to 44% at the beginning of July, even though this was at the peak of Obama's advertising. But during July, the trend line was flat. At the end of July, the percentage of voters with a favorable view of Romney was 40%—the same as three months prior.[92] The RAND data, which began July 11 and allow a fine-grained day-by-day analysis, also showed no change in the candidates' standing during the period when Bain Capital was so much in the news. In fact, if anything, Obama's lead over Romney was slightly higher before the *Boston Globe* story broke than it was a week later, after all of the controversy. Some small number of people may have shifted their preferences during this time, but if so, the shifts canceled one another out and produced steady poll numbers overall.

We can drill down even further to assessments of Romney's specific qualities. During the summer months, there was no trend in whether people thought Romney was "likable" or whether he "says what he believes" (versus "what he thinks people want to hear"). And the indicators most intimately connected to the Bain attacks—which measured Romney's empathy—were similarly stable. We noted earlier that Romney faced the disadvantage that many Republican presidential candidates have faced: the perception that he was less concerned about the poor and middle class than about the wealthy. The Bain attacks seemed designed to magnify this perception. But no such thing occurred. The percentage of the voters who thought that "cares about people like me" described Romney somewhat or very well was 42% in early January, 38% in early April, 42% in June, and 40% at the end of July. The same stability was evident in the other items: cares about the poor, cares about the middle class, and cares about the wealthy.

The relationships among these different items were also fairly stable. Earlier we noted two relationships in particular: between believing Romney was personally wealthy and believing he cared about the wealthy, and between believing Romney cared about the wealthy and believing he did not care as much about the middle class or "people like me." The coverage of Romney's time at Bain Capital could have made those relationships stronger. Certainly the Obama campaign was trying to connect Romney's wealth and business practices (outsourcing, profits earned from Bain Capital deals, Cayman Islands tax havens, etc.) to an alleged lack of concern about the middle class ("If Romney wins, the middle class loses"). But these relationships were relatively static.[93]

The coverage of Romney and Bain Capital could have mattered in another way: by strengthening the connection between vote intentions and beliefs about Romney's wealth and empathy. This, too, would be a plausible goal for Obama and Priorities USA. Given that Obama had the advantage in this domain—more people believed he cared about the middle class than believed that about Romney—the Obama campaign would have wanted this domain to become more central in people's decision about which candidate to vote for. Many academic studies have documented how political campaigns can "prime" certain decision-making criteria in this way.[94] We calculated the difference between evaluations of Obama and Romney on each of these empathy dimensions (cares about people like me, cares about the poor, cares about the middle class, cares about the wealthy, is personally wealthy) and looked to see if these differences became more strongly related to vote intention in July. They did not (see the appendix to this chapter).

Did the Early Ads Matter?

So far we have described a summer of feverish campaigning that produced mostly stable trends in public opinion overall. There are two possible explanations for this stability. One is that the ads and other electioneering simply had no effect on anyone—they were, to be frank, a waste of money. The other possibility is that the Obama ads shifted votes to Obama in places where Obama out-advertised Romney and, simultaneously, Romney ads shifted votes to Romney in places where he out-advertised Obama. The result was no net advantage for either candidate. If so, the money spent on ads was not wasted. Quite to the contrary, it was vital. If one candidate had stood down, the polls might have shifted to the other candidate.

Sorting out which of these two patterns was underlying the stability requires investigating the relationship between candidate advertising and people's vote intentions. To identify whether and how the ads might have mattered, we could exploit variation in when and where Obama or Romney was airing more ads. Because both candidates focused their advertising in battleground states, with few national advertising buys, and because Obama and Romney each had the lead in different media markets at different times, this variation existed: voters outside the battleground states saw few if any ads, while voters in the battleground states may have seen more Obama ads or more Romney ads, depending on where they lived and when they were surveyed.

The advertising data that we analyzed were obtained from the Nielsen Company and were measured in "gross rating points" (GRPs), a metric that captures the expected penetration of ads in a given market.[95] To measure advertising advantage, we calculated the difference in each candidate's total GRPs for each day. We included not only candidate ads but ads paid for by the RNC—the Democratic National Committee (DNC) did not air its own advertisements in the presidential race—and by the major independent groups supporting one of the candidates: for Obama, Priorities USA Action; for Romney, Restore Our Future, American Crossroads, Crossroads GPS, and Americans for Prosperity.

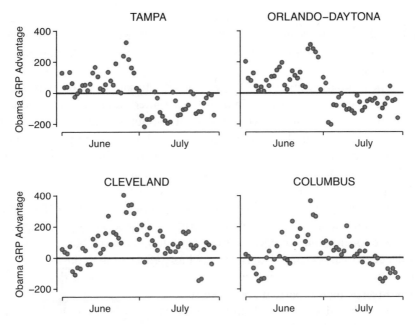

Figure 5.7.
Difference in advertising GRPs during June and July in selected markets.
The figure depicts the balance of gross rating points in four battleground state media markets. Positive numbers represent an Obama advantage and negative numbers a Romney advantage. The data are from The Nielsen Company.

During the summer months, despite the initial push by Obama, the advertising advantage actually shifted back and forth between Obama and Romney. This pattern of call-and-response can be seen in four competitive media markets in two battleground states, Florida and Ohio. Figure 5.7 shows Obama's increasing advantage and then Romney countering that advantage and eventually establishing his own. These variations in advertising advantage help us uncover effects of the ads among people living in different markets but also show how difficult it was for Obama or Romney to get a large and durable advantage on the airwaves. The tug-of-war was well under way in June and July.

We combined these advertising data with weekly YouGov polls from June through November, thereby matching each respondent to the advertising in his or her media market. We estimated the effect of advertising on the day that each respondent was interviewed, as well as the five days before. It may seem surprising to have included only the ads aired so close to the day of interview, but studies of campaign advertising have found that the effects of ads do not last long, perhaps no more than a few days.[96] We then estimated a statistical model to determine whether advertising was associated with vote intention, over and above other factors. Further details are in the appendix to this chapter.

When either Romney or Obama was able to air more advertisements than the other, it did shift votes in their favor. Other things equal, a candidate who had a 100-GRP advantage in a market—about one ad per capita more than his opponent aired—could expect to gain almost an additional point of vote share, compared to a market in which the two candidates were at parity in their television advertising. A 200-GRP advantage, or two additional ads per capita, was associated with almost 2 points of vote share.[97] We also examined the separate effects of Obama's and Romney's ads, rather than combining them into a single measure of relative advantage. Each candidate's ads appeared to shift votes in his direction, as we might expect, but there was no evidence that either candidate's ads were more effective than the other's. This belies the notion, prominent during and after the campaign, that Obama's early advertising was particularly powerful.[98]

But if the advertising did shift vote intentions, why were its effects not clearly visible in the poll numbers that horse-race junkies were following? For one, it was rare for the candidates to have a consistent and substantial advantage in advertising. Across all 210 media markets during the sixty-one days in June and July—a total of 12,810 "market-days"—Obama had a 2:1 advantage (or better) only 15% of the time and Romney had this advantage only 23% of the time. In only those markets and on only those days that saw at least some advertising—a total of about 6,650 market-days—Obama had at least a 2:1 advantage 23% of the time and Romney about 45% of the time (largely due to the spike in his ads at the end of July). Large ad imbalances across long periods of time or across all markets were not that common and did not consistently favor either Obama or Romney. Because neither candidate had a durable advantage, it was difficult to move the polls in either candidate's favor.

A second reason is that the effects of advertising decayed rapidly. We found no statistically meaningful impact of ads aired the five days before the respondents were interviewed. Only the ads aired on the day closest to the interview mattered. Most of the effects of the ads were gone within a day, consistent with what other studies have found. This fast decay meant that any boost from an advertising advantage was a very temporary one. And because neither candidate had a consistent advertising advantage, day in and day out, it was not surprising that the polls were so stable. To return to the tug-of-war metaphor, the hundreds of thousands of ads in the summer signified that each candidate was pulling hard on the rope. Their efforts did move people's vote intentions, but neither candidate was able to pull hard enough for long enough to change the dynamics of the race, which were not much different after this barrage of early advertising. The two campaigns largely neutralized each other's efforts.

Romney's Gamble: The Ryan Pick

At 7:07 AM EST on Saturday, August 11, 2012, anyone who had installed the Romney campaign's smart-phone app saw this message: "Mitt's choice for VP is Paul Ryan. Spread the word about America's Comeback Team." About a half hour later, @MittRomney tweeted: "I am proud to announce @PaulRyanVP as my VP. Stand with us today . . . #RomneyRyan2012."[99] Meanwhile, in Norfolk, Virginia, a crowd was gathering in front of the USS *Wisconsin*, a World War II battleship turned museum, where Mitt Romney and Paul Ryan would make their first joint appearance as the "Comeback Team." After a summer of trailing Obama in the polls—and a string of campaign gaffes that, however inconsequential to voters, were not what the Romney campaign wanted—a comeback could not come at a better time.

The choice of the USS *Wisconsin* was not an afterthought. Almost immediately people learned about Paul Ryan's upbringing and life in Wisconsin. He went to Catholic churches and schools and took care of his aging grandmother, who suffered from Alzheimer's disease, while his mother attended college in Madison. He managed all of this after finding his father dead in their home after a fatal heart attack. Ryan was just fifteen at the time. He was a star in school—at sports, in school government, and in class. He worked at McDonald's, and he saved his Social Security survivor's benefits to help pay for his college education at Miami University of Ohio. After working in Washington, D.C., for Jack Kemp and Senator Sam Brownback of Kansas, he returned to Wisconsin and in 1998, at the age of twenty-eight, was elected to represent Wisconsin's 1st congressional district. He had served for seven terms and risen to chair the Budget Committee, where he drafted the most prominent Republican alternative to the White House's budget proposals—also known as the "Ryan budget." Back home, he made his own bratwurst and hunted with a bow, sometimes growing a beard during hunting season to mask his scent while in the woods. He was only forty-two years old when Romney picked him as his running mate.

In many ways, Ryan's upbringing set him apart from Romney—the son of a governor and presidential candidate and a titan of private equity. But the two were apparently simpatico. One friend of Romney's said that Romney picked "someone he felt comfortable with and who appealed to his intellect and wonkier side—rather than someone who helped with, say, Hispanics or

Ohio," reported *Politico*.[100] One of Romney's advisors said: "Mitt sees a bit of himself in Ryan. They're both data guys, policy guys, details guys. It's fun to watch them together—sometimes they go into wonk-world together." This pick did seem to be Romney's alone; his advisors apparently opposed it.[101] Afterward, however, they were diligently limning the strategic value of picking Ryan. It was "bold"—one that signaled "seriousness" and "bigness," said a Romney advisor. Such boldness brought risks. The Romney campaign said that they had done no polling about potential running mates. If they had, they would have seen that as of August 2012, very few Americans knew much about Paul Ryan, but among those who did, unfavorable opinions of him outnumbered favorable opinions, even relative to the other candidates Romney might have chosen.

In several YouGov polls conducted between April and August, respondents were asked their opinion of various people who had been suggested as vice-presidential candidates. On average, 43% of survey respondents said they had not heard of or had no opinion of Paul Ryan. In mid-July, 52% could not even guess whether he was a member of the House of Representatives, a senator, secretary of state, or a governor. Only 32% of Americans got it right, not much better than chance. (Even among Republicans, only 42% got it right.) The 57% who did have an opinion of Ryan were evenly divided between those with favorable and unfavorable views, although those with strongly held views were more likely to view him unfavorably. Even among Republicans, only 54% had a favorable opinion of Ryan, with most of the rest unsure. Opinions of Ryan were less favorable than those of previous vice-presidential nominees.[102]

How did Ryan compare to other potential contenders for the VP slot? Figure 5.8 displays opinion about each of the contenders mentioned in these polls, compared in terms of their familiarity—the percentage who expressed an opinion about them—and the net favorability of those opinions—the percent favorable minus the percent unfavorable.[103] Former secretary of state Condoleezza Rice and General David Petraeus were the most widely known and most favorably viewed. Another group of potential candidates—New Hampshire senator Kelly Ayotte, Ohio senator Rob Portman, South Dakota senator John Thune, South Carolina governor Nikki Haley, and Virginia governor Bob McDonnell—were not well-known at all. Potential nominees like Florida senator Marco Rubio, Louisiana governor Bobby Jindal, and New Jersey governor Chris Christie were about as well-known as Ryan but more popular. Ryan was somewhat similar to Jeb Bush, in that both had neutral net favorable ratings and at least some visibility, although Bush was familiar to more people than was Ryan.

In the weeks immediately after his introduction in Norfolk, opinions about Ryan became less favorable on average. As people began to form

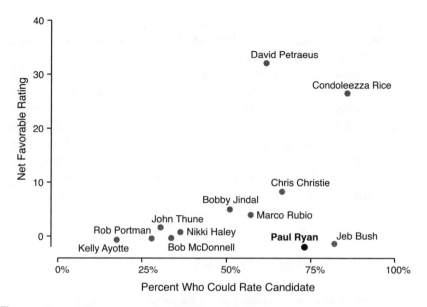

Figure 5.8.

Opinions of Paul Ryan and other vice-presidential contenders.

The graph depicts voters' familiarity with potential Republican vice-presidential nominees (the percentage who expressed an opinion about them) and the net favorability of those opinions (the percent favorable minus the percent unfavorable). The data are from YouGov polls conducted July 21–23, July 28–30, and August 4–6.

opinions about him—the percentage that had no opinion dropped from 50% to 19% in three weeks—more people developed an unfavorable than favorable opinion. The percentage with an unfavorable view grew from 28% to 44%, while the percentage with a favorable view grew more slowly (from 27% to 38%).

But opinions about Ryan among the broader public or among Republicans generally may have been less important if Romney was seeking to appeal to one group in particular: conservative Republicans unenthused about a "Massachusetts moderate." If so, this amounted to a solution in search of a problem: conservative Republicans were not the voters Romney needed to woo.[104] It was the moderates and liberals in the party who were the bigger problem for him. We already noted that Republican voters coalesced around Romney quickly, but those who remained undecided tended to be more moderate, not more conservative. Moreover, conservative Republicans tended to be more, not less, excited about voting in this election than liberal and moderate Republicans. In July, 72% of Republicans who called themselves "very conservative" were either "extremely enthusiastic" or "very enthusiastic" about voting in the upcoming November election—compared to 66% of Republicans who were "somewhat conservative" and 50% of liberal or moderate Republicans.

Even if more voters had a negative than a positive view of Ryan, this was unlikely to matter much come November. Vice-presidential picks have had at most a small influence on modern presidential elections. They have not provided a consistent boost to the ticket in pre-election polling—and Ryan's pick did not give Romney one.[105] They also have provided, at best, a very modest boost to the ticket on Election Day, both overall and in their home states. Political science studies have confirmed this over the years.[106] The question was not whether Ryan himself would matter but how his selection might have affected broader aspects of messaging and strategy—both Romney's and Obama's—and thereby shifted the dynamics of the race.

Lend Me a Hand, or Leave Me Alone?

At this point in time, both Romney and Obama seemed to be running clarifying campaigns by focusing on the economy. As Romney said in early August after the latest jobs report, "When you see what this President has done to the economy in just three years, you know why America doesn't want to find out what he can do in eight."[107] But the Ryan pick elevated the secondary theme in his campaign, the one that seemed more like an insurgent issue: the size of government and the national debt. This theme was sometimes framed around a broader vision of the role of government, as in these lines from Ryan's speech at the USS *Wisconsin*:

> America is more than just a place . . . it's an idea. It's the only country founded on an idea. Our rights come from nature and God, not government. We promise equal opportunity, not equal outcomes. This idea is founded on the principles of liberty, freedom, free enterprise, self-determination and government by consent of the governed. This idea is under assault. So, we have a critical decision to make as a nation. We are on an unsustainable path that is robbing America of our freedom and security. It doesn't have to be this way.[108]

This theme was also framed around the country's fiscal health. The "unsustainable path" was a reference to the national debt in particular, which Ryan referred to earlier in that speech as "crushing debt" alongside support for "fiscal discipline" and a reference to Romney's ability to balance budgets as governor of Massachusetts.

Ryan's language in this speech, and his inclusion in the ticket, seemed to suggest not only the potential for an insurgent campaign but possibly a successful one. The few successful insurgent campaigns often linked their messages on the specific insurgent issues to a broader argument about the future of the country—à la John Kennedy's New Frontier in 1960. In Norfolk, Ryan essentially asked, what kind of America do we want to be? Answering this question might have shifted emphasis away from jobs, jobs, and jobs to a more philosophical statement about what America was or should be. Ryan was suggesting a simple answer: not what it is now. At a time when two-thirds of Americans thought the country was headed in the wrong direction, such a message would have been in line with public opinion.

A critique of Obama's record on spending and the deficit was also in sync with what most Americans thought. In May, June, and July, YouGov asked respondents how much they approved of Obama's performance on fourteen different issues ranging from the deficit to the economy to immigration to abortion to Afghanistan. The budget deficit was Obama's worst issue. Only 36% approved of his handling of the deficit.[109] In a separate survey, voters were asked how the outcome of the election would affect the federal budget deficit.[110] The plurality, 46%, said that it would be higher if Obama was re-elected. Only 17% thought it would be higher if Romney was reelected. (The rest thought the election would make no difference.)

Other polling suggested that the broader Romney-Ryan message about the role of government could resonate, too. Romney and Ryan were essentially calling for government to get out of the way—hence Ryan's affirmation of "free enterprise" and "self-determination" in Norfolk. Obama was arguing for government's positive role, which was the point of "you didn't build that." On its face, the public seemed to side with Romney and Ryan. In a September Gallup poll, a majority of Americans (51%) said that the federal government had "too much power," 40% said it had about the right amount of power, and 8% said it had too little.[111] In this same poll, 54% said that the government was "trying to do too many things that should be left to individuals and businesses" while 39% said that government "should do more to solve our country's problems." An August YouGov poll put the question even more succinctly, asking Americans what message they would send to the federal government if they could say only one of two things: "lend me a hand" or "leave me alone." Fifty-seven percent said "leave me alone."[112]

The deficit and spending had the makings of a potentially successful insurgent issue. Romney and Ryan's view appeared closer to that of the majority of Americans than did Obama's. And Obama could not easily wriggle out of his position; he was constrained by his record. Government spending and the deficit had gone up under Obama, even if the policies of George W. Bush had contributed more to the total size of the debt. It seemed as though Romney and Ryan were on to something.

But they confronted an important challenge. In the minds of many Americans, opposition to government in the abstract coexists with significant support for government in reality. Americans may say "leave me alone," but when it comes to many specific programs, they say "lend me a hand." Political scientists Christopher Ellis and James Stimson have described these voters as "symbolic conservatives" but "operational liberals."[113] Indeed, once voters are confronted with a list of government programs or areas of spending—education, Social Security, Medicare, national defense, agriculture, and so forth—it is typically hard to find majority support for cutting spending on any of them. (The exception is foreign aid, but of course it is a miniscule fraction of the federal budget.) Among Republicans as of 2012, less than half wanted to cut most of these programs.[114] When faced with the explicit trade-off between cutting the deficit and leaving Medicare and Social Security as they are, 51% of the public chose the latter. There was not majority support among Republicans for cutting the deficit once this trade-off was made clear.[115]

Even more troubling for Romney and Ryan was that the "Ryan budget" was most well-known for restructuring and/or cutting spending on two of the most popular government programs: Medicare and Social Security. The prospect that Ryan's place on the presidential ticket would draw attention to his budget plan made even Republicans nervous. Four days after Ryan was picked, House Speaker John Boehner had to address "concerns that many of the party's down-ballot candidates would be left vulnerable to attacks tying them to Ryan's controversial plan to rework the nation's entitlement programs."[116] If the debate over government spending was framed around Ryan's (and perhaps therefore Romney's) budget plan instead of the general theme of smaller government, Obama was on much safer ground—in two senses.

First, he was on the Democratic Party's turf. The Democratic and Republican parties have developed reputations for being good at handling certain issues, and Democrats have been more trusted to handle Social Security and Medicare. They "own" the issue.[117] A February 2012 George Washington University Battleground Poll found that 52% of respondents trusted Democrats to handle "Social Security and Medicare," while 43% trusted Republicans. An August YouGov Poll found a similar 7-point advantage for Democrats on Medicare. When the question was posed not in terms of the two parties but in terms of Obama and Romney, Obama was favored by a similar margin among adults and registered voters and by a bit less among likely voters.[118]

Second, the Ryan plan—although unfamiliar to most people—was not popular. In an August 2012 YouGov poll, we asked this question:

Republican vice presidential candidate Paul Ryan has proposed a plan to change Medicare, the federal government's health insurance program for older Americans. Which of the following most accurately describes Ryan's proposal for Medicare?

- Gradually end the Medicare program over the next forty years
- Turn Medicare into a government voucher program for the purchase of private insurance
- Transfer control of the Medicare program from the federal government to the states
- Have not heard about Ryan's plan

The plurality (43%) said that they had not heard, while 40% picked the correct answer (voucher program). Among those who picked voucher program, 58% opposed it and 34% favored it. The intensity of opinion favored opponents: 53% strongly opposed it. Naturally Democrats were more likely than Republicans to oppose it, and Democrats' opinions were more intense. Among independents, 60% opposed it. Other polls generated similar findings. For example, August *New York Times* polls in Florida, Ohio, and Wisconsin asked:

> Which of these two descriptions comes closer to your view of what Medicare should look like for people who are now under 55 who would be eligible for Medicare coverage in about 10 years? Medicare should continue as it is today, with the government providing older Americans with health insurance. OR, Medicare should be changed to a system in which the government would provide older Americans with a fixed amount of money toward buying private health insurance or Medicare insurance.

Majorities ranging from 59% to 64% wanted to keep Medicare as it is.[119] In sum, most Americans opposed Ryan's plan for Medicare.

Romney and Ryan thought they had a way to overcome the challenges posed by the Democrats' ownership of these issues and the strong support for traditional Medicare: argue that the Affordable Care Act, "Obamacare," would necessitate $716 billion in cuts to Medicare.[120] One attempt to test this message against a Democratic counterargument—that Republicans would end Medicare by privatizing it—found that the parties would fight to a draw.[121] For the GOP, a draw on Democratic turf was probably as good as a win.

But other attempts at message-testing did not produce such comforting findings. In an August NBC/*Wall Street Journal* poll, respondents were read a description of Ryan's proposal to reform Medicare—but with no mention of Ryan or Romney—and then asked their opinion. Most (51%) were not sure, 30% thought it was a bad idea, and 15% thought it was a good idea.[122] They were then asked whether they agreed with Romney's argument that this proposal would "strengthen Medicare" by "giving future seniors more control over their own health care dollars and a choice between traditional Medicare and a variety of private plans," or whether they agreed with Obama's argument that this proposal would "end Medicare as we know it by turning it into a voucher system." Many more agreed with Obama's argument than Romney's argument (50% versus 34%).

None of these surveys was necessarily dispositive. The problem with message-testing in any pre-election survey is that it is like testing someone's reaction to a blizzard by holding an ice cube against their skin. The swirling, blinding mess of campaign discourse is distilled to a clear identifiable cue. But taken together, all of these polling data suggested that Romney and Ryan were fighting an uphill battle on Medicare. Obama, for his part, seemed willing to debate the issue. Within a week of Romney's nomination, he aired an ad attacking the Ryan plan for "undermining" Medicare.[123] He also created a website, www.medicarefacts.com.

Ultimately an insurgent campaign centered on spending and deficits—much like a clarifying campaign centered on the economy—did not offer a clear advantage to either side. A lot would depend on the precise vantage point through which voters saw these issues. If it was simply about the incumbent's performance with regard to the budget deficit, or the abstract question of whether government should do more or less, Romney and Ryan had the edge. But the Ryan pick only magnified a danger Romney was already facing: that Obama could center the discussion on government programs that were popular—programs long associated with the Democratic Party—and tie Romney to the proposed cuts to these programs that Ryan and many other congressional Republicans supported. In the summer of 2012, voters were as ambivalent about the role of government as they were about who could turn around the economy.

Game Same

On May 1, Obama had a 1.5-point lead over Romney in the Pollster average. On August 27, the day the Republican National Convention began, Obama had the exact same 1.5-point lead. Nearly four months of vigorous campaigning had left the race essentially where it had been at the outset—with only a few net changes to the polls at any point throughout this period.

To point out this stability after having found little of lasting consequence from the summer campaign might appear to confirm the stereotype that political scientists think campaigns "don't matter." And it was true that parts of the summer campaign did not matter much. Some events, like certain candidate "gaffes," did not register with most voters. Many were loyal partisans and did not change their minds easily or at all. And the people paying closer attention to politics, the ones more likely to see a gaffe played and replayed on the news, were the least likely to change their minds.

But the lesson of this chapter is not that presidential campaigns are irrelevant. If Obama or Romney had simply taken the summer off—hanging out at Camp David or Lake Winnipesaukee or wherever—the polls would likely have moved toward the candidate still out campaigning. The reason that the polls were so stable was that the Obama and Romney campaigns were fairly evenly matched. It may seem strange even to say that because so much news coverage and commentary during presidential campaigns seek to identify which candidate is getting the better of the other. But it is typically hard for one high-quality, well-financed presidential candidate to consistently "out-campaign" the other. The stability in the polls from May to August was a testament to this.

Consider the major gambits of that summer. Obama spent a lot of money "front-loading" his advertising in May and June and was able to gain an edge over Romney for several weeks. The ads arguably helped him a little bit. But their impact was short-lived. And soon thereafter, in July and August, the Republicans were often outspending Obama. Political advertising in a presidential race is rarely one-sided for long.

Consider the news coverage of Romney's time at Bain Capital. A combination of investigative reporting by the *Boston Globe* and opportunistic campaigning by Obama meant that Romney had several days of news coverage that he would sooner forget. But it was also short-lived. News coverage of Obama soon became less favorable, too. More important, focusing on who is winning the news cycle on any given day or week obscures the larger picture. Over time, the news coverage of presidential candidates tends to be balanced, unless the race is simply a landslide, in which case coverage tends to favor the front-runner.[124] In the summer of 2012, when no landslide seemed imminent, news coverage did not consistently favor Romney or Obama.

Based on the data we presented in Figure 5.3, Romney received an average of 10,650 mentions each day between May and August, while Obama received about 8,900 mentions—a small gap at best. The measure of tone that we used can be converted into an easy-to-interpret measure that ranges between –100 (the least favorable) and 100 (the most favorable). The averages for this period were 7 for Romney and 1 for Obama. What did that mean? It meant that the coverage of both candidates was slightly positive. It meant that coverage of both candidates was very close to the hypothetical neutral point of zero—as you might expect given that much of the news media is still governed, believe it or not, by norms of objectivity. Finally, it meant that, on this 200-point scale, the two candidates were only 6 points apart. Neither was covered much more positively or negatively than the other.[125] This is consistent with many other studies of news coverage of presidential campaigns, which have tended to find little systematic bias in favor of one party or candidate.[126]

Whether a campaign "matters" depends on the scenario that serves as the point of comparison. If that scenario is, "Obama plays golf and doesn't hold a single rally or spend a dime on advertising," then the actual 2012 summer campaign did matter. Obama's campaigning was important in neutralizing Romney's. Of course, this scenario is also far-fetched.

One could imagine other, more realistic scenarios. But not all of these would necessarily suggest a big campaign effect. For example, one might ask: even if Obama's early ads did not appear to have large or lasting effects, could they have prevented something else from happening? Did they prevent Romney from gaining ground in the polls? Possibly, but we tend to doubt it, especially since Romney was not gaining in states where there were no ads being aired. Another scenario: did attention to Bain Capital help distract from storylines potentially more conducive to Romney, such as public pessimism about the economy? Again, possibly. But note that there were several points at which the prevailing storyline favored either Romney or Obama—and none of these produced major shifts in polls. Moreover, the tendency toward balance in news coverage meant conducive storylines rarely lasted long anyway.

There are other scenarios, of course. So to say that the particular configuration of campaign strategies and news coverage in the summer of 2012 did relatively little to reshape the race is not to say that no configuration could have done so. On the other hand, one other fact about the summer of 2012 stands out: the race was very much in line with the underlying fundamentals, which predicted an Obama victory. Campaigns are often most effective when the polls are out of line with the fundamentals—when one candidate is doing much better or much worse than he "should" be, which means that some voters have not lined up behind the candidate that prevailing national conditions, or these voters' own beliefs, would predict. This was not the case as the Republican National Convention approached.

Still, this observation would not have provided much solace to Romney, who seemed unable to put a dent in Obama's small but seemingly durable lead. In fact, on the eve of his formal nomination, Romney was viewed not only less favorably than Obama but less favorably than every other presidential candidate since 1984—less favorably even than eventual losers like Walter Mondale and Michael Dukakis.[127] If there was a Romney comeback in the offing, it had not yet begun.

But one was only weeks away.

CHAPTER 6

The Action

It was the week before their national convention, and Republicans were worried. Romney had not put a significant dent in Obama's lead, which was narrow but seemingly durable. John Boehner had argued a couple months before that Romney's image was secondary to the president's economic performance, saying, "The American people probably aren't going to fall in love with Mitt Romney," but some Republicans were beginning to think Romney's image needed an overhaul.[1] At such moments, anonymous "party strategists" always come out of the woodwork, and August 2012 was no exception. On August 28, the first day of the convention, *Politico*'s John Harris and Alexander Burns wrote, "Republicans believe Obama's governing defects should make a GOP victory virtually inevitable, but Romney's political defects make it only a long-shot possibility." Romney needed a "reintroduction"— something that would make his image more "appealing."[2] Former Mississippi governor Haley Barbour said that all voters knew about Romney was what Obama had told them: "He's a wealthy plutocrat married to a known equestrian." Romney's advisors seemed to agree that "a more combative footing" was necessary.[3]

Meanwhile, the Obama camp remained confident. Mark Halperin of ABC News had talked with Obama's advisors in May and visited them again on the eve of the Republican convention. In an interesting turn, they seemed more bullish on Romney's candidacy than Republicans were:

Romney, Team Obama concedes, has shown himself to be a better candidate than expected. He has displaced Obama as the most prolific fundraiser in the nation's history. He has, with few exceptions, exhibited discipline and precision in the months since he secured the nomination. He showed genuine boldness and purpose with his Veep pick (even while giving the Obamans ammunition in the process). And he has improved his performance on the stump.

But this newfound respect for Romney did not sap Team Obama's confidence. Said Halperin, "the Obama people don't seem to believe they can lose."[4]

In the fall campaign, the Republicans would ultimately get their wish—a more appealing image for Romney—and the confidence of the "Obamans" would be shaken. After a summer of relative stability, there would be larger shifts in the polls. We have argued that such shifts do not come often during presidential general election campaigns; the candidates tend to be too evenly matched and thus each struggles to secure any advantage. The story of the fall campaign, however, is precisely about which moments finally gave Obama or Romney that kind of advantage—thereby disrupting, at least temporarily, the dynamic equilibrium. Moments that many thought would matter—the attacks in Benghazi, Hurricane Sandy—were less consequential. This is not to suggest that these moments failed to move any voters. As was sometimes true in the summer, potentially persuadable voters did shift in reaction. But these voters were not numerous enough, and the shifts not always large enough, to upend the horse race.

More important were the party conventions, especially the Democratic National Convention, and the first debate. That the party conventions mattered conforms to a well-established pattern in presidential campaigns over the last several decades, one documented in political science research. The impact of the debates was equally predictable: debates can move the polls but rarely determine the winner of the election. And so Romney's apparent victory in the first debate vaulted him back in the race but ultimately did not propel him to victory. In fact, many of the people who moved toward Romney after that first debate were people who had previously been his supporters but had wavered after the release of video containing his remarks about "the 47%." The debate looked like a pivotal moment, but it was really just a return to the status quo—the equilibrium from which the race had departed because of the 47% video. The same happened to Democrats: a few wavered after the first debate but rallied to Obama by the end of the campaign. As they did so, the race began to open up. By the end, a surprising number of pundits remained baffled by where the race stood, but the outcome on November 6 was no surprise.

The Conventions

As the party conventions drew near, the spate of positive media coverage for Romney, generated by choosing Paul Ryan as his running mate, had dissipated and most of the media coverage Romney had garnered since then was negative. After the Ryan pick, the first event that generated more coverage of Romney came on August 23, when the website Gawker released internal audits and other records that provided some details about Romney's personal finances and specifically where his wealth was physically located—what was described in one news account as "a convoluted series of holding companies in tax havens including the Cayman Islands and Luxembourg."[5] The second event occurred the following day, August 24, when Romney appeared to joke about Obama's birth certificate by telling an audience in his home state of Michigan that "No one's ever asked to see my birth certificate. They know that this is the place that we were born and raised." Many Americans, mostly Republicans, did not believe or were not certain that the president was born in the United States, in the face of much evidence to the contrary. While Romney's supporters likely cheered the line, the media took it as an overt appeal to Americans' prejudices. Such messaging can be effective when subtle and implicit, but not when overt and explicit.[6] The joke appeared to generate most of the negative coverage of Romney—consistent with headlines like "Romney Birth Certificate Remark Sets off Firestorm."[7] Figure 6.1 displays these trends.

The Republican National Convention offered Romney the chance to change the dynamics of the race. The party conventions have been, year in and year out, the most influential events in presidential campaigns, at least as measured by changes in the polls. These changes are sometimes known as "convention bounces" or "bumps."[8] There has been more instability in the polls during the conventions than at any other time during the campaign. Typically, the poll standing of the candidate being nominated has increased by 5–6 points.[9] On its face, this may seem surprising. Party conventions have become devoid of any suspense, as backroom dealings have been replaced with a coronation that is carefully stage-managed for television. Despite the effort to produce packaged television moments, most of the major networks no longer interrupt other programming to cover conventions, and even cable coverage of the conventions features pundits talking about strategy more than the actual events on the convention floor. Of course, careful stage management has made for boring television, causing the audience for convention coverage to shrink as well.[10]

But conventions still matter for two reasons: they generate a spike in coverage for the candidate being nominated and the coverage tends to reflect positively on this candidate.[11] (That stage management is not for nothing, after

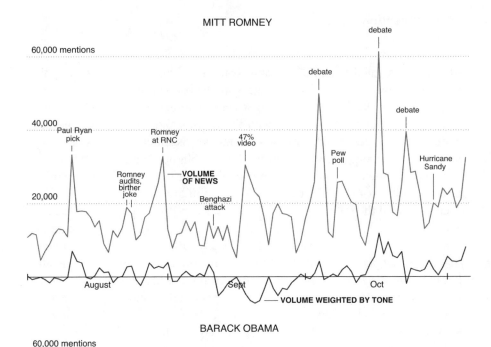

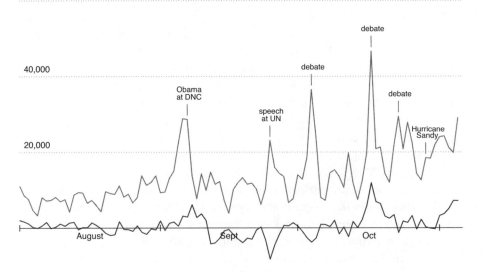

Figure 6.1.

Trends in Romney's and Obama's news coverage.

The gray line represents the volume of mentions of each candidate. The black line represents the volume of mentions, weighted by the tone of the coverage. When the black line is above 0, the coverage is net positive; when it is below 0, the coverage is net negative. The data span the period from August to Election Day.

all.) This mode of news coverage departs from most other times during the campaign when, as we argued in chapter 5, the news covers the candidates in roughly equal measure and often in a balanced fashion that gives neither a consistent advantage. The imbalance in the news coverage opens the door for changes in the polls, as we saw during the nominating process.

Going into the conventions, at least one factor suggested Romney could expect a bigger bounce than Obama would receive. The party whose convention goes first—the party not occupying the White House—has usually received a bigger bounce, perhaps because the challenger has been less familiar than the incumbent and thus voters actually learned more about the challenger during the convention. When there were weeks between the two conventions, the imbalance in media coverage and new information about the challenger boosted him in the polls. But when the conventions were held in successive weeks, as in 2008 and 2012, the advantage of going first was muted.

One other thing might have dampened Romney's hopes. The size of convention bounces has also depended on where the polls stand relative to what the underlying fundamentals predicted.[12] If one candidate had a lead that seemed "too large" given the fundamentals, the outcome of the two conventions shrank that candidate's lead. In other words, some of the polling shifts in past elections were the result of the convention bringing the race in line with fundamentals like the state of the economy. As the Republican convention got under way, Obama was leading Romney by approximately 1.5 points, which, as we have argued, was not terribly out of line with the fundamentals. If the Republican convention was going to produce a large shift toward Romney, it would have to be a blockbuster.

If either convention proved to be consequential, its effects would reverberate until Election Day. The phrase "convention bounce" suggests something temporary, but in actuality the bounces have been "bumps." They have not abated quickly like the changes we saw among susceptible voters in chapter 5. Conventions have left a more permanent imprint on the race. On average, the party that has gained ground after the conventions has kept those gains through Election Day.[13]

The Republican National Convention, although it began late after the first day was canceled due to Hurricane Isaac, mimicked the traditional pattern. As Figure 6.1 shows, Romney became more visible in the news than in the week before the convention and more visible than Obama. This coverage spiked on August 31, the day after Romney's speech to the convention. The balance of coverage was also favorable, while coverage of Obama tended to be less favorable—as one might expect given that much of this coverage was quoting from GOP convention speakers criticizing him. All of this was true even though Romney's speech was preceded by an ad-libbed speech by the actor

Clint Eastwood, during which he pretended to speak to an invisible Obama sitting in an empty chair, something that many commentators found strange. Eastwood received an enormous spike in coverage the following day—about 17,000 mentions in the news outlets tracked by General Sentiment, compared to about 32,000 for Romney—and coverage of Eastwood more negative than positive. But coverage of Romney was much more positive than negative, suggesting that the Eastwood speech did not necessarily overshadow Romney's own performance.

The same pattern was evident when the Democratic convention began the following week—spikes in coverage, especially the day after Obama's speech, and coverage of Obama that was more favorable than coverage of Romney. This pattern then persisted for several days thereafter.[14]

This apparent symmetry in news coverage of the conventions did not lead to a symmetrical reaction in the polls. As was the case in 2008, having the two conventions close together mitigated the advantage of going first and gave the governing party the bigger bump. Just as John McCain got this bump, and briefly took the actual lead in the wake of the 2008 Republican National Convention, Barack Obama got a bump of about 3 points while Romney got none. This is visible in Figure 6.2, which plots the polling averages developed by Pollster and denotes various events in August, September, and October.

Because the polling averages are "smoothing" the many polls to separate signal from noise, the lines appear to shift before the Democratic convention started, but some apples-to-apples comparisons show that the Democratic convention itself generated Obama's bump. For example, in a YouGov poll conducted the weekend before the Republican National Convention, 46% supported Obama and 47% supported Romney. The weekend after the Republican convention, those numbers were virtually unchanged: 47% for Obama and 46% for Romney. Potentially persuadable voters—those who were originally undecided or supported a candidate other than Obama and Romney when first interviewed in December 2011—moved a bit more. They became less favorable to Obama but not enough to put Romney in the lead.[15]

By contrast, the weekend after the Democratic convention, Obama was up 49%–45%. The movement in the polls was particularly evident among Democrats. In the two weeks after the convention, Democratic support of Obama increased by 6 points. Democrats also became more enthusiastic about voting. The week before the convention, 56% of Democrats said they were very or extremely enthusiastic about voting. Two weeks after the convention, 73% said this. These trends show how, as we noted in the previous chapter, campaigns rally partisans—in this case bringing Democrats "home" to Obama and stoking their excitement. Persuadable voters shifted as well, both in terms of how favorably they viewed Obama and Romney and in terms

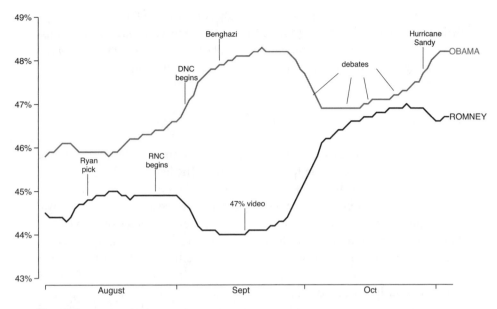

Figure 6.2.
Poll standing of Obama and Romney in the fall of 2012.
The figure presents averages from state and national polls developed and presented
by the *Huffington Post*'s Pollster site.

of their vote intentions.[16] In fact, the gains for Romney among susceptible voters after his convention (7 points) were negated by the gains for Obama among these voters after his convention (9 points). This is one more instantiation of the tug-of-war between presidential candidates.

It is tempting to interpret Obama's larger bump as suggesting that the Democrats' convention was "better" than the Republicans'—that the speakers were more compelling, that Eastwood ruined Romney's night, and so on. Certainly there was what *Politico*'s Mike Allen and Jim VandeHei called "public griping and internal sniping" about "Romney's convention stumbles."[17] Unfortunately, the available polling data can neither confirm nor disprove this impression. On balance, public evaluations of the two conventions were similar—at least according to Gallup's polling—but these and the other post-convention polls do not allow us to separate out the effects of each individual night's speeches, to say nothing of separating out the effects of two speeches given on the same night, as were Eastwood's and Romney's.[18] What may have been more important was simply timing. Both candidates got the spurt of favorable news coverage that conventions have typically produced, but any benefits that Romney may have gotten from that coverage were quickly obscured by the Democratic convention. By contrast, the favorable coverage that Obama got did boost his poll numbers. The party conventions, by advantaging the candidate whose convention was last and who was favored by the underlying fundamentals, made Obama's reelection that much more likely.

Benghazi

September was, on its face, a bad month for both Romney and Obama but one that would do relatively little to move the polls. The bad news began on September 11 with a surprise attack on the American diplomatic mission in Benghazi, Libya, which killed four Americans, including the ambassador to Libya, Christopher Stevens, and injured several others. News coverage of both candidates became more negative in the wake of the attack. For Obama, the attack immediately raised multiple questions, such as whether his administration had provided enough security in Benghazi. The administration's initial statements also erroneously suggested that the attack was spontaneous and was sparked by protests in Cairo over an anti-Islamic video that was filmed in the United States. Subsequently the administration revised that assessment and concluded that the attack was a premeditated assault by an organized terrorist group. Republicans, many of whom believed from the outset that the attack had been planned, criticized the administration's response. Although news stories were more likely to report the administration's initial framing of the attack as spontaneous than Republicans' belief that it was a planned attack, coverage discussing the security problems at the embassy was even more prominent.[19] This may help explain why the news coverage of Obama, which had been positive since the convention, became more negative in the wake of the attack.

But Romney himself also came in for criticism. On the evening that the shooting took place and again at a news conference the next day, he repeated a perennial criticism: that Obama was "apologizing" for America. (Romney himself had penned a 2010 book titled *No Apology: The Case for American Greatness*.) In this case, Romney was reacting to a statement condemning the video that was put out by the American embassy in Cairo before both the Cairo protests and Benghazi attack. On the evening of the attack, Romney's statement read, "It's disgraceful that the Obama administration's first response was not to condemn the attacks on our diplomatic missions but to sympathize with those who waged the attacks." At the news conference, he said: "I think it's a terrible course for America to stand in apology for our values, that instead when our grounds are being attacked and being breached, that the first response of the United States must be outrage at the breach of the sovereignty of our nation. An apology for America's values is never the right course."

This response generated its own controversy and thus negative news coverage for Romney (see Figure 6.1). For one, fact-checking organizations argued that Romney misrepresented the order of events and incorrectly characterized the Cairo embassy's statement as an "apology."[20] Second, some news stories questioned whether it was appropriate to criticize the president so soon after a crisis. For example, a *Washington Post* story written after Romney's news conference began:

> Crises overseas tend to create moments of joint resolve back home, a time to pause from the daily bickering of partisan politics. But as news was streaming in about attacks on U.S. diplomatic missions in Egypt and Libya, Mitt Romney broke from that protocol.
>
> Statements that the Republican presidential nominee made slamming President Obama led to a day of tumult for Romney, with leading voices in his party criticizing him and his top aides scrambling to prevent further damage.[21]

The presence of criticism from within the party—the article noted that even Paul Ryan's comments after the attack were less critical of Obama than were Romney's—likely led to more negative coverage than if Republicans had united behind Romney, leaving only Democrats to criticize him.

Given that news coverage of both candidates was negative, it is unsurprising that, among voters, neither candidate emerged the clear winner of this exchange. In a YouGov survey conducted September 15–17, immediately after the attack, 86% of respondents reported hearing about the attack, suggesting that news about it had reached most Americans. Their opinions about both Obama and Romney were mixed. For example, 47% approved of Obama's handling of the crisis, 44% disapproved, and 9% were not sure. Most did not think that Romney would have handled it any better: 37% said better, 12% the same, and 43% worse. The public was also evenly divided on Romney's response—specifically the question of whether it was "right for a candidate to criticize the President's handling of a foreign policy crisis during an election campaign": 22% said it was "always right" to do so, 22% said it was "always wrong," and 47% said "it depends." A second poll conducted around this time suggested that, on balance, more people approved of Obama's handling of the situation (45%) than approved of Romney's comments (23%).[22] But a few weeks later, opinions about Obama had become a bit less favorable: 35% approved of Obama's handling of the crisis, 38% disapproved, and 27% were not sure.[23] Democrats and Republicans were predictably polarized on this issue; independents tilted somewhat toward disapproval, but a third of them had no opinion whatsoever. Although it is difficult to disentangle the impact of the Benghazi attack from the broader aftermath of the Democratic convention, there is not much evidence that either candidate benefited, especially among persuadable voters, whose vote intentions were no different several days before and several days after the attack. Neither candidate appeared to derive an immediate political advantage from the attack and ensuing controversy.

The 47% Video

The Benghazi attack was soon overshadowed by the release of what would become known as the "47% video." On September 17, *Mother Jones* magazine posted video footage of Romney speaking at a fund-raising dinner in Boca Raton, Florida, on May 17. The video, secretly filmed by a bartender, Scott Prouty, was approximately sixty-eight minutes long. Most controversial was a passage in which Romney spoke about the "47 percent."[24]

> There are 47 percent of the people who will vote for the president no matter what. Alright, there are 47 percent who are with him, who are dependent upon government, who believe that they are victims, who believe the government has a responsibility to care for them, who believe that they are entitled to health care, to food, to housing, to you-name-it. That's an entitlement. The government should give it to them. And they will vote for this president no matter what. And I mean the president starts off with 48, 49 . . . he starts off with a huge number. These are people who pay no income tax. Forty-seven percent of Americans pay no income tax. So our message of low taxes doesn't connect. So he'll be out there talking about tax cuts for the rich. . . . My job is not to worry about those people. I'll never convince them they should take personal responsibility and care for their lives. What I have to do is convince the 5–10% in the center that are independents, that are thoughtful, that look at voting one way or the other depending upon in some cases emotion, whether they like the guy or not.

Obama responded on David Letterman's television show by saying, "My expectation is if you want to be president, you've got to work for everybody, not just for some." For his part, Romney, while acknowledging that his comments were "not elegantly stated," did not back away from the substance of what he said: "The president believes in what I've described as a government-centered society, where government plays a larger and larger role, provides for more and more of the needs of individuals. And I happen to believe instead in a free enterprise, free individual society where people pursuing their dreams are able to employ one another, build enterprises, build the strongest economy in the world."[25] But inside the Romney campaign, there was "a palpably gloomy and openly frustrated mood."[26]

And no wonder. Romney's comments in the video elicited harsh words from across the political spectrum. Even some conservatives criticized Romney or his campaign, such as the *Wall Street Journal*'s Peggy Noonan ("incompetent") and the *New York Times*'s David Brooks ("depressingly inept").[27] Other commentators simply declared the Romney campaign over within hours of the video's release. *Bloomberg*'s Josh Barro wrote: "You can mark my prediction now: A secret recording from a closed-door Mitt Romney fundraiser, released today by David Corn at *Mother Jones*, has killed Mitt Romney's campaign for president."[28] *Talking Points Memo*'s Josh Marshall wrote: "It's rare when the impact of some gaffe or embarrassment or revelation isn't overstated on first blush. But this may just be that rare exception. This tape strikes me as absolutely devastating."[29] To commentators used to thinking of campaigns like a boxing match, this was another "knock-out blow."

Such comments are consistent with the overall tone of news coverage, depicted in Figure 6.1. News coverage of both candidates was already unfavorable, but Romney's coverage both increased and became even more unfavorable in the wake of the video's release. The volume of coverage of Romney increased nearly sixfold from the day before the video's release to the day after its release. If you combine the volume and tone of coverage, the week after the video's release was the worst week of news coverage for the Romney campaign between May and November.

What, then, was the impact of the video and related news coverage on voters? In the previous chapter, we discussed how the impact of campaign gaffes was routinely overstated. Somehow the 47% video seemed different, however. For one, it was not really a "gaffe" in the sense that Romney misspoke. Romney clearly intended to say what he said. Second, the 47% video also captured Romney unawares, thereby seeming to offer more insight into his real opinions than the scripted language he used on the stump. Third, the content of the video was particularly controversial—especially since the "47%" seemed to include Americans whose use of government benefits is typically seen as justified, such as veterans and senior citizens. Finally, the video seemed potent because it dovetailed precisely with the characterization of Romney that Obama's early ads, and some of Romney's previous comments, seemed to further: that of a wealthy guy unable to relate to average Americans. As one editorial put it: "Romney's captured remarks reinforce a narrative that he is an out-of-touch elitist who doesn't care about the plight of the average American, and that his allegiance is primarily to his class rather than to his country."[30]

The public's reaction to the video tended to be unfavorable but not to an extent that would suggest the video was "absolutely devastating." When asked in a Pew survey which candidate had "made comments describing 47% of the population as dependent on government and paying no taxes," the majority (67%) identified Romney.[31] But that means one-third of the public did not know this; most of these people were simply unsure who had said it. As we saw with Obama's comments like "the private sector is doing fine," not every American registers even campaign events that commenters consider dramatic.

The initial reaction to Romney's comments tended to be negative but not overwhelmingly so. When asked whether their reaction was "positive" or "negative," more than twice as many respondents in this Pew survey said negative (55%) than positive (23%). A negative reaction was most prevalent among Democrats, but independents also reacted negatively (55%–18%).[32] However, a September 22–24 YouGov poll that asked whether Romney's comments were a "serious mistake," a "minor mistake," or "not a mistake" generated more ambiguous findings. A large plurality, 39%, said that Romney's comments were a "serious mistake"—but the vast majority of these people (85%) were Democrats and therefore not likely to vote for Romney anyway. Their predictably partisan responses illustrated how partisanship can shape responses to gaffes rather than the other way around. The rest of the sample said that Romney's comments were either a minor mistake (19%) or "not a mistake" (38%), with the latter category populated mainly by Republicans. Political independents were more likely to say that it was "not a mistake" (44%) than that it was a "serious mistake" (26%).

All of these polls also asked whether the 47% video would make you more or less likely to vote for Romney. Majorities said it would not affect their vote, but among those who said it would, more said it make them less likely to vote for Romney. However, despite the ubiquity of this type of survey question in public polling, it is not particularly useful for understanding the impact of an event. People are not good at reporting on their own mental processes, and sometimes what they say are the reasons they arrived at their opinions are just rationalizations of opinions that already existed.[33] Rather than ask people whether the 47% video changed their mind, we should measure whether their minds actually changed.

In terms of the most important decision—who to vote for—there was no consistent evidence that much changed. In YouGov polling, Romney's numbers did drop: Obama had a 49%–44% lead in the September 15–17 poll, with the rest undecided or supporting another candidate; two weeks later, in the

September 29–October 1 poll, his lead was 49%–41%. This trend was particularly sharp among persuadable voters. The week after the video aired, support for Obama among these voters increased about 14 points. There were similar shifts in how favorably these voters viewed Obama and Romney.[34] Romney's support also dropped 5 points among those who actually favored him when first interviewed in December 2011. But these wavering supporters did not move to support Obama but instead said they were undecided—suggesting that they could be won back over to Romney's side.

In other polls, however, there was little movement after the video's release. In the Gallup polls conducted the week prior to the video's release, Obama had a 3-point lead (48%–45%). The week after the release, Obama had a 2-point lead (48%–46%) and the week following a 4-point lead (49%–45%). Rasmussen polls also showed no trend. The average of all the public polls (Figure 6.2) shows that they were stable in the wake of the video's release. Obama had about a 4-point lead on the day the video was released. A week later, his lead had not changed. Two weeks later, his lead had actually shrunk by a point or so.[35] Thus it is far from clear that the video's impact really changed anyone's mind.

But, as when Obama attacked Romney's record at Bain Capital in July, it may be more important to examine perceptions of Romney's empathy—the trait that seemed most implicated by comments like "It's not my job to worry about those people," where "those people" meant nearly half of the American public.[36] We have already examined these perceptions —such as how much the candidates "care about people like me"—and in Figure 6.3, we now do so for the entire period from January through the weekend before Election Day. Obama's advantage on this dimension stands out once again. Over these ten months, people perceived that he cared more about "people like me," the poor, and the middle class than did Romney. By contrast, and by a large margin, Romney was perceived as caring more about the wealthy.

However, these differences did not change after the 47% video was released. Indeed, they were stable over the entire ten-month period. Imagine that voters were rating Obama and Romney on a 100-point scale. In the first poll in which we asked these questions, when Newt Gingrich's and Rick Perry's attacks on Romney's time at Bain Capital had just begun, voters rated Obama a 47 and Romney a 40—a 7-point advantage for Obama. The weekend before the election, they rated Obama a 53 and Romney a 44—a 9-point advantage. All of the discussion of Bain Capital, Romney's wealth, Romney's tax returns, and the 47% video did not appear to give Obama much more of an advantage on this dimension. *Washington Post*/ABC News polling also found no significant shift toward Obama after the video's release in perceptions of who "better understands the economic problems people in this country are having."[37]

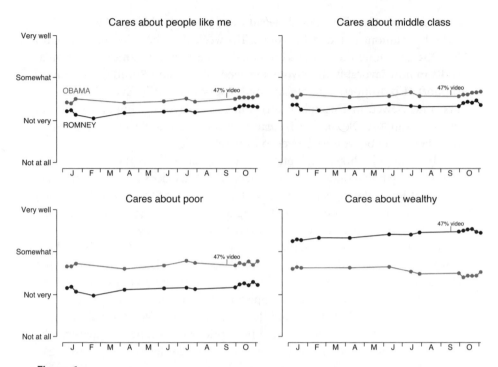

Figure 6.3.
Perceptions of empathy.
The poll questions asked how well each of the phrases (e.g., "cares about people like me") described each candidate. The trend lines represent the average perception on the 4-point scale ranging from very well to not at all well. Data from YouGov polls between January and November 2012.

All of these data belie many of the claims made about the effects of this video—for example, that it "pierced the national consciousness in a way that few blunders do" and became "a defining element of Romney's candidacy."[38] It may have been that voters did not need to be told much about Romney in order to perceive him as less empathetic than Obama. Perhaps this was a perception that predated much of the campaign. Or perhaps this was simply a case in which partisan stereotypes—Democrats care about the average person, Republicans care about the wealthy—motivated at least some voters' perceptions.

Whatever the explanation, it was striking that this video, a supposed bombshell, detonated with so little apparent force in the minds of voters. Of course, a possible rejoinder involves hypotheticals. If not for the video's release, could Romney have campaigned more on his preferred message rather than doing damage control? It is certainly true that had the 47% video never come to light, the conversation during the last two weeks of September would have been different. But how beneficial would that conversation have been to Romney? It was true that the 47% video generated particularly negative coverage. Without that video, would the coverage have been favorable to Romney? Or would other events in September, like Romney's reaction to the Benghazi attacks and Obama's lead in the polls, have continued to cast a shadow? We cannot know, but it is not obvious that, without the video's release, the weeks after the Democratic National Convention would have been so much more favorable to Romney as to change the dynamics of the race. As our analyses to date have shown, news coverage and electioneering—except for the Democratic convention—have not had large or durable effects on public opinion to this point. If so, then it seems unlikely two weeks of campaigning without the specter of the 47% video would have helped Romney all that much.

But perhaps the best evidence that the 47% video was not fundamentally devastating to Romney was how quickly its apparent impact was undone a few weeks later in Denver.

The Denver Debate

As September came to a close and the first debate approached, Romney lagged Obama in the national polls and in key states—even if the 47% video had not clearly hurt his image among voters. Right-leaning pundits started looking for people to blame for Romney's nomination. Conservatives like RedState's Erick Erickson blamed "elitist Republicans" and "elitist jerks" who "hold the base of the GOP in contempt."[39] Relative moderates like Daniel Larison blamed conservatives.[40] Even Romney's own advisors were not exactly complimentary. "Lousy candidate; highly qualified to be president," said one. "He's a great leader, but he's not a great politician," said another.[41] Romney needed something to rehabilitate his image, and quickly. The debates were about all he could count on.

Could the debates propel Romney to victory? It was a long shot. For all the hype about presidential debates—they were yet another potential "game-changer" in 2012—there is little historical evidence that they could have changed the game in the way Romney needed.[42] That is, they have rarely propelled the candidate who was lagging in the polls to victory. The best cases for a game-changing debate effect were in 1960 and 2000, when they appeared to give large enough nudges to Kennedy and George W. Bush for them to win—although it is hard to say whether the debates alone deserve the credit. But many other stories about game-changing debates amount to folklore.[43] It has been quite common for debates to move the polls, but rare for them to determine the winner of the election. As political scientists Robert Erikson and Christopher Wlezien put it in their study of the 1952–2008 presidential campaigns, "the best prediction from the debates is the initial verdict before the debates."[44] In other words, in the average election year, you can accurately predict where the race will stand after the debates by knowing the state of the race before the debates.

Why is that? In part, it is because most voters have made up their minds and come away from the debate convinced that—surprise!—their party's candidate won. Another part of it has to do with the format of the debate itself. Unlike during conventions, when one candidate dominates the news, debates are deliberately structured to put the candidates on relatively equal footing. Time limits and the moderator help ensure that neither candidate can dominate the discussion.

In fact, if anything puts the candidates on unequal footing, it is not the debate itself but the media's reaction. Pundits and commentators take on the role of theater critic, and the consensus that sometimes forms can shape how voters respond. For example, in 2004, political scientist Kim Fridkin and other researchers at Arizona State University randomly assigned people to see one of three types of debate footage: the third presidential debate between John Kerry and George W. Bush and no media coverage at all, the debate plus twenty minutes of post-debate commentary on NBC, or the debate plus twenty minutes to read commentary on CNN's website. The NBC commentary was more favorable to Bush than CNN's, according to analysis done by Fridkin and colleagues. People watching the debate tended to think that Kerry had won, as did those who read analysis on CNN. But those who watched the NBC postmortem tended to think Bush had won.[45] The media's reaction in 2012 would be equally relevant.

The first debate, held at the University of Denver, took place on October 3. More than seventy million Americans watched it—more than had watched any first debate since 1980 (though lower as a fraction of the total population).[46] On paper, it read as fairly even-keeled. The discussion was often remarkably substantive—a "wonky blizzard of facts, statistics and studies," said one postmortem.[47] Perhaps the most memorable line was Romney's pledge that he was going to end federal funding of public television, even though he did "like Big Bird."[48]

Nevertheless, a consensus quickly developed in the news media that Romney had not only won the debate but completely dominated. The *National Journal*'s Ron Fournier said that Obama was "peeved and flat" while Romney was "personable, funny, and relentlessly on the attack."[49] *Washington Post* reporters David Nakamura and Philip Rucker perceived Romney's victory in spin-room body language: Republicans like Marco Rubio "paraded

triumphantly" while Obama's advisor David Plouffe looked "tired and uncertain" and needed a "handler" to guide him into the room.[50] Among some
liberal pundits and Obama supporters, the reaction was anguished. Andrew
Sullivan of the *Daily Beast*, who had just written a *Newsweek* cover story predicting that Obama would become "the Democrats' Reagan" and an "iconic
figure" if he were reelected, concluded his live-blog of the election with these
descriptions of Obama's performance: "meandering, weak, professorial arguments" ("professorial" is, alas, not a compliment when applied to a politician
or perhaps even to a professor), "effete, wonkish lectures," "tired, even bored,"
"entirely defensive."[51] MSNBC's Chris Matthews wailed, "Where was Obama
tonight?" and "What was he doing tonight?" He said, "I don't know what he
was doing out there."[52] In fact the "torrent of criticism," as Michael Shear of
the *New York Times* put it, created perhaps the most bipartisan moment of
the campaign, "with Republicans, as well as many Democrats, accusing Mr.
Obama of delivering a flat, uninspired and defensive performance."[53]

That the news media scored this debate as a resounding Romney win
is evident in Figure 6.1. It shows the sharp spike in coverage of both candidates that the debate generated, although the spike was larger for Romney
(nearly 50,000 mentions compared to about 36,500 for Obama). Even more
important was the divergent tone of that coverage, with Romney's mostly positive and Obama's mostly negative. This divergence was the largest that would
occur at any point between August and November.[54] If the 2012 campaign was
going to have a game-changing moment, it looked like this would be it.

The media consensus about Romney's victory likely helped produce
a consensus in the public as well. Although the majority of Americans had
predicted that Obama would do a better job in the debate, the majority believed that Romney had won.[55] In debate night polls, Romney came out ahead
among a CNN poll of debate watchers (67% said he won versus 25% who
said Obama) and in a CBS News poll of undecided voters who watched the
debate—although there the margin was closer: 46%–22% (the remainder said
it was a tie). In a Gallup poll conducted among likely voters during the two
days after the debate, the margin was more lopsided (72%–20%).[56] In an October 4–7 Pew poll, it was 66%–20%; among self-reported debate watchers it
was 72%–20%.[57] If one averages the two debate night polls and compares them
to the average of the Gallup and Pew polls, it does appear that the percentage
who believed Romney won increased after the debate—as we would expect
when so many in the news media declared him the winner.

The first debate also appeared to shift vote intentions. In the public polls,
the lead Obama had had since the Democratic convention dwindled, leaving
the two candidates nearly tied (see Figure 6.2). The apparent reduction in
Obama's lead suggested a swing of about 4 points, which was somewhat large

by historical standards.[58] Some polls even put Romney in the lead—most famously, an early October Pew poll, in which Romney, previously down by 8 in Pew's September survey, was now up by 4 points. The Pew poll appeared to cause another spike in media coverage of Romney (see Figure 6.1) and not a little consternation among Obama supporters. Andrew Sullivan wrote "Did Obama Just Throw the Entire Election Away?"[59] Before long, it was Democratic strategists' turn to come out of the woodwork and criticize the Obama campaign. James Carville and Stanley Greenberg, best known for their work on the 1992 Clinton campaign, penned a memo titled "Getting to the Bold Policy Offer Winning Now Requires," which said that "in the first debate, Obama did not make a bold case for the bold policies he would offer in the next four years" and that he "must offer a bold narrative, bold policies, and a clear choice for the future focused on restoring the middle class."[60]

Some further sleuthing suggests who exactly was shifting toward Romney. In YouGov polling, the debate bump came from those who were undecided. Their numbers dropped 4 points as Romney's increased by the same amount. Many of these undecided voters were Republicans who were apparently returning to the fold. They had previously supported Romney, wavered after the 47% video and became unsure about their vote, and now had come back to him after this debate. The number of undecided Republicans had increased in YouGov polls from 4% to nearly 12% in the two weeks after the 47% video was released, but in the first poll after the debate only a bit more than 1% was undecided and Romney's support was 8 points higher than just before the debate. This same trend was evident in the Obama campaign's own polling.[61] The impact of this debate showed, once again, how quickly even dramatic moments like the 47% video's release could be undone by new events as the tug-of-war between the candidates continued. The losses Romney appeared to suffer after the video's release actually made subsequent events like the debates more likely to bring him gains, assuming that these undecided Republicans would return to Romney.

The shift in vote intentions was attributed by some commentators to Romney's embrace of moderate positions on issues during the debate. This was what one Romney advisor had suggested Romney could do in the general election campaign after having spent the primary appealing to conservative voters: "Everything changes. It's almost like an Etch-A-Sketch. You can kind of shake it up and restart all over again."[62] After the debate, David Brooks wrote a celebratory column titled "Moderate Mitt Returns!"[63] Bill Clinton said sarcastically, "Wow, here's old moderate Mitt. Where ya been, boy?"[64] The Obama campaign called Romney "more brazenly dishonest."[65]

But in contrast to these comments, voters' reactions had much more to do with style than substance. In Figure 6.4 we present a variety of assessments of

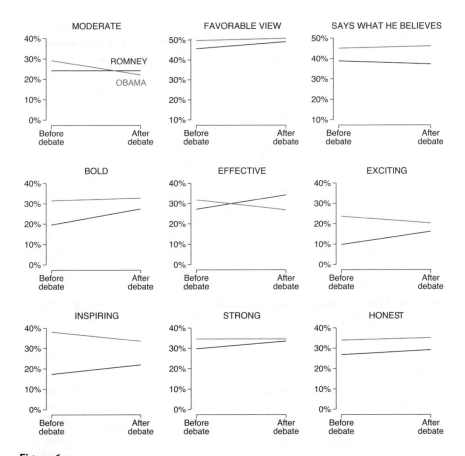

Figure 6.4.

Perceptions of Romney and Obama, before and after the first debate.

The graph presents the percentage of respondents who gave each assessment of Obama and Romney before and after the first debate. "Moderate" indicates those who identified the candidates as "moderate" on a 5-point category measure ranging from "very liberal" to "very conservative." "Favorable view" indicates those who had a very or somewhat favorable view as opposed to a very or somewhat unfavorable view. "Says what he believes" indicates those who chose this option rather than "says what he thinks people want to hear." For the other traits, respondents were shown these among a list of 16 adjectives and asked whether they did or did not describe Romney and Obama. Respondents could also leave these items blank, indicating no opinion. These items were not asked in the context of the debate itself but overall. Data from YouGov polls conducted September 29–October 1 and October 6–8, 2012.

the two candidates. In fact, voters did not perceive Romney's ideology differently. The graph labeled "moderate" shows no change in the proportion that said Romney was moderate.[66] Romney's attempted shift to the center was not as apparent to voters as to *New York Times* writers or former presidents. In fact, perceptions of Obama's ideology changed a bit more: fewer said he was moderate but more said he was liberal. And despite any apparent "Etch-a-Sketching," voters did not change their views of Romney's sincerity. Perceptions of whether he "says what he believes" or was "honest" did not change either.

Instead, voters came to perceive Romney more positively in terms of other traits. The fraction with a generally favorable view of Romney increased, bringing him nearly to Obama's level. The fraction of voters that perceived Romney as "bold," "effective," "exciting," "inspiring," and "strong" also increased, while the fraction of voters perceiving Obama this way either did not change or actually declined. Among independents, these trends were even sharper, giving Romney the advantage on several of these dimensions.[67] Republicans also saw Romney more positively. Perhaps the most striking finding concerned Democrats, whose assessments of Obama became less positive on many of these dimensions, such as "effective" and "exciting." This is unusual. As we have noted, and as the Democratic convention demonstrated, most campaign events serve to reinforce or increase party polarization, making Democrats and Republicans love their candidate more and the other candidate less. In this case, Republicans followed this pattern but Democrats did not, even if their reaction was not quite as dramatic as that of Chris Matthews.

There is no doubt, then, that the reaction of commentators and the apparent shift in polls will likely make this debate go down in lore. But it is important to sound one cautionary note because some other evidence shows that this may be wrong, or at least exaggerated.

There are two reasons why public polls of likely voters registered the change they did after the debate. One is that people's minds changed: some people who supported Obama or were undecided now supported Romney. The other is that people's minds did not change but more Romney supporters declared themselves likely to vote, changing the composition of voters in the samples of these polls. Here is one piece of evidence for the latter. YouGov had an electoral college forecasting poll in the field in twenty-five states in September, in which 33,000 people were interviewed. After the debate, 25,000 of these people were reinterviewed. Measuring changes in the same people helps mitigate the problems that arise from comparing samples of different voters—namely, are differences between the polls due to changes in attitudes or to changes in the composition of the sample? This was the problem endemic in measuring the debate's effect using the other public polls. These polls did weight their samples to match demographic benchmarks in the Census, but those weights alone may not have been enough to make the samples comparable—especially since most pollsters did not weight based on party identification, and this may have been the crucial characteristic that determined whether people participated in surveys.

The YouGov poll found almost no change across the two waves of interviews. "The Romney bounce was tiny," wrote YouGov's president, Peter Kellner.[68] But had YouGov adopted the practice of simply weighting to demographic benchmarks like other pollsters, they would have shown a 5-point swing toward Romney. Why was there this discrepancy? One reason is that Romney supporters in the September YouGov survey were more likely to answer the October YouGov survey than were Obama supporters from September: 80% of Romney supporters did so, but only 74% of Obama supporters.[69] This may help explain why, for example, the partisan composition of the early October Pew survey tilted slightly toward Republicans (by 1 point) while the sample in the September survey tilted much more toward Democrats (+8 points). Such swings in party identification are unlikely to occur in such a short time. More plausible is that more Republicans were willing to respond to polls at a moment when the Republican candidate was doing well. Any polls that did not account for this might have overestimated the shift to Romney. Only if Republicans' willingness to respond to polls signaled a greater motivation to vote on Election Day was the shift in the composition of the samples important.

The first debate of 2012 may therefore have been less of a "game-changer" than originally thought. Of course, few knew it at the time. And certainly Obama would not take the chance of believing it.

Fight Nights

One reason that presidential debates have not necessarily vaulted the underdog to victory is that a single debate victory has not been enough. Other debates have followed, and it has proven difficult to run the table and win them all. Indeed, there is tentative evidence that the opposite has happened: the candidate who performed well early did worse later on, and the candidate who initially struggled then improved.[70] That was what happened to Obama. And the consequence was the mirror image of what happened after the first debate. Whereas that debate helped rally Republicans who wavered in the weeks after the release of the 47% video, later debates helped rally Democrats who wavered after Obama's performance in the first debate and the media's reaction to it. These movements illustrate two points we have emphasized: the campaign's tug-of-war often makes advantages and disadvantages short-lived, and partisans tend to be predictable. Even when they waver, they frequently come back to the decision we would otherwise expect them to make.

After the first debate, Obama benefited almost immediately from the jobs report released two days later. The report showed an unexpected drop in the unemployment rate, from 8.1% to 7.8%—the lowest since Obama had taken office. News coverage of the report was positive. The *New York Times* characterized it as a "jolt" to the presidential race, saying "the improvement lent ballast to Mr. Obama's case that the economy is on the mend and threatened the central argument of Mitt Romney's candidacy, that Mr. Obama's failed stewardship is the reason to replace him."[71] This account was typical of Obama's news coverage. After two days of post-debate coverage that was more negative than positive, coverage over the weekend was slightly more positive than negative (see Figure 6.1), roughly similar to Romney's. A *Washington Post*/ABC News poll showed that Democratic perceptions of Obama, which had suffered after the first debate, became more favorable over the weekend, after the jobs report had been released.[72] This was one manifestation of predictable partisanship.

However, as the impact of the debate became fully manifest, a small group of Democrats continued to waver. In the week after the debate, as most polls showed a tighter race and some—especially the Pew poll—showed a Romney lead, Democratic support for Obama fell about 6 points in YouGov surveys.[73] To regain his footing, Obama needed to rally these Democrats.

The Obama campaign readied a different, more aggressive strategy for the debates that were to come. Some reporting suggested that Obama did not particularly care for debates to begin with—viewing them, perhaps correctly, as "media-driven gamesmanship"—and that his preparation for the first debate had been interrupted by events he needed to attend to as president.[74] This time around, his preparation was more intense. Obama himself averred that he had been "just too polite" in the first debate.[75] Obama advisor Robert Gibbs promised that Obama would be "more energetic."[76]

The newly aggressive posture began a week after the first debate, when Vice President Joe Biden and Paul Ryan debated. It was "the debate that President Obama and Mitt Romney did not have a week ago." The two "fiercely quarreled" with Biden "using the cutting attack lines against the Republican ticket that Mr. Obama did not" while Ryan delivered "a spirited case for the conservative policies that Mr. Romney had soft-pedaled."[77] The debate itself did not move the polling average (see Figure 6.3) or succeed in rallying these wavering Democrats, but vice-presidential debates rarely have much effect.[78] This debate did, however, set the stage for what Obama would do in the following weeks.

In the October 16 presidential debate, structured in the town-hall style with questions from the audience, Obama was "aggressive" and a "feistier" candidate who "ripped into Mitt Romney's economic blueprint" and "challenged" Romney and "accused him of shifting positions."[79] As Romney responded in kind, "their town-hall-style engagement felt more like a shouting match than a presidential debate."[80] Unlike in the first debate, there were no sharp divergences in the tenor of news coverage, which was slightly more positive for Obama than Romney. The post-debate polling reflected the news coverage, inasmuch as Obama went from the apparent loser of the first debate to the narrow winner of this one.[81] Most important, Obama's performance seemed to bring back the wavering Democrats. In the YouGov survey conducted October 20–22, Obama gained back the 6 points of Democratic support that he had lost after the first debate.[82]

The third debate, held on October 22 and focused more on foreign policy, was framed by the news coverage in much the same way. Obama was "ready to take the fight to" Romney, and Romney mostly responded in kind: "President Obama and Mitt Romney clashed repeatedly over foreign policy here Monday night, with the president arguing assertively that Romney has lacked the consistency or clarity of vision to lead the country while the Republican nominee charged that Obama has been weak and ineffective in the face of growing turmoil in the world."[83] News coverage of both candidates was less plentiful and less positive than in the first two debates. Obama was judged by more voters to be the winner and by a larger margin than in the second debate.[84] His support among Democrats notched 3 points higher after this debate, according to YouGov's polling—making Democrats as loyal to Obama as they were before the first debate. They would remain so for the rest of the campaign.

The sum total of the debate season, then, was to create a tighter race but not put Romney in the driver's seat. This was consistent with history and the academic literature: debates have moved the polls but rarely determined the winner of the election. In 2012 as in past years, this was due to the tug-of-war dynamic: candidates who had a bad outing in one debate improved in the others. In part, this was also due to the gravitational pull of partisanship. For the vast majority of voters, partisanship solidified their vote intentions and helped them ignore or rationalize new information that might have made them change their minds. But for the small group of partisans who wavered, the campaign helped bring them back into the fold.

Of course, all of this presumes that a candidate who struggles in one debate will do better in others. What if, in the eyes of the news media and many voters, Obama had performed as poorly in the second or third debate as in the first? Would the debates have mattered more then? Could Romney have won the election on the basis of more than one convincing victory? These questions are unknowable. But history suggests that such scenarios are, at a minimum, unlikely. It has been relatively rare for presidential candidates to lose one debate as badly as Obama appeared to lose the first one. Most candidates have been competent debaters—their sand-bagging before the debate notwithstanding—and have prepared diligently ahead of time. It has been even rarer for a candidate to lose more than one debate by a wide margin. The candidates have tended to fight to something like a draw. To be sure, the 2012 debates were not quite a draw. The net impact of the debates helped Romney. But they did not make him the clear front-runner, and Obama was able to gain back some of what he lost after the first debate. For Romney, time was running out.

Hurricane Sandy

As the closing weeks of the campaign began, there were still about 5–7% of voters who remained "persuadable," as we have defined it. In this final stretch, two events dominated news coverage of the campaign. One was about something that never happened: Romney's sudden "momentum." The other was about something that did, but did not appear to matter much for the election: Hurricane Sandy. Believing Romney had momentum heading into the last week of the campaign might lead one to think that Sandy somehow shifted the momentum back to Obama. But the polls showed neither momentum for Romney nor a clear shift to Obama because of the hurricane.

The Romney momentum narrative emerged right about the time of the third debate. An October 22 *Politico* story said this:

> It's momentum vs. the map. With a little more than two weeks left until judgment day, Barack Obama's campaign is embracing a fundamentally defensive strategy centered on winning Ohio at all costs—while unleashing a new barrage of blistering attacks against Mitt Romney aimed at mobilizing a less-than-fired-up Democratic base. A surging Romney is suddenly playing offense all over the map, and the upward movement since the Denver debate gives him the luxury of striking what his advisers—and more than a few Democrats—think is a more positive, presidential, "Morning in America" tone.[85]

A *New York Times* story the following day also seemed to suggest that Romney had momentum, citing "some polls suggesting that Mr. Romney is closing the gap." Other outlets made similar claims.[86]

If "momentum" is to mean something in this context, it should be grounded in polling. A candidate may seem to have momentum in some other respect—maybe their campaign rallies appear to have more "energy"— but if voters are not noticing, what is the difference? The problem for the Romney momentum narrative was that there had been no recent movement in the polls—not since the first debate three weeks prior to the *Politico* story. That debate did help "close the gap," but the polls had remained stable since that point. There was nothing on or about October 22 that changed. If "some polls" showed the gap closing further, some other polls did not—which is why the average of the polls was stable, as in Figure 6.3. This episode seemed like a classic case of "rooting for the story"—writing news coverage that asserted a trend was occurring, thereby making the news account more compelling, even without much evidence for that trend.

Indeed, when asked whether Romney truly had momentum, one reporter for a major newspaper admitted to us that the story was really about what other reporters were saying, not about any actual change in the polls. This reporter said, "What we call momentum is more like narrative, and we're buying into that." And as with many a narrative built on sand, it soon crumbled. Not three days later, *Politico* suddenly declared that Romney's "Big Mo" had become "Slo Mo."[87]

The following week—Monday, October 29—Hurricane Sandy brought destructive winds and flooding along the Eastern Seaboard, particularly in New Jersey and New York. Given the storm's toll—it killed 131 people and caused billions in damage—it inevitably seems crass to focus on its impact on the election. But natural disasters have influenced elections. Voters have punished incumbents for droughts, floods, and tornadoes, presumably believing that more could have been done either to prevent the damage before the disaster or to address them after. This historical pattern would obviously implicate Obama after Sandy.[88] Inclement weather also appears to depress Democratic turnout, something that David Axelrod expressed concern about after Sandy hit.[89] But there was a potential upside for Obama: disaster declarations by the president and federal disaster relief appear to mitigate the effects of the disaster and can boost turnout by the president's party.[90] But with only a week to go until the election, it was not clear how much potential there was for punishment or reward. Running water and electricity did not return to many homes by Election Day, much less tangible federal disaster relief.

Obama did not take any chances. Having flown to Florida on Sunday, October 28, to campaign—including at a joint rally with Bill Clinton scheduled for Monday afternoon—he instead left Florida on Monday morning, flying back to the White House on the morning of October 29 and spending the day in contact with state officials like New Jersey governor Chris Christie.[91]

On Tuesday morning he presided over a meeting in the White House Situation Room and visited the Red Cross. On Wednesday he and Christie toured the devastation together. "We are here for you, and we will not forget," said Obama.[92] Romney also canceled campaign events and turned a campaign rally already scheduled in Dayton for October 29 into a less political "storm relief event."[93]

There was reason to assume Obama would have the upper hand at this moment. He could be and act "presidential," mobilizing the trappings of his office to show concern and support for the victims. Presumably, then, news coverage of Obama would be more favorable. In fact, the evidence is mixed. Across the thousands of news outlets our data summarize, there was not much difference in the coverage of the two candidates (Figure 6.1). Analyzing a smaller sample of elite media, the Project for Excellence in Journalism did find that Obama received more coverage and more positive coverage during the last week of the campaign than he had in prior weeks. But this was not due to Hurricane Sandy. Relatively few stories about Hurricane Sandy mentioned Obama. Instead, the shift toward more favorable coverage of Obama was evident in horse-race stories.[94]

Another piece of evidence supports the idea that any favorable coverage of Obama was being driven by favorable numbers in the horse race. This evidence derives from examining the relationship between poll numbers and news coverage—as we have been doing throughout. In the previous chapter, we found no relationship during the period from May through August: news coverage did not appear to drive poll numbers, and poll numbers did not appear to drive news coverage. Once we extend the analysis to consider the fall campaign as well, we continue to find no evidence that news coverage drove poll numbers, but better poll numbers do appear to produce a larger volume of positive news coverage. (The appendix to this chapter provides further detail.) This is consistent with what the Project for Excellence in Journalism found in its analysis of news coverage at the end of the campaign. It is also consistent with a host of scholarship on news coverage of elections, which argues that news coverage tends to emphasize the horse race and thus pays a great deal of attention to polls. So it is not surprising that as the polls shifted, the news coverage followed along.[95]

Given that news coverage did not seem to drive poll numbers, it is also unsurprising that after Sandy hit, the polls did not move very much. *The Guardian*'s Harry Enten examined the polls and found no consistent evidence of movement toward Obama after Sandy.[96] Looking at the national polls, Enten found that the majority of pollsters found that Obama had lost points, gained no points, or gained only 1 point after Sandy. In the state polls, Obama gained in only three of twelve states, or in twenty-five of the sixty-seven instances where a pollster had polls in the field pre- and post-Sandy. There was not even a notable shift toward Obama in the states hit hardest by Sandy, New York and New Jersey. We also examined persuadable voters in the YouGov sample—those who might be the most affected by Sandy-related news coverage—and found no significant shift toward Obama.

The idea that Hurricane Sandy changed the dynamic of the race was largely contingent on the misperception that Romney had momentum immediately before Sandy made landfall. Of course, there are always the what-ifs. What if Sandy turned out into the Atlantic and sent no more than a bit of rain to the East Coast? Romney strategist Stuart Stevens suggested that the hurricane prevented them from closing out the campaign as they had planned:

> After the storm, I never had a good feeling. Not that the storm impacted things so much, per se, but these races—a race like this is a lot like an NBA game. It's all about ball control at the end. . . . We went from having these big rallies around the country to literally sitting around in hotel rooms and there was just nothing we could do about it.[97]

At the same time, the hurricane did not keep Romney sitting around for long. After canceling some events on the day after the hurricane hit, he resumed campaigning on the following day—holding three events in Florida on Wednesday, October 31—and kept up a busy schedule through Election Day. Nor did Romney or Obama pull their ads when Sandy hit. As destructive as the hurricane was, it was at best a short-lived disruption in the campaign.

The Ad Blitz

Romney had one remaining hope: a last-minute ad blitz in the battleground states. The timing certainly seemed right: we have already shown how quickly the effects of political advertising wear off. As Democratic campaign consultant Aaron Strauss has put it: "The effects of any campaign activity are ephemeral. Just because you touched someone in, let's say, the beginning of October doesn't mean they'll be with you two weeks or even one week later."[98] Late advertisements could therefore have proven crucial, and waiting until late in the campaign was apparently Romney's strategy. One Republican strategist close to the Romney campaign said: "The goal has always been 'let's get to October and be within striking distance.' We're going to have a financial advantage these last two months in the air wars, from the campaign as well as the third-party independent groups."[99] In late September, Republicans were saying that they expected to "dominate the airwaves through November."[100]

Figure 6.5 presents the advertising volume on both sides separately for candidates and groups. The repeated bumps in the graph indicate that the campaigns tended to advertise much more on weekdays than weekends. Throughout the entire campaign, Obama out-advertised Romney, but GOP groups dominated Democratic groups. In August the GOP maintained an overall advantage, except during the week of the Olympics. The GOP also aired very few ads during the Republican National Convention—a common strategy historically, though one that the Obama campaign ignored, running ads during both conventions in 2012. (Both campaigns aired almost no advertising on September 11 in recognition of the terrorist attacks of September 11, 2001.)[101] After the conventions, the Democrats continued to maintain an advantage in September and part of October. Only at the very end of the campaign did the Republicans pull ahead, just as the Romney campaign intended. In total, the Republicans aired more ads than Obama and his allies on every day from October 22 until Election Day.

Despite early concerns that Obama would be vastly outspent in the fall campaign, several things helped him remain competitive on the airwaves. For one, Romney's reliance on advertising by super-PACs and outside groups put him at a disadvantage because those groups pay higher rates than candidates. Under the law, candidates are entitled to the "lowest unit rate"—that is, the lowest rate that stations charge to air an ad at any particular time—during the sixty days prior to the November election. But outside groups do not get this advantage and were often paying several times more. For example, on September 23, the Obama campaign paid $4,500 for a thirty-second ad to air during *60 Minutes* in the Tampa media market. The GOP group American Crossroads paid $14,000.[102]

Second, in some instances the Romney campaign was itself paying higher rates than the Obama campaign. These gaps arose because the two campaigns employed different strategies for buying advertising time. The Obama campaign sought a more efficient strategy than simply buying time during television programs believed to be popular among the voters they were targeting. Instead, they bought detailed information about the viewing habits of millions of cable subscribers and then matched this information to their own data about voters' opinions. They claimed that this enabled them to find programs, or more specifically, times of day on particular channels, where they could reach targeted voters but at much lower costs.[103] For a campaign afraid of being outspent, this sort of efficiency was crucial. It also may have given the Obama campaign a little additional advantage on the airwaves, since it was airing ads when and where Romney was very unlikely to be advertising. People tuning into these programs would thus see only one side's ads.

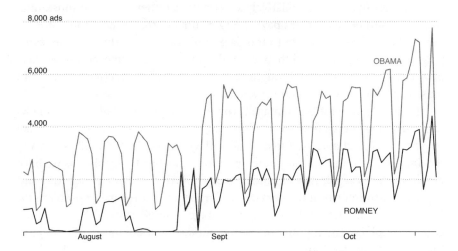

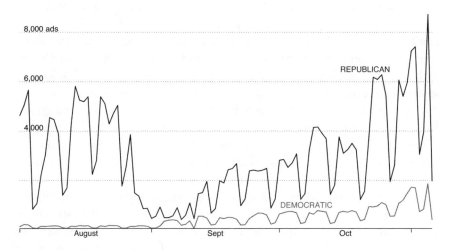

Figure 6.5.
Volume of television advertising in the fall of 2012.
The figure depicts the estimated daily number of ads aired in the presidential race
from August 1 until Election Day, November 6. The top panel includes ads by Obama
and Romney. The bottom panel includes ads by the party organizations and major
outside groups: Priorities USA Action on the Democratic side, and Restore Our Future,
Americans for Prosperity, American Crossroads, Crossroads GPS, and the Republican
National Committee on the Republican side. Data from The Nielsen Company.

By contrast, the Romney campaign often paid more for advertising be-cause it was buying ads on relatively short notice, rather than with substantial lead time, and because it was paying larger sums so that its ads would not get bumped as prices rose close to the date of air time.[104] To the Romney cam-paign, this strategy allowed them to be flexible and adaptable, adjusting their buys based on where they thought ads would be most effective, rather than making guesses weeks or months ahead of time.

Did the Democratic advantage throughout most of the fall, or the Repub-lican advantage in the final week, ultimately affect voters? Based on the model we presented in chapter 5, a five-ad advantage per capita (500 GRPs) on any day increased Romney's vote share by approximately 4 points. But as we have emphasized, these effects were short-lived—mostly gone by the next day and replaced by the effects of the next day's ad imbalance. The further problem for Romney was that he rarely had an advantage as large as five ads per capita. After multiplying the number of media markets by the number of days after the conventions, we found that on less than 1% of these "market-days" did Romney have an advantage this large or larger. In the last week of the cam-paign, when the Romney ad blitz was under way, Romney had this advan-tage on less than 3% of market-days. Even smaller advantages than these were hard to come by: in the last week of the campaign, Romney had an advantage equivalent to one ad per capita on about one-fourth of the market-days. (In markets that saw at least some ads during that final week, he had that advan-tage on only one-third of market-days.) Despite the advantage that Obama had early on, and that Romney had in the closing days, it was still difficult to sustain a large advantage in a large number of markets simultaneously.

To help visualize the symmetry in ad balance over the fall campaign and the challenge of using ads to move the polls, we plot the GRP differences in Figure 6.6. Each dot in the figure is a media market and the spread of dots on any given day shows the variation across markets in terms of the advertising balance. The solid lines trace the population-adjusted average daily balance of ads in the nation as a whole and in the battleground states alone. For illustra-tion, at three points we note the shift in vote intentions associated with a given ad imbalance. Despite the large imbalances on some days in some markets, the average national differences hover close to zero, even in the battleground states, although the average differences are bigger there. Thus, despite the fact that Obama or Romney had advertising advantages on some days in some places, the average advantage was small and the effects of any advantage even smaller and short-lived. Relying on advertising to move the polls was very hard—mainly because the candidates were so effective at neutralizing each other.

For Romney, the fall ad blitz simply did not give him enough of an advan-tage, especially given Obama's lead in the polls in the battleground states and

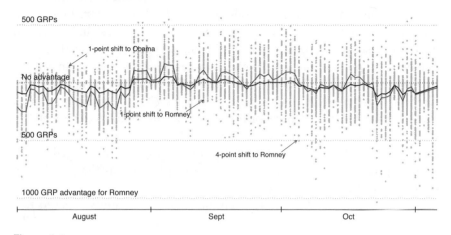

Figure 6.6.
Advertising imbalance and illustrative effects on voters.
The dots represent the balance of GRPs in media markets on each day. Markets with no advertising are clustered at zero, although we do not show that clustering visually. The black line is the population-adjusted average balance of GRPs nationwide. The gray line is the population-adjusted average balance of GRPs in the battleground states. The estimated shift in the polls associated with different ad imbalances are illustrated. Data are from The Nielsen Company.

the fact that a substantial number of voters—approximately 32%—had already voted by the time this blitz was under way.[105]

Endgame

As Election Day drew closer, this was where the race stood. Based on the economic and political fundamentals, Obama had been the favorite early on. He maintained a narrow lead for virtually the entire campaign, one that expanded after the Democratic convention but shrank after the first debate. For a few weeks in October the race was close to a tie, but more in the national polls than in battleground state polls, where Obama's lead was generally larger and more durable. Toward the end of the campaign, Obama opened a slightly larger lead in the national polls as well.

At that point, and arguably even beforehand, the race was not hard to call. Virtually everyone aggregating the public polls believed Obama was going to win, and with a very high probability. Nate Silver of the *New York Times* 538 blog was perhaps the most visible, and sometimes vilified, person making this argument, but his view was shared by Stanford political scientist Simon Jackman, who was working for Pollster at the *Huffington Post*, Emory political scientist Drew Linzer, who maintained Votamatic.org, and Princeton neuroscientist Sam Wang at his site, the Princeton Election Consortium. Pre-election polls provide an increasingly accurate forecast of the outcome as the election draws nigh.[106] They may not call the final margin on the nose, but rarely do they miss it entirely. (Such misses are a bit more common, though hardly typical, in presidential primaries or down-ballot races.) Indeed, it would have taken an unprecedented level of bias in the public polls for them to miss this election.[107] Americans seemed to have put all this together: the majority predicted an Obama victory and, history has shown, their prediction tends to be correct.[108]

On the other hand, some Republicans and conservatives believed that the polls were biased. Their argument was that many polls overestimated the Democratic composition of the electorate and that Obama's middling approval ratings and Romney's apparent advantage with independent voters meant he was certain to win. Perhaps most famously or at least infamously, a Virginia Republican named Dean Chambers created a website, unskewed-polls.com, that reweighted public polls to reflect a more pro-Republican electorate. Skepticism about the polls is perhaps why some commentators and pundits were confident in a Romney victory. Dick Morris predicted not only a Romney victory but a "landslide." Karl Rove, Michael Barone, George Will, and others also predicted that Romney would win.[109]

Perhaps this disagreement between poll aggregators and poll deniers created something akin to the "fog of war"—a state in which a battle becomes so confusing that its participants cannot figure out what is going on. Certainly some reporting and commentary seemed foggy. On the day before the election, the *Wall Street Journal*'s Peggy Noonan wrote, "We begin with the three words everyone writing about the election must say: Nobody knows anything. Everyone is guessing."[110] (Noonan predicted a Romney victory. "The vibrations are right," she wrote.) *Time*'s Joe Klein penned a column titled "I Don't Know" and said, "Anyone who claims to know who is going to win is blowing smoke."[111]

There should not have been any fog at all. The polls were clear. Even the Romney campaign's internal numbers suggested that victory was a long shot. One senior Romney strategist told us that his simulations based on the campaign's internal polls gave Romney an 18% chance of winning by the end. It is not surprising, then, that the fog cleared quickly on Election Day. As the returns began to roll in, there was remarkably little drama. By 11 PM Eastern or thereabouts, networks began calling the election for Obama. Obama won 332 Electoral College votes to Romney's 206, winning every battleground state except North Carolina. After all the votes were counted, Obama beat Romney by 3.9 points in the popular vote. If anything, the polls had underestimated Obama's margin, rather than overestimating it as Chambers and unskewed-polls.com suggested. The major polling aggregators proved extraordinarily accurate, calling all fifty state outcomes correctly.

We have likened the presidential general election campaign to a tug-of-war in which it is rare for one candidate to pull much harder than the other and shift the polls in his direction. Only in a few such moments—after the Democratic National Convention and then the first presidential debate—did that clearly happen. But even the effect of each of those events could be undone, as persuadable voters moved back and forth or as partisans who wavered temporarily came back home.

Meanwhile, the daily ebb and flow of candidate advertising and news coverage was arguably less relevant because it was largely balanced. In both the summer and fall, a candidate with a substantial advantage in advertising could move the polls. The problem is that the effect of the ads was very short-lived. The further problem is that it was hard to get a substantial advantage. In a race where both candidates spent about a billion dollars, their respective advertising blitzes in the battleground states were largely cancelling each other out. News coverage, although it likely helped shift the polls after the Democratic convention and the first debate, was not driving the polls over the entire fall. Instead, if anything, the polls were driving it—a dynamic different than what was true for several of the candidates in the Republican primary. This again reflects the relative balance in news coverage of the candidates, with neither covered substantially more often, or more favorably, than the other.

On election night, Romney took the stage to concede, saying, "I have just called President Obama to congratulate him on his victory. His supporters and his campaign also deserve congratulations. I wish all of them well, but particularly the president, the First Lady, and their daughters." Obama expressed similar sentiments in his speech: "I just spoke with Governor Romney and I congratulated him and Paul Ryan on a hard-fought campaign. We may have battled fiercely, but it's only because we love this country deeply and we care so strongly about its future." The debates of this campaign were finally over, but it some ways the most important debate was about to begin. It was a debate about why Obama won, why Romney lost, and what it meant for the next four years.

CHAPTER 7

The Winning Hand

Why did Barack Obama win the 2012 presidential election? Was it that he ran a "great campaign" or even a "formidable campaign"—one with "a much more potent organizational arsenal than in 2008"? Or was it something specific that he did? Was it that he "articulated a set of values that define an America that the majority of us wish to live in"? Was it "spending an enormous amount of money to discredit Romney in the swing states" during the spring and summer? Or maybe Obama just gave "gifts" to crucial constituencies like "the African-American community, the Hispanic community, and young people."[1]

Why did Mitt Romney lose the 2012 presidential election? Was it because he "ran a bad campaign"? Was it that he failed "to sell voters on the candidate's personal qualities and leadership gifts"? Was it that he "really screwed up on the immigration issue" by moving too far to the right and alienating Latinos? Or was he not conservative enough—a "meandering managerial moderate"? Or maybe "any explanation that centers on Mitt Romney is mistaken." Perhaps "Romney was not a drag on the Republican party" but "the Republican party was a drag on him." And what was the party's problem? Was it that some Republicans' comments about abortion, same-sex marriage, and racial minorities suggested that the party was just "mean" and "nasty"? Or was Romney's loss beyond even the party's control, as a "demographic time bomb" blew up in its face?[2]

The weeks and months after the 2012 election saw these and many other explanations put forth by politicians, commentators, and journalists. After any election, such explanations quickly ossify into conventional wisdom and therefore history, becoming the things that "everyone knows" mattered in an election. Our goal is to assess some of these explanations in light of our arguments thus far and systematic data about voters and campaign activity. We do not evaluate every explanation, but we can begin to shed light on some of them.

We have already begun to do so in chapters 5 and 6. The postmortems that emerged after the election confirmed much of what we have already argued. For example, despite the credit that Obama's early advertising received, the Obama campaign's own data mirrored our finding that the ads never really moved the polls. Here is Obama's chief strategist, David Axelrod, four days after the election:

> What's been interesting to watch is that our data has been remarkably consistent really from last spring forward, and our battleground polls really didn't fluctuate much. There were times when it would dip to where we had a 2-point lead in the battleground states. There's one poll over the course that we had a 1-point lead. By and large, we've been 3 and 4 points ahead in the battleground polls.[3]

David Simas, the Obama campaign's director of opinion research, said the same thing.[4] And despite hopes (or fears) that the 47% video would be Romney's undoing, Obama's campaign did not see it as all that momentous either. Obama's deputy campaign manager, Stephanie Cutter, said that whatever small fraction of voters moved away from Romney after the video's release eventually came back to him: "No one believed us at the time. We were saying that as this two percent moved away from Romney it wasn't ours. The race was closer than people thought at the time."[5] This is precisely what we found: Republicans who shifted away from Romney after the video's release came back to him after the first debate.

Now we tackle several different explanations. We selected these based in part on the sixty-plus years of political science research on American presidential elections. It gave us a sense of which explanations were likely to have merit. We also selected some of the explanations offered by pundits, commentators, and the two campaigns themselves in the weeks after the election. These explanations were often stated as fact but were really no more than conjecture. We want to know how much truth they contain. We consider six explanations in particular, acknowledging that these are not exhaustive. Our argument, in a nutshell, is this:

- *Political and economic fundamentals.* The campaign made partisanship and the economy even more salient to voters than they already were, and this arguably helped Obama win.

- *"Gifts" to key partisan constituencies.* Contrary to what some commentators and Romney himself said, the Obama administration's support for the auto "bailout," for reproductive rights and contraception, and for granting residency status to children of illegal immigrants did not appear crucial to shoring up support among the Democratic constituencies who may have favored these policies—the Rust Belt working class, women, and Latinos, respectively.
- *Romney's "severe conservatism."* Some commentators suggested Romney moved so far to the right to appeal to conservative voters in the Republican primary that he damaged his appeal among general election voters. But in the general election it was actually Obama, not Romney, who was ideologically further from the most voters. Romney's "extreme" ideology did not appear to be a significant factor in his loss.
- *Likability and empathy.* Commentators also pointed to Romney's deficits in terms of whether voters liked him and believed he understood their problems. The campaign closed some of these gaps, and those that remained were not large enough to cost Romney the race. Had he been perceived as favorably as Obama, he likely would have lost anyway.
- *Race and religion.* Negative attitudes toward African Americans appeared to depress support for Obama in the 2008 election, and we find that the same was true in 2012. But attitudes toward Mormons had a much smaller effect on support for Romney.
- *Obama's "formidable" campaign.* The ads and field organizations of the campaign made a small difference to the outcome but did not decide the election. Eliminating any advantages Obama or Romney had in terms of the air war and the ground game likely would have left Obama's victory intact.

It is tempting to believe that one can isolate each of these factors, estimate its precise effect on the election's outcome, and then add up these effects to something like a "recipe" for Obama's victory—a tablespoon of economic fundamentals, a teaspoon of empathy, and . . . voila! But any election is too complex a phenomenon for cookbook precision. Our goal is more modest: to offer plausible evidence about whether these factors mattered and, if so, rough estimates of how much they mattered. Our estimates are necessarily rough because often we are addressing hypotheticals like "What if Romney had been considered as empathetic as Obama?" or "What if Romney had matched Obama's ground game?" We will never know the answers to such questions. Had these things been true, the campaign would likely have been different in other ways that we cannot anticipate or account for. So we try to be appropriately cautious about our evidence.

Nevertheless, even a little progress toward evaluating these explanations helps separate fact from folklore as we seek to identify what exactly was in Obama's winning hand.

The Fundamentals

To understand Obama's victory, the first place to begin is "the fundamentals"— the central political and economic factors that undergird voters' choices and election outcomes. We have argued that Obama was forecast to win on the basis of these fundamentals alone, and that forecast was borne out on November 6. However, the success of the forecast was not preordained. Had the candidates made different choices or had things gone differently during the campaign, our forecast, as well as several others, might have been wrong. But that did not happen in 2012.

A simple but telling illustration of the role of economic fundamentals in this and earlier presidential elections is displayed in Figure 7.1. Here we compare presidential election outcomes from 1948 to 2012 to the change in gross domestic product during the first two quarters of the election year. The diagonal line captures the relationship between economic conditions and election outcomes for all years *except* 2012. If 2012 were close to what we would predict based on this historical relationship, it should fall close to that diagonal line. And indeed it does. To be sure, there is no reason to suspect that this one economic statistic would provide such an accurate forecast every election year. But nothing about 2012 was out of line with the forecast.[6]

The forecasting model that we described in chapter 2 was also accurate. This model combined growth in gross domestic product with changes in two other economic indicators—unemployment and real disposable income—as well as presidential approval and an indicator for whether the incumbent's party had occupied the White House for only one consecutive term (as was true in 2012) or more than one term. Based on where these factors stood at the end of 2011, our forecast was that Obama would win almost 52% of the major-party vote (that is, the vote for either the Democratic or Republican candidate, excluding third parties). Based on some plausible guesses of what presidential approval and economic growth would be in the first half of the election year itself, our forecast was that Obama would win 52.9% of the vote. We can now go back and generate a forecast based on what presidential approval and economic growth actually were. That forecast gives Obama 52.7% of the vote.[7] In actuality, Obama won almost 52% of the major-party vote—a figure slightly lower than our forecast but well in line with it.[8]

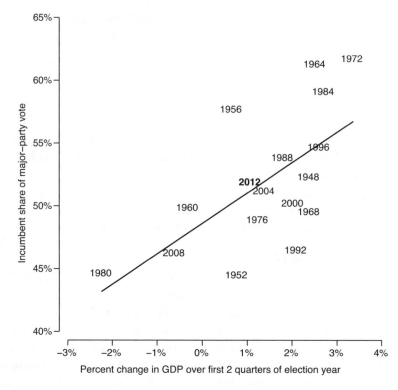

Figure 7.1.
Economic growth and presidential election outcomes, 1948–2012.
Note: The relationship between change in GDP and the vote—the diagonal line—is estimated without the 2012 election included. This shows how close the 2012 outcome was to what we would predict based on the historical relationship between GDP and the vote from 1948 to 2008.

In fact, the election's outcome was not much different than where the polls stood almost a year before it. When YouGov surveyed 45,000 Americans in December 2011—well before the general election and before the factors in our forecasting model were even in place—Obama garnered 52% of the vote among registered voters who preferred Obama or Romney, almost exactly his major-party vote share on Election Day. But it was no given that this 52% figure would remain consistent throughout the election year, thereby rendering our forecast accurate. By taking stock of the economic and political landscape in December 2011, we can identify what would have needed to happen to change the polls and, perhaps, render our forecast inaccurate. Five features of the landscape stand out:

- The slowly growing economy.
- A high degree of party loyalty among "decided voters."
- A group of "persuadable" voters large enough to decide the election.
- A campaign centered on the economy.
- A Democratic advantage in party identification and thus potentially among voters.

We will discuss the first four of these in turn, saving the fifth for later.

The slowly growing economy. As of December 2011, the economy was growing, but not quickly. For our forecast to be accurate, the economy needed to remain in a fairly steady state. Had there been a large economic shock of some kind, one that our forecasting model failed to capture, then the outcome could have been different than what we predicted.

That did not come to pass. Economic trends during 2012 might be best described as "more of the same." There was never a point at which the economy plunged back toward a recession or began to grow rapidly. In the first half of 2012, the economy slowed somewhat, as we discussed in chapter 5. The small increase in unemployment in April was perhaps the most visible manifestation of the slowdown. Had this slowdown continued, it might have put Obama's reelection in doubt. Instead, beginning in August, the economy began to rebound. The improvement is visible in Figure 7.2, which shows the

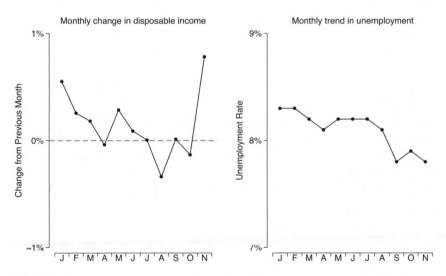

Figure 7.2.
Election-year trends in the national economy.
Data are from the Bureau of Economic Analysis and the Bureau of Labor Statistics.

monthly change in real disposable income and the monthly unemployment rate. Both improved in the fall. For example, the unemployment rate dropped from 8.1% to 7.8% in September. The monthly jobs reports had already been attracting significant news coverage—even though these reports present early estimates that often end up being revised—but this one seemed more dramatic, especially since it helped change the subject after Obama was judged to have performed so poorly in the first debate.

But more notable is just how stable the economy was. Consider the change in gross domestic product, the indicator we present in Figure 7.1. It grew 1% in the third quarter of 2011 and 0.5% in the fourth quarter—about the time when Obama claimed 52% of the major-party vote in the December poll. In 2012, GDP grew 0.3% in the first quarter but 0.8% in the third—a bit slower than in late 2011 but not so much slower that the economy appeared headed toward recession. Throughout the campaign, there was much speculation as to whether late changes in the economy would reshape the presidential race. This has rarely been the case. As Robert Erikson and Christopher Wlezien noted in their study of presidential elections from 1952 to 2008, "the economic cake is baked" relatively early in the election year.[9] Had there been a major shock—for example, had a sudden outbreak of war in an oil-producing region produced a large spike in gas prices—then perhaps the cake would have needed to bake a bit longer, as it were. But those shocks are uncommon. From the standpoint of election forecasting, even the financial crisis in the fall of 2008 was less of a shock than it might seem because the economy had already been in a recession for ten months at that point (of course, the crisis was important in many other ways). The predictability of the 2012 election hinged on the stability of the economy throughout the election year.

Party loyalty among the "decided" voters. When asked about a hypothetical Obama-Romney matchup in December 2011, Democrats and Republicans were already remarkably loyal partisans. About 80% of each party's voters chose their party's candidate. So for the state of the race in December to resemble that on Election Day, these decided voters needed to stick with that decision and remain faithful to their party. Had there been numerous defections in a direction that benefited either Romney or Obama then the outcome may have deviated from what voters said in December and from forecasts like ours. As it turned out, the behavior of decided voters manifested impressive stability, and the small number of defections did not overwhelmingly benefit either candidate. In fact, decided voters brought their political attitudes more in line with their party identification and vote intentions as the campaign went on. That campaigns reinforce partisanship is a decades-old finding in the political science literature, and 2012 was no exception.

Table 7.1.
The Stability of Candidate Preferences
from December 2011 to November 2012

December 2011 vote intention or party identification	December sample (%)	November 2012 vote choice			
		Obama (%)	Romney (%)	Other (%)	Did not vote (%)
All respondents					
Obama	43	74	2	2	22
Romney	38	4	77	2	17
Other or undecided	19	21	21	10	47
Other candidate	4	15	35	26	24
Undecided	15	23	17	5	55
Democrats	46	70	6	2	22
Independents	14	26	24	7	43
Republicans	40	6	74	4	16
Self-reported voters					
Obama	44	95	3	2	
Romney	41	5	92	3	
Other or undecided	15	41	40	19	
Other candidate	4	20	46	33	
Undecided	11	51	37	12	
Democrats	48	89	8	3	
Independents	10	45	42	13	
Republicans	42	7	88	4	

Note: Data are from YouGov polls. YouGov polled 44,998 people in December 2011 and then reinterviewed 35,408 of them after the November 6 election. Independents who lean toward a party are coded as partisans.

Table 7.1 depicts the stability of decided voters by comparing the vote intentions of YouGov respondents who were originally interviewed in December 2011 with their actual choices in the election, as they reported when interviewed again later in November 2012. Among those who identified as Obama supporters in December 2011, 74% reported voting for him, 22%

reported not voting, and only 2% reported voting for Romney. Romney supporters in December 2011 were very similar: 77% voted for him, 17% did not vote, and only 4% voted for Obama.[10] Thus, although not every supporter ended up voting, it was rare for voters to end up voting for the candidate they did not already prefer in December. This is even clearer when we examine only self-reported voters. Among those who supported Obama in December, 95% voted for him in November. Romney supporters were similarly loyal (92%). A small fraction of voters changed their minds: about 3% switched from Obama to Romney, and 5% from Romney to Obama—thereby providing a small benefit for Obama (less than 1 point of vote share). Ultimately, it was possible to predict how the vast majority of Americans would vote from what they said ten months before the actual election.

Much of this stability illustrates the power of partisanship in contemporary American politics. We have emphasized that most voters are partisans and most partisans end up supporting their presidential candidate. That was true in 2012, much as in other recent presidential elections. As Table 7.1 shows, 89% of Democrats who reported voting chose Obama, and 88% of Republicans who reported voting chose Romney—rates higher than in December 2011, which also suggests something about the behavior of the undecided voters we will discuss momentarily. The rate of partisan loyalty among voters in the exit poll was slightly higher: 92% among Democrats and 93% among Republicans. (The exit poll does not ascertain whether independents lean toward a party, so their measure of partisanship differs from ours.) According to the exit poll, party loyalty was even higher in 2012 than in 2008.

Such stability and predictability did not mean that the campaign was irrelevant. When partisans wavered, as some Republicans did after the release of the 47% video, campaign events helped reinforce their partisan inclination. The campaign also helped ensure partisans' loyalty by bringing other attitudes in line with partisanship. One example was candidate favorability. Among people who, as of December 2011, already supported Obama and then were reinterviewed during the last two weeks of the campaign, strongly favorable views of Obama increased by 8 points (from 60% to 68%) and strongly unfavorable views of Romney increased by 27 points (from 39% to 66%). The same polarization was evident among early Romney supporters. Their views of Obama did not change much—78% already had strongly unfavorable views of him in December—but strongly favorable views of Romney increased 26 points (from 30% to 56%). These shifts show how people react to new information in ways that conform to their preexisting opinions: if you were an early Obama supporter, most of what you learned about Mitt Romney during the presidential campaign made you oppose him all the more. Early Romney supporters had the opposite reaction.

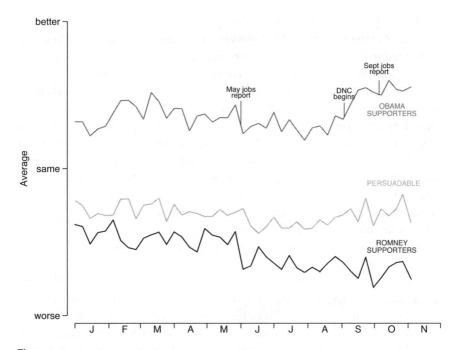

Figure 7.3.
The trend in perceptions of the economy.
The graph presents average response on a three-point scale ("worse," "same," "better")
for each group. "Persuadable" voters include those who were undecided as well as those
who preferred a candidate other than Romney and Obama. Data from YouGov polls.

Views of the economy also manifested this same pattern of polarization. As a result, trends in economic perceptions depended more on partisanship and vote intentions than the actual objective economy. Relying on the vote intention respondents originally stated in December 2011, Figure 7.3 displays the trends for Obama supporters, Romney supporters, and persuadable voters. (The results are similar if we compare Democrats, independents, and Republicans.)[11] Obama supporters came to have more favorable views of the economy as the campaign progressed. This was not in response to actual economic events, such as the poor May jobs report or the encouraging September jobs report. The economic perceptions of Obama supporters actually began to improve before the drop in unemployment. The key event was the Democratic National Convention. In the YouGov poll fielded over the weekend before the convention, 43% of Obama supporters said that the economy was getting better. The weekend after the convention, 54% said so. A week later, 60% said so. That fraction remained fairly constant for the rest of the campaign.[12]

Romney supporters moved in the opposite direction. They became more pessimistic in the wake of the May jobs report and this trend continued throughout the rest of the campaign.[13] The September jobs report had no real impact on them. In fact, many did not believe it. On the Friday the report was released, former General Electric CEO Jack Welch tweeted, "Unbelievable jobs numbers . . . these Chicago guys will do anything . . . can't debate so change numbers."[14] His suggestion of a government conspiracy—"Chicago guys" referred to Obama's campaign headquarters—was widely circulated. An October poll found that 85% of Republicans believed that the unemployment statistics had been manipulated, compared to only 23% of Democrats.[15] Partisanship affected not only how people perceived the economy but whether they thought partisanship had corrupted the measurement of the economy. Both findings demonstrate how partisanship filtered information during this campaign, as in politics generally, and helped keep "decided" voters from changing their minds.[16]

Persuadable voters. Obama's 52% of the December vote was only among respondents who preferred Obama or Romney. They were the majority of respondents but not all: 10% of registered voters, and 19% of all respondents, were undecided or preferred one of the other candidates in the race. These were the "persuadable voters," as we have called them. The question is why these persuadable voters ended up voting as they did. As of December, they were evenly balanced in their partisanship: 26% were Republicans, 47% independents, and 27% Democrats. They were somewhat pessimistic about the economy: 44% said it was getting worse, 47% said it was the same, and 8% said it was getting better. Their views of Obama were slightly more favorable than their views of Romney, but more striking is the fraction that had no opinion of Obama (25%) or Romney (41%). In December 2011, they truly seemed up for grabs. What these voters decided would affect how well the fundamentals forecast the outcome.

As Table 7.1 illustrates, many of them did not vote, but among those who did most chose either Romney or Obama, including those who originally said they preferred some other candidate. In fact, they were evenly split between Obama and Romney: 41% to 40%. (This belies the hoary conventional wisdom that undecided voters always "break for the challenger"—a rule that was widely debunked before 2012 but was still in regular circulation during the campaign.)[17] The even split of these voters helped ensure that neither Romney nor Obama gained much advantage from them.

The main reason these voters split evenly was because they arrived at a predictable decision—one largely consistent with their partisanship. Although many of these voters harbored concerns about their party's candidate, as we noted in chapter 5, the campaign appeared to allay those concerns.

Persuadable voters who were interviewed in December and then again in the last two weeks of the campaign became more favorable toward their party's candidate. In December, only 10% of persuadable Democrats had a very favorable opinion of Obama, but by the end 39% did. Most of the rest, 32%, had a "somewhat" favorable view. If we combine the "very" and "somewhat" categories, Obama's "favorables" increased nearly 30 points among persuadable Democrats—not to a level equal to that of Democrats who initially supported Obama but certainly to a level that made supporting Obama more palatable. The movement of persuadable Democrats to Obama was aided by their deteriorating views of Romney. In December, only 38% had a very or somewhat unfavorable view of Romney; 33% had no opinion. By the end of the campaign, 58% had an unfavorable view, and only 13% had no opinion. Persuadable Republicans behaved similarly: Romney's favorables jumped 19 points over the course of the campaign, while views of Obama—already unfavorable to begin with—became even more so.

Persuadable Democrats also came to hold views of the economy that were more in line with their partisanship. As Figure 7.3 shows, views of persuadable voters as a whole became, at most, a bit more positive during the campaign. This was largely because Democrats became less pessimistic: in December 2011, 40% said the economy was getting worse, 47% said it was the same, and 13% said it was getting better. By the end of the campaign, only 12% said the economy was getting worse, 70% said it was the same, and 19% said it was better. Persuadable Republicans and independents did not change their views. At the end of the campaign, 55% of these Republicans thought that the economy was getting worse, as did 42% of these independents. The majority of these independents, 52%, thought that the economy was about the same.

Given how partisanship came to shape persuadable voters' views of the candidates and the economy, it is not surprising that it shaped their votes as well. Among persuadable Democrats who reported voting, 71% ended up supporting Obama, 16% Romney, and the rest someone else. Among persuadable Republican voters, 69% ended up supporting Romney and 14% Obama. Persuadable independent voters broke 42%–31% in favor of Obama. We can track the increasing impact of partisanship on the vote intentions of persuadable voters by calculating the relationship between partisanship, measured in December, and vote intentions in each month before the election (further details are in the appendix). The top half of Figure 7.4 shows how the effect of partisanship, while important even in January, increased across these ten months. Because persuadable Republicans turned out at a higher rate than persuadable independents or Democrats, the combination of these three groups produced the 41%–40% split in Table 7.1.[18] Predictable partisanship among both decided and persuadable voters was the norm.

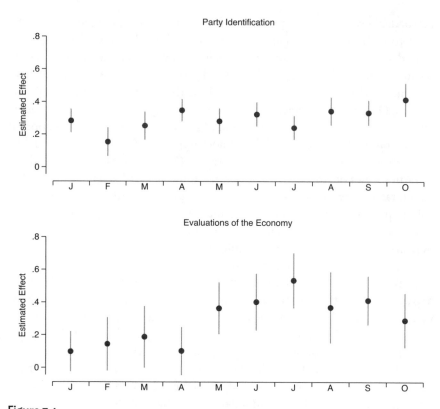

Figure 7.4.
Estimated effect of party identification and economic evaluations on the vote intentions of persuadable voters.
The figure presents the monthly estimated effect of party identification and economic perceptions on vote intentions, with 95% confidence intervals to capture the uncertainty in these estimates. Persuadable voters are those who said they were undecided or preferred a candidate other than Romney or Obama when first interviewed in December 2011. Data from YouGov polls.

We can go one step further to identify potential reasons why partisanship became more relevant for these persuadable voters. Thus far, we have been talking about how "the campaign" helped accentuate partisanship. But what about the campaign was important? Was it the ads, fieldwork, and other electioneering in the battleground states? Or was the increased relevance of partisanship a nationwide phenomenon—one perhaps attributable to the news coverage, debates, and other information that reached all the states? Using the post-election interviews, we compared how persuadable voters of different partisan stripes voted, both in battleground states and non-battleground states.[19] Living in a battleground state did not matter much for persuadable Republicans. But it did matter for persuadable Democrats—increasing their support of Obama by 7 points (to 76% in the battleground states from 69% in the other states). And it mattered for persuadable independents as well but in the opposite direction: they were about 7 points less likely to support Obama and 2 points more likely to support Romney (with the remaining difference going to another candidate).[20] All told, Obama did about 4 points better among persuadable voters in the battleground states than in the other states.

A campaign centered on the economy. The relationship between economic fundamentals and election outcomes—depicted in Figure 7.1—may not be inevitable. It may depend on the campaign. That campaigns can make fundamental factors more salient is a mainstay of the academic research on campaigns.[21] But this also depends on the decisions of the candidates themselves. In the 2000 presidential election, Al Gore was reticent to run on the Clinton administration's record, even though Clinton had presided over robust economic growth. Gore's campaign focused on issues besides the economy, largely domestic policy, and he ended up underperforming the economic fundamentals (see Figure 7.1) and ultimately losing the Electoral College. There was little chance of this in 2012, however, as we discussed in chapter 5. Both Obama and Romney centered their campaign messages on the economy, and it was prominent in news coverage as well.

Because of this, the relationship between people's initial views of the economy and their vote intentions should have become stronger over the course of the campaign. That is, views of the economy should have become a stronger influence on people's decision about whether to support Obama or Romney. This should be especially true for persuadable voters, whose views were not initially as strongly anchored by partisanship—although they became more so as the campaign went on. We examined the effect of views of the economy on the vote intentions of persuadable voters in each month from January through October, using the entire set of YouGov polls at our disposal. (Again, the appendix to this chapter provides further detail.) The bottom half of Figure 7.4 shows the trend in the estimated effect of economic evaluations.

As with party identification, the effect of economic evaluations strengthened over the course of the campaign. From January through April, the effects were small. But in May, the effect nearly doubled in size. It then peaked in July before falling somewhat in the fall, though remaining meaningful throughout.[22] To envision what these numbers mean, imagine a measure that ranged a total of 100 points—with someone who intended to vote for Romney scored 0, someone who intended to vote for Obama scored 100, and someone who was undecided or preferred another candidate scored in between, at 50. As of October, our results suggest that people who believed the economy was getting better would score 30 points more favorable to Obama on this scale relative to someone who thought the economy was getting worse.

An interesting question is why the effect was largest in July, especially since the bulk of the campaign advertising occurred in the fall. One reason is that the battleground state campaigning did not appear to make the economy more salient to voters. The effect of economic evaluations on vote intentions was not greater in battleground states than in other states.[23] A second, and admittedly speculative, reason has to do with how voters respond to economic bad news versus economic good news. In particular, they seem far more responsive to bad news.[24] For example, incumbents tend to be punished more for economic downturns than they are rewarded for economic growth. This is relevant to 2012 because, as Figure 7.2 demonstrates, the late spring and summer saw some of the worst economic news of the year, but the news began to improve in the fall. This may explain why the economy seemed more salient to persuadable voters earlier in the general election campaign than later.

Obama's victory was not necessarily unpredictable or surprising given the fundamentals. Such a statement might seem to suggest that the campaign did not matter at all. But that is not our argument. Several things could have gone off-track during the campaign to make that forecast wrong. One was the economy itself, but instead it continued plodding along—not growing quickly but growing quickly enough to reelect an incumbent. Another concerned partisanship: had significant numbers of decided or persuadable voters defected from the party they identified with, and especially if the defections had favored Obama or Romney, the ultimate outcome would have been less predictable. But as is typically true in presidential elections, the campaign itself helped ensure that did not happen. Finally, during the campaign, the economy itself became more salient to persuadable voters, although not necessarily as a direct result of campaigning by Romney and Obama. Had events made some other issue salient—as a terrorist attack could have made foreign policy and national security salient—a forecast based on economic indicators could have been wrong.

The key point is that fundamentals influence elections in part because the campaign brings them to the foreground. In some sense, the 2012 campaign helped "make" pre-election predictions like ours come true. It is noteworthy, too, that our argument conforms to what the campaigns were seeing. Here is one description of internal data from the Obama campaign:

> For the most part, however, the analytic tables demonstrated how *stable* the electorate was, and how *predictable* individual voters could

be. Polls from the media and academic institutions may have fluctu-
ated by the hour, but drawing on hundreds of data points to judge
whether someone was a likely voter proved more reliable than using
a seven-question battery like Gallup's to do the same. "When you
see this Pogo stick happening with the public data—the electorate is
just *not that volatile*," says Mitch Stewart, director of the Democratic
campaign group Organizing for America. The analytic data offered a
source of calm.[25]

Emphasis ours.

The "Gifts"

About a week after the election, Mitt Romney held a conference call with
fund-raisers and donors to his campaign. He credited Obama's victory to
"gifts" that the Obama administration had given Democratic constituencies—
"especially the African-American community, the Hispanic community, and
young people." Romney went on to single out such policy "gifts" as "forgive-
ness of college loan interests," "free contraceptives," and "Obamacare" as mobilizing young people. He cited Obamacare as mobilizing black and Hispanic
voters. He also suggested that "the amnesty for children of illegals"—Obama's
June 15 decision to allow children of illegal immigrants to live and work in
the United States without fear of deportation—helped Obama with Latinos.[26]

Romney's argument was roundly criticized, even by Republicans. Newt
Gingrich called it "just nuts." On *Meet the Press*, Senator Lindsay Graham
said, "We're in a big hole. We're not getting out of it by comments like that.
When you're in a hole, stop digging. He keeps digging." But Romney's argument was actually much more widely accepted than these comments would
suggest. Numerous postmortems suggested that the Republican Party needed
to soften its stance on immigration and moderate on issues like contraception
and abortion.

Underlying these prescriptions is what we might call the "what have you
done for me lately?" theory of voting behavior: the notion that demographic
groups choose candidates based on which candidate is better for their members' self-interest. Under this theory, certain demographic groups supported
Obama for idiosyncratic reasons. Young women gravitated to Obama because
of his stance on contraception. Latinos gravitated to Obama because of his
stance on immigration and health care reform. Working-class voters in Rust
Belt states gravitated to Obama because the government bailed out General
Motors and Chrysler. And so on.

There are two problems with this argument, however. The first is that so-cial science research has struggled to show that self-interest affects all political attitudes.[27] People are more likely to ground their attitudes in broader political predispositions and values. So whether they supported the Affordable Care Act, for example, was less about whether the act would "give" them health care and more about whether they supported government regulation generally or, even more simply, identified as Democrats. The second problem is that the "what have you done for me lately?" theory overestimates the relevance of the idiosyncrasies of individual groups and underestimates the broader national trends that affect all groups in similar ways. Campaigns often worry about what needs to be done to "shore up" loyalties among various groups, and advances in micro-targeting suggest that they can send groups of voters messages tailored directly to them. But national forces that are largely out of the candidates' con-trol, like the economy, also move groups around and arguably more so.

The evidence for these national forces can be seen in how similarly groups shifted between 2008 and 2012. The "swing" between these two elections was remarkably uniform across groups. Figure 7.5 shows Obama's margin among thirty-five different demographic groups in the 2008 and 2012 exit polls. If his margin were identical in each year within a particular group, that group's data point would fall right on top of the diagonal line. Most groups are below this line—indicating that Obama did worse among almost every group in 2012 relative to 2008, largely because the fundamentals did not work as strongly in his favor. When confronted with a pattern like this, Occam's razor suggests focusing on what groups had in common rather than supposing that most of them moved in similar ways but for completely different reasons.

Nevertheless, it is worth delving more deeply into the behavior of several of these groups, particularly ones that Romney believed received "gifts." Part of the reason is that at least one of these groups, Latinos, apparently bucked the trend: they were more supportive of Obama in 2012 than in 2008. And part of the reason is one other finding from political science research on self-interest and public opinion: self-interest can be a bigger influence on politi-cal attitudes when the benefits of policies are clear, visible, and tangible. One could argue that the gifts Obama allegedly gave to Democratic constituen-cies met this definition. We will examine three constituencies in particular: working-class voters who could have benefited from the auto bailout, women who may have supported the Obama administration's policies on contracep-tion and abortion, and Latinos who may have supported health care reform and the Obama administration's immigration policy.

The Rust Belt and the auto bailout. Did the government loans to General Mo-tors and Chrysler help Obama win votes in crucial battleground states like Ohio? In the wake of the election, many people thought so. Writing from

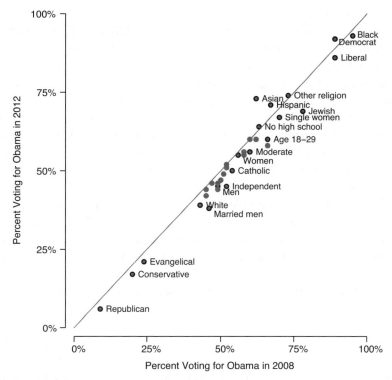

Figure 7.5.
The voting behavior of demographic groups in 2008 and 2012.
Source: National exit polls. Note: "single women" includes all non-married women.
Labels correspond to points with solid black outlines.

Columbus, *USA Today*'s Dennis Cauchon began his story thusly: "President Obama won the nation's most important swing state Tuesday with the help of one controversial issue—the auto bailout." The main evidence for this claim was: Obama won Ohio, the majority of Ohio voters in the exit poll said they supported the auto bailout, and Obama did better among union households in Ohio relative to 2008.[28]

But that is circumstantial evidence at best. Just because a majority of Ohioans said they supported the bailout does not mean that it was the cause of their vote. Better evidence would come from examining Obama's actual vote share in the Rust Belt and whether it was higher in places where there were auto plants. That is a much more precise measure of where the auto bailout might have helped auto workers, their families, their neighbors, and so on. If Obama did better in those places, relative to 2008, than in counties without plants, then we have clearer, though not conclusive, evidence that the auto bailout helped him.

Political scientist Dan Hopkins did exactly this analysis, both for the midwestern states often associated with the Rust Belt—Missouri, Illinois, Indiana, Michigan, Ohio, and West Virginia—and for much of the nation as a whole. Moreover, Hopkins accounted for other factors that might distinguish counties with auto plants from those without. For example, counties with auto plants—like Wayne County, Michigan, where Detroit is located—often have large populations of black voters who might support Obama for other reasons. Once other factors had been incorporated into the analysis, Obama did not do significantly better in counties with auto plants than in those without. There was no evidence that the auto bailout earned Obama additional votes in precisely the places where its effect should have been largest.[29]

This does not mean the bailout was irrelevant, however. Perhaps its effect on the election had less to do with the economics of the Rust Belt and more to do with the overall economy. Had there been no bailout, the resulting loss of jobs and personal income may have weakened the economy even further, thereby endangering Obama's reelection bid. But if so, this would have been more evidence for the importance of the national economy, not the "what have you done for me lately?" theory.

Women, and the "war" on them. The election year presented the Republican Party with a series of incidents that, to many observers, damaged its standing among women. In January, a controversy arose about whether the Obama administration would require religious institutions to provide contraception to employees—leading to a White House compromise on February 10. In the wake of this, the House Committee on Oversight and Government held a hearing on contraception and was attacked for inviting no women to testify. At about this time, presidential candidate Rick Santorum spoke out against birth control, saying it is "a license to do things in the sexual realm that is counter to how things are supposed to be." A prominent supporter of Santorum's campaign, Foster Friess, then suggested that women could hold an aspirin "between their knees" as a form of birth control. Two weeks later, House Democrats organized their own hearing on contraception and invited Sandra Fluke, a Georgetown University law student who was not allowed to appear at the earlier hearing and advocated for including contraception coverage in the university's health care plan. In response, talk radio host Rush Limbaugh called Fluke a "slut" and a "prostitute" who "wants to be paid to have sex." Obama then called Fluke to express his support. Meanwhile, House Democrats began fund-raising around the slogan "The War on Women."

Once the general election campaign was under way, Obama ran commercials attacking Romney on these issues. In one ad, a woman said that it was "scary time to be a woman" and that Romney was "so out of touch." The ad said that Romney opposed requiring insurance companies to cover contraception and supported a bill that would outlaw abortion even in cases of rape or incest.[30] On August 19, this very topic came up again after Republican Senate candidate Todd Akin of Missouri was asked about abortion in cases of rape. He said, "First of all, from what I understand from doctors, that's really rare. If it's a legitimate rape, the female body has ways to try to shut that whole thing down," before going on to suggest that it was the rapist, not the child, that should be punished. This resulted in a firestorm of protest, and Akin's poll numbers dropped by several points. (He went on to lose to incumbent Claire McCaskill.) Then, in the second presidential debate on October 16, Romney responded to a question about fair pay for women by asserting that, as Massachusetts governor, he had actively tried to find women to serve in his cabinet: "I went to a number of women's groups and said, 'Can you help us find folks,' and they brought us whole binders full of women." The "binders" comment was also mocked and went on to become an Internet meme. Finally, on October 23, Republican Senate candidate Richard Mourdock of Indiana said in a debate that "even if life begins in that horrible situation of rape, that is something God intended to happen." No wonder, then, that the Obama campaign believed the issues of abortion and contraception benefited them. Press Secretary Jen Psaki said, "The more we're talking about women's issues, women's healthcare, the differences between the candidates, the better it is for us."[31]

Before we examine the "War on Women" and its impact in 2012, one piece of context is important to understand. The well-known gender gap in partisanship and voting behavior—whereby women are more likely than men to identify as Democrats and vote for Democratic candidates—did not emerge because of changes in women's behavior. The gender gap has grown because *men* have changed their political views, becoming more Republican over the last several decades.[32] In 1952, 59% of women identified with or leaned toward the Democratic Party. In 2008, almost the same fraction, 55%, did so. By contrast, Democratic Party identification dropped 13 points among men during this period (from 60% to 47%).[33] Thus we should not unwittingly fall prey to what writer Katha Pollitt calls the "Smurfette Principle"—"boys are the norm, girls are the variation"—and assume that any differences between women and men derive only from the interests or values of women, or from how women respond to information during a campaign. In this case, men are the variation.[34]

A first piece of evidence involves how men and women differed in their attention to controversies about contraception and abortion. When we asked about two specific contraception controversies during the campaign, women were *less* likely than men to know about these controversies. In a March 3–6 poll, respondents were asked to pick which of three statements was Santorum's

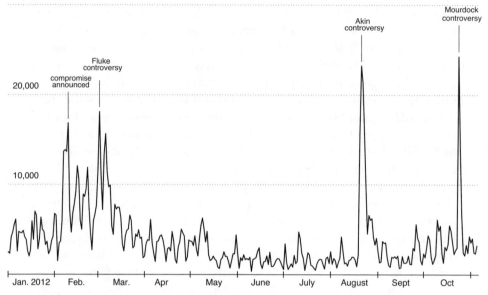

Figure 7.6.

Media coverage of topics related to contraception and abortion.

The figure includes mentions of "contraception," "contraception mandate," "contraception coverage mandate," "birth control," "birth control mandate," "abortion," "rape," "Sandra Fluke," "Todd Akin," and "Richard Mourdock." Data from General Sentiment.

position on birth control, one of which was the statement quoted earlier. Only 36% of men and 26% of women picked the correct statement; most said they did not know. We also asked who had called "a female Georgetown University law student" after Limbaugh attacked her. About 57% of men, but only 44% of women, said that it was Obama. This does not suggest that women were particularly attentive to news about contraception.[35]

To understand how women did or did not respond to all of the controversies in 2012 about contraception and abortion, we begin by charting news media attention to these controversies. Figure 7.6 presents the number of mentions of the prominent figures in this debate—Fluke, Akin, and Mourdock—as well as general mentions of issues like contraception and abortion.[36] The figure shows how the debate about health care reform's contraception mandate initially created attention to these topics, culminating in the February 10 compromise. Afterward the controversies surrounding Fluke and Limbaugh, Akin, and Mourdock generated additional spikes in news coverage.

Did any of this coverage affect attitudes about the presidential race? We matched respondents in YouGov surveys to the volume of coverage that aired around the time they were interviewed. The question is whether attitudes about Obama and Romney were different when this coverage spiked and, if so, whether women's attitudes shifted—in particular, whether they shifted in ways that favored Obama. We subdivided women into two groups—those under forty-five and those forty-five and older—to capture any differences based on the likelihood of future childbirth.

We could find no consistent relationship between the volume of coverage about contraception and abortion and a host of attitudes: vote intentions, overall views of the candidates, approval of Obama's job performance, approval of Obama's performance on abortion, or enthusiasm for voting in November. This was true both for older and younger women. (The appendix to this chapter has further details.)

For the general election period, June–November, we also compared the vote intentions of people living in battleground states to those living in other states. Perhaps women living in battleground states—who were more likely to have seen ads about contraception and abortion or be contacted by the campaigns about these issues—were distinctive. We found little evidence of this as well. We also looked month by month, in case the differences between non-battleground and battleground states increased with time as the campaign became more vigorous. Only in July did women in battleground states appear even slightly distinctive: relative to women in non-battleground states, they were about 3 points more favorable toward Obama if we imagine vote intentions as a 100-point scale.[37] Interestingly, July was when the Obama campaign began its advertising on abortion. But there were no differences between women in battleground and non-battleground states in later weeks, perhaps because abortion was rarely mentioned in Democratic ads after the summer. Given the short-lived effect of ads generally, any effects of these July ads likely did not persist for months on end.

Here is one last test of whether the issue of abortion in particular boosted Obama's support among women. We know from the December 2011 interview whether people were initially Obama supporters, Romney supporters, supporters of some other candidate, or undecided. We can then see how their attitudes toward abortion, along with other factors, affected whom voters in each of these four groups ended up supporting when interviewed after the election in November 2012. That is, we can see how attitudes toward abortion affected any shifts in vote decisions, as it might have if the "War on Women" changed people's minds. We can address various questions. Did support for abortion help ensure that Obama's initial supporters, especially his female supporters, stuck by him in the end? Did support for abortion end up driving Romney's initial supporters, especially his female supporters, to Obama? Were attitudes toward abortion consequential in how undecided voters broke? Most important, we seek to estimate the overall effects of all of these processes: how much did abortion attitudes contribute to Obama's vote share in November?

Perhaps unsurprisingly, given the issue's longstanding salience in American politics, abortion attitudes were related to the voting decisions of both men and women. Among men, the most important consequence of a pro-choice attitude was to reinforce the loyalties of initial Obama supporters. The most pro-choice man who supported Obama in December 2011 was 9 points more likely to support him in November, compared to the most pro-life man. But among women, the most important consequence of a pro-choice attitude was to build support for Obama among those who did not initially support him. Compared to the most pro-life woman, the most pro-choice woman was only 2 points more likely to support Obama on Election Day if she initially supported Obama, but 9 points more likely if she initially supported Romney, 31 points if she initially supported another candidate, and 30 points if she initially was undecided. The apparent impact of abortion attitudes exists over and above other influences that may have induced changes in voting behavior over these months—such as party identification or attitudes about government regulation of the economy. Clearly, then, abortion attitudes helped account for how both men and women voted—and how they ended up at their final choices. (The appendix to this chapter has further detail.)

But did the impact of abortion attitudes affect the candidates' *overall* vote share? That is a very different question. Just because pro-choice and pro-life voters tended to make different decisions on Election Day does not mean that the issue of abortion gave either candidate a net advantage. If, for example, undecided female voters were evenly split between pro-choice and pro-life attitudes, then any influence of abortion attitudes on their ultimate decision would send equal numbers of female voters into the Romney and Obama camps. We therefore estimated the contribution of abortion attitudes to the total vote share of each candidate. This calculation is specific to the particular measures, model, and sample in our analysis, so we must be cautious in any generalizations.

With that caveat stated, here is the striking finding: abortion attitudes appeared to contribute more to Obama's vote share among men, not among women. Among men, the contribution of abortion attitudes was about 1 point of vote share. This was mainly due to the fact that abortion attitudes helped ensure that men who were initially Obama supporters remained Obama supporters. Because most of this group leaned to the pro-choice side, the combination of that leaning and the impact of abortion attitudes produced a net advantage for Obama from this issue.

But among women, abortion attitudes contributed very little to Obama's overall vote share. Among women who initially supported Romney or another candidate, abortion attitudes benefited Romney more than Obama—mainly because these women leaned to the pro-life side. Among women who initially supported Obama or were undecided, abortion attitudes ended up benefiting Obama. Altogether, neither candidate gained much of an advantage from this issue. It ultimately netted Obama less than a tenth of a point of vote share. To see why Obama did not benefit all that much, consider women who were originally undecided in December 2011. Their attitudes toward abortion were not tilted much to either side: 27% called themselves pro-life, 28% called themselves pro-choice, 29% said they were both, and the rest said neither or were unsure—to draw on one of the questions we used to measure attitudes toward abortion. The salience of abortion helped Obama a little bit among this group, but ultimately it produced new supporters for both Obama and Romney, not Obama alone.

Ultimately, despite the Obama campaign's claim that women's health was an advantageous issue for them, news coverage of the controversies about contraception and abortion did not appear to change women's vote intentions or views of the candidates. And although attitudes about abortion were related to how vote decisions evolved over the course of the campaign, this did not produce much advantage for either candidate—at least in the particular data we have analyzed. None of this means that the controversies surrounding Sandra Fluke, Todd Akin, and Richard Mourdock—and, by extension, Mitt Romney—were things that the Republican Party can afford to repeat. These controversies may have cost the Republicans two Senate seats, after all. But the impact of the "War on Women" in the presidential election appears to have been muted at best.

Latinos. On Election Day, the strength of Latino and Asian voters' support for Obama surprised many observers. Although Obama's winning margin was over 3 points lower in 2012 than in 2008, it was 4 points greater among Latinos and 11 points greater among Asians according to the exit poll.[38] This led to a variety of theories as to why. One was that Romney took a position on immigration during the Republican primary that was too conservative. The *National Journal's* Ronald Brownstein made this argument:

> Of all Romney's primary-season decisions, the most damaging was his choice to repel the challenges from Perry and Gingrich by attacking them from the right—and using immigration as his cudgel. That process led Romney to embrace a succession of edgy, conservative positions anathema to many Hispanics, including denouncing Texas for providing in-state tuition to the children of illegal immigrants; praising Arizona's immigration-enforcement law; and, above all,

promising to make life so difficult for the estimated 11 million illegal immigrants that they would "self-deport."[39]

The *Wall Street Journal*'s editorial board said that Romney's "single worst decision may have been to challenge Texas Governor Rick Perry in the primaries by running to his right on immigration."[40] Quite quickly, this theory became accepted as fact. One *New York Times* piece began: "After a presidential election in which Latino voters rewarded President Obama while punishing Republicans for their positions on immigration, Republican leaders and prominent conservatives moved quickly this week to shift to new ground, saying they could support some kind of legislation to fix illegal immigration."[41] As that piece made clear, even Republicans believed, without any definitive evidence, that their stance on immigration was hurting the party. Some in the Romney campaign also believed as much.[42]

Another theory about Latinos focused on Obama and his "gifts." According to this theory, Obama's health care plan and especially his June 15 executive action to allow the children of illegal immigrants to remain in the United States without fear of deportation boosted his support among Latinos.[43] Latinos were, to be sure, very supportive of Obama's action. The vast majority of them supported giving undocumented children and youth permanent resident status as well as a path to citizenship.[44] But that alone was no guarantee that this issue or immigration generally drove Latinos' votes on Election Day.

To assess the behavior of Latinos in this election, it is important to go beyond the exit poll. Exit polls are very useful instruments, but they are not designed to produce reliable samples of subgroups within the electorate. This fact has bedeviled exit poll samples of Latinos in particular. In 2004, George W. Bush won a vaunted 44% of the Latino vote in the major national exit poll. But this figure was strangely out of line with nearly every pre-election poll—in which Kerry led Bush among Latinos by a much larger margin than in the exit poll, as he did among almost every Latino subgroup, including likely voters, college graduates, and other groups that would be more predisposed to turn out.[45] The same thing may have happened in 2010.[46] In 2012, there was no such discrepancy—the exit poll was in line with pre-election polls of Latinos, such those by the firm Latino Decisions, which had Obama winning 73%–24% in its last pre-election poll. This gave more credence to the exit poll results in 2012, but the general point still holds: we should be cautious about taking exit poll estimates at face value. Moreover, even if the exit poll was accurate, the mere fact that Latinos supported Obama at a slightly higher rate in 2012 than 2008 tells us nothing about *why* they did so. We need to probe more deeply.

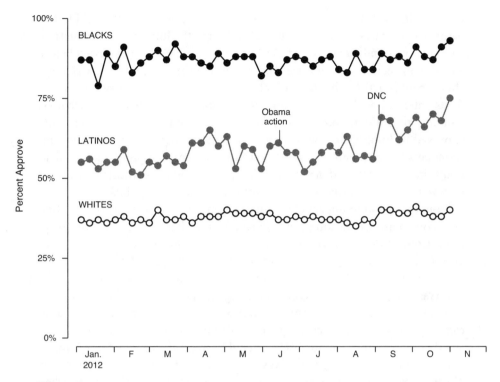

Figure 7.7.
Obama approval among whites, blacks, and Latinos.
Data are weekly aggregates from Gallup polls. "Obama action" denotes his June 15 decision to allow undocumented children to remain without threat of deportation. "DNC" denotes the first day of the Democratic National Convention.

If Obama's "gifts" mattered, we would expect that Latinos' perceptions of the candidates or their vote intentions shifted in the wake of Obama's executive action on June 15. Figure 7.7 shows Obama's approval rating during 2012 among whites, blacks, and Latinos, drawing on weekly Gallup surveys. There was no bump in approval among Latinos in the immediate aftermath of Obama's announcement. Indeed, a few weeks after the announcement, his approval among Latinos was actually several points lower than before it—although there is no reason to attribute this dip to the announcement. More important in rallying the support of Latinos was the Democratic National Convention. This is not surprising: most Latinos identify as Democrats, and we have already shown that the convention improved Obama's standing among Democrats.

It may be, though, that Obama's action on immigration improved how Latinos evaluated his handling of immigration specifically. In a fortunate bit of timing, a Latino Decisions/America's Voice poll was in the field in five battleground states from June 12 to 21, bracketing the June 15 executive action. Although respondents were not randomly assigned to be interviewed before and after the action, and thus we must be cautious in interpreting any changes after Obama's action, the data reveal an interesting pattern. Among respondents interviewed before the June 15 decision, 45% approved of Obama's handling of immigration. Among those interviewed after the decision, 61% approved of him.[47] There was similar movement after June 15 in Latino respondents' vote intentions and enthusiasm: Obama's support increased 10 points in a head-to-head matchup with Romney, and the percentage who said they were "very enthusiastic" about voting increased by 7 points.

But the apparent impact of Obama's action was only temporary. In Latino Decisions national tracking polls, Obama's vote share did notch upward in July—from a 66%–23% lead to a 70%–22% lead. But his lead faded by August. In an August 24–30 poll, Obama's lead was 64%–30%. After that, Obama began to gain ground as the Democratic convention got under way.

Was this later rally to Obama among Latinos tied to immigration? It seems unlikely on its face. Immigration was not a very prominent issue in campaign advertising: according to the Campaign Media Analysis Group, less than 1% of either Democratic or Republican ad airings mentioned immigration. Moreover, immigration was not the highest priority among Latinos. The economy was a higher priority regardless of whether Latinos were asked their priorities in an open-ended fashion or whether they chose from a set list of policies.[48] This is not to say that it was unimportant—it was the second most cited issue when Latino Decisions asked the open-ended question—but it may not have been paramount.

A more direct test of how much Obama's "gifts" propelled Latinos toward Obama involves two steps. First, we assess the impact of attitudes toward both immigration and health care reform in December 2011, before much of the fall campaign but after the passage of health care reform as well as Romney's statements about immigration in the early primary debates. Second, as in the previous analysis of abortion attitudes and the vote decisions of men and women, we assess how immigration and health care attitudes may have affected whether and how Latinos changed their votes between December and November 2012—and ultimately how much each issue contributed to Obama's vote share. We compare Latinos to non-Hispanic whites (Anglos) to get a sense of whether any patterns among Latinos were distinctive. We measured attitudes toward immigration with a scale combining answers to three questions: whether illegal immigrants make a contribution to American society or are a drain, whether there should be a pathway to citizenship for illegal immigrants, and whether it should be easier or harder for foreigners to immigrate to the United States. We measured health care attitudes with items asking whether respondents agreed that it was "the responsibility of the federal government to see to it that everyone had health care coverage" and whether they wanted the health care reform law to be expanded, repealed, or kept the same. (Further details are in the appendix to this chapter.)[49]

In December 2011, attitudes toward both immigration and health care reform were associated with vote intentions, and among both Latinos and Anglos. However, the net impact of those issues differed across the two groups. Among Latinos, who tended to have pro-immigration and pro-Obamacare attitudes, the impact of these issues advantaged Obama—netting him over a point of vote share. Among whites these issues, especially health care reform, netted Romney about 3 points of vote share. This is even after we accounted for the influence of other powerful factors affecting vote intentions, such as party identification and attitudes toward other economic and social issues. Thus both issues appeared to be important, and, among Latinos, favored Obama—as the "gifts" hypothesis might suggest.

But this hypothesis falls short in another respect. There is little evidence that attitudes toward immigration or health care reform helped Obama gain much vote share during the campaign itself. When we examined how vote decisions changed from December 2011 to November 2012, immigration attitudes were important among Latinos—and more so than among Anglos—but they contributed only about an additional half a point of vote share to Obama within this group. With health care attitudes, the opposite happened. The total impact of this issue on changes in vote decisions was in Romney's favor, not Obama's—netting Romney about 3 points of vote share among Latinos. This is because health care attitudes mattered most among Latinos who initially supported Romney or another candidate. These Latinos tended to oppose health care reform, and thus the overall impact of the issue was to keep them in or move them to Romney's camp.[50]

The "gifts" theory focused on how Latino support for immigration or health care reform advantaged Obama—and both issues did to some extent, as was apparent at the end of 2011. These issues appeared to help voters make an initial vote choice but did little to gain Obama votes over the course of the campaign—and may even have cost him votes. Had health care reform mattered less, some of these Latinos might have moved toward Obama. We emphasize "might have" because our analysis cannot definitively establish any such hypothetical. But it is worth considering whether if most Latinos who supported health care reform lined up behind Obama early, the remaining Latinos may have been pushed toward Romney in part because of their own concerns about health care reform.

To be sure, our analysis—any analysis—is limited. To pick one limita-tion, our measures of attitudes toward immigration could have been more extensive. They tapped relevant debates about this issue but not every debate, such as the one over the DREAM Act. Another caveat is that our analysis cannot speak to alternative scenarios or counterfactuals, including the most important: what if Romney had adopted more moderate positions on immi-gration rather than attacking Perry from the right? It is an open question. Romney certainly seemed to regret his stance, saying after the election that "we weren't effective in taking my message primarily to minority voters—to Hispanic-Americans, to African-Americans, other minorities. That was a real weakness."[51]

We are skeptical, however, that Romney himself was the central problem. Part of the challenge that Romney faced among Latinos was the Republican Party's challenge—just as Romney's "empathy gap" has been endemic to his party, as we noted in chapter 5. The GOP was not in high standing among Latinos well before Romney was the nominee. For example, in a Latino De-cisions poll conducted in May 2011, 48% said that the Democratic Party was doing "a good job reaching out to Latinos," but only 12% said that of the Re-publican Party.[52] To be sure, a substantial minority was not happy with the Democrats—31% said that Democrats "don't care too much" about Latinos—but clearly the Republicans fared worse. It is not clear Romney could have undone that single-handedly. For Romney to do much better with Latinos, the Republican Party probably needed to be doing much better before the presidential race began. For that reason, nothing about our analysis should be construed as arguing that Republicans can safely ignore a fast-growing de-mographic like Latinos. If Republicans want to make enduring gains among Latinos, they will need a more sustained initiative within the party and not simply a presidential nominee who says all the right things.

There is also a larger lesson to be drawn from the behavior of demo-graphic groups in 2012, such as the many we present in Figure 7.5. Much as partisans behaved in predictable ways in 2012, so did the constituent elements of each party's coalition. That is, much as the campaign rallied partisans, it also reconstituted the party coalitions. During elections we often read stories about whether a candidate is "losing" a group of voters who supported him in a previous election. In 2012, there were stories about whether Obama was losing young people and Jews, to name two examples.[53] But in reality, there are no big swings from election to election among most groups. And what swings do exist depend a great deal on factors *common* to almost all groups, such as the fundamental conditions in the country. This is not to say that any one group's particular interests or opinions are by definition irrelevant. There is more variation in election-to-election swings among smaller subgroups—for example, older low-income whites living in the South.[54] But these variations should not obscure the general pattern. And to the extent that swings among demographic groups are similar, it begs a final question: despite the increasing ability of campaigns to "micro-target" voters using detailed demographic and political data, what if voters respond more to broad, untargeted messages and information? The ability of campaigns to micro-target has not been matched by evidence that microtargeted appeals are more effective.[55]

Was Romney Too Conservative?

"If I hear anybody say it was because Romney wasn't conservative enough I'm going to go nuts." So said Republican senator Lindsay Graham the day before the election.[56] He was talking about a potential Romney loss and what it should mean for how Republicans thought about the party's ideology and positions on issues. After the election, moderates and conservatives each insisted that Romney's loss vindicated their personal beliefs. To moderates, Romney's conservatism was the problem. To conservatives, he was a "meandering moderate." But there was one thing that no one seemed to notice: compared to Obama, Romney was ideologically closer to more voters all along.

In December 2011, the 45,000 YouGov respondents were shown a five-category ideological scale—ranging from "very liberal" to "very conservative"—and asked to place themselves, Romney, and Obama on that scale. If we imagine that the scale runs from 0 to 100, where 100 means very conservative, then the average respondent was almost at the midpoint—labeled "moderate"—with a score of 55 (although 13% were not sure and did not place themselves). On average, respondents placed Obama at 26 but Romney at 62. That is, Romney was perceived to be only 7 points away from the average respondent, but Obama was perceived to be 29 points away.

However, more respondents (26%) were not sure about where to place Romney than were unsure about where to place Obama (16%). This makes sense: Obama was a more familiar figure than Romney at that point. Did the campaign help give voters more information about the candidates, allowing some to form perceptions of the candidates' ideologies and perhaps shifting the perceptions of those who already had some idea? Both things occurred. The percentage who were unsure where to place the candidates declined over the course of the campaign. By the weekend before Election Day, 17% could not place Romney and 9% could not place Obama.

Perceptions also changed, as we show in Figure 7.8. The average respondent did not waver much, remaining slightly right of center. Perceptions of Obama and Romney grew more polarized. In the first survey in which these

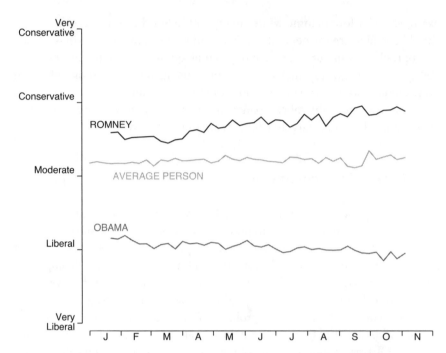

Figure 7.8.
Perceptions of Obama's, Romney's, and voter's own ideological position.
The lines are where, on average, respondents placed themselves, Romney, and Obama
on this ideological scale. Data are from YouGov polls.

questions were included—in mid-January 2012—respondents placed Obama
at an average of 29 on the hypothetical 100-point scale. By the end of the
campaign, perceptions of Obama shifted 5 points in the liberal direction. For
Romney, the trend was in the opposite direction and a bit more pronounced:
average perceptions shifted from approximately 65 in January to 61 in March
but then increased by 11 points to 72 at the end of the election.[57] But even this
shift in perceptions of Romney still left him significantly closer to more voters
than Obama was. The weekend before the election, 52% of voters placed themselves closer to Romney than Obama, while 38% placed themselves closer to
Obama. The rest saw themselves as equally close to both. Romney also had
this advantage, as he did throughout the campaign, among potential groups
of swing voters, such as true independents or voters who as of December 2011
did not prefer either Obama or Romney.

   We can quantify more precisely what Obama's greater distance from the
average voter might have cost him. We focus here on truly independent voters,
who, because they are not influenced by partisanship, appear able to vote in

relatively unbiased ways based on where they perceive the candidates to stand ideologically.[58] For the sake of a simple illustration, imagine that these voters made their decisions in November based only on how far they stood from where they believed each of the two candidates to be. Thinking about voting this way means assuming that voters choose candidates based on where they think those candidates stand rather than choosing a candidate and then "relocating" the candidates ideologically to rationalize that choice—such as by imagining that their preferred candidate is now ideologically closer to them. Even for independents without strong partisan biases, this assumption may not hold.

But if we proceed with this illustration, it suggests that Obama's greater distance from the average independent could have cost him vote share. The further independent voters were from either Romney or Obama, the less likely they were to support him.[59] Had each independent perceived Obama to be at the same ideological position that he or she perceived Romney to be, Obama would have gained nearly 17 points. Again, this is assuming that only ideological perceptions drove voting, so 17 points is higher than it would have been in reality. And other factors may have mattered more for voting than ideology, making Obama's ideological disadvantage less of a liability. The point of this exercise is simply to show that Obama's greater distance from the average independent voter was plausibly consequential.

Of course, we could attach even more caveats to this analysis. For example, these omnibus measures of ideology did not capture specific issues, like Medicare or immigration. But the basic finding deserves consideration. In the weeks and months after the election, almost all of the conversation about ideology and issues centered on whether Romney was too extreme. Wrote *Slate*'s Jacob Weisberg, "Romney is not a right-wing extremist. To win the nomination, though, he had to feign being one."[60] Whether Obama was too extreme rarely, if ever, came up. But Obama appeared to be the candidate more ideologically out of step with American voters in 2012.

Obama's Race

"Making the Election about Race." That was the title of an August column in the *New York Times* by Thomas Edsall. It was occasioned by two Romney campaign advertisements. The first attacked Obama for allegedly "gutting" the requirement that people who received welfare benefits seek work. The second said that the Affordable Care Act ("Obamacare") would cut over $700 million from Medicare to create a "massive new government program that's not for you." In both ads, Edsall saw "a racially freighted resource competition pitting middle class white voters against the minority poor."[61]

The influence of race has been a chronic feature of Obama's campaigns for president and indeed his presidency. Even as Obama's presence on the Democratic ticket did seem reduce the level of racial prejudice among Americans during the 2008 campaign, it increased again after the campaign was over and he took office.[62] Moreover, Obama's candidacy in 2008 and his subsequent presidency made racial attitudes far stronger predictors of political attitudes. People's attitudes toward blacks have been related to many things associated with Obama, including not only their vote in the 2008 election but also their attitudes toward policies he has promoted, such as health care reform—even their attitudes toward his dog.[63] As we described in chapter 2, the net impact of racial attitudes seems to hurt Obama: that is, he loses more because of sentiments less favorable to blacks than he gains from sentiments more favorable to blacks. The question is whether this was true in the 2012 election as well.

Using the measure of racial attitudes that we introduced in chapter 2—"racial resentment"—we compared how racial attitudes were associated with the vote in both 2012 and 2008. In 2008, YouGov administered a similar election survey that included this same measure of racial resentment. Across the two surveys, there was very little change in the level of racial resentment. If we imagine racial resentment as a 100-point scale, the mean as of December 2011 was only 2 points lower than in 2008.[64] (These items were asked in the first interview with respondents.)

The effect of racial attitudes on vote decisions in the 2012 election resembled the predictable pattern others have uncovered: among whites, those with more positive attitudes toward blacks were more likely to vote for Obama than were people with more negative attitudes. This finding comes from a model of vote decisions in both years that also accounted for several other political and demographic factors, which we describe further in the appendix to this chapter. The apparent effect of racial resentment among whites was slightly smaller in 2012 than in 2008 but still quite potent. In 2008, a white person who expressed the least positive attitudes toward blacks according to this measure was 38 points less likely to vote for Obama than was a white person who expressed the most positive attitudes. In 2012, the comparable effect was 30 points.[65] Above and beyond factors like party identification and ideology, racial attitudes were strongly related to attitudes toward Obama in both elections.

Did racial resentment in 2012 affect not only how people voted in November but also whether and how their vote decisions evolved over the course of the campaign? As in previous analyses, we estimated how much racial resentment was associated with any shifts in the decisions of white voters between December 2011 and November 2012. After accounting for other political and demographic factors, we found that whites with less favorable views of blacks were more likely to shift away from Obama if they initially supported him in December 2011, to remain supportive of Romney if they initially supported Romney, and to end up supporting Romney if they supported another candidate or were undecided in December 2011—that is, were "potentially persuadable voters." The apparent impact of racial resentment on transitions was much larger among these persuadable voters, all else equal. And because persuadable voters' views of blacks were more unfavorable than favorable, on average, racial resentment may have cost Obama as much as 6 points among these voters.

Was the impact of racial resentment during the 2012 campaign, particularly among persuadable voters, a consequence of advertising or news coverage of issues related to race, like Romney's welfare ad? We lack a systematic test of this proposition, but several pieces of evidence make us skeptical. For one, when voters were interviewed after the election, the association between racial resentment and their reported votes was not any greater in battleground states than non-battleground states—as one might expect if advertising and other electioneering had made race more salient. For another, the association between racial resentment and any changes in vote decisions over the campaign was also no greater in battleground states and non-battleground states.

Why were differences between battleground states and other states so muted? One possible explanation is that the campaign's discourse did not have the racial undertones that some commentators perceived in Romney's attacks regarding welfare and Medicare. Or perhaps any racial undertones did not affect voters in profound ways. This seemed true with regard to voters' reactions to the welfare ad, for example. In an August YouGov poll, respondents were randomly assigned to watch this ad or not to watch it via a video embedded in the online survey instrument. They were then asked a series of questions about whether Romney and Obama's policies would help or hurt the poor, the middle class, the wealthy, African Americans, and white Americans. Among those who saw the ad, racial resentment became more strongly related to beliefs about whether Romney's policies would be good for the poor, the middle class, and blacks. But there was no such effect on views of Obama's policies, which likely were already strongly tied to racial attitudes. Ultimately, racial messages in the 2012 campaign may not have been sustained or potent enough to make attitudes toward Obama much more racialized than they already were. The impact of race may have been more a chronic feature of how some people think about a black president and not something magnified by battleground state campaigning.

Could racial attitudes have cost Obama at the ballot box in 2012? To answer this question, we first simulated Obama's vote share given racial attitudes as they were and then after shifting all voters' racial attitudes toward a hypothetical neutral position (the midpoint of the racial resentment scale). That is, we "replaced" both favorable and unfavorable attitudes with neutral attitudes. When we performed such a simulation in chapter 2, we found that Obama's approval rating increased by almost 4 points—suggesting that unfavorable attitudes toward blacks were, on the whole, depressing support for Obama. That finding paralleled some published analyses of voting behavior in the 2008 election. In the 2012 election, this same simulation produced almost exactly the same effect: a 4-point increase in Obama's vote share. We also simulated the effects of eliminating only unfavorable attitudes toward blacks and replacing them with neutral attitudes. This produced a slightly larger 5-point increase in Obama's vote share.[66]

As we noted in chapter 2 and will emphasize here, such simulations are inherently limited. They are based on simple statistical models and involve fairly unrealistic hypotheticals. One cannot infer, for example, that had a white Democratic candidate run against Romney, that candidate would have outperformed Obama by 4 or 5 points—thereby winning in a veritable landslide. Other factors may have limited that white Democrat's appeal. In 2008, for example, some simulations suggest that Hillary Clinton would not have done substantially better than did Barack Obama had she been the nominee.[67] Similarly, in a world in which racial attitudes were less strongly associated with attitudes toward Obama, other factors might have come to the fore and held Obama to roughly the same vote share that he earned in 2012. The upshot of these simulations is only that racial attitudes are prevalent and salient enough to plausibly (though not conclusively) depress support for Obama.

The Obama presidency has always presented the possibility of a "post-racial America"—one in which negative feelings toward or stereotypes about African Americans play a smaller role in our politics. In reality, the opposite has happened: Obama's 2008 campaign and first term as president heightened the role of racial attitudes—in presidential approval, in attitudes toward certain public policies, and at the ballot box. The substantial impact of racial attitudes in the 2012 election, while not as large as in 2008, only confirmed the ongoing salience of race.

The Stained Glass Ceiling

In a survey conducted during the 2008 Republican presidential primary, the political scientists David Campbell, John Green, and Quin Monson did an experiment. They gave people information about Mitt Romney and then asked them if this information made them more or less likely to support Romney. Everybody was told that Romney was a businessman, the former governor of

Massachusetts, and the head of the 2002 Winter Olympics. They also heard that he had been married for thirty-nine years and had raised five sons. One random subset of people was then told that he was "a local leader in his church." A different random subset of people was told that Romney was "a local leader of the Church of Jesus Christ of Latter-day Saints, often called the Mormon Church." Being told that Romney was merely a church leader had no effect on people's willingness to vote for him. But being told that he was a Mormon church leader reduced people's willingness to vote for him by 30 points. Campbell and colleagues concluded that this helped explain why Romney could not break the "stained glass ceiling" in 2008.[68]

Fast-forward to 2012, and it seemed as if little had changed. Nearly 20% of Americans said that they would not vote for a Mormon for president—a number exceeded only by the fraction who would not vote for a Muslim or an atheist.[69] Larger numbers said that they would be less likely to vote for a candidate who was Mormon.[70] Almost a third of Americans said that they did not believe that Mormons were Christians, as did 42% of white evangelicals—an important part of the Republican base. All of this raises the question: did his Mormonism hurt Romney at the polls in November?

There was actually reason to think it would not. About 40% of registered voters did not even know that Romney was Mormon in the first place. And Mormonism, while present in some news coverage, was not a major theme of either campaign.[71] At one point in the summer of 2011, the Obama campaign appeared to threaten that they would at least allude to Romney's religion, as one Obama advisor said that "There's a weirdness factor with Romney, and it remains to be seen how he wears with the public."[72] This created a hue and cry, and the Obama campaign never said much about Romney's religion afterward. Meanwhile, Romney himself spent most of the campaign avoiding the subject of the Mormon Church, having been shocked by the anti-Mormonism he encountered on the trail in 2008.[73] He worked mainly behind the scenes to earn the support of prominent evangelical leaders like Franklin Graham (and was successful).[74] Only toward the end of the campaign, starting around the Republican National Convention, did Romney change his mind, inviting Mormons to offer testimonials at the convention, citing his experience as a missionary and pastor in the second debate, inviting the press to attend church with him, and so on.

On its face, Mormonism did not seem much of a hindrance. For example, Romney's support among white evangelicals was comparable to that of recent Republican presidential candidates, and the white evangelical percentage of the exit poll sample was also comparable to that of previous years.[75] This appeared to confirm early evidence that Romney's Mormonism was not costing him support among Republicans or white evangelicals: in July, roughly equal numbers supported him no matter whether his Mormonism made them "uncomfortable" or not.[76] Even more interestingly, Campbell, Green, and Monson repeated their experiment from 2008 in 2012. They found that telling people about Romney's Mormon faith had a much smaller impact than it had in 2008.[77]

But we want to push further to identify the potential effects of attitudes about Mormons in the overall electorate, including not only whether people voted for Romney but whether they voted at all. When YouGov first interviewed respondents in December 2011, they were asked a simple question: How favorably or unfavorably would you rate Mormons on a 0–100 scale? The average among non-Mormon respondents was 55—just slightly on the favorable side—which was more favorable than the average rating of Muslims (47) but less favorable than the average views of Jews (71) or Christians (74). Of course, Mormons consider themselves Christians, although some Americans do not believe this. In this survey, we merely included the terms "Mormons" and "Christians" in a longer list of groups that respondents evaluated—including not only Muslims and Jews but also whites, blacks, Latinos, Asians, and gays and lesbians. We left it to respondents to define those terms as they wished.

On average, views of Mormons were more positive among Republicans (62) than among Democrats (51) or independents (52). Among people who said they were born again—a proxy for identifying evangelicals—views of Mormons were a bit less favorable but only among Republicans. The average for born-again Republicans was 58, compared to 64 among Republicans who were not born again. One challenge in asking about Mormons at this point in time was that people's answers may have depended on their feelings toward Romney, arguably the most prominent Mormon in the news. This, and not general feelings toward a group perceived as culturally conservative, may explain why Democrats rated Mormons less favorably than Republicans. But the difference that being born again created among Republicans also suggests that people were thinking at least in part about Mormons and not solely along party lines. And one advantage of asking people their views of Mormons before much of the campaign occurred is that it mitigated (although did not eliminate) the possibility that they would later change their views of Mormons based on their feelings toward Romney. If that happened, then the causality would be reversed: rather than Romney being helped or hurt by people's attitudes toward Mormons, their attitudes toward Mormons would be helped or hurt by their feelings toward Romney.[78]

For the moment, we proceed on the assumption that feelings toward Mormons could have affected people's feelings toward Romney. To estimate the role that Mormonism might have played, we modeled both whether and how people voted based on what they reported in the post-election interview. The factors in the model were all from the first interview with these people in December 2011, and they included not only attitudes toward Mormons but other factors known to be associated with turnout and voter choice. For example, the model of voter choice also included people's party identification, their feeling toward African Americans, measures of their views on both social issues and economic issues, and several demographic variables. (See the appendix to this chapter for more details.) Merely including these factors did not ensure that we accurately estimated any impact of attitudes toward Mormons, and there were plausibly important factors we did not include. But this model at least provided a somewhat rigorous test.

When it comes to whether people voted in the first place, attitudes toward Mormons were significantly related to turnout, but to such a small extent that their effects were not very consequential. Other things equal, a person with a fairly favorable view of Mormons—75 on the 0–100 scale—was about 2.4 points more likely to vote than someone with a fairly unfavorable view of 40. (About 25% of the sample had views less favorable than 40; 25% had views more favorable than 75.) What did such differences add up to? Not much. If somehow every voter viewed Mormons as favorably as Christians generally—which would have lifted the average favorability of Mormons by almost 20 points—this model predicted that turnout would have increased by about 1.4 points. Of course, this simulation represents a dramatic and unlikely shift in attitudes. Less dramatic shifts would produce even smaller increases in turnout.

Moreover, most of the people who had relatively unfavorable views of Mormons and stayed home on Election Day would not have voted for Romney anyway. We examined people who were interviewed in the last month of the campaign and then reported that they did not vote when they were interviewed again after the election. Among those who expressed an unfavorable view of Mormons—defined as scores on the 0–100 scale below the average of 55—only 11% reported that they preferred Romney, whereas 59% supported Obama and 30% were undecided or supported some other candidate. In short, there was not a large group of people who were otherwise predisposed to support Romney but stayed home on Election Day because they disliked Mormons.

Were attitudes toward Mormons associated with the choices of those who did vote? They were, but again this did not put Romney at a significant disadvantage. Holding other factors constant, a person with a relatively favorable view of Mormons was about 1.3 points more likely to support Romney than was someone with a relatively unfavorable view (using the values of 75 and 40 again). To estimate the overall consequences of attitudes toward Mormons, we again simulated the effect of making attitudes toward Mormons as favorable as attitudes toward Christians generally. This increased Romney's support by 0.8 points—a very modest amount given how transformative such a shift in attitudes toward Mormons would be.[79]

Even these small effects may be too big. If attitudes toward Mormons were more a consequence than a cause of support for Romney, or there was something that we have left out of the model but was related to both attitudes toward Mormons and voting, we have overstated the possible impact of attitudes toward Mormons in this race. We are not suggesting that Mormons can safely run for office without any fear of religious prejudice hurting their chances. We must study more races involving Mormon candidates before drawing firm conclusions. But in 2012, Romney's religion appeared to be a minimal factor in his loss.[80]

The Favorability Gap

During and after the election, commentators returned again and again to the question of Romney's personality and biography—and whether these were somehow obstacles he could never overcome. We noted in chapter 5 that at the end of the summer Romney was not only viewed less favorably than Obama but less favorably than other presidential candidates since 1984. This prompted the *Washington Post*'s Ruth Marcus to write: "Is Romney Likable Enough to Win?"[81] For some, the election seemed to answer the question. The *National Review*'s Daniel Foster asked, "Could the Romney campaign have done more to make their guy likable when it counted?"[82]

Other commentators, including even some rueful Republicans, zeroed in on the empathy gap we have described. According to this theory, Romney's problem was that he was not perceived as "caring" enough about ordinary Americans' problems—a notion often connected to his time at Bain Capital and prominent in Democratic attacks on him. We have shown that these attacks appeared not to shift the polls in notable ways. In fact, the empathy gap was essentially no different on the eve of the election than it had been at the beginning of 2012. But the election made it seem crucial. Commentators frequently cited the exit poll in which 21% of voters selected "cares about me" as the most important from a list of important traits that the candidates should have, and those voters broke for Obama 81%–18%. The *Weekly Standard*'s Jay Cost said, "Obama's campaign against Romney, which portrayed him as an out-of-touch plutocrat, appears largely to have been successful."[83]

Was Romney's loss really about likability or empathy? This is a hard question to answer, and the reason—as we have discussed throughout this chapter—is the classic challenge of separating correlation from causation. Did people form perceptions of Obama and Romney and then decide who to vote for based on those perceptions? Or did they decide who to vote for based on some other criteria—like simple partisan loyalty—and then arrange their perceptions of the candidates to fit their vote intentions?[84] The exit poll can shed no light on this question. Our data cannot resolve this issue either, but they can take us further toward an answer.

Romney had one thing going for him as the campaign drew to a close. Even if the empathy gap remained, the favorability gap narrowed and was perhaps even eliminated. In YouGov surveys, views of Obama remained stable as views of Romney became more favorable. This is evident in the first panel of Figure 7.9, which shows the average favorability ratings of each candidate on a 4-point scale ranging from "very unfavorable" to "very favorable." Neither candidate was evaluated particularly favorably, but Romney did narrow what was a persistent gap, largely because of his performance in the first debate. The small edge that Obama had in the last pre-election YouGov poll was mirrored in the other public polls as well.[85]

We have already described how partisan loyalties appeared to drive trends in perceptions of the candidates. Figure 7.9 illustrates this again. The second panel of the figure breaks down Romney's average favorability rating by whether respondents were Romney supporters, Obama supporters, or undecided or third-party supporters as of their first interview in December 2011. Viewed this way, it is clear where most of the increase in Romney's favorability came from: people who already supported him and just decided that they liked him more. Democrats moved in the opposite direction, although not quite as much. Undecided voters bounced around largely because there were relatively few in each week's survey, creating more random fluctuation. But if we smooth out these fluctuations, there is very little secular trend. The reason for this is evident in the third panel of Figure 7.9, which breaks down these undecided voters by whether they were Republicans, Democrats, or independents. Given the small number of undecided voters, the trends are presented monthly rather than weekly. Once again, the same pattern emerges, one consistent with the growing power of partisanship among undecided voters that we documented earlier: undecided Republicans came to feel better about Romney, while undecided Democrats moved in the opposite direction. Ultimately Romney became more popular largely because Republicans came to like him more.

All of this illustrates the challenge in sorting out correlation from causation. To make some headway, we relied on statistical modeling similar to what we employed to study the relationship between economic evaluations and vote intentions (see the appendix). We examined respondents who were interviewed in October after the first presidential debate and then reported

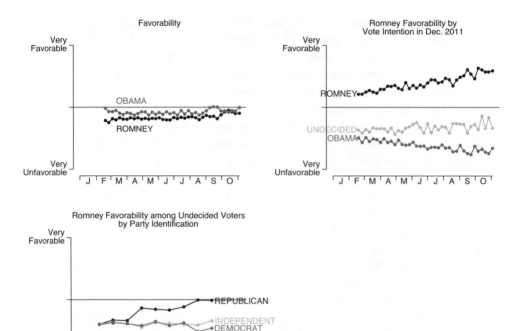

Figure 7.9.
Candidate favorability and its relationship to preexisting partisan loyalties.
Each graph depicts average candidate favorability. The upper left-hand panel displays
favorability for Romney and Obama among all respondents. The upper right-hand panel
displays favorability for Romney, with respondents broken down by the candidate they
supported in their first interview in December 2011. The lower left-hand panel focuses
only on voters who were undecided or favored a third-party candidate in December
2011, and displays average Romney favorability each month broken down by the party
with which these voters identified. The figure shows how trends in favorability appear to
reflect preexisting loyalties to a candidate or a party. Data from YouGov surveys.

voting when interviewed again after the election. We modeled the vote decisions they reported in the post-election interview as a consequence of three
factors: their vote intentions in the initial December 2011 interview, and their
views of Obama and Romney in terms of favorability or empathy, which
were measured in October. To measure empathy, we rely on assessments of
whether the candidates "cared about people like me." By measuring favorability and empathy in October, relatively close to the election, we likely captured
the way respondents felt about the candidates when they voted.

Because views of the candidates may have been in part a consequence of vote decisions, we drew on these respondents' original ratings of candidate favorability in December 2011 as a proxy for—or, in statistical lingo, an "instrument" for—their ratings of the candidate favorability in October. The idea is that by drawing on ratings very early in the campaign, before vote intentions may have been fully solidified for some voters, we can estimate the effect of favorability on vote choice more accurately, with less threat from reverse causation (vote intentions affecting perceptions of the candidates). Even this kind of statistical model cannot fully eliminate such threats, but it is arguably better than proceeding as if those threats do not exist. Unfortunately, we do not have measures of empathy in the December 2011 interview, so the estimated impact of empathy cannot be modeled in this same way. (Further details are in the appendix to this chapter.) Note that this model did not control for many other things and thus likely overestimated the effects of favorability and empathy. If favorability and empathy were not decisive based on this model, then it is not likely they would be once other relevant factors were taken into account.

As expected, how people felt about the candidates was strongly associated with how they voted. The key question is what any favorability or empathy gap cost Romney overall. One way to think about this is to "adjust" perceptions of him to be more positive and see what consequence might have resulted. This is a hypothetical exercise, but an instructive one. Romney faced two potential disadvantages: despite his gains in favorability, he was not viewed quite as favorably by Republicans as Obama was viewed by Democrats, and he was not viewed as favorably by independents as Obama was. This was even more true in people's assessments of empathy.

If we adjust Romney's favorability to eliminate his disadvantage, what happens? Very little. Obama loses only a tenth of a point of vote share. If we adjust both Romney's favorability and empathy to eliminate his larger empathy disadvantage, what happens? Obama is estimated to lose almost 1 point in this simulation. This would have been enough to tighten the race—theoretically, shrinking Obama's winning margin from nearly 4 percentage points to just about 2 points—but would not have tipped the race clearly in Romney's favor. And, again, given the simplicity of the model, this is likely an unrealistically large estimate. Accounting for a few other factors that were plausibly associated with vote decisions—for the sake of illustration, we added to the model attitudes toward blacks, a set of economic issues, and a set of social issues—reduced the benefits that Romney received in this hypothetical scenario to 0.8 points, well short of what he needed to eke out even the narrowest of victories.

Over the years, Republican presidential candidates have both won and lost elections while suffering from an empathy gap relative to their Democratic opponents. Closing this gap was therefore not necessary for Romney in 2012. And it probably would not have been sufficient, as this analysis suggests. This leads to a broader point about presidential elections: although much about the presidential campaign helps us "get to know" the candidates—their strengths, weaknesses, quirks, and foibles—it is not necessarily the case that the candidates will win or lose the election because of who they are as people. When political scientist Larry Bartels studied how voters perceived the candidates on a variety of trait dimensions in the 1980–2000 presidential elections—honesty, leadership, empathy, and others—he found only one election, 2000, where the elimination of gaps in how voters assessed the opposing candidates could have shifted the outcome.[86] This is not surprising. Perceptions of the candidates seem to be much more the consequence, and not the cause, of how people vote.

Obama's Formidable Campaign

When an election is over, almost no time passes before the victor's campaign gets the credit. The day after Obama was first elected in 2008, the front-page *New York Times* story said, "The story of Mr. Obama's journey to the pinnacle of American politics is the story of a campaign that was, even in the view of many rivals, almost flawless."[87] And the day after Obama was reelected, *Slate's* John Dickerson wrote, "What was ratified on election night was the benefit of a permanent campaign and the talent of the Obama team. The much vaunted Obama ground game appears to have been a real thing. . . . His campaign team was so formidable that it made up for all the inadequacies, vulnerabilities, and missteps (remember that first debate?) of a weak incumbent president in a sputtering economy."[88] Granted, Obama's 2012 campaign was no longer "almost flawless," only "formidable," but the logic is the same: winners win because they run great campaigns. The corollary, of course, is that losers never do.

We have argued throughout that general election campaigning can matter. This was evident in how the Democratic National Convention and the debates shaped people's views of the candidates. This was also evident in how television advertising could leave an imprint—albeit a fleeting one—on vote intentions during the summer and fall. Now our task is to assess the impact of not only the advertising—the "air war" of campaigns—but the "ground game," the field organizations that Dickerson referred to. The field operation of the Obama campaign has been justifiably lauded. It reflected an intensive and innovative effort to target the right subset of voters, the staff necessary to contact voters (often face-to-face), and the tactics and techniques that have been shown—often via rigorous experimentation—to both persuade people to support a candidate and then get them to the polls.[89] The field operation was credited in bringing enough Democrats to the polls so that the electorate looked much like it did in 2008, despite the doubts of many—particularly Romney supporters—who thought that the 2008 electorate was an aberration. The challenge is to figure out how much all this campaigning mattered.

As we noted in chapter 6, the Romney campaign's disadvantage in television advertising disappeared as the campaign drew to a close, with a particularly large spike in Romney ads right before Election Day. Romney and his allies bought a big chunk of advertising in battleground states as well as some ads that aired nationally. But Romney's disadvantage in terms of field organization was large and durable. We can quantify his disadvantage simply by considering the number of field offices that each campaign had opened up—data we gleaned from each candidate's webpage. Obama had 786 offices; Romney had 284. This meant that not only did Obama tend to have more offices in areas where Romney also had offices, but Obama had many offices in places where Romney did not. There were 187 counties in the United States that had at least one Obama field office but no Romney field office. Figure 7.10 maps each candidate's field offices and shows Obama's advantage.[90]

The location of Obama's and Romney's field offices also offers a clue as to each campaign's goals. Obama's offices were located predominantly in

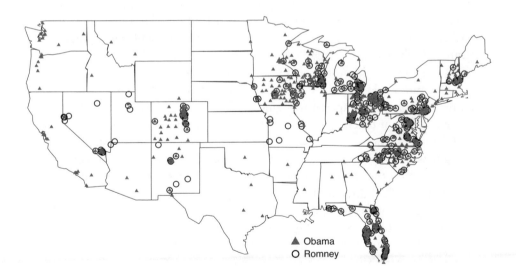

Figure 7.10.
The location of Obama and Romney field offices.
Data on field office location were gathered from the Obama and Romney websites.
The graph is by Brian Law.

Democratic-leaning counties—suggesting that the goal of these offices was to boost Democratic turnout. A county in which Obama won 75% of the vote in 2008 was nearly 40 percent more likely to have at least one Obama office in 2012 than a county where Obama won only half the vote. Romney's offices, however, were located in a mix of Republican-leaning counties and swing counties. A county in which McCain won 75% of the vote was only 7 points more likely to have at least one Romney field office than a county where McCain won 50% of the vote. The location of Romney's offices appeared to reflect the desire to both boost Republican turnout and persuade swing voters to support him.[91]

Obama seemed to have another advantage in terms of the orientation within each field office. The *Atlantic*'s Molly Ball traveled to field offices in various swing states and summarized her reaction thusly: "The Obama offices were devoted almost entirely to the president's reelection; the Republican offices were devoted almost entirely to local candidates, with little presence for Romney." In large part this was because Romney had outsourced his field operation to the Republican National Committee (RNC), who was charged with mobilizing support for Republican candidates up and down the ballot.[92] Ball's assessment fits with what we saw after visiting several field offices in Cuyahoga, Lake, and Medina counties in Ohio in October. At the Obama office in Parma, Ohio, there were many different kinds of Obama signs and stickers available for people to take home, including bumper stickers with ethnic identifiers that would appeal to the neighborhoods around Parma. At the Romney office not far away in Independence, Ohio, there were traditional Romney signs and stickers alongside yard signs and materials for other Republican candidates running in the state, particularly state treasurer Josh Mandel, who was hoping to oust incumbent Senator Sherrod Brown from office.

Of course, field offices are not the full story about field organization. Certainly the Romney campaign was quick to dismiss their disadvantage in the sheer number of offices. Rick Wiley, the political director of the RNC, told Ball: "The Obama campaign thinks, 'If we put 100 offices in this state, we're going to win.' We take a smaller, smarter approach, just like we do for government." Even for the Obama campaign, field offices were just part of the equation. Obama's field director, Jeremy Bird, explained to Ball how they also did organizing out of "staging locations" that could be nothing more than a volunteer's living room in a battleground state neighborhood. But the presence of field offices was likely correlated with the reach and vigor of the broader field operation.

Our goal, then, was to estimate the potential impact of both advertising and field offices on Obama's vote share. In 2008, Obama's advantage in both advertising and field offices appeared to matter. In one study, political scientists Michael Franz and Travis Ridout found that an advantage for Obama of 1,000 ads over the month before the election translated into an additional six-tenths of a point of vote share.[93] In addition, two studies of field offices in 2008 found that they garnered votes for Obama, perhaps enough to swing the outcomes in a three swing states.[94] However, no study has yet to estimate the impact of both advertising and field offices simultaneously.

We did so by analyzing county-level election returns from all 3,156 counties in the continental United States plus Hawaii (including the District of Columbia). Using the county-level election returns has several advantages. Most important, we could study not pre-election surveys—whose respondents may or may not vote—but actual vote share (people who showed up and voted). By analyzing actual vote share, we directly assessed the impact of campaign activity on the election's outcome.

For each county, we recorded how many Obama or Romney field offices were present: none, one, or two or more. (Few counties had more than two.) We also recorded the balance of advertising in that county on the day prior to Election Day—Monday, November 5, when there was a particularly big advantage for Romney—and the balance of advertising in the five days prior to that. We expected that the balance of advertising on Monday was more potent than the earlier ads, given how quickly advertising effects appeared to dissipate. We also took account of various other county characteristics: how well Obama did in that county in 2008; demographic characteristics such as the percentage of blacks and Latinos living in the county; and the change in unemployment in the year before the election. (More information and the results of the model are in the appendix to this chapter.)

The relationship of ads to vote share resembled what we found previously: a greater ad imbalance improved vote share for the candidate airing more ads, but the effect of ads appeared to decay quickly. Ads on the day before the election appeared to produce small but measurable gains in vote share—although we cannot estimate this effect with much precision. The largest advantage that Obama had in any one county—the equivalent of an additional three ads per capita on that Monday, relative to Romney's advertising—translated into an additional three-tenths of a point of vote share. The largest advantage that Romney had—the equivalent of nine additional ads per capita—translated into almost an additional point of vote share. By contrast, the effects of the previous five days of ads had a much smaller effect. According to our estimates, it would have taken about eighty additional ads per capita over the course of those five days to generate the same increase in vote share that an advantage of three ads per capita produced the day before the election. At one point, Obama advisor David Axelrod argued that early advertising was more important than late advertising, suggesting that Romney's ad blitz was wrongheaded. Axelrod said: "By September, people are disregarding ads.

They back-loaded. We front-loaded."[95] We find that back-loading—airing ads close to the election—was actually more effective than front-loading—airing ads early in the campaign—if the goal was to influence voters on Election Day.

We also found some effect of field offices, but only the Obama field offices. Compared to counties with no Obama field offices, Obama's vote share was about three-tenths of a point higher in counties where Obama had one field office and six-tenths of a point higher in counties where Obama had two or more field offices. Romney's field offices, by contrast, had an effect that was only half this big and could not be estimated with as much statistical confidence. This is consistent with the impression that Obama's field operation was more effective than Romney's. Essentially, our best guess is that Romney would have needed two offices in a county to match the effects of one of Obama's offices, all else equal.

Putting these two sets of results together generates some interesting conclusions about the relative effectiveness of ads and field offices. If the apparent impact of the Obama field offices indicates what effective field organization can produce, then in 2012 placing one field office in a county was worth about as much as an advertising advantage of roughly 3 additional ads per person on the day before the election.[96] Obama had that large of an advertising advantage in eighteen counties on the eve of the election—suggesting that there was considerable value for him in organizing and sustaining a large field operation. The Romney campaign's strategy of a last-minute ad blitz also makes sense, given this result. Without the organizational strength on the ground, it needed to do more work through the airwaves. Of the 983 counties in the battleground states, Romney had a last-minute 3:1 or greater advantage in 144 counties.

Ultimately, then, the results suggest two things. First, an advertising advantage on the day before the election likely increased vote share, and much more than did advertising prior to that point. Second, the Obama field offices also appeared to increase vote share. We use the phrase "the results suggest" deliberately. Our results are based on statistical models that may not account for every important factor, although we have included arguably the most important (especially Obama's vote share in 2008). But if the campaigns were targeting their advertising and ground game in part based on factors that we have not accounted for, then our results may overestimate the impact of all this campaign activity.[97] On the other hand, we may not have captured all of the impact of the ground game—particularly if the staff at some field offices worked outside of the county in which the field office was located. For example, staff in field offices in some non-battleground states likely worked to contact voters in battleground states. And within a battleground state, there was obviously nothing preventing staff from one field office from crossing county boundaries.

With those caveats stated, it is worth addressing two hypotheticals about the race. First, how much additional late advertising would Romney have needed to win? Second, what if Obama had not had an advantage in the field? What do our data and models suggest might have happened? For Romney to win the election, assume that he would have sought only the minimum winning number of Electoral College votes (270) and that he would have targeted states where Obama's winning margin was the smallest. One strategy would then be to win Florida, New Hampshire, Ohio, and Virginia. But to win even this handful of states, Romney would have needed truly massive advantages in advertising. As we have noted, it was not common for Romney to have even a 3:1 advantage on the day before the election. The most he had anywhere was about a 9:1 advantage. Based on our model, he would have needed to expand his advertising advantage in Florida by an additional 4:1 margin, in Ohio by an additional 16:1 margin, in Virginia by an additional 22:1 margin, and in New Hampshire by an additional 31:1 margin. He might have been able to advertise a bit less at the end of the race if he had maintained a larger advantage in the week leading up to that last day, but he still would have needed an incredible boost at the very end given that many of the battleground state outcomes were not very close. Even if Romney had mustered the resources to buy that much advertising, there was likely not enough space on the airwaves to rack up margins of that size. A Romney strategist told us that at the end of the campaign, their campaign bought ads in Pennsylvania solely because there was nothing else left to buy in places like Ohio. In short, Romney's problem was not necessarily that he was too late with his advertising—as Axelrod suggested—but that he had too little. Given the practical limits on how much additional advertising could have been aired, it seems doubtful that advertising alone could have vaulted Romney to victory.

What about Obama's advantage in field offices? How decisive was it? If Obama had established only as many field offices as Romney had in all of these counties, we again estimate that the outcome of the election would not have changed very much. Obama would have lost an average of almost a tenth of a point of vote share across the states, and no state outcome would have changed. Obama would have lost about 123,000 total votes in this scenario.

Overall, we estimate that Obama gained roughly an additional 248,000 votes from his field operation. Given where those votes were located, we estimate that Obama would have lost Florida by a very narrow margin in this scenario. This is consistent with estimates from 2008. Political scientists Joshua Darr and Matthew Levendusky have estimated that Obama's 2008 field operation won him about 275,000 votes in total and could have been responsible for his victory in North Carolina.[98] A similar analysis by political scientist Seth Masket found that Obama's 2008 field operation may have been consequential in North Carolina, Florida, and Indiana.[99]

Given the attention Obama's field operation received in both 2008 and 2012, it might seem odd that his field operation—at least as we have measured it here—likely did not decide the election. Certainly our findings call into question headlines like "Obama Won Ohio with Ground Game."[100] Of course, we should be cautious about our findings, especially because counting the number of field offices is a blunt way to measure a field operation. But two points help explain why field organization may not have decided the election. First, many people who vote in presidential elections do so out of habit—that is, they do not need to be contacted by a volunteer. And others may become motivated to vote by the general hullabaloo of the campaign, not by direct outreach from a field office. Second, studies of field organization and mobilization suggest that, at most, effective mobilization will increase turnout by a single-digit number of percentage points—perhaps as much as 8–9 points, and often less—among those who are contacted.[101] The phrase "among those who are contacted" is important, since obviously campaigns contact only a subset of voters and, indeed, only intend to do so. We do not know how many voters were contacted by either campaign, nor do we know whether their contacts increased turnout by 8–9 points or less. But some provisional back-of-the-envelope math suggests why a field organization may not be decisive. For example, in Ohio, Obama beat Romney by 166,272 votes. Assume, very generously, that the Obama field organization increased turnout by 9 points in 2012. Such an effect would presume face-to-face contact between an Obama field staffer and each targeted voter, since other forms of contact are less effective. To generate a winning margin of over 166,000 votes assuming a 9-point boost from voter mobilization efforts, the Obama campaign would have had to contact 1.8 million voters in this labor-intensive face-to-face fashion and do so very close to when each Ohioan could or did vote, since the effects of contact likely also wear off. That is a massive number to contact in such a short time, equivalent to a third of all of voters in Ohio that year. Perhaps this is why in 2008 Obama advisor David Plouffe referred to a field operation as a "field goal unit"—implying that it was valuable but not necessarily the game-winner unless the margin was close.[102] In 2012, the election did not appear close enough for either the ads or field organization to be decisive.

Comparing Electioneering and the Fundamentals

We have made much of the advantages bestowed on an incumbent party candidate when the economy is growing or on the challenger when the economy is contracting. Along the way, we have been careful not to suggest that campaigning is irrelevant. In fact, the tug-of-war metaphor is meant to suggest the opposite. Campaigns affect voters, but both sides tend to neutralize each other. The effects of ads were appreciable but fleeting. Obama and Romney needed consistently to air many more ads than the other to win votes, and neither could do this for long. The effects of field offices were also notable but perhaps not as large as many people believe.

Another way to think about the effects of the campaign is to compare them directly to the impact of the underlying fundamentals. This allows us to investigate a different hypothetical: could campaigning alone have neutralized the advantage that Obama had because of the underlying fundamentals? In other words, could Romney have overcome Obama's structural advantage by campaigning? Addressing this hypothetical requires several assumptions, but here is how the calculation might go.

We can begin with an estimate of the advantage Obama received from the economy, using a model based only on GDP change and incumbency status. In previous presidential elections dating back to 1948, the incumbent party's candidate would be expected to receive an additional 2.4 points of vote share if the economy grew by 1.1% in the first six months of the election year, as it did in 2012. If so, then how much campaigning would Romney have needed to gain 2.4 points at the polls and neutralize Obama's advantage from the economic fundamentals in any given county?

In terms of advertising, Romney would again have needed an enormous advantage—one far greater than he achieved with his final push at the very end of the race. Based on the model we discussed previously—in which we estimate how much advertising affected vote share in each county—ads on the day before the election were most potent. To offset Obama's structural advantage, Romney would have needed to run 27 more ads per capita than Obama.[103] Even if Romney had been out-advertising Obama by 10 ads per capita on each of the five days (Tuesday–Sunday) leading up to that final day (Monday), he still would have needed to air 24 ads per capita more than Obama on this final day.[104]

If Romney had added more field offices, it would have helped but probably not enough. Adding an additional field office in a county would earn him only .15 points (and even that estimate was accompanied by a lot of uncertainty). He would still have needed the same 10 ad per capita advantage in advertising from Tuesday to Sunday before Election Day, plus a 23 ad per capita advantage on the day before Election Day. An additional two field offices still would have required a 10 ad per capita advantage on that Tuesday through Sunday and a 21 ad per capita advantage on that Monday as well.

Thus to neutralize the effects of even a slowly growing economy, Romney would have needed a massive investment in advertising and a field operation probably two to three times the size of the one he had. And we have not even begun to account for other fundamental factors benefiting Obama, such as incumbency. Incumbents typically get 3 points of vote share just for being the incumbent, over and above any advantage for the economy. For Romney to have made up another 3 points of vote share would have been nearly impossible. This calculation underscores once more what a tough battle Romney faced.

Conclusion

Why did Obama win the 2012 election? Here is what we know or at least suspect. He did not win because of "gifts" to demographic groups, or because voters had prejudices about Mormons, or because Romney was perceived as too conservative. He won in spite of lingering racial prejudice. He won in part because he was perceived more favorably than Romney and in part because he had an effective ground game—but neither of these was likely decisive. As former George W. Bush campaign strategist Matthew Dowd put it: "All of this raises the question of whether campaigns and tactics matter. They do, but only in a very limited way, and they are insignificant compared with the overall political environment and the grand movements of the world and our country."[105]

In 2012, Obama won in part because the environment favored him. The economy was growing enough for an incumbent to win reelection, and little during the election year pushed the outcome far from what the economy would predict. Indeed, one of the important effects of the campaign was to make a fundamentals-based prediction come true. Although the most visible manifestations of campaign activity, such as television ads and field organizations, were not necessarily deciding factors, the campaign did matter in subtler ways—for example, by rallying partisans and making the economy more salient to undecided voters.

The Wednesday morning after a presidential election is filled with the quarterbacking that usually takes place on a Monday morning during football season. In 2012, pundits and politicians alike were quick to condemn Romney and his campaign for a host of sins—not likable enough, too conservative, not conservative enough, and so on. Some condemnations appeared to reflect misguided expectations. A much-discussed piece by former Republican White House veterans Michael Gerson and Peter Wehner began with this: "By all rights, Barack Obama should have lost the 2012 election. The economy during his first term in office was weak from beginning to end."[106] But this is a misunderstanding of what the fundamentals suggested, thereby calling into question whether Romney could have won even if the Republican Party had taken all of Gerson and Wehner's advice. Indeed, what strikes us is how much judgments of any losing candidate are the consequences, not the causes, of losing. Winning candidates do not face such scrutiny. After all, if they had committed such sins, they never would have won, right?

One implication of our analysis, however, is that there was not necessarily any grave mistake that Romney made, one momentous enough to cost him the election. Of course, without the benefit of a time machine and the ability to rerun the campaign different ways, we cannot know for sure. But Romney's personality, biography, platform, and campaign organization—whatever their limitations—did not appear to have been the reason he lost. Although some decisions may have cost him votes, they did not necessarily cost him the race.

CHAPTER 8

Cashing In

A few weeks after the election, conservative activists filled a ballroom to hear newly elected Texas senator Ted Cruz muse on the election. Cruz lit into Mitt Romney, praising him as a "man of character" but saying this about Romney's references to the "47 percent": "I cannot think of an idea more antithetical to the American principles this country was founded on." Out in the room, the mood was bleak. One lobbyist said, "Oh yes, we are all very sad. Some of us have turned to drugs; others are in therapy." Public opinion polls confirmed that a little therapy might be in order: Republicans' assessments of the quality of their lives dropped sharply after the election—to a level not seen since, well, the first time Barack Obama was elected. Republicans were not only unhappy but angry, too. Cruz's remark was indicative of the accusations, recriminations, and self-flagellation within the party. *Politico* even created an entire category of news called "GOP Civil War."[1]

This sort of reaction is predictable. Americans with long memories may remember way back in 2004, when John Kerry's loss to George W. Bush occasioned the same sort of intraparty hand-wringing—about whether Democrats could win over the "values voters" that were allegedly responsible for Bush's victory, about whether the Democrats could ever win anything again, period. That the Democrats won decisively in the 2006 and 2008 elections suggests a lesson that many commentators seem not to learn, year after year: just as elections are not actually full of game-changing moments, elections themselves may not be game-changers. Commentators often believe that elections foreshadow a sweeping transformation, and, to be sure, they do have policy consequences. It matters whether Republicans or Democrats control the White House and Congress. But we should not lose sight of the ways in which elections maintain the status quo. They can be "game-samers," too.

Perhaps the two most common mistakes in interpreting an election are assuming that it constitutes a mandate for the winner's policy agenda and assuming that it constitutes a permanent realignment of the electorate. These mistakes are most frequently made by the winning side because winners like to believe that they won because people agreed with them and because they like to believe that their victory means their side will keep on winning. Neither is usually true. As the winning side soon discovers when it goes to cash in its chips, it did not win quite as much as it thought. After the 2012 election, despondent Republicans could take heart in one thing: even if it was not the outcome they wanted, the 2012 election was no sea change in the Democrats' favor either. This puts a very different light on how much the Republican Party must overhaul itself in order to retake the White House. A slowing economy, not a renovation within the party, might be the quickest ticket to 1600 Pennsylvania Avenue.

Understanding that presidential campaigns are not full of game-changers and presidential elections are not necessarily game-changers themselves leads to useful lessons for candidates and the news media alike. A more modest perspective on what campaigns can accomplish can inform not only whether candidates run and how they campaign but also how journalists write about the election. A little more "moneyball" can help both in ways that dovetail their overriding goal: for candidates, to win; for journalists, to see beyond the spin and get the story right.

If it seems boring to live through a campaign without that many game-changers, ask yourself: would our elections be better with more game-changers? That is a tricky question to answer, but we are inclined to say no. The predictability and stability that we have documented—underpinned by economic fundamentals and party loyalty—might be preferable.

No Mandate

After his reelection in 2004, George W. Bush famously said, "I earned capital in this election, and I'm going to spend it." Then he embarked on an unsuccessful effort to reform Social Security and saw the increasingly unpopular Iraq War and a worsening economy drag his approval rating down to a low of 22%. After Barack Obama's election in 2008, his supporters were similarly triumphant. *New York Times* columnist Paul Krugman said, "This year, however, Mr. Obama ran on a platform of guaranteed health care and tax breaks for the middle class, paid for with higher taxes on the affluent. John McCain denounced his opponent as a socialist and a 'redistributor,' but America voted for him anyway. That's a real mandate."[2]

The aftermath of the 2008 election reflected anything but a mandate for Obama's policies. As we described in chapter 2, although Obama and congressional Democrats accomplished much by dint of controlling the House, Senate, and White House, they reaped few political benefits. Commentators who had celebrated the 2008 election as a victory for liberal ideas—the *New Republic*'s John Judis published a piece titled "America the Liberal"—were soon lamenting Obama's missed opportunities, as Judis did in a 2010 article called "The Unnecessary Fall."[3]

Despite the apparent lessons of Obama's first term, the mood among some Democrats and liberals after his victory in 2012 was no less exuberant than after his victory in 2008. Krugman, writing a month before the election, had not changed his tune: "This election is . . . shaping up as a referendum on our social insurance system, and it looks as if Obama will have a clear mandate for preserving and extending that system."[4] And when Obama won, the rhetoric reached new heights. Bob Moser, executive editor of *The American Prospect*, wrote:

> The right will not wither or relent in response to the message this election has delivered. But progressives can now take heart. The conservative consensus that took hold of America with Ronald Reagan's election in 1980 is over. The idea that government is the enemy no longer prevails. Obama may not have created a new liberal movement—and he may not do so in the next four years. But the emerging liberal majority can.[5]

A *BuzzFeed* headline put it even more succinctly: "Welcome to Liberal America."[6]

Why is this interpretation of the election as wrong in 2012 as in 2008 or 2004? It begins with what a "mandate" means and why it is very rare. The most common meaning of mandate implies a theory about voters: that voters have fixed opinions about a range of political issues, learn the candidates' opinions on those issues, and then vote for the candidate who shares their opinions. Thus the winning candidate should believe that if he implements his policy agenda, the majority of voters will approve.

That would be a reasonable belief if this was how voters made choices. In reality, political science research has shown that voters often do not have fixed opinions about policy and do not know the candidates' opinions either. Of course, candidates do not make it easy for voters to learn, often preferring vague formulations about "helping working families" to specifics about their

plans for, say, entitlement reform. When voters do learn, often the causal relationship runs in the direction opposite to what the mandate interpretation
implies: voters adjust their opinions about issues to match those of the candidate they have decided to support for other reasons.[7]

The mandate interpretation is complicated further by another tendency
that voters have: to serve as "thermostats" for public policy. Voters move
in the *opposite* direction as the party controlling the White House—to the
left under Republican administrations and to the right under Democratic
administrations. It is as if when the government does too much, or is "too
hot," the public says "cool it." When the government does too little, or is
"too cold," the public says "turn up the heat in here." So although the mandate interpretation was that Obama's victory in 2008 suggested an "emerging liberal majority," thermostatic public opinion soon moved against him.
This is demonstrated in Figure 8.1, which uses an omnibus measure of the
public's support for government programs that is derived from hundreds
of different survey questions.[8] Under Reagan, for example, the public became more liberal, in contrast to the notion that Reagan's two terms and

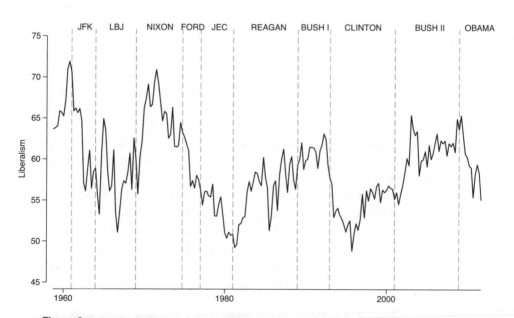

Figure 8.1.

The ideological mood of the American public.

The figure displays the public's overall support for government spending, based on
a combination of hundreds of survey questions. Higher values indicate more liberal
opinion. The data are from James Stimson.

skills as a communicator succeeded in shifting the public to the right. Under Clinton, there was a sharp shift to the right and then back to the left under George W. Bush.

During the Obama administration, as under Clinton, there was another shift to the right. Far from ushering in a liberal majority, the Obama administration's agenda—which included an economic stimulus, greater regulation of the banking industry, and, most important, health care reform—led the public to prefer less government, not more government. Obama helped increase the conservatism of the American public more than Reagan ever did, ironically enough. It is true that there are countervailing trends to the public's increasing conservatism, such as growing support for same-sex marriage and the legalization of marijuana—two trends that seemed particularly salient on Election Night when voters in Maine and Maryland ratified same-sex marriage and voters in Colorado and Washington ratified marijuana legalization. But those trends are the exception rather than the rule. Thus it is perhaps no surprise that Obama was perceived further to the left of the average voter than Romney was perceived to the right.

Even if there was no mandate coming from voters, Obama could hope that Republicans would still interpret his victory as a mandate. In their book *Mandate Politics*, political scientists Lawrence Grossback, David Peterson, and James Stimson note another meaning of mandate: a "shared conclusion that derives from public interaction over the interpretation of an election."[9] In their telling, it is less important what voters did or did not want and more important what policymakers believe voters want. After elections perceived to convey a mandate, members of Congress change how they would normally vote, thus shifting policy in the direction the president favors. However, according to Grossback and colleagues, only the 1964 and 1980 presidential elections were truly "mandate" elections, and, even then, the effects of the election on congressional voting were short-lived.

Little about either the 2008 or 2012 election suggested that Republicans believed Obama had a mandate. Republicans quickly coalesced in opposition to Obama's first-term agenda. In the wake of the 2012 election—at least as of this writing—the dynamics did not seem much different. Looming deadlines, including the need to raise the debt ceiling and the expiration of the tax cuts passed under George W. Bush, did create some pressure on Republicans to compromise. The result was a raise in the debt ceiling and the extension of the Bush tax cuts on all individuals making less than $400,000 a year. Some Republicans also embraced immigration reform, believing it central to winning votes among Latinos.

On many other issues, however, Republicans did not appear ready to compromise. The budget sequestration, which Obama had thought Republicans wanted to avoid because of its cuts to defense spending, did not bring Republicans to the bargaining table. In fact, the budget plan drawn up by Paul Ryan and supported by most House Republicans proposed even further cuts to discretionary spending—especially to programs that Obama and Democrats generally support. After the tragic shooting in Newtown, Connecticut, and a strong push by Obama for new gun control measures, Senate Republicans mostly voted against those measures. In short, Republicans remain quite far apart from the Obama administration on big issues. Their posture is not unexpected. The week after the election, Paul Ryan dismissed the possibility that Obama had won a mandate, saying, "I don't think so" and noting that voters "also reelected House Republicans."[10] Thus the 2012 election seemed to produce only more of the slow grind of divided government, without any lubrication from a perceived mandate for Obama.

No Realignment

When one party wins control of the White House—and especially if that party has congressional majorities as well—some commentators cannot resist the presumption that this arrangement must always last. After the 2004 election the writer Michael Lind declared, "Karl Rove is an evil political genius, but he is a political genius. As he hoped, 2004 was a realigning election like 1896. . . . The Democratic Party is not a national party anymore."[11] And then in 2008, Lind had no problem changing his tune about a party that was "not a national party" only four years before: "The election of Barack Obama to the presidency may signal more than the end of an era of Republican presidential dominance and conservative ideology. It may mark the beginning of a Fourth Republic of the United States."[12]

The shift of power between the 2004 and 2008 elections—indeed the general seesawing of party power in recent decades—might suggest that elections do not have such grand consequences. But after 2012, similar pronouncements were made, exemplified by *New York Times* columnist Ross Douthat's calling the election "the Obama realignment." The 2012 election appeared to validate an influential 2002 book by John Judis and Ruy Teixeira called *The Emerging Democratic Majority*. After the 2008 election, Judis had declared that the election was a "radical realignment" that was "predicated on a change in political demography and geography."[13] Then after the 2012 election, Judis said "Barack Obama's reelection is evident of a Democratic realignment that dates back almost two decades."[14]

The problem with such conclusions is that they are based on the shopworn notion of "realignment"—a concept that once held sway among some political scientists but by now has largely been cast aside. The term was always a bit mushy, used in different ways by different scholars. But at its core, the notion of realignment refers to the profound changes wrought by certain distinctive or "critical" elections, occurring occasionally but regularly. "Realigning" elections crystallize a new coalition of voters and, at least in some accounts, bring about unified party control of government and thus major shifts in government policy. The main feature of realignments is their durability. Indeed, the original conception of realignment suggested that after each realigning election, the newly dominant party would hold sway for twenty or thirty years, until societal and political forces threw out the old order and created a new one.[15]

The reason that realignment has lost its sway among political scientists is simple: it does not describe what has happened. Scholars have looked for evidence that "critical" or realigning elections really ushered in permanent change and found that they did not. Even canonical realigning elections, like the 1896 election that Lind cited, did not have this effect. Political scientist Larry Bartels surveyed 128 years of presidential elections, and though one or two facts corresponded to conventional understandings of realigning elections—the impact of the 1932 election, for example—the overall pattern did not. There were no sharp breaks caused by realignments, followed by periods of relative stability.[16]

Instead, Bartels found a pattern directly at odds with what realignment suggests—and what commentators suggested about 2012. The realignment idea suggests that winning an election should be associated with continued success. Bartels found the larger the size the winning party's margin of victory in one election, the *smaller* that party's margin in subsequent elections. Winning did not begat more winning. It begat losing. Bartels described this as a tendency toward "equilibration"—that is, a tendency not toward periods of one-party dominance but consistent two-party competition, or what Bartels called "fairly regular alterations between Republican and Democratic possession of the White House."[17] This is analogous to the "dynamic equilibrium" of the general election campaign. Just as two well-funded presidential candidates often compete without one of them achieving a sustained advantage over the months of a campaign, so do the two parties compete without achieving a sustained advantage over multiple elections.

This is exactly what recent elections have illustrated. The presidency has oscillated between Democratic and Republican control. This has often occasioned some scrambling among those certain that a realignment was afoot. After Al Gore lost the 2000 election, Judis and Teixeira wrote that George W. Bush was going to confront a sputtering economy that might "easily be the final catalyst for a new realignment" in favor of the Democrats.[18] After

Republicans expanded their majority in the House in 2002 and Bush was re-elected in 2004, Teixeira blamed both Gore and John Kerry for their inability to "connect in a genuine fashion" with white working-class voters.[19]

Moreover, one party's victory in a presidential election has sometimes been followed by victories for the opposite party in midterm elections. According to Judis and Teixeira, the Republican takeover of the House in 1994—which interrupted the realignment signaled by Clinton's victory in 1992—was just "the Indian summer of an old realignment rather than the spring of a new one." If so, it has been the longest Indian summer on record. By the next midterm election in 2014, Republicans will have controlled the House for sixteen of the last twenty years. To Judis, elections like 2002 or 2010 are just "speed bumps" in the ongoing Democratic realignment.[20] Perhaps, but given that the 2010 midterm election delivered more House seats to the Republican Party than any election since 1938, "speed bump" may not be the most appropriate metaphor; "brick wall" comes to mind.

At this moment, the still-emerging Democratic realignment is twenty years old. It has lasted as long as the period *between* realignments was supposed to last, according to the classic works in the field. And yet it has not yielded what realignments are supposed to yield. Control of the White House has oscillated between the Democratic and Republican parties—largely following the economic fundamentals in each election year. Control of Congress has oscillated as well, with the Democrats having control in the Senate about half the time but Republicans controlling the House for most of this period. And even Judis believes that this realignment will not bring Democrats to power in Congress any time soon or bring about policy shifts in the liberal direction because of the "machinery of interest groups and lobbies."[21]

But what about the future? Perhaps the Democratic realignment that thus far seems elusive is only now picking up steam, as the electorate is comprised more and more of groups—especially younger voters and Latinos—that lean Democratic. Will current demographic trends finally bring about a Democratic realignment at last? We are skeptical, or at least far more cautious than some commentators.

Both proponents and skeptics of the emerging Democratic majority seem to agree on this much: 2012 hardly suggests that the Democrats can rest on their laurels. The growth in demographic groups that currently lean Democratic is slow enough that they are best thought of as a thumb on the scales in the Democrats' favor, and no more. The changing complexion of the electorate will not insulate Democrats from a year in which the fundamentals favor Republicans. We agree with Teixeira himself, who wrote several months after the election:

Political reality is far more complicated than suggested by the neat orderly progression of classic realignment theory, political scientists argue. Nothing is inevitable in American politics; everything is contingent. There are no automatic majorities and certainly no permanent majorities.

I am open to all this. Democrats will certainly *not* win every election for decades, no matter how big their demographic advantages. Decisions made by parties and the consequences of those decisions (e.g., for economic growth and distribution) certainly *will* be central to the ability of any party to win elections in a sustained fashion.[22]

This leaves the issue of whether and how much, despite the continued relevance of the economy and other short-term factors, the underlying terrain has shifted in the Democrats' favor. In part, this depends on the answers to two questions.

First, will the constituent groups of the "Obama coalition," such as young people and Latinos, remain as loyal to the Democratic Party and as motivated to vote as they were in 2008 or 2012? The good news for Democrats is that this generation of young people will likely remain disproportionately Democratic. Political identities tend to crystallize in early adulthood and remain stable over the lifespan. A thirty-year-old Democrat will probably be a Democrat when he or she is eighty.

There is an important qualification, however. The political leanings of any generation tend to reflect the political events they experienced in late adolescence and young adulthood. This generation of young people came of age during a time that was hardly favorable to the Republican Party. There was a lengthy and inconclusive Iraq War, a punishing recession, and an unpopular Republican president, George W. Bush. However, the next generation may come of age during an unsuccessful Democratic administration or a successful Republican administration—and then end up tilting toward the Republicans, as did young people who came of age during the Reagan administration. Indeed, early surveys of high-school age youth suggest that they are not as favorable to Obama as are young adults. Of course, we want to be cautious extrapolating from the views of high school students to their views as young adults. But we should also be cautious extrapolating the views of today's young adults to the generations that come after them.[23]

The future political tilt and motivation of racial and ethnic minorities are also uncertain. The "Obama realignment" may prove to involve only a coalition specific to Obama. When he is no longer at the top of the ticket, will groups like Latinos and African Americans turn out in such numbers and with such strong support for the Democratic candidate? Although 79% of

African Americans are "very enthusiastic" about the Democratic Party now, only 47% say they will be after Obama's presidency ends.[24] It is unlikely that African Americans are going to vote for a Republican candidate in large numbers, but will they turn out at such a high rate for whichever Democrat wants to succeed Obama?

The second question is whether the Republicans can make inroads into this coalition. The GOP does not need to win 75% of the Latino vote to win a presidential election. Even 40% might suffice. Is that possible? It is true, as we noted in chapter 7, that Latinos view the Republican Party as less concerned about them than the Democratic Party. But this does not mean that a particular Republican candidate could not win more of their votes than did Romney. For example, in a January 2012 Latino Decisions poll, Jeb Bush had a 67% approval rating among Hispanics in Florida, while Romney had a 40% rating and Obama a 60% rating. Another piece of data: in the Latino Decisions exit poll, 31% of Latino voters said they would be more likely to vote for the Republican Party if it supported comprehensive immigration reform.[25]

Of course, these data speak to hypothetical outcomes, and Republicans may need to do more than just embrace immigration reform and nominate Jeb Bush. But these findings should also give Democrats pause. Party coalitions are fairly stable election to election, and it is unlikely that Latinos will suddenly swing en masse to the Republican Party. But can the Republican Party do well enough among Latinos to win the White House? What about in a year when economic fundamentals are in Republicans' favor? Latinos' Democratic leaning does not mean they will ignore the fundamentals. Questions such as these make us unwilling to declare a Democratic realignment under way.

Ultimately, politics has much more contingency than notions of realignment suggest. As political scientist David Mayhew has written, "Any kind of contingency-free theorizing about real politics has serious limitations."[26] The fortunes of political parties rise and fall with the underlying fundamentals. Each political party adapts to counter the advantages of the other. It did not do the Democrats any favors to imagine their victory in 2008 was a mandate, and it will not do them any favors to imagine that 2012 was either a mandate or a realignment. The same will apply to Republicans the next time they win a presidential election. The country remains too closely divided politically for either party to assume we are at or approaching the End of History.

The Republican Reboot

The lesson that many people draw when a party loses a presidential election is that the party needs to change. The Republican Party certainly received no end of advice after the 2012 election. There were frequent calls for the party to embrace (or re-embrace) immigration reform (or not), same-sex marriage (or not), economic policies that would appeal to the middle class rather than the wealthy (or not), and so on.[27] Perhaps some of that advice was sensible. Maybe support for immigration reform is a necessary, if not sufficient, step in gaining votes from Latinos in future elections. And it may make sense to support same-sex marriage, simply to be on the right side of majority opinion.

Nevertheless, the lessons we draw are somewhat different. If the 2012 was no mandate for Obama and presaged no Democratic realignment and if, as we have argued, Obama's victory was consistent with the underlying economic fundamentals, then this puts a very different light on how the Republican Party should have reacted to its loss.

The 2012 election was not one that Republicans "should" have won. This is not to say that they were destined to lose, just that the fundamentals in the country favored Obama. Romney may not have been the strongest candidate on every dimension—likability, for instance—but simply eliminating such disadvantages relative to Obama probably would not have won him the election. Given all of this, Republicans could have looked back on the election and said, "Well, it is no fun losing, but it is hard to beat an incumbent president when the economy is growing even slowly. We needed to be exceptional to win and he only needed to be average." Paul Ryan even acknowledged this in September 2012, saying, "it's never easy to beat an incumbent" (though of course he promised that "we're going to beat him").[28]

Moreover, the same fundamentals suggest that Republicans can be at least somewhat optimistic about their chances in 2016. Although a lot will hinge on the rate of economic growth that year, Republicans can take heart in this: since the passage of the Twenty-Second Amendment limiting an incumbent president to two consecutive terms, only once—the period 1980–92—has one party controlled the White House for more than two consecutive terms. This regularity—present in our forecasting model in chapter 2—boosts the Republican Party's chances in 2016.

Another question that the Republican Party is debating is whether it needs to change its ideological stripes. Every faction within the party—moderate, conservative, and so forth—believes that the party would do better if only it would move in their direction. But maybe the problem is not really ideology. We have shown that the public has grown more conservative, not more liberal, during Obama's presidency, excepting issues like same-sex marriage where there are broader secular trends afoot. We have shown that Romney was arguably among the more moderate of the Republican presidential hopefuls and that he was perceived as ideologically closer to more voters during the general election than was Obama.

All of this suggests that the Republican Party's loss in 2012 was *mainly* about performance—specifically, that Obama had "performed" well enough, as judged by the fundamentals—and less about policy. It may be that the Republicans would benefit from endorsing same-sex marriage or immigration reform, and endorsing those policies is no small matter, as those positions will provoke opposition within some parts of the party. But those steps alone do not amount to a fundamental rethinking of the party's platform. Winning back the White House may not require it.

A final piece of advice often given to the Republican Party has little to do with message and more to do with tactics. Many Republicans envied the Obama campaign for its sophisticated use of data, its sprawling field operation, its innovative new digital tools. These Republicans argued that the GOP needs a reboot in terms of its campaign mechanics. Often this argument targeted the "old guard" of Republican consultants, especially the senior strategists of the Romney campaign.[29] This argument was often a bit diffuse and at times silly. Romney strategist Stuart Stevens was criticized for, of all things, not tweeting enough.

One could perhaps distill a more sensible lesson within this critique, however: play "moneyball." This means that the Republican Party needs to catch up to the Democratic Party in its ability to target voters and figure out how best to mobilize and persuade those voters. We agree that there is value in doing so, inasmuch as social science—whose findings have been incorporated and extended by groups working on the political left—can provide rigorous evidence about effective campaign tactics. Certainly the Obama campaign's innovations made it more efficient, thereby generating more bang for the buck. For example, the Obama campaign learned how to raise more money by experimenting with the text of email solicitations. It also used more detailed data on television viewing habits to place advertisements during television programs that did not command an expensive rate for advertisers but were watched by significant numbers of voters the campaign was targeting. This greater efficiency actually echoes how the Oakland Athletics used "moneyball": to find players that were not only talented but cost a lot less.

But we have also shown that campaign tactics alone were likely not responsible for Obama's victory. The Obama campaign, for all its innovations, was not necessarily the deciding factor in this race. Thus Republicans may find in 2016 that even if their campaign does not emulate Obama's in every respect, they may win anyway. Campaigning may move votes, much as it did in 2012, but not necessarily enough votes to constitute the winning margin.

In sum, it is rash to write off the Republican Party as a spent electoral force. If the economy slides backward before the 2016 election, they may find themselves favored. Of course, even with the economy on their side, this does not mean that the Republicans could nominate just any candidate and win. As the experiences of Barry Goldwater and George McGovern suggest, candidates who are perceived as ideologically out of step with the electorate are punished at the ballot box.[30] Fortunately, history suggests that losing parties are smarter than this: the longer a party is out of the White House, the more moderate its nominees become.[31] Guessing who the nominees will be is little better than a parlor game at this point, and we will not speculate. The point is simply this: history tells us that the combination of the fundamental conditions in the country, the qualities of the two candidates at the top of the ticket, and the strength of their respective campaigns could just as easily favor the Republicans in 2016 as they could favor the Democrats—even if the Republican Party does not reinvent itself between now and then.

The Math We Do

About 11:25 PM on Election Night, November 6, Karl Rove was in the Fox News studio alongside anchors Chris Wallace and Megyn Kelly, and he was not pleased. The night had been remarkably free of drama so far but not in the way Rove had hoped: Barack Obama appeared to be winning handily. And now the Fox News decision desk, consisting of two political scientists and other elections data analysts, had just made a consequential call: Obama would win Ohio, securing him the presidency. Then the drama began.

The Romney campaign immediately emailed Wallace to object, and Rove agreed, directly contradicting the decision desk and saying: "We gotta be careful about calling things when we have like 991 votes separating the two candidates and a quarter of the vote yet to count. Even if they have made it on the basis of select precincts, I'd be very cautious about intruding in this process." At 11:32, Kelly was then dispatched to the decision desk to interview its staff on air, one of whom, Arnon Mishkin, confirmed that they were "quite comfortable" with the call. When Kelly returned to the studio and Rove continued to object, he implicitly answered a question Kelly had asked Rove earlier in the evening, when things already looked grim for Romney: "Is this just math that you do as a Republican to make yourself feel better or is this real?"

This episode was a microcosm of a broader debate about the state of the horse race in the fall of 2012—the one pitting most election forecasters and polling aggregators on one side, and the "unskewed polls" adherents on the other. A central lesson of this book is "do the math," which is precisely what Rove and devotees of the "unskewed polls" did not want to do. We have made clear that "the math" does not generate perfect answers or complete certainty. But we have shown that it can take us far in understanding presidential campaigns and elections. Doing the math can help candidates and the media alike.

For candidates, "the math" has two implications. One has to do with the fundamentals. Many a campaign begins and then unceremoniously ends because candidates do not grasp what the fundamentals suggest about their campaign. In the primary, candidates need broad support within the party, what is most visibly expressed in endorsements from party leaders. It is hard to win with media and momentum alone, as Perry, Cain, Gingrich, and Santorum all discovered. It is also hard for candidates to believe this. We talked with strategists for one ultimately unsuccessful Republican candidate on the eve of the Iowa caucus. They outlined this candidate's path to victory, which entailed a stronger-than-expected showing in Iowa, then a victory in South Carolina, and then several other more steps. The more we listened, the more this plan sounded like the equivalent of a trick shot in billiards—stunning but improbable. The point is not that candidates with a small chance of winning should not run. There may be reasons for candidates to run for their party's presidential nomination even when they lose—and competition in elections is usually a good thing. The point is that candidates do themselves no favors when they do not appear to understand what it really takes to win.

In the general election, both parties' nominees can do nothing but campaign hard, even if the underlying fundamentals are not favorable. But understanding the fundamentals accurately can help the campaign strategize smarter. The Romney campaign's laser-focus on the economy suggested that they believed that the economy favored them. But it arguably favored Obama, which suggests that the Romney campaign needed to do more than blame the president for the pace of the economic recovery.

The other lesson for candidates, and campaign practitioners too, is to have a more modest view about what the campaign itself can do. At times, practitioners acknowledge the limitations in what they can accomplish. They talk about how few voters are really up for grabs, or how they expect television ads or the field organization to produce only a small effect—the proverbial "field goal unit," as Obama advisor David Plouffe said. But then after the campaign is over, the loser's campaign receives too much blame and the winner's campaign too much credit—including from the winners themselves. After the election, Bill Burton, the head of the Priorities USA, praised their ads attacking Romney for his time at Bain Capital: "They were emotional. People could connect on a visceral level." He went on to say that the Obama campaign was "strategic and had a clear sense of what they wanted to say about who Mitt Romney was." He added, "We were relentless."[32] In reality, campaign advertising had a measurable impact in 2012, but not one that likely determined the outcome, no matter how "relentless" the Obama campaign was.

Our view is that candidates should and indeed must campaign vigorously. It is precisely when one side out-campaigns the other that the polls may shift in its direction. But the combination of two vigorous campaigns is often a tie, as the two sides offset each other. It may seem perverse for a candidate to spend more than a billion dollars only to ensure a tie, but to do otherwise amounts to unilateral disarmament. We have also shown that most of the effects of campaign advertising wear off quickly. This might suggest that a campaign should wait and spend most of its money in the final week. We would not advise that either. We have documented the short-lived effects of ads only amid a hotly contested campaign. For one side to cede the airwaves to the other side until the end would create a very different campaign—one that has not been observed in contemporary presidential elections and one that we could only speculate about. In such a campaign, the candidate who did advertise might build up enough of a lead in the battleground states that a late and powerful blitz by the other candidate would be insufficient. While most of the effects of campaign advertising wear off quickly, a small fraction remains and builds. This long-term accumulation, coupled with the effects of new advertising every day, makes a sustained advertising advantage important. But sustaining that advantage is difficult in a competitive race. In short, presidential candidates can expect their campaigning to make some difference, but because both sides do so much of it with approximately the same level of skill, neither side can expect its campaign to outweigh any advantage or disadvantage bestowed by the fundamentals.

The lesson of this book for the media is that the tools of political or social science—the extant research, the reliance on hard data—can actually serve the incentives of journalists. To say so might sound surprising. It is often assumed that political science is of little use to journalists, precisely because it casts doubt on the campaign "game-changers" that make for great headlines. But drawing on political science and incorporating quantitative rigor serve two other goals that journalists have.

One is accuracy. Journalists want to get the story right. Consider this from a *Politico* article published the week before the election:

> Gov. Mitt Romney's campaign says it still has momentum. President Barack Obama's campaign says that's all spin. Meanwhile, there isn't a single well-informed pundit between them who can tell you who's right . . . pundits know that the trajectory of the campaign can turn on a dime. A change in a candidate's message, new revelations unearthed by the media, an unfortunate gaffe—all of these things could

change voter sentiment in Ohio, Florida, Virginia or any of the other battleground states and tip the scales in the last days of the election.[33]

In actuality, "well-informed" people had a very good idea of who was going to win the race. All of the major aggregations of public polls showed that Obama was likely to win. Moreover, studies of previous presidential elections have showed that polls conducted a week before the election have had a very good track record of predicting who would win.[34] Perhaps "pundits" were unable to see that, but journalists have the ability to go beyond what pundits say and examine the data and research themselves.

Another goal of journalists is to be skeptical about what the candidates and their campaigns say. Campaigns are forever pushing their own spin on events, and journalists know better than to believe it. This produces any number of news stories that investigate, fact-check, and critique the candidates' claims. So when candidates or their spokespersons go around promoting some moment as a potential game-changer, journalists can draw on moneyball—from political science, poll numbers, history, and so on—to identify that as spin, too. For example, the Romney campaign was free to go around claiming that they had momentum late in the race. Indeed, since they were behind at that point, it made sense for them to claim to be gaining ground. But there was no reason for reporters to imply that this was true when the polls had not moved for three weeks. The lesson is simple. Journalists have to report what the campaigns are saying and doing on any given day—that is their job—but when journalists *evaluate* what the campaigns are saying and doing, they can use social science and a closer look at the available data to separate truth from spin.

A World with Fewer Game-Changers

In this book, we have made three arguments about presidential campaigns. First, the relevant fundamentals structure outcomes in both the primaries and the general election. The candidate whom the fundamentals advantage tends to win. Second, media coverage and electioneering by the candidates can affect voters. But this occurs only when these things strongly favor one candidate at the expense of the other. This happens with some frequency in presidential primaries—and certainly it happened in 2012—but it happens much more rarely in presidential general elections. Third, when one side out-campaigns the other, the differences have an impact but one that is often short-lived. An advantage that one side has today may be gone by tomorrow. Thus to have a durable impact, one side must sustain this advantage—something that is not easy to do in the general election campaign.

We have put forth these arguments as a counterpoint to a view of presidential campaigns that constantly emphasizes "game-changers." Game-changing moments, especially ones that affect who wins or loses, are few and far between. This raises a final question: is the lack of game-changers a good thing or a bad thing for our democracy? Would elections be better or worse as links between the governed and those who govern them if things like television advertising, candidate debates, and inadvertent gaffes were *more* important than they seem to be? In other words, would elections be better or worse if there were more game-changers? A complete answer would require another book, but we will hazard a short answer that can at least serve as a provocation if nothing else.

The answer depends a great deal on what the game-changer is and how or why voters respond. What if a candidate made an innocuous mistake that was somehow decisive for many voters? Surely there are better criteria for choosing a candidate than some flub or off-the-cuff remark that commentators deemed a "gaffe." But what if the candidate made a comment like Todd Akin's about "legitimate rape"? That may be a more credible basis for voters to change their minds, since it signals something about Akin's views on abortion, a public policy issue of some consequence. (Akin's defenders would argue his comment was misconstrued.) The same is true of ads or debates. If some ads stretch or misrepresent the truth, then it is good that the effects of an advertising advantage are probably too small and temporary to determine the winner. If the debates are framed as theater by the media—as when one commentator opined that "Romney looked and sounded presidential" after the first debate—and voters therefore react more to the theater than the substance of what either candidate said, then it is good that presidential debates rarely decide the winner.[35] But ads can be truthful and contain useful information, and debates often feature substantive exchanges that reveal important differences between the candidates.

Of course, the "right" criteria for voting are not easy to agree on. One could argue that "the fundamentals" are not perfect criteria either. After all, the president has at best a limited impact on the nation's economy and deserves far less credit or blame than he receives. But given that a lot of the allegedly game-changing moments in 2012 did involve gaffes that were not all that revealing and ads that were half-true at best, we may be better-off in a world of "game-samers."

APPENDIX TO CHAPTER 2

Consumer Sentiment

The quarterly consumer sentiment data in Figure 2.2 are available here: http://www.sca .isr.umich.edu/data-archive/mine.php. Information about how the index is constructed is here: http://www.sca.isr.umich.edu/documents.php?c=i. These are the means and standard deviations for each president. For Obama, these include all data through the fourth quarter of 2011. The dates for the recessions indicated on Figure 2.2 are from the National Bureau of Economic Research.

	Mean	Standard deviation
Kennedy	94.9	3.0
Johnson	97.1	4.7
Nixon	81.4	8.8
Ford	76.2	11.5
Carter	74.4	10.9
Reagan	87.0	11.3
Bush I	82.3	9.2
Clinton	97.8	8.7
Bush II	85.9	9.9
Obama	68.5	5.2

Approval of Obama

The presidential approval data in Figure 2.3 were gathered from publicly available polls compiled by Pollster.com, a polling clearinghouse hosted by Huffington Post. We thank Mark Blumenthal for his help in acquiring these data.[1] The graph includes every poll that was taken after Obama's inauguration on January 29, 2009, and before December 31, 2011. The averaged trend line was estimated using a lowess smoother with a bandwidth of 0.05.

Forecast of Obama Approval

The analysis underlying Figure 2.4 drew on presidential approval data gathered by George Edwards and Gary Jacobson and then updated by us. We thank Jacobson for sharing data with us. For Presidents Truman through Clinton, the data include only Gallup polls. For President George W. Bush, the data include both Gallup and CBS News/*New York Times* polls. For Obama, they include all publicly available polls compiled by Pollster. The approval data contain overall approval among all respondents, as well as approval among Democrats, Republicans, and independents. Independents who lean toward a party were counted as independents. We aggregated the presidential approval data to quarters, dropping two quarters—the fourth quarter of 1963 and the third quarter of 1974—in which presidents overlapped due to Kennedy's assassination and Nixon's resignation. For six quarters there were no Gallup data (1948Q3, 1948Q4, 1949Q4, 1964Q3, 1972Q3, and 1976Q3). We imputed the approval rating for these quarters via linear interpolation. The data range from 1948 through the first quarter of 2012.

The economic indicators used in the analysis come from data collected and disseminated through the St. Louis Federal Reserve's FRED Database. These included the following indicators:

- Gross domestic product. This was calculated as the percentage change from the previous quarter.
- The unemployment rate. The model included the unemployment rate from the previous quarter, which has been a stronger predictor of approval than the unemployment rate in the current quarter.
- The consumer price index, which measures inflation. This was calculated as the percentage change from the previous quarter.

The analysis also included several other measures. Two were counts of salient events in each quarter that may have affected presidential approval in either a positive or a negative direction. These events were drawn from previous studies of presidential approval.[2] For the Obama administration, we coded the second quarter of 2011, when Osama bin Laden was killed, as containing a salient event in a positive direction. A second measure was a dummy variable that captured the effects of Watergate (coded 1 for the first quarter of 1973 through the second quarter of 1974, and 0 otherwise). A third measure was the number of American military casualties in each quarter between 1964 and 1968.[3] A fourth measure was the presence of divided government, coded 0 for unified government and 1 for divided government. (Presidential popularity has tended to be higher under divided government.)[4]

Because the data are both cross-sectional (across presidents) and over-time (across quarters), we estimated a fixed effects model that included a measure of approval lagged one quarter, the three economic indicators, the measures capturing Vietnam casualties, Watergate, and divided government, the numbers of positive and negative events, and the number of quarters the president had been in office at that point.[5]

To generate Figure 2.4, we estimated this model for every presidential administration before Obama's and then generated predicted approval ratings for Obama. As an illustration, here are the results from a model estimated on the data from 1948 through the first quarter of 2012. The results show that presidential approval is associated with all of these factors, although the effect of negative events is estimated somewhat imprecisely.

	Coefficient	Standard error
Approval rating in previous quarter	0.76	0.04
Unemployment rate in previous quarter	−1.10	0.44
Percentage change in GDP since previous quarter	0.93	0.40
Percentage change in inflation rate since previous quarter	−0.85	0.25
Watergate	−5.27	.77
Vietnam deaths	−.0009	.0003
Number of quarters in office	−0.21	0.06
Positive event	2.83	0.60
Negative event	−.63	0.43
Divided government	3.40	0.47
Constant	19.20	4.00

Note: Number of observations = 243. Number of presidents = 12. Overall R^2= 0.87. Standard error of the estimate = 4.57.

Below are the average differences between actual and predicted approval, as well as the average standard error of that difference, for each president.

	Difference (actual − predicted)	Standard error
Truman	−.70	6.02
Eisenhower	1.37	1.03
Kennedy	2.93	1.36
Johnson	−1.56	.78
Nixon	−2.40	.74
Ford	−.93	1.71
Carter	−.60	1.61
Reagan	1.73	1.04
Bush I	.70	2.33
Clinton	−.56	.88
Bush II	1.56	1.68
Obama	2.70	.55

To generate Figure 2.5, we used the 1948–2008 data and estimated models with the same factors, except we focused on approval ratings for Democrats, independents, and Republicans. We then predicted values for Obama for each partisan group.

Racial Attitudes and Presidential Approval

This analysis drew on a YouGov survey conducted April 14–17, 2011. The measure of racial attitudes, known as "racial resentment" in the political science literature, combined answers to four questions:

- "Over the past few years, blacks have gotten less than they deserve."
- "Irish, Italian, Jewish, and many other minorities overcame prejudice and worked their way up. Blacks should do the same without any special favors."
- "It's really a matter of some people not trying hard enough; if blacks would only try harder they could be just as well off as whites."
- "Generations of slavery and discrimination have created conditions that make it difficult for blacks to work their way out of the lower class."

This measure of racial attitudes is widely used although not without controversy.[6] However, other measures of racial attitudes—such as views of interracial dating or direct measures of racial stereotypes—are also strongly correlated with attitudes toward Obama.

In addition, the model included party identification (on a 7-point scale ranging from strong Republican to strong Democrat), self-reported ideology (on a 5-point scale ranging from strong conservative to strong liberal), sex, race, and income. Approval of Obama was a four-category measure that we collapse to two categories (approve or disapprove) to be consistent with the other analyses of presidential approval in this chapter. Below are the coefficients from the model.

	Coefficient	Standard error
Racial resentment	−0.64	0.11
Party identification	0.67	0.07
Ideology	0.75	0.15
Female	0.27	0.21
Black	1.00	0.43
Hispanic	0.27	0.37
Other race	−0.46	0.39
Income	0.04	0.03
Constant	−3.50	0.75

Note: Cell entries are logit coefficients and standard errors. Number of observations = 830. Pseudo-R^2 = 0.47.

The model predicted that Obama's approval rating would be 48.9% (in actuality, it was 48.2% in this sample, suggesting that the model's prediction was accurate). When racial attitudes were shifted to neutrality, his predicted approval rating was 52.8%. The difference between the two predicted values was statistically significant ($p < .001$). When we focused only on respondents who were not black, we obtained virtually the same result.

Blame for the Economy and Presidential Approval

This analysis also drew on the April 14–17 YouGov survey. In this survey, respondents were asked, "How much is each of the following people or groups to blame for the poor economic conditions of the past few years?" In random order, people were asked about

Obama, George W. Bush, Democrats in Congress, Republicans in Congress, "Wall Street bankers," and "Consumers who borrowed too much money." The response categories were: a great deal, a lot, a moderate amount, a little, and not at all. We subtracted the blame given to Obama from the blame given to Bush, so that higher values on the measure indicated more blame for Bush relative to Obama.

We then estimated a model of Obama approval, focusing only on those respondents who identified as independents and did not lean toward a major party. The model included this blame measure in addition to self-reported ideology, sex, race, and income. Below are the coefficients from the model.

	Coefficient	Standard error
Blame for economy	0.94	0.18
Ideology	−0.28	0.34
Female	0.17	0.45
Black	1.26	0.90
Hispanic	0.90	0.87
Other race	−0.81	0.80
Income	−0.10	0.07
Constant	0.40	1.19

Note: Cell entries are logit coefficients and standard errors. Number of observations = 142. Pseudo-R^2 = 0.30.

The model predicted that Obama's approval rating would be 40.1% (his actual approval rating among independents was 36.5% in this sample). Under the assumption that every respondent blamed Bush and Obama equally, his predicted approval rating was 30.8%. The difference between the two predicted values was statistically significant ($p < .001$). For more elaboration of this analysis, see: http://today.yougov.com/news/2012/04/27/blame-game/.

Presidential Election Forecast for 2012

The forecasting model focused on the incumbent party's share of the major-party vote in presidential elections from 1948 to 2008. The factors we included in the model were:

- Presidential approval in June of the election year. We calculated the average if there were multiple polls in that month.
- The percentage change in GDP between January and July of the election year. (Note that the results did not change much if we substituted GDP per capita or if we annualized the percentage change.)
- The percentage change in real disposable income per capita between January and July of the election year.
- The percentage point change in the unemployment rate between January and July of the election year.
- An indicator for whether the incumbent party had held the White House for only one term or for two or more terms.

The forecasting model always included presidential approval and the incumbent party's tenure in office. We estimated models including different combinations of the three economic indicators and then averaged the results together using a procedure called Bayesian model averaging. This technique is especially useful when there is not a strong reason to prefer a particular model and it makes more sense to evaluate a variety of plausible alternatives. We employed the technique because any or all of these economic indicators could plausibly have influenced presidential election outcomes. Here are the model's parameters after averaging:

	Coefficient	Standard error
Approval rating	0.21	0.06
Time in office	−3.65	1.51
Percentage change in GDP	1.12	0.92
Percentage change in RDI	0.37	0.62
Change in unemployment rate	0.10	1.86
Constant	45.33	4.83

Note: Number of observations = 16.

APPENDIX TO CHAPTER 3

Media Data

We relied on extensive media data collected by General Sentiment and the Project for Excellence in Journalism (PEJ). The General Sentiment data were discussed in the text. Here we describe the PEJ data in more detail.[1] After sampling stories from a range of print, broadcast, and cable news sources, the PEJ determined whether each of the presidential candidates was the focus of at least 25% of the story. They then calculated the share of the week's stories in which each candidate was featured at that level (where a week was defined as Monday through Sunday). PEJ also calculated the tone of news stories, albeit in a different fashion than they calculated news share and in a different fashion than does General Sentiment. PEJ staff members coded a set of news stories as positive, negative, or neutral toward the various candidates. Stories that were unambiguous in tone were then used to "train" a computer algorithm developed by the company Crimson Hexagon.[2] Like General Sentiment, Crimson Hexagon examined a large number of news sites (more than 11,500 in total) and then, drawing on its training by PEJ staff members, placed content from these news organizations in the categories positive, negative, or neutral. This methodology is different than General Sentiment's, which relies not on human coders to help the algorithm identify tone but on dictionaries of words with positive or negative connotations. Unlike General Sentiment, the PEJ methodology did not generate an overall "score" but percentages in each category of positive, negative, and neutral. We used both sources of information in an attempt to triangulate on the tone of news coverage.

Statistical Analyses

In the text we argued that salient events drove news attention to candidates. When this happened for the first time for any candidate—what we called "discovery"—the data suggested that news attention created a subsequent increase in poll numbers. At that point, news attention and poll numbers may have begun to reinforce each other, meaning that increasing news coverage helped drive poll numbers but increasing poll numbers helped drive news coverage. We attempted to get some purchase on the relationship between news coverage and polls using a technique called vector auto-regression (VAR). VAR is a way of modeling two factors that could simultaneously cause each other—that is, where you cannot assume that Factor #1 causes Factor #2 but not the other way around. A VAR model stipulates that each factor is caused by previous values of that factor as well as previous values of the other factor. In other words, a candidate's poll standing on Wednesday might be due to his standing on Monday and Tuesday, as well as news coverage on Monday and Tuesday.

To estimate these models, we followed these steps. First, we generated a measure of the candidate's national poll standing that helped separate movement in the polls from sampling fluctuation and provided us a daily measure, even though the national polls were episodic (as Figures 3.2–3.5 show). We first "smoothed" the polls using a technique called local regression or lowess, which helped "even out" the bumps and wiggles that may have arisen because of sampling fluctuation. Given the rapidity with which the candidates' poll numbers sometimes changed, we made the smoothed measure relatively sensitive to changes in poll numbers.[3] For days that did not have polling data, we interpolated poll numbers in a linear fashion. If polls showed a candidate at 15% on Monday and 18% on Thursday, we assumed that the candidate's standing was 16% on Tuesday and 17% on Wednesday. If anything, this method of smoothing likely underestimated the extent to which polls responded to news coverage of salient events. Even a relatively sensitive smoother may not have captured the abrupt changes that characterized polling during this primary and thus suggested erroneously that polls were moving even before the event and subsequent news coverage took place. Nevertheless, this was the best we could do without creating a measure that assumed that the polls could not move until after the event—which would essentially have meant creating a measure designed to confirm our theory.

Second, to capture news coverage, we relied on the measure of news share that was weighted by tone, as presented in Figures 3.2–3.5. We chose this measure because the figures suggest that poll numbers responded not only to the volume of coverage but also to its tone.

Third, we needed to choose the appropriate number of previous values. Because a candidate's poll standing and news coverage may have depended on his earlier poll standing and/or news coverage, we had to answer the question "how much earlier?" To do so, we examined various numbers of previous values and chose the model that best fit the available data.[4] Typically this meant including values from the previous two, three, or four days.

Having estimated these models, we then examined a statistic—the chi-squared statistic—that suggested whether each factor appeared to be causing the other. This statistic was generated from a test created by the statistician Clive Granger and is sometimes called a test of "Granger causality." Essentially it conveys how useful each factor was in predicting the other. If the chi-squared value was statistically significant, this did not necessarily imply strict causality, which we could not have ascertained without randomized experiments. But it did suggest how polls and news coverage were related.

In the table below we present the chi-squared statistics for Perry, Cain, Gingrich, and Romney from July to December 2011. For Cain, the model included the days through December 3, when he suspended his campaign.

For Perry, the results suggest a reinforcing cycle. More (and more favorable) news coverage was associated with higher poll numbers and vice versa. Although Perry's poll

	Polls → News	News → Polls
Perry	27.3*(2)	10.8*(2)
Cain	6.0(4)	12.8*(4)
Gingrich	21.3*(3)	5.7(3)
Romney	3.6 (4)	2.7(4)

Note: Cell entries are chi-squared statistics from Granger causality tests. Degrees of freedom are in parentheses. Number of observations for Perry, Gingrich, and Romney is 184; for Cain, it is 156.

*$p < .05$

numbers did not initially increase until after the news coverage did, after that it did appear that each helped sustain the other. For Cain, however, news coverage was associated with poll numbers but not the reverse. This may have been because the trends in Cain's coverage were driven less by success in the polls and more by discrete events—the Florida straw poll, the debates, and the allegations of sexual misconduct.

For Gingrich, the opposite was true: his rising poll numbers appeared to shape news coverage, but news coverage did not shape polls. This is consistent with what we found earlier, where there was a modest increase in his poll numbers in October even though news coverage had not increased. Moreover, his slow gain in the polls was noticed and cited by reporters. Later coverage in November also cited poll numbers, which could mean that the poll numbers themselves helped motivate the coverage, even though the coverage cited other factors besides poll numbers as reasons for the renewed attention to Gingrich.

Finally, for Romney an entirely different dynamic held. As we argued, news coverage of Romney and his poll numbers did not exhibit the same pattern as that of the other candidates. There was no apparent cycle of discovery, scrutiny, and decline but instead relative stability.

APPENDIX TO CHAPTER 4

Analysis of South Carolina and Florida Polls and Advertising

To estimate the possible effects of advertising in South Carolina and Florida, we combined pre-primary polls with data on advertising in each state's media markets. In South Carolina, we relied on three Public Policy Polling (PPP) surveys of likely Republican voters conducted January 5–7, 11–13, and 18–20 (right before the primary). In Florida, we relied on two Survey USA polls of likely Republican voters—one from January 8 (before the New Hampshire primary) and one from January 27–29 (right before the Florida primary). The advertising data were gathered by the Campaign Media Analysis Group. These data were measured at the level of sponsor, week, and market. So, for example, the data could tell us how many ads were aired by Mitt Romney in the Miami media market in the week ending

January 15. Because both sets of polls identified the county in which each respondent lived, we then matched respondents to their corresponding media markets and thus to the volume of advertising they could have seen.

South Carolina

Here were the trends in candidate favorability and preferences across the three PPP polls.

	January 5–7 poll	January 11–13 poll	January 18–20 poll
Views of Gingrich			
Favorable	50%	50%	55%
Unfavorable	38	37	36
No opinion	12	13	9
Views of Romney			
Favorable	62%	59%	54%
Unfavorable	27	26	39
No opinion	11	15	7
Candidate Preference			
Huntsman	4%	5%	0%
Gingrich	23	25	38
Romney	32	30	30
Paul	7	12	12
Perry	5	6	0
Santorum	19	14	14
Other/no opinion	10	8	5

The major trends are: a small increase in the percent of voters expressing a favorable opinion of Gingrich (50% to 55%), a larger increase in the percent expressing an unfavorable view of Romney (27% to 39%), and a large increase in the proportion planning to vote for Gingrich (23% to 38%).

The question was whether these trends differed across the various South Carolina media markets, depending on the balance of advertising in those markets. To estimate the apparent effects of advertisements, we estimated models in which candidate favorability and preference depend on three factors:

1. Whether the respondent was interviewed in the January 18–20 poll or in one of the earlier polls. This measure combined respondents to the two earlier polls because there was very little change in opinion between these polls.
2. The balance of pro- versus anti-Gingrich ads or pro- versus anti-Romney ads in the week prior to each poll. Given the relatively fast decay of advertising effects, the previous week's ads should be most effective, if the ads have any effect at all.[1] The CMAG data categorized ads by whether they supported or attacked a candidate and then reported the dollars spent on each category. We calculated the proportion of spending on that category and multiplied the total number of ads by that proportion. We then subtracted the estimated number of anti-candidate ads from the estimated

number of pro-candidate ads. Thus larger values indicated a larger number of positive ads related to negative ads. The analysis then applied the appropriate candidate-specific measure—for example, we assumed that attitudes toward Gingrich are only affected by advertisements supporting or opposing him.

3. The interaction between the first two factors. This indicated if the trend, which is captured by when the respondent was interviewed (i.e., in which poll), varied depending on the balance of advertising in the respondent's media market.

The models also included variables for the various media markets (not shown in the models below) to capture aspects of these markets besides the advertising that aired in them. We estimated models of four quantities: favorability toward Gingrich (coded 1-favorable and 0-otherwise), favorability toward Romney, preference for Gingrich (coded 1 for Gingrich and 0 for other candidates or no opinion), and preference for Romney. Here are the results:

	Gingrich favorability	Gingrich vote	Romney favorability	Romney vote
Last poll	0.18	0.68	−0.27	−0.07
	[0.19]	[0.10]	[0.06]	[0.06]
Ad balance	0.10	−0.11	0.05	0.02
	[0.07]	[0.10]	[0.05]	[0.05]
Last poll × ad balance	−0.08	0.08	−0.002	0.05
	[0.09]	[0.09]	[0.09]	[0.07]
Constant	0.16	−0.83	0.33	−0.80
	[0.08]	[0.05]	[0.09]	[0.05]

Table entries are logit coefficients with standard errors clustered by media market in parentheses. The models also include fixed effects for each media market, which are not shown.

N = 3,455

The coefficients for "Last poll" demonstrate that in markets where the ad balance was even, Gingrich's vote share increased between the first two and the third polls, while Romney's favorability decreased. But as the interaction terms demonstrate, this effect did not vary alongside the ad balance. The trends in South Carolina Republicans' opinions were not associated with the advertising that targeted or supported either Romney or Gingrich.

Florida

In Florida we estimated similar models drawing on the two Survey USA polls. We focused on candidate favorability because these polls did not capture the important trends in vote choice. The earlier Survey USA poll occurred before Gingrich's surge heading into the South Carolina primary, and because the later poll occurred after his numbers had declined, the proportion intending to vote for Gingrich was the same in each poll. Here were the trends in favorability across these two polls:

	January 8 poll	January 27–29 poll
Views of Gingrich		
Favorable	50%	44%
Unfavorable	22	34
Neutral	24	21
No opinion	3	1
Views of Romney		
Favorable	58	53
Unfavorable	19	25
Neutral	22	21
No opinion	2	0

Both candidates came to be viewed less favorably, although the shift was larger for Gingrich (whose unfavorables increased by almost 12 points) than for Romney (about 6 points).

For the statistical models, we collapsed these ratings into a measure coded 1 for unfavorable and 0 otherwise, since the changes in these ratings mainly involve a shift from favorable, neutral, or unfamiliar into unfavorable. The advertising measures again included only ads that aired in the week before each survey.

	Gingrich favorability	Romney favorability
Last poll	−1.34	0.38
	[0.27]	[0.71]
Ad balance in prior week	−0.19	−0.63
	[0.25]	[1.13]
Last poll × ad balance	0.50	0.50
	[0.23]	[1.13]
Constant	−0.43	−2.15
	[0.11]	[0.60]

Note: Table entries are logit coefficients with standard errors clustered by media market in parentheses. The models also include fixed effects for each media market, which are not shown.

$N = 1,107$

The results demonstrate that the trend across the two polls did vary by the level of advertising.[2] For example, the increase in the probability of having an unfavorable impression of Gingrich was negligible when the balance of pro- and anti-Gingrich ads in the respondents' market was most favorable to Gingrich (which was actually still not very favorable—about 300 more anti-Gingrich ads than pro-Gingrich ads). But in markets where the balance of ads tilted most strongly against Gingrich—about 800 more anti- than pro-Gingrich ads— the probability of an unfavorable opinion increased by about 0.34.

However, there was no effect of pro- and anti-Romney ads on the relatively small trend across these two polls. This is evidence that the anti-Gingrich ads did hurt Gingrich, but the anti-Romney ads did not hurt Romney.[3]

The Relationship between National Polls and News Coverage of the Candidates

As in the previous chapter, we examined the relationship between the news coverage of the candidates—in this case, Gingrich, Romney, and Santorum—and their national poll numbers. This helped reveal whether news coverage appeared to drive poll numbers, polls appeared to drive news coverage, or both simultaneously. The measures we employed and the methodology are discussed in more detail in the appendix to chapter 3. Here we report the Granger causality tests:

	Polls → News	News → Polls
Gingrich	11.3*	2.3
	(3)	(3)
Romney	1.7	3.2
	(4)	(4)
Santorum	11.3*	21.4*
	(4)	(4)

Note: Cell entries are chi-squared statistics from Granger causality tests. Degrees of freedom are in parentheses. Number of observations for Gingrich and Romney is 117; for Santorum it is 96 (January 1–April 9).

$^*p < .05$

The results parallel those from the previous chapter. For Gingrich, although news coverage after the South Carolina debates appeared to catalyze his poll numbers, overall his poll numbers appeared to drive news coverage, perhaps because of the dynamics of his decline after Florida. For Santorum, there appeared to be a reciprocal relationship between polls and news—much as there was for Perry in the fall of 2011—but here news coverage appeared to have the stronger effect, as judged by the magnitude of the chi-squared statistics. For Romney, there was no systematic relationship between news coverage and poll numbers, which once again suggests how the cycle of discovery, scrutiny, and decline applied much less to him.

APPENDIX TO CHAPTER 5

The Relationship between News Coverage and National Polling

As we did in chapters 3 and 4, we examined the relationship between news coverage and polling using vector auto-regression. The polling data were the Pollster averages presented in Figure 5.4. News coverage was the tone-weighted measure of volume presented in Figure 5.3. We estimated models for Obama and Romney separately, as well as for the difference between them to capture whether the difference in their news coverage was related to the margin between them in the polls. The data spanned the period from May 1 to August 31. The results suggested no statistically significant relationship between news and polls.

	Polls → News	News → Polls
Obama	2.9	4.8
	(4)	(4)
Romney	2.1	4.3
	(4)	(4)
Difference (Obama − Romney)	1.0	3.4
	(3)	(3)

Note: Cell entries are chi-squared statistics from Granger causality tests. Degrees of freedom are in parentheses. $N = 119$

Models of Vote Intention and Empathy

Did the attention to Romney's experience at Bain Capital during the summer of 2012 make "empathy" a more salient criterion for voters in choosing between Romney and Obama? To answer this question, we took measures related to empathy and examined their relationship to vote intention in successive polls via regression modeling. If those relationships strengthened, it should have been evident in the size of the regression coefficient, which would have increased through the spring and summer.

In this model, vote intention was coded −1 for Romney, 0 for those who are undecided or preferred another candidate, and 1 for Obama. Those who initially said they were undecided but in a follow-up question indicated that they leaned toward a candidate were coded as supporting that candidate. Empathy was measured with five questions asking how well each of the following described Obama and Romney: is personally wealthy, cares about people like me, cares about the wealthy, cares about the middle class, and cares about the poor. The possible responses were "very well," "somewhat well," "not very well," or "not at all well." We then computed the difference between evaluations of Obama and Romney on each dimension. In the first model, we examined the effects of each dimension separately. In the second model, we computed the average difference across all dimensions—a summary measure of empathy perceptions. (The reliability of this summary measure is 0.79.) Both models also included party identification as a factor.

For the period through August 2012, these measures of empathy were available in seven YouGov polls, stretching back to the weekend before the New Hampshire primary and continuing until the surge of advertising and news coverage of Bain Capital had concluded. We would expect to see stronger relationships between these measures and vote intention in July in particular, which was when Bain Capital took center stage in the campaign.

In fact, there was very little by way of secular trends across this time period. In the first model, the "cares about people like me" measure had a somewhat stronger relationship to the vote in June and July than in April, but the apparent increase between April and June predated most discussion of Romney and Bain. In the July surveys, when that discussion was most intense, the relationship did not change very much. The "cares about the middle class" measure actually had a stronger relationship to vote intention *before* June and July. The other three measures were more weakly associated with vote intentions throughout this period and manifested no discernible trend. The second model, using the summary measure, confirmed this finding. There was no secular trend in the summary measure's apparent effect, and certainly no increase in July.

	Dates of poll						
	Jan. 7–10	Jan. 14–17	Jan. 21–24	April 7–10	June 9–11	July 14–16	July 28–30
Model 1							
Personally wealthy	−0.10	−0.05	−0.10	0.02	−0.05	−0.02	0.09
	(0.07)	(0.06)	(0.07)	(0.06)	(0.07)	(0.06)	(0.07)
Cares about people like me	0.53	0.55	0.48	0.38	0.69	0.79	0.70
	(0.08)	(0.08)	(0.10)	(0.09)	(0.09)	(0.08)	(0.08)
							(continued)

	Dates of poll						
	Jan. 7–10	Jan. 14–17	Jan. 21–24	April 7–10	June 9–11	July 14–16	July 28–30
Model 1							
Cares about poor	0.12	0.03	0.05	0.15	−0.07	0.02	0.03
	(0.08)	(0.07)	(0.08)	(0.07)	(0.06)	(0.06)	(0.06)
Cares about middle class	0.38	0.42	0.39	0.39	0.29	0.23	0.24
	(0.09)	(0.09)	(0.09)	(0.08)	(0.09)	(0.08)	(0.08)
Cares about wealthy	0.01	−0.06	−0.03	0.05	0.03	−0.09	−0.13
	(0.06)	(0.05)	(0.05)	(0.05)	(0.05)	(0.05)	(0.05)
Model 2							
Summary of empathy perceptions	1.55	1.55	1.39	1.37	1.39	1.53	1.39
	(0.09)	(0.07)	(0.08)	(0.07)	(0.06)	(0.06)	(0.06)

Note: Cell entries are OLS regression coefficients, with standard errors in parentheses. The model also controlled for party identification.

The Effects of Television Advertising on Vote Intention

Below are some descriptive statistics about presidential television advertising during June and July 2012. We broke down the advertising data by the sponsor of the ad and whether it appeared on broadcast television, national cable, or local cable. We included the total number of ads and GRPs. Our statistical model used GRPs and thus did not include local cable ads.

	Broadcast	Cable	Local cable
Obama for America			
Ads	137,604	16,170	16,155
GRPs	439,366	9,760	
			(continued)

	Broadcast	Cable	Local cable
Priorities USA Action			
Ads	11,195	0	6,293
GRPs	292,253	0	
Romney for President			
Ads	56,324	0	0
GRPs	202,772	0	
RNC			
Ads	10,077	0	1,227
GRPs	38,063	0	
Crossroads/GPS			
Ads	40,562	3,872	8,338
GRPs	144,918	2,916	
Americans for Prosperity			
Ads	14,136	20,526	2,414
GRPs	8,250	62,105	
Restore our Future			
Ads	8,002	0	669
GRPs	33,231	0	
Total Romney			
Ads	166,111		
GRPs	492,255		
Total Obama			
Ads	187,417		
GRPs	478,773		

Note: The data are statistics on advertising volume across 210 media markets between June 1 and July 30. These data were provided by The Nielsen Company under a licensing agreement with Lynn Vavreck and John Geer. Local cable advertising is measured in advertising units (number of airings) only. GRPs are gross rating points and are equal to the ad's percent reach multiplied by its frequency. For example, 100 GRPs could mean that 100% of TV households in a given market saw the ad once.

The balance of Democratic and Republican GRPs was matched to survey respondents by their media market and day of interview. Respondents were interviewed throughout the day. We would have liked to match each respondent to ads that ran in his or her market up to the exact time of interview and not after. Unfortunately, the GRP data were summed over the calendar day. This meant, for example, that respondents who took the survey between midnight and 3:00 AM on Tuesday could have seen many ads over the course of Monday evening, but few or none on the calendar day (Tuesday) they took the survey. We could not eliminate this problem but significantly ameliorated it. The few people who completed interviews between midnight and 3:00 AM were assigned to ads from the previous calendar day. Everyone else was coded as potentially exposed to some of the ads on their calendar day of interview.

Having matched respondents to advertising data in their market, we then estimated a statistical model of vote intention—specifically, an ordered probit model where respondents were coded as supporting Obama, undecided, or supporting Romney. We ignored the small fraction of respondents who supported another candidate. The model included the ad balance on the day of interview and the previous five days (positive values favor Obama). The model also included these attributes of individuals: party identification, self-reported ideology, education, age, race, gender, income, political knowledge, and interest in news. We included the week of interview to account for factors, like the tenor of news coverage, that may have varied week to week across all media markets. We accounted for whether a respondent's media market saw no presidential advertising at all on the day of interview as well as the state respondents lived in, which helped capture other kinds of campaign activity in the battleground states, like field organizations, and the media markets in which they lived. Below are the coefficients and standard errors.

	Coefficient	Standard error
Day of interview ads	.06	.03
Previous 5 days' ads	−.003	.003
Party ID (3 categories)	.97	.02
Ideology (3 categories)	−1.1	.03
Latino	−.22	.06
White	−.35	.04
Female	.06	.03
Education (3 categories)	.05	.03
Political knowledge	−.11	.02
Income	−.02	.007
Over 55	.06	.04
Attention to news scale	1.4	.11
Racial attitudes	−.60	.02
Battleground	−.19	.43
No ads in market	.11	.05
Cut 1	−.25	.43
Cut 2	.05	.43

Note: This model is a variation of the model in Hill et al. (2013), "How Quickly We Forget." The dependent variable is vote intention measured in three categories: Romney, undecided, Obama. The advertising variables are measured using GRPs and are the difference in each candidate's total advertising on the day and in the market corresponding to a respondent's interview and location. Estimation is an ordered probit. Not shown are the coefficients for week of interview and for respondents' media markets and states of residence. Also not shown is the coefficient for a dummy variable for declining to state a household income level (these respondents are included at the midpoint of the income scale). The data are from The Nielsen Company and YouGov, Inc. for the Cooperative Campaign Analysis Project. The model explained about 57% of variation in vote intention. $N = 15{,}881$.

APPENDIX TO CHAPTER 6

The Relationship between News Coverage and Poll Standing

In the table that follows we report the results of vector auto-regressions of poll standing—specifically the tests of Granger causality. The polling data are the Pollster averages presented in Figure 6.2. News coverage is the tone-weighted measure of volume presented in Figure 6.1. We report the results for Obama and Romney separately, as well as for the difference between them to capture whether the difference in their news coverage is related to the margin between them in the polls. The data span the period from May 1 to November 5.

	Polls $\rightarrow$ News	News $\rightarrow$ Polls
Obama	8.3*	3.1
	(3)	(3)
Romney	10.9*	3.4
	(4)	(4)
Difference (Obama – Romney)	15.5*	5.4
	(3)	(3)

Note: Cell entries are chi-squared statistics from Granger causality tests. Degrees of freedom are in parentheses. $N = 185$.

*$p < .05$

APPENDIX TO CHAPTER 7

Analysis of Economic Perceptions and Vote Intention

To measure how the association between economic perceptions and vote intentions evolved over the campaign, we constructed a statistical model that leveraged the earlier interview with respondents in December 2011. Vote intentions were coded 1-Obama, 0-undecided, and –1-Romney. The statistical model included party identification, which was measured in December 2011 (coded 1-Democrat, 0-independent, and –1-Republican, with independents who leaned toward a party coded as partisans). The statistical model also included economic perceptions (coded 1-economy getting better, 0-economy the same, and –1-economy getting worse). However, because economic perceptions may themselves have been the consequence, rather than a cause of, vote intentions—due to the partisan activation process we discussed—we employed an instrumental variables framework, using economic perceptions in 2011 as the "instrument" for perceptions during the campaign. This framework helps reduce the bias in the estimated effect of the factor whose causal status is less clear. Typically, it shows the estimated effect to be smaller than if its causal status were ignored.[1] In the table below we present the estimated effects of economic perceptions and party identification for each weekly survey, focusing only on persuadable voters. These numbers underlie Figure 7.4.

Month	Economic Evaluations		Party Identification	
	b	s.e.	b	s.e.
January	0.10	0.06	0.28	0.04
February	0.14	0.08	0.15	0.04
March	0.19	0.09	0.25	0.04
April	0.10	0.07	0.35	0.03
May	0.36	0.08	0.28	0.04
June	0.40	0.09	0.32	0.04
July	0.53	0.08	0.24	0.04
August	0.37	0.11	0.34	0.04
September	0.41	0.07	0.33	0.04
October	0.29	0.08	0.41	0.05

Note: Cell entries are estimated coefficients and standard errors from a two-stage least squares model estimated separately for each month's data. Persuadable voters are those who were undecided or preferred a candidate other than Obama and Romney when first interviewed in December 2011. Data from YouGov polls.

Analysis of Abortion, Contraception, and the Political Attitudes of Women and Men

The analysis we present in this section is in two parts. First, to estimate the effects of news coverage of abortion and contraception on political attitudes, we modeled several different attitudes as a function of news coverage, whether the respondent was a man, a woman age 18–44, or a woman age 45 or above, and the interaction of the two. This allows us to see whether the differences between the attitudes of women and men were greater when there was extensive news coverage of these issues. We also controlled for several other factors: age, education, party identification, and ethnicity. The five different types of attitudes we examined were vote intention, net favorability (favorability toward Obama minus favorability toward Romney), Obama job approval, Obama job approval on abortion, and enthusiasm for voting in the general election. Each of these variables was coded –1 to +1, with higher values indicating more pro-Obama attitudes or more enthusiasm for voting. Below is a sample set of results, where news coverage was measured as the number of mentions (in 10,000s) of these issues in the week before the day of interview.

	Vote intention	Net favorability	Obama approval	Obama approval (abortion)	Enthusiasm for voting
Women age 18–44	0.019	−0.003	0.031	0.005	−0.162
	[0.022]	[0.017]	[0.015]	[0.016]	[0.032]
Women age 18–44 × News coverage	0.0004	−0.003	−0.0003	0.0002	0.008
	[0.005]	[0.005]	[0.004]	[0.004]	[0.009]
Women age 45+	0.040	0.040	0.075	0.043	−0.142
	[0.013]	[0.012]	[0.011]	[0.014]	[0.024]
Women age 45+ × News coverage	−0.004	−0.005	−0.004	0.003	0.013
	[0.003]	[0.003]	[0.003]	[0.004]	[0.007]

(continued)

	Vote intention	Net favorability	Obama approval	Obama approval (abortion)	Enthusiasm for voting
News coverage	0.003	0.004	0.005	−0.0001	−0.008
	[0.003]	[0.002]	[0.002]	[0.002]	[0.005]
Constant	−0.011	0.103	0.267	0.176	0.446
	[0.030]	[0.020]	[0.020]	[0.020]	[0.064]
R-squared	0.63	0.58	0.52	0.34	0.11
Observations	36,347	33,300	42,934	42,648	15,302

Note: Cell entries are ordinary least squares regression coefficients and standard errors clustered by day of interview. Not shown are the coefficients for age and education as well as dummy variables for party identification and ethnicity. News coverage is the sum of coverage (in 10,000s of mentions) in the week before the day of interview.

The most important coefficients—for the interactions between being a woman and news coverage—are almost all substantively small in size and statistically insignificant. Perhaps the only exception is that women age 45 and older expressed more enthusiasm about voting during periods when news coverage of abortion and contraception was prevalent. But the bump in enthusiasm was small. If we think of enthusiasm as a 100-point scale and compare women interviewed when this coverage was at its minimum to women interviewed when the coverage was at its maximum, the shift in enthusiasm was only 6 points. In general, the differences between men and women did not grow larger as the volume of coverage increased.

We estimated alternative models with measures of news coverage from the day of interview, the day of interview plus the previous two days, and the previous three days combined. This did not produce any consistent changes in our conclusions. We also examined only the period between June and November, when Romney was known to be the Republican nominee. Again, our conclusions remained the same. We then examined only "persuadable voters"—those who said they were undecided or preferred a third-party candidate when originally interviewed in December 2011. There were no significant effects of news coverage among these voters.

The second part of the analysis looked at the effect of abortion attitudes on vote intentions and vote choice. Here we leveraged a useful feature of the data: in December 2011, YouGov first measured abortion attitudes and vote intentions, and then, in November 2012, YouGov measured vote choices after the election. This allowed us to compare the effects of abortion attitudes within the same respondents, but at two points in time. In particular, we modeled transitions from initial vote intentions in December 2011—which had four categories: Obama, Romney, another candidate, or undecided—to final vote reports in November 2012. We interacted each explanatory factor with each category of initial vote intention to ascertain how much each factor may have helped change vote decisions.[2] To measure abortion attitudes, we constructed a scale from two questions: whether abortion should be legal in all cases, legal/illegal in some cases, or illegal in all cases; and whether respondents called themselves pro-life, pro-choice, both, or neither. The resulting scale ranged from −1 (someone who said illegal in all cases and pro-life) to +1 (someone who said legal in all cases and pro-choice). Our statistical model also took account of attitudes toward economic issues (whether there is too much, too little, or the right amount of government regulation of business, and whether taxes should be raised on families earning over $200,000 per year), racial resentment (discussed in the appendix to chapter 2), party identification, age, and ethnicity. (For simplicity's sake, we do not include economic evaluations, which are at least somewhat endogenous to vote intentions and vote choice and thus require a more complicated instrumental variables model, as we presented earlier.) Given the highly interactive structure of the model, we estimated it using ordinary least squares, also for simplicity's sake. Below we show the results of this model separately for men and women.

	Men		Women	
	b	se	B	se
Obama supporter (Dec. 2011)	0.874	(0.015)	0.954	(0.016)
Romney supporter (Dec. 2011)	0.159	(0.014)	0.251	(0.019)
Other candidate supporter (Dec. 2011)	0.756	(0.051)	0.433	(0.070)
Undecided (Dec. 2011)	0.471	(0.028)	0.724	(0.029)
Obama × abortion attitudes	0.045	(0.005)	0.010	(0.005)
Romney × abortion attitudes	0.006	(0.005)	0.044	(0.005)
Other × abortion attitudes	0.045	(0.016)	0.155	(0.022)
Undecided × abortion attitudes	0.020	(0.012)	0.151	(0.011)
Obama × economic attitudes	0.039	(0.007)	0.014	(0.007)
Romney × economic attitudes	0.061	(0.005)	0.063	(0.005)
Other × economic attitudes	0.101	(0.018)	0.088	(0.022)
Undecided × economic attitudes	0.120	(0.011)	0.003	(0.013)
Obama × racial resentment	−0.024	(0.006)	−0.019	(0.006)
Romney × racial resentment	−0.057	(0.007)	−0.051	(0.009)
Other × racial resentment	−0.348	(0.025)	−0.031	(0.029)
Undecided × racial resentment	−0.163	(0.017)	−0.118	(0.015)
Obama × Democrat	0.010	(0.010)	0.033	(0.011)
Romney × Democrat	0.099	(0.014)	0.158	(0.015)
Other × Democrat	0.225	(0.032)	0.313	(0.040)
Undecided × Democrat	0.313	(0.018)	0.139	(0.017)
Obama × Republican	−0.127	(0.015)	−0.163	(0.018)
Romney × Republican	−0.042	(0.009)	−0.063	(0.012)
Other × Republican	−0.151	(0.025)	−0.204	(0.033)
Undecided × Republican	−0.351	(0.018)	−0.263	(0.017)
Obama × education	0.004	(0.002)	0.0003	(0.002)
Romney × education	0.002	(0.002)	−0.002	(0.002)
Other × education	−0.008	(0.007)	0.003	(0.009)
Undecided × education	0.023	(0.005)	−0.011	(0.005)
Obama × age	0.0004	(0.000)	−0.0004	(0.000)
Romney × age	−0.001	(0.000)	−0.001	(0.000)
Other × age	−0.004	(0.001)	−0.001	(0.001)
Undecided × age	0.0005	(0.000)	−0.002	(0.000)
Obama × black	0.037	(0.007)	0.008	(0.008)

(continued)

	Men		Women	
	b	se	B	se
Romney × black	0.015	(0.020)	0.131	(0.027)
Other × black	−0.165	(0.089)	0.057	(0.080)
Undecided × black	0.246	(0.027)	0.199	(0.029)
Obama × Latino	0.025	(0.009)	0.009	(0.010)
Romney × Latino	−0.037	(0.010)	0.004	(0.013)
Other × Latino	−0.176	(0.027)	0.050	(0.104)
Undecided × Latino	−0.004	(0.028)	0.259	(0.017)
Obama × Asian	−0.018	(0.018)	0.006	(0.020)
Romney × Asian	−0.005	(0.030)	−0.033	(0.035)
Other × Asian	0.270	(0.147)	−0.377	(0.094)
Undecided × Asian	0.070	(0.044)	0.097	(0.046)
Obama × other race	0.031	(0.013)	−0.028	(0.014)
Romney × other race	0.004	(0.010)	−0.039	(0.017)
Other × other race	−0.049	(0.030)	0.128	(0.051)
Undecided × other race	0.086	(0.036)	−0.045	(0.032)
R-squared	.92		.91	
Observations	12,599		13,479	

Note: Cell entries are ordinary least squares coefficients with standard errors in parentheses. The dependent variable is coded 0-Romney or 1-Obama. Abortion and economic attitudes are coded so that higher values correspond to more liberal attitudes.

To calculate the effects we present in the text, we first drew on the method proposed by political scientists Michael Hanmer and Kerem Ozan Kalkan.[3] This provided an estimate of the differences between pro-life and pro-choice respondents. These are average effects of abortion attitudes across the respondents included in any model, given observed values on each variable for each respondent. Second, we calculated the "contribution" of abortion attitudes to the candidates' overall vote share by multiplying the coefficient for abortion attitudes by the mean on the abortion attitudes scale. We did this separately for each of the four groups defined by their December 2011 vote intention. This is a method for assessing the "level importance" of a variable.[4]

Analysis of Latinos and Attitudes toward Immigration

The analysis of the vote choices of Latinos and other ethnic groups paralleled that of men and women above. The main difference was that we include three additional measures. One is a scale that combined three questions about immigration:

- Overall, do you think illegal immigrants make a contribution to American society or are a drain? (mostly making a contribution, neither, mostly a drain)
- Do you favor or oppose providing a legal way for illegal immigrants already in the United States to become U.S. citizens? (favor or oppose)
- Do you think it should be easier or harder for foreigners to immigrate to the United States legally than it is currently? (much easier, slightly easier, no change, slightly harder, much harder)

In addition, we included a measure of attitudes toward health care, which combined whether or not respondents agreed with this statement: "it is the responsibility of the federal government to see to it that everyone has health care coverage" and whether they thought that health care reform should be repealed, expanded, or kept the same. The measure of social attitudes combined the two questions about abortion included in the previous analysis as well as support for same-sex marriage. As in the analysis of women's and men's voting behavior, all of the variables in this model were measured in December 2011.

The first set of models examined vote intentions in the December 2011 interview. These were coded 0 for Romney, .5 for undecided voters or those supporting another candidate, and 1 for Obama. Below are models for both Hispanic and non-Hispanic white respondents.

	Hispanics		Non-Hispanic whites	
	b	se	b	se
Immigration attitudes	0.037	(0.010)	0.055	(0.003)
Health care attitudes	0.115	(0.009)	0.155	(0.003)
Social attitudes	0.022	(0.009)	0.075	(0.003)
Economic attitudes	0.036	(0.009)	0.066	(0.003)
Racial resentment	−0.164	(0.012)	−0.037	(0.004)
Democrat	0.248	(0.013)	0.203	(0.005)
Republican	−0.186	(0.016)	−0.191	(0.005)
Education	−0.010	(0.004)	0.001	(0.001)
Age	−0.001	(0.000)	−0.001	(0.000)
Female	0.017	(0.010)	−0.013	(0.003)
Constant	0.608	(0.021)	0.535	(0.007)
R-squared	0.53		0.65	
Observations	3,971		31,729	

Note: Cell entries are ordinary least squares coefficients with standard errors in brackets. The dependent variable is coded 0-Romney, .5-undecided or other candidate, or 1-Obama. All attitudinal measures are coded so that higher values correspond to more liberal attitudes.

The second set of models focused on reported vote decisions after the election, in the November 2012 wave, and how those related to vote intentions in December 2011, a host of other factors, and the interaction between these factors and vote intentions. This model thus resembles the model used to estimate the impact of abortion attitudes on men's and women's vote decisions.

	Hispanics		Whites	
	b	se	b	se
Obama supporter (Dec. 2011)	0.932	(0.030)	0.867	(0.014)
Romney supporter (Dec. 2011)	0.139	(0.034)	0.262	(0.013)
Other candidate supporter (Dec. 2011)	0.711	(0.150)	0.619	(0.049)
Undecided (Dec. 2011)	0.923	(0.046)	0.590	(0.024)
Obama × immigration attitudes	0.015	(0.010)	−0.004	(0.005)
Romney × immigration attitudes	−0.015	(0.012)	0.025	(0.005)

(continued)

	Hispanics		Whites	
	b	se	b	se
Other × immigration attitudes	−0.253	(0.059)	−0.014	(0.018)
Undecided × abortion attitudes	0.261	(0.019)	−0.026	(0.012)
Obama × health care attitudes	−0.007	(0.010)	0.035	(0.005)
Romney × health care attitudes	0.114	(0.016)	0.151	(0.006)
Other × health care attitudes	0.444	(0.076)	0.067	(0.019)
Undecided × health care attitudes	0.213	(0.015)	0.095	(0.010)
Obama × social attitudes	0.012	(0.009)	0.041	(0.006)
Romney × social attitudes	−0.014	(0.013)	0.027	(0.004)
Other × social attitudes	0.028	(0.052)	0.128	(0.016)
Undecided × social attitudes	0.021	(0.018)	0.140	(0.010)
Obama × economic attitudes	0.016	(0.011)	0.027	(0.007)
Romney × economic attitudes	−0.002	(0.012)	0.015	(0.004)
Other × economic attitudes	−0.204	(0.061)	0.110	(0.017)
Undecided × economic attitudes	−0.028	(0.021)	0.072	(0.011)
Obama × racial resentment	0.001	(0.010)	−0.017	(0.006)
Romney × racial resentment	−0.027	(0.020)	−0.013	(0.007)
Other × racial resentment	−0.138	(0.099)	−0.104	(0.024)
Undecided × racial resentment	0.019	(0.026)	−0.157	(0.015)
Obama × Democrat	0.037	(0.023)	0.017	(0.010)
Romney × Democrat	0.179	(0.026)	0.095	(0.012)
Other × Democrat	0.230	(0.089)	0.302	(0.030)
Undecided × Democrat	0.014	(0.030)	0.178	(0.015)
Obama × Republican	−0.357	(0.039)	−0.075	(0.014)
Romney × Republican	−0.019	(0.020)	−0.043	(0.008)
Other × Republican	−0.439	(0.070)	−0.166	(0.023)
Undecided × Republican	−0.44	(0.025)	−0.275	(0.015)
Obama × education	−0.001	(0.003)	0.001	(0.002)
Romney × education	0.006	(0.005)	0.001	(0.002)
Other × education	0.039	(0.020)	−0.016	(0.006)
Undecided × education	−0.060	(0.008)	0.008	(0.004)
Obama × age	0.0002	(0.000)	0.0003	(0.000)
Romney × age	−0.001	(0.000)	−0.001	(0.000)
Other × age	−0.004	(0.003)	−0.002	(0.001)
Undecided × age	−0.005	(0.001)	0.000003	(0.000)
Obama × female	0.002	(0.010)	0.015	(0.005)
Romney × female	0.041	(0.013)	0.006	(0.005)
Other × female	0.005	(0.085)	−0.019	(0.018)
Undecided × female	0.348	(0.027)	−0.022	(0.012)
R-squared	.96		.89	
Observations	2,289		18,906	

Note: Cell entries are ordinary least squares coefficients with standard errors in parentheses. The dependent variable is coded 0-Romney or 1-Obama. Immigration, health care, social, and economic attitudes are coded so that higher values correspond to more liberal attitudes.

Analysis of Racial Attitudes

To estimate the effect of racial attitudes, we leveraged both the 2012 survey as well as a 2008 survey that was also conducted by YouGov. The 2008 survey impaneled 20,000 people over several waves of interviews in 2008 and was representative of registered voters.[5] In 2008, the racial resentment measure was asked in the September wave of the survey. For the 2012 project, it was asked in the December 2011 wave. The 2008 survey also contained alternative measures of prejudice, but the 2012 study contained only racial resentment so we limited our attention to this measure. We jointly scaled the four racial resentment items for both. The scale's reliability was 0.86. Higher values indicated less favorable attitudes toward blacks.

We estimated a model of vote choice in the November 2008 and 2012 waves, focusing only on white voters and using a handful of political and demographic variables that were common to both survey instruments: party identification (dummy variables for Democratic and Republican respondents, including those who lean toward a party), ideology (a five-category measure ranging from very conservative to very liberal), education, age, and gender. In both surveys, these other variables were measured in the initial wave of the survey (December 2007 and December 2011). Below are the results of the models:

	November 2008	November 2012
Racial resentment	−0.984	−0.870
	[0.045]	[0.039]
Republican	−1.094	−0.942
	[0.056]	[0.047]
Democrat	0.759	1.124
	[0.052]	[0.046]
Ideology	−0.479	−0.594
	[0.026]	[0.023]
Education	0.020	0.017
	[0.013]	[0.011]
Age	−0.006	−0.006
	[0.001]	[0.001]
Female	−0.052	0.028
	[0.040]	[0.032]
Constant	2.179	2.295
	[0.124]	[0.105]
Observations	11,378	17,437

Note: Cell entries are probit coefficients, with standard errors in brackets. The dependent variable is coded 1-Obama and 0-Romney/McCain. Only white voters are included in these models. The data are from YouGov polls.

The individual-level effects of racial resentment—for example, the difference between people with unfavorable and favorable views of blacks—that we present in the text are based on the same kinds of calculations described in the sections on the voting behavior of women: these are average effects across respondents, given observed values on each variable for each respondent.

The second model we discussed in the text considered how racial resentment and other factors were associated with changes from December 2011 vote intentions to November 2012 vote decisions. Below are the results of that model, which was estimated only on whites and is similar in structure to models estimated in the previous sections of the appendix. We excluded from this model measures of attitudes toward issues, like health care reform, which may have originated at least in part from racial attitudes.

	b	se
Obama supporter (Dec. 2011)	0.923	(0.018)
Romney supporter (Dec. 2011)	0.304	(0.018)
Other candidate supporter (Dec. 2011)	0.885	(0.061)
Undecided (Dec. 2011)	0.821	(0.039)
Obama × racial resentment	−0.035	(0.006)
Romney × racial resentment	−0.053	(0.007)
Other × racial resentment	−0.139	(0.023)
Undecided × racial resentment	−0.151	(0.016)
Obama × Democrat	0.025	(0.010)
Romney × Democrat	0.159	(0.012)
Other × Democrat	0.376	(0.030)
Undecided × Democrat	0.198	(0.016)
Obama × Republican	−0.100	(0.015)
Romney × Republican	−0.047	(0.009)
Other × Republican	−0.221	(0.025)
Undecided × Republican	−0.281	(0.017)
Obama × ideology	−0.011	(0.004)
Romney × ideology	−0.034	(0.004)
Other × ideology	−0.093	(0.011)
Undecided × ideology	−0.110	(0.009)
Obama × education	0.005	(0.002)
Romney × education	−0.002	(0.002)
Other × education	−0.011	(0.007)
Undecided × education	0.026	(0.004)
Obama × age	0.001	(0.000)
Romney × age	−0.001	(0.000)
Other × age	−0.002	(0.001)
Undecided × age	0.001	(0.000)
Obama × female	0.006	(0.005)
Romney × female	0.013	(0.005)
Other × female	−0.010	(0.020)
Undecided × female	0.038	(0.013)
R-squared	0.89	

Note: Cell entries are ordinary least squares coefficients with standard errors in parentheses. The dependent variable is coded 0-Romney or 1-Obama. Ideology is coded so that higher values correspond to more liberal attitudes. Only white voters are included in this model. The data are from YouGov polls. *N* = 16,897.

In the text, we report the aggregate impact of racial attitudes among persuadable voters. This was calculated by the same "level importance" statistic that we described in the previous section on abortion attitudes and the vote decisions of women.

To determine whether the impact of racial attitudes was greater in battleground states than non-battleground states, we first estimated a model of November 2012 vote decisions identical to the one in the first table above but including an interaction between racial attitudes and battleground state status. That interaction term was not statistically significant ($p = .61$). We also estimated this same model but added a measure of respondents' December vote intentions—thereby allowing us to measure changes in vote decisions. In this model, the interaction of racial attitudes and battleground state residence was also insignificant ($p = .38$). We then estimated the more elaborate model of changes in vote decisions presented in the second table but separately for battleground states and other states. Conditional on December 2011 vote intentions, the impact of racial resentment was very similar in both groups of states.

To assess the aggregate-level consequences of shifts in the distribution of racial resentment, we estimated the models in the first table above, generated a predicted value, replaced the values of racial resentment as discussed in the text, and generated a second predicted value. Then we compared the averages of the predicted values to gauge the possible impact on Obama vote share of these changes to racial resentment.

Analysis of Favorability toward Mormons

To estimate the apparent effect of attitudes toward Mormons, we relied on self-reported turnout and vote choice in the post-election wave. Approximately 75% of the sample reported voting, a high number that likely reflected the well-known tendency of survey respondents to over-report turnout. Among major-party voters, 53% of the sample reported voting for Obama. We coded turnout so that 1 indicated a self-reported vote and 0 no vote. We coded vote choice so that 1 indicated a vote for Obama and 0 a vote for Romney. The measure of attitudes toward Mormons was the 0–100 scale where 100 indicated very favorable attitudes.

In addition to the variables we have described previously, the turnout model also included several additional measures. One was simply whether the respondent lived in a battleground state (CO, FL, IA, MI, NC, NH, NV, OH, PA, VA, or WI). Two others were measures of political engagement. Political information captured whether respondents knew the positions held by Eric Cantor, Nancy Pelosi, John Roberts, Harry Reid, Mitch McConnell, John Boehner, and Joe Biden (the options were representative, senator, cabinet member, vice president, or judge). The measure summed up the number of correct answers. Political interest was respondents' self-reported interest in "politics and current affairs" (very much, somewhat, or not much interested). Strength of partisanship was coded: independent, independent-leaning partisan (Democrat or Republican), weak partisan, or strong partisan. We also included a measure of family income, as well as a dummy variable for those who refused to state their income. As before, all of the variables in the model came from the initial interview with these respondents in December 2011. The results are below. All of these analyses excluded a small number of Mormon respondents.

	Turnout	Vote choice
Attitude toward Mormons	0.003	−0.003
	[0.0003]	[0.001]
Lives in battleground state	0.080	
	[0.020]	
Political information	0.099	
	[0.006]	
Political interest	0.472	
	[0.014]	
Strength of partisanship	0.225	
	[0.009]	
Income	0.062	
	[0.004]	
Refused to state income	−5.577	
	[0.333]	
Racial resentment		−0.707
		[0.036]
Economic attitudes		1.008
		[0.027]
Social attitudes		0.505
		[0.028]
Democrat		0.861
		[0.041]
Republican		−0.810
		[0.042]
Education	0.171	0.008
	[0.007]	[0.010]
Age	0.011	−0.007
	[0.001]	[0.001]
Female	0.183	0.041
	[0.019]	[0.031]
Born again	0.056	−0.051
	[0.020]	[0.036]
Black	0.162	0.670
	[0.030]	[0.064]
Latino	0.107	0.204
	[0.032]	[0.052]
Asian	−0.720	−0.049
	[0.053]	[0.110]
Other race	0.033	−0.068
	[0.043]	[0.076]
Constant	−2.967	0.518
	[0.054]	[0.091]
Observations	30,257	23,516

Note: Cell entries are probit coefficients with standard errors in brackets.

For the simulations reported in the text, we estimated each model and generated a predicted level of turnout or vote share. Then we substituted each respondent's attitude toward Christians for their attitude toward Mormons, generated a second prediction based on the model, and compared the two predictions.

Analysis of Candidate Favorability

To model the effect of candidate favorability on vote intentions, we focused on respondents who were interviewed in October 2012 after the first debate and the subsequent increase in Romney's favorability. The dependent variable was their self-reported vote choice in the post-election interview. (We thereby excluded those who did not vote.) The key variables in these models were the difference in their favorability or empathy ratings of Obama and Romney, as measured in October. (Empathy was measured with the "cares about people like me" item.) In each model, we also controlled for vote intentions in the initial interview in December 2011 (dummy variables for an Obama vote intention or a Romney vote intention, with those supporting another candidate or undecided the excluded category. One model also controlled for the measures of racial, economic, and social attitudes employed in the analysis of attitudes toward Mormonism. In the two-stage least squares model, we instrumented for October favorability ratings using favorability ratings in December.

	(1) OLS	(2) 2SLS	(3) OLS	(4) OLS
Difference in favorability	0.27	0.19	0.18	0.17
	[0.01]	[0.02]	[0.01]	[0.01]
Difference in empathy			0.14	0.12
			[0.01]	[0.01]
Intend to vote for Obama (Dec. 2011)	0.27	0.35	0.27	0.24
	[0.02]	[0.02]	[0.01]	[0.02]
Intend to vote for Romney (Dec. 2011)	−0.26	−0.31	−0.20	−0.19
	[0.01]	[0.03]	[0.02]	[0.01]
Racial resentment				−0.03
				[0.01]
Economic attitudes				0.04
				[0.01]
Social attitudes				0.02
				[0.01]
Constant	0.50	0.49	0.47	0.48
	[0.01]	[0.01]	[0.01]	[0.01]
R-squared	0.88	0.88	0.89	0.90
Observations	3164	3147	3126	3122

Note: Cell entries are coefficients and standard errors from ordinary least squares or two-stage least squares models. Data from YouGov polls. Differences in favorability or empathy are created by subtracting ratings of Romney from ratings of Obama. The dependent variable is vote choice in the November post-election interview, coded 1-Obama and 0-Romney.

The simulations reported in the text, which manipulated favorability or empathy ratings, involved these steps. First we estimated the model and a predicted probability of voting for Obama for each respondent. Then we altered the favorability or empathy ratings as discussed in the text—improving Romney's rating overall—and estimated a second predicted probability based on the same model. Then we compared the means of the two sets of probabilities to estimate how much Obama's vote share would have changed if favorability or empathy ratings had been different. The first simulation we report, which manipulated only the candidates' favorability ratings, was based on model 2 in the table above. The second simulation, which manipulated both favorability and empathy ratings, was based on model 3. The final simulation, based on a model that also accounted for several other factors, was based on model 4.

Analysis of Candidate Advertising and Field Offices

The analysis of advertising and field offices consists of county-level political and demographic data merged with county-level data on the number of field offices and media market-level data on campaign advertising. The county-level election data were obtained from Dave Leip's website (uselectionatlas.org). In these models, we analyzed Obama's share of the major-party vote. The field office data were collected from the Obama and Romney campaigns' webpages and coded into variables measuring the presence of field offices—specifically, whether a county had zero, one, or two or more Obama or Romney offices. The advertising data were obtained from The Nielsen Company and are the same data we analyzed in chapters 5 and 6. These data included advertising by Obama, Romney, the Republican National Committee, and the major super-PACs or independent groups. Again, we denominated advertising volume in gross rating points (GRPs) and calculated the balance of advertising in each market (subtracting Romney's advertising from Obama's), including a dummy variable to capture markets in which no Obama ads aired (since Romney alone ran several days of national broadcast ads in the week before the election). We assigned each county to the media market that contained the county's geographic center-point using U.S. Census shape files for counties and a market shape file provided by GeoCommons (http://geocommons.com/overlays/275440). In the model below, we include the advertising balance on the day before the election (Monday, November 5), and the balance in the five days preceding that (Wednesday, October 31 through Sunday, November 4).

In addition, the model includes Obama's share of the two-party vote in 2008, the percentages of the county that are black, Hispanic, have no high school degree, have a bachelor's degree, and are under the age of 18; the median income in the county; the 2011 population in the county (in millions) and the growth in population between 2008 and 2011; and the change in the unemployment rate in the year before the election. In addition, the models include indicators for each state to capture any state-level dynamics that might affect all of the counties (such as a salient statewide race). The model is estimated with ordinary least squares, with standard errors clustered by media market to account for any non-independence among counties within a market. The combination of indicators for each state and clustered standard errors makes this model a fairly conservative test of whether campaign activity was associated with vote share.

	Effect on Obama major-party vote share
Advertising balance on day before election	0.09
	[0.07]
Advertising balance on previous 5 days	0.004
	[0.03]
No Obama advertising	−0.79
	[0.33]
Number of Obama field offices	0.27
	[0.12]
Number of Romney offices	−0.15
	[0.13]
Obama 2008 two-party vote share	0.98
	[0.01]
Percent black	0.10
	[0.01]
Percent Latino	0.08
	[0.01]
Percent with bachelor's degree	0.02
	[0.01]
Percent with no high school degree	−0.08
	[0.02]
Percent under age of 18	0.06
	[0.03]
Median income (in $1000s)	−0.05
	[0.02]
Size of 2011 population (in millions)	0.33
	[2.91]
Growth in population 2010–11	0.00
	[0.00]
Change in unemployment in election year	−0.38
	[0.15]
Constant	−0.95
	[0.83]
Observations	3,082
R-squared	0.98

Note: Cell entries are least squares regression coefficients, with standard errors clustered by media market in brackets. The model also includes fixed effects for states.

NOTES

Chapter 1: Ante Up

1. Tim Murphy, "Every Single Political Game-Changer of the 2012 Election," *Mother Jones*, November 4, 2012; Richard Dunham, "The 12 Worst Political Clichés of 2012," *Albany Times-Union*, November 5, 2012; Jen Chaney, "Game Changer: Lindsay Lohan Has Endorsed Mitt Romney," *Washington Post* Celebritology blog, October 12, 2012.

2. This quote was uttered by a senior Obama staff member at the RootsCamp2012 conference, as reported by EngageDC in this slidedeck: http://www.engagedc.com/inside-the-cave/.

Chapter 2: The Hand You're Dealt

1. The transcript of the interview is here: http://today.msnbc.msn.com/id/28975726/ns/today-today_people/t/obama-were-suffering-massive-hangover/#.

2. Overall, changes in GDP explain about 40% of the year-to-year variation in presidential election outcomes.

3. The value of the Dow Jones was 10,831.07 on October 1, 2008, and 8776.39 on December 31.

4. Bureau of Economic Analysis, "Frequently Asked Questions: Why Has the Initial Estimate of Real GDP for the Fourth Quarter of 2008 Been Revised Down So Much?" August 5, 2011, http://www.bea.gov/faq/index.cfm?faq_id=1003.

5. The Editor's Desk, Bureau of Labor Statistics, "Payroll in January 2009," February 9, 2009, http://www.bls.gov/opub/ted/2009/feb/wk2/art01.htm.

6. The ad can be viewed here: http://www.youtube.com/watch?v=EU-IBF8nwSY.

7. Adam Clymer, "G.O.P. Senators Prevail, Sinking Clinton's Economic Stimulus Bill," *New York Times*, April 22, 1993, http://www.nytimes.com/1993/04/22/us/gop-senators-prevail-sinking-clinton-s-economic-stimulus-bill.html?pagewanted=all&src=pm.

8. Noam Scheiber, "Obama's Worst Year: The Inside Story of His Brush with Political Disaster," *The New Republic*, February 10, 2012, http://www.tnr.com/article/politics /100595/obama-escape-artist-excerpt.

9. Dana Milbank, "The Republicans Are Smiling, But They're Not Buying," *Washington Post*, January 28, 2009.

10. Congressional Budget Office, "Estimated Impact of the American Recovery and Reinvestment Act on Employment and Economic Output from October 2011 through December 2011," 2012, http://www.cbo.gov/publication/43013.

11. Carmen Reinhart and Kenneth Rogoff, *This Time Is Different: Eight Centuries of Financial Folly* (Princeton: Princeton University Press, 2009).

12. Pew Research Center for the People & the Press, "Auto Bailout Now Backed, Stimulus Divisive," February 23, 2012, http://pewresearch.org/pubs/2202/ government-loans-automakers-banks-financial-institutions-economic-stimulus-tarp.

13. Kaiser Family Foundation, "Kaiser Health Tracking Poll, March 2011," March 18, 2011, http://www.kff.org/kaiserpolls/upload/8166-F.pdf.

14. Kaiser Family Foundation, "Kaiser Health Tracking Poll, August 2011," August 29, 2011, http://www.kff.org/kaiserpolls/upload/8265-F.pdf.

15. Michael Bailey, Jonathan Mummolo, and Hans Noel, "Tea Party Influence: A Story of Activists and Elites," *American Politics Research* 40, no. 5 (2012): 769–804.

16. Brendan Nyhan, Eric McGhee, John Sides, Seth Masket, and Steven Greene, "One Vote Out of Step? The Effects of Salience Roll Call Votes in the 2010 Election," *American Politics Research* 40, no. 5 (2012): 844–79. This analysis accounted for other factors besides support for the ACA that may have influenced the election or defeat of Democratic incumbents.

17. Gary C. Jacobson, "Legislative Success and Political Failure: The Public's Reaction to Barack Obama's Early Presidency," *Presidential Studies Quarterly* 41, no. 2 (2011): 220–43.

18. Major Garrett, "Top GOP Priority: Make Obama a One-Term President," *National Journal*, October 23, 2010, http://nationaljournal.com/member/magazine/top-gop -priority-make-obama-a-one-term-president-20101023.

19. Steve Kornacki, "Obama's Comeback Mirage?" *Salon*, December 22, 2011, http:// www.salon.com/2011/12/22/obamas_comeback_mirage/singleton/.

20. The standard deviation in Obama's approval rating for 2009–11 was about 6 points. Johnson's "first term"—from Kennedy's assassination until his inauguration in 1965—saw even less volatility (a standard deviation of 2.6 points), although he was arguably benefiting from an extended honeymoon due to Kennedy's assassination. The lack of volatility in Obama's approval rating makes him similar to Clinton, Nixon, and Eisenhower, who had slightly lower standard deviations (about 5 points) in their first terms. Evaluations of Kennedy, Ford, Reagan, and both Bushes varied more over time (standard deviations from 7 to 13 points).

21. We calculated standard errors for the difference between actual and expected approval in this fashion. For actual approval, we calculated the standard error of the average of the polls in each quarter. For the predicted approval, we calculated the standard error of the predicted value in each quarter. We then calculated the standard error of the difference between expected and actual approval as: $\text{s.e.}_{\text{diff}} = \sqrt{(\text{se}^2_{\text{actual}} + \text{se}^2_{\text{expected}})}$. Across the first three years of Obama's presidency, the standard error of the difference averaged 1.65 (minimum = 1.24; maximum = 1.79). In most quarters, the difference between actual and expected approval was between 1.5 and 3.6 times larger than this standard error. This suggests that the difference between actual and expected approval is statistically meaningful.

22. For each of the presidents besides Obama, we formally tested the hypothesis that the mean difference between Obama's actual and expected approval was greater than his. The associated p-values for these tests were: Eisenhower ($p = .14$), Kennedy ($p = .57$), Johnson ($p < .001$), Nixon ($p < .001$), Ford ($p = .01$), Carter ($p = .04$), Reagan ($p = .22$), George H. W. Bush ($p = .22$), Clinton ($p = .003$), and George W. Bush ($p = .28$). (Note that we do not have first-term approval data for Truman.) We can therefore have at least some statistical confidence, and in several cases quite a bit of confidence, that Obama's better-than-expected approval rating distinguished him from previous presidents.

23. Benjamin Highton, "Prejudice Rivals Partisanship and Ideology When Explaining the 2008 Presidential Vote across the States," *PS: Political Science and Politics* 44 (2011): 530–35; Donald R. Kinder and Allison Dale-Riddle, *The End of Race? Obama, 2008, and Racial Politics in America* (New Haven: Yale University Press, 2012); Josh Pasek et al., "Determinants of Turnout and Candidate Choice in the 2008 U.S. Presidential Election," *Public Opinion Quarterly* 73, no. 5 (2009): 943–94; Brian F Schaffner, "Racial Salience and the Obama Vote," *Political Psychology* 32, no. 6 (2011): 963–88; Seth Stephens-Davidowitz, "The Effects of Racial Animus on a Black Presidential Candidate: Using Google Search Data to Find What Surveys Miss" (unpublished manuscript), http://www.people.fas .harvard.edu/~sstephen/papers/RacialAnimusAndVotingSethStephensDavidowitz.pdf.

24. Nolan McCarty, Keith T. Poole, and Howard Rosenthal, *Polarized America: The Dance of Ideology and Unequal Riches* (Cambridge, MA: MIT Press, 2006).

25. Alan I. Abramowitz and Kyle L. Saunders, "Is Polarization a Myth?" *Journal of Politics* 70, no. 2 (2008): 542–55; Marc J. Hetherington, "Resurgent Mass Partisanship: The Role of Elite Polarization," *American Political Science Review* 95, no. 3 (2001): 619–31; Matthew Levendusky, *The Partisan Sort: How Liberals Became Democrats and Conservatives Became Republicans* (Chicago: University of Chicago Press, 2009); Pew Research Center for the People & the Press, "Trends in American Values: 1987–2012," June 4, 2012, http:// www.people-press.org/files/legacy-pdf/06-04-12%20Values%20Release.pdf.

26. Gary Jacobson, *A Divider, Not a Uniter: George W. Bush and the American People* (New York: Pearson Longman, 2006).

27. Gallup Politics, "Obama Ratings Historically Polarized," January 27, 2012, http:// www.gallup.com/poll/152222/obama-ratings-historically-polarized.aspx.

28. John Fund, "The Carter-Obama Comparisons Grow," *Wall Street Journal*, September 22, 2010, http://online.wsj.com/article/SB10001424052748704129204575505822 147816104.html.

29. We focus on blame with regard to the economy, but leaders can also escape blame for wars that began under a predecessor from another party. See Sarah E. Croco, "The Decider's Dilemma: Leader Culpability, War Outcomes, and Domestic Punishment," *American Political Science Review* 105 (2011): 457–77.

30. Gallup Politics, "In U.S., Slight Majority Now Blame Obama for U.S. Economy," September 21, 2011, http://www.gallup.com/poll/149600/slight-majority-blame-obama -economy.aspx; *Washington Post*/ABC News poll, January 12–15, 2012, http://www .washingtonpost.com/wp-srv/politics/polls/postabcpoll_011512.html.

31. Maureen Dowd, "Captain Obvious Learns the Limits of Cool," *New York Times*, January 9, 2010, http://www.nytimes.com/2010/01/10/opinion/10dowd.html?_r=1.

32. John Sides, "Is Obama 'Not Connecting?'" *The Monkey Cage*, January 21, 2010, http://themonkeycage.org/blog/2010/01/21/is_obama_not_connecting/.

33. James Fallows, "Obama, Explained," *The Atlantic*, March 2012, http://www.the atlantic.com/magazine/archive/2012/03/obama-explained/8874/.

34. We helped design a somewhat similar forecasting model for the *Washington Post*. An interactive widget is here: http://www.washingtonpost.com/wp-srv/special/politics /2012-election-predictor/.

35. Alan Abramowitz, "Forecasting the 2008 Presidential Election with the Time-for-Change Model," *PS: Political Science and Politics* 41, no. 4 (2008): 691–95.

36. Larry M. Bartels, *Unequal Democracy: The Political Economy of the New Gilded Age* (Princeton: Princeton University Press, 2008).

37. Larry M. Bartels and John Zaller, "Presidential Vote Models: A Recount," *PS: Political Science and Politics* 34, no. 1 (2001): 9–20.

38. Specifically, we estimated multiple different models and averaged the results together via a statistical procedure called Bayesian model averaging. More details are in the appendix to this chapter. See also Bartels and Zaller, "Presidential Vote Models: A Recount."

39. We measured outcomes in a fashion standard in the forecasting literature: as the incumbent party's percent of the votes won by major-party candidates. Forecasting models of presidential elections usually do not attempt to predict the votes won by third parties or independent candidates.

40. On average, the model's prediction differed from the actual election results by 3.3 points in absolute value when using conditions from the previous year. When using election-year conditions, it differed by only 1.7 points.

41. A prominent survey of forecasters suggested that the economy would grow by about 2.4% in 2012, which translates into 1.2% growth in the first two quarters. They also forecasted a 0.2-point drop in unemployment, which translates into a 0.1-drop in this time period. http://www.philadelphiafed.org/research-and-data/real-time-center/survey -of-professional-forecasters/2011/spfq411.pdf. The estimate of income growth assumed income was to grow at the same rate in 2012 as it did in 2011. (It grew about 0.6% from 2010 to 2011, or from $32,481 to $32,667. See Table 2 of this report by the Bureau of Economic Analysis: http://www.bea.gov/newsreleases/national/pi/2012/pdf/pi0312.pdf.)

Chapter 3: Random, or Romney

1. Erick Erickson, "Mitt Romney as the Nominee: Conservatism Dies and Barack Obama Wins," *RedState*, November 8, 2011, http://www.redstate.com/erick/2011/11/08/ mitt-romney-as-the-nominee-conservatism-dies-and-barack-obama-wins/.

2. "Rev. Franklin Graham: Romney Not a Christian," *Newsmax*, February 21, 2012, http://www.newsmax.com/Newsfront/franklin-graham-Romney-Mormon/2012/02/21/ id/430049; "Romney's Mormon Faith Likely a Factor in Primaries, Not in a General Election," *Pew Forum on Religion and Public Life*, November 23, 2011, http://www.pewforum .org/Politics-and-Elections/Romneys-Mormon-Faith-Likely-a-Factor-in-Primaries-Not -in-a-General-Election.aspx.

3. Ian Schwartz, "Krauthammer: Romney 'Not the Kind of Guy Who Sends a Thrill Up Your Leg,'" *Real Clear Politics*, February 7, 2012, http://www.realclearpolitics.com /video/2012/02/07/krauthammer_romney_not_the_kind_of_guy_who_sends_a_thrill _up_your_leg.html; Jonah Goldberg, "Most Boring Guy Wins Most Boring Debate?" *The Corner*, January 23, 2012, http://www.nationalreview.com/corner/289031/most-boring -guy-wins-most-boring-debate-jonah-goldberg.

4. Steve Holland, "Romney's Struggles Fuel Talk of a Brokered Convention," Reuters, February 17, 2012, http://www.reuters.com/article/2012/02/17/us-usa-campaign -convention-idUSTRE81G1ZF20120217.

5. In a May 2011 YouGov poll, only 9% could not rate Romney, compared to the 72% who could not rate Huntsman and 40% who could not rate Pawlenty. Similarly, in a September 2011 Gallup poll, about half of Republican voters said they were not familiar with Herman Cain, Rick Santorum, or Jon Huntsman, and approximately a quarter were not familiar with Rick Perry. Only 14% said this of Romney.

6. Michael Cooper and Megan Thee-Brenan, "Congress Seen as Top Culprit in Debt Debate," *New York Times*, August 5, 2011, A1.

7. Carl M. Cannon, "What Makes the 2012 GOP Field So Weak?" May 20, 2011, *Real Clear Politics*, http://www.realclearpolitics.com/articles/2011/05/20/what_makes_the _2012_gop_field_so_weak_109933.html.

8. Ryan Witt, "Rush Limbaugh Admits GOP Presidential Field Is Very Weak," Examiner.com, March 7, 2011, http://www.examiner.com/political-buzz-in-national/rush -limbaugh-admits-gop-presidential-field-is-very-weak-audio.

9. Charles Krauthammer, "Relax, Republicans, It's a Fine Field," *Real Clear Politics*, October 26, 2007, http://www.realclearpolitics.com/articles/2007/10/relax_republicans _this_is_a_fi.html.

10. Gary Jacobson and Samuel Kernell, *Strategy and Choice in Congressional Elections* (New Haven: Yale University Press, 1983).

11. Those who lost were William Howard Taft in 1912, Herbert Hoover in 1932, Gerald Ford in 1976, Jimmy Carter in 1980, and George H. W. Bush in 1992. The tabulation of winners and losers counts any sitting president who ran for reelection as an incumbent, even if he was not elected in the first place (i.e., he took office as a result of the president's death or resignation).

12. Federal Reserve Bank of Philadelphia Research Department, "Forecasters Predict Slower Growth over the Next Four Years," *Survey of Professional Forecasters*, May 13, 2011, http://www.phil.frb.org/research-and-data/real-time-center/survey-of-professional -forecasters/2011/spfq211.pdf?CFID=35590062&CFTOKEN=60515431&jsessionid=ac30 493448616b1b895822624b1db2a7c366.

13. Martin Cohen, David Karol, Hans Noel, and John Zaller, *The Party Decides: Presidential Nomination Before and After Reform* (Chicago: Chicago University Press, 2008).

14. Mark Blumenthal, "Sarah Palin Can't Win, Shouldn't Run, HuffPost-Patch GOP Power Outsiders Say," *Huffington Post*, August 31, 2011, http://www.huffingtonpost.com /2011/08/31/sarah-palin-polls_n_943615.html.

15. See Cohen et al., *The Party Decides*, 170–72.

16. See, for example, the reaction to South Carolina governor Nikki Haley's endorsement of Mitt Romney, which led Rush Limbaugh to issue a "blistering broadside" against her and attracted the ire of Tea Party leaders as well. Reid J. Epstein, "Nikki Haley's Mitt Romney Endorsement Catches Flak," *Politico*, December 16, 2011, http://www.politico .com/news/stories/1211/70580.html.

17. Jo Ling Kent, "Huntsman on Romney's McCain Endorsement: 'Nobody Cares,'" *First Read on NBCNews.com*, January 4, 2012, http://firstread.msnbc.msn.com/_news /2012/01/04/9952876-huntsman-on-romneys-mccain-endorsement-nobody-cares.

18. Cohen et al., *The Party Decides*.

19. Endorsements that were made earlier than this—for example, in 1994 for the 1996 primary and 2010 for the 2012 primary—appear in quarter 1. Endorsements that were made in the election year itself but before the Iowa caucus appear in quarter 4.

20. Cohen et al., *The Party Decides*, 194.

21. Mark Blumenthal, "Mitt Romney Is Presidential, Electable, HuffPost-Patch GOP Power Outsiders Say," *Huffington Post*, September 14, 2011, http://www.huffingtonpost .com/2011/09/14/mitt-romney-presidential-electable-power-outsiders_n_962167.html.

22. Mark Blumenthal, "Michele Bachmann Can't Win, HuffPost-Patch GOP Power Outsiders Say," *Huffington Post*, September 21, 2011, http://www.huffingtonpost.com/2011 /09/21/michele-bachmann-polls_n_973995.html?ref=power-outsiders.

23. Tom Bevan and Carl Cannon, *Election 2012: The Battle Begins* (New York: Crown, 2011).

24. Mark Blumenthal, "Rick Perry Is a Leader Who Can Beat Obama, HuffPost-Patch GOP Power Outsiders Say," *Huffington Post*, September 7, 2011, http://www.huffington post.com/2011/09/07/rick-perry-polls-huffpost-patch-gop-power-outsiders_n_952823 .html?ref=power-outsiders.

25. The picture can be viewed here: http://instagr.am/p/HP8bWNLdxN/.

26. Karl Rove, "Donald Trump and Our Debate Mania: Why This Presidential Contest Has Been the Most Unpredictable Contest of My Lifetime," Rove.com, December 15, 2011, http://www.rove.com/articles/355.

27. Julie Hirschfeld Davis and Michael Tackett, "Romney's Road to Nomination Rocked by Voters Shredding Rulebook," Bloomberg, February 17, 2012, http://www .bloomberg.com/news/2012-02-17/romney-s-road-to-republican-nomination-rocked-as -voters-shredding-rulebook.html.

28. David Carr, "Who's Leading the Republican Presidential Race? Mr. Random, Of Course," *New York Times Media Decoder*, February 21, 2012, http://mediadecoder.blogs .nytimes.com/2012/02/21/whos-leading-the-republican-presidential-race-mr-random-of -course/.

29. Pew Research Center for the People & the Press, "Republican Candidates Stir Little Enthusiasm," June 2, 2011, http://pewresearch.org/pubs/2012/poll-republican -presidential-candidates-2012-romney-palin-gingrich-paul-cain.

30. See, among others, Larry Bartels, *Presidential Primaries and the Dynamics of Public Choice* (Princeton: Princeton University Press, 1988). More generally, see John Zaller, *The Nature and Origins of Mass Opinion* (Cambridge: Cambridge University Press, 1992).

31. See, for example, Henry E. Brady and Richard Johnston, "What's the Primary Message: Horse Race or Issue Journalism?" in Gary R. Orren and Nelson W. Polsby, eds., *Media and Momentum: The New Hampshire Primary and Nomination Politics* (Chatham, NJ: Chatham House, 1987).

32. Tom Rosenstiel, Mark Jurkowitz, and Tricia Sartor, "How the Media Covered the 2012 Primary Campaign," Journalism.org, April 23, 2012, http://www.journalism.org/ analysis_report/romney_report.

33. Shanto Iyengar, Helmut Norpoth, and Kyu Hahn, "Consumer Demand for Election News: The Horserace Sells," *Journal of Politics* 66, no. 1 (2004): 157–75.

34. The debate schedule can be viewed here: http://www.2012presidentialelectionnews .com/2012-debate-schedule/2011-2012-primary-debate-schedule/.

35. Dana Milbank, "The Media ♥ Newt Gingrich," *Washington Post*, January 31, 2012, http://www.washingtonpost.com/opinions/the-medias-codependent-relationship-with -newt-gingrich/2012/01/31/gIQArTADgQ_story.html.

36. It is also possible that campaigning in individual caucus or primary states can lead to surges in state polls, which then drive national news coverage, which in turn drives national polls. This dynamic appears to characterize Santorum's surge before the Iowa caucus, as we document in the next chapter.

37. There is a vast social science literature on media framing. One example is Shanto Iyengar, *Is Anyone Responsible? How Television Frames Political Issues* (Chicago: Chicago University Press, 1991).

38. Bartels, *Presidential Primaries*. See also Diana Mutz, "Mechanisms of Momentum: Does Thinking Make It So?" *Journal of Politics* 59, no. 1 (1997): 104–25.

39. Positive horse-race coverage can also help a candidate's fund-raising, although we do not investigate that possibility here. See Diana C. Mutz, "Effects of Horse-Race Coverage on Campaign Coffers: Strategic Contributing in Presidential Primaries," *Journal of Politics* 57, no. 4 (1995): 1015–42.

40. Bartels, *Presidential Primaries*, 39.

41. Huma Khan, "Newt Gingrich's Moment in the Sun: Will It Last?" ABC News/*The Note*, November 15, 2011, http://abcnews.go.com/blogs/politics/2011/11/newt-gingrichs -moment-in-the-sun-will-it-last/.

42. That Ron Paul was never considered a front-runner may help explain why, as we show later, his news coverage was generally favorable. There was less incentive for either other candidates or the news media to scrutinize him.

43. This is one reason why it is misguided to assume that any other Republican candidate could have entered the race late and been a kind of savior for the unenthusiastic party. Scrutiny of those candidates would have likely revealed their shortcomings as well.

44. Stephanie Condon, "Rick Perry Surges to Front in Latest GOP Poll," CBS News/ *Political Hotsheet*, August 24, 2011, http://www.cbsnews.com/8301-503544_162-20096796 -503544.html.

45. Naureen Khan, "Can the 'Wizard behind the Curtain' Save Rick Perry?" *National Journal*, December 10, 2011, http://www.nationaljournal.com/2012-presidential-campaign/ can-the-wizard-behind-the-curtain-save-rick-perry--20111210?mrefid=election2012.

46. For the sake of brevity we do not examine the brief surges of Donald Trump and Michele Bachmann.

47. The PEJ's data confirm this. In the seven days before Perry's announcement, he was featured in about 20% of stories. After his announcement, he was featured in 75% of stories.

48. Jeff Zeleny and Jackie Calmes, "Perry Links Federal Reserve Policies and Treason," *New York Times*, August 16, 2011, http://www.nytimes.com/2011/08/17/us/politics/17perry .html.

49. Brian Montopoli, "Rick Perry Tiptoes away from Social Security Stance," CBS News/*Political Hotsheet*, August 22, 2011, http://www.cbsnews.com/8301-503544_162 -20095591-503544.html?tag=contentMain;contentBody.

50. The PEJ data confirm this. In the four weeks between August 15 and September 11, roughly one-third of stories about Perry were positive, and twice as many as were negative. (The rest were judged neutral in tone.)

51. In the PEJ data, the proportion of negative stories increased by 10 points, to 25%, although 31% were still positive.

52. Susan Page, "Cain Upsets Perry at Florida Straw Poll," *USA Today*, September 25, 2011, http://content.usatoday.com/communities/onpolitics/post/2011/09/florida-straw -poll-2012-perry-romney-paul/1#.T8li2cX7R8E.

53. Jane Sutton and Steve Holland, "Cain Upsets Perry in Florida Republican Straw Poll," Reuters, September 24, 2011, http://www.reuters.com/article/2011/09/24/us-usa -campaign-winner-idUSTRE78N2RE20110924.

54. "Herman Cain Upsets Gov. Rick Perry to Win Florida GOP Straw Poll," Fox News, September 24, 2011, http://www.foxnews.com/politics/2011/09/24/perry-says-rivals-made -mistake-by-skipping-florida-test-vote/.

55. Again, the PEJ data confirm this. In the week after the Florida straw poll, 35% of Cain's coverage was positive and 20% was negative. The ratio increased slightly—to 36–18—in the first full week of October. In that same week in October, 34% of Perry's coverage was negative and only 26% was positive. This was the first week that his negative coverage outweighed his positive.

56. Stephanie McCrummen, "At Rick Perry's Texas Hunting Spot, Camp's Old Racially Charged Name Lingered," *Washington Post*, October 1, 2011, http://www.washingtonpost .com/national/rick-perry-familys-hunting-camp-still-known-to-many-by-old-racially -charged-name/2011/10/01/gIQAOhY5DL_story.html.

57. Philip Rucker and Amy Gardner, "Romney Keeps Solid Footing in GOP Race," *Washington Post*, October 12, 2011.

58. Michael A. Fletcher, "Experts See Surprise in Cain's 9-9-9 Plan," *Washington Post*, October 14, 2011.

59. Jonathan Martin, Maggie Haberman, Anna Palmer, and Kenneth P. Vogel, "Herman Cain Accused by Two Women of Inappropriate Behavior," *Politico*, October 31, 2011, http://www.politico.com/news/stories/1011/67194.html.

60. "Gingrich Apologizes to Paul Ryan for 'Right-Wing Social Engineering' Criticism," Fox News, May 17, 2011, http://www.foxnews.com/politics/2011/05/17/gingrich -apologizes-paul-ryan-right-wing-social-engineering-criticism/.

61. The PEJ data confirm this. In every week in October, Gingrich was featured in no more than 4% of campaign stories.

62. Karen Tumulty, "Newt Gingrich: GOP's Consummate Survivor Is Back on His Feet," *Washington Post*, October 29, 2011, http://www.washingtonpost.com/politics/newt -gingrich-gops-consummate-survivor-is-back-on-his-feet/2011/10/29/gIQAG6rYTM _story.html.

63. Richard Oppel Jr., "Gingrich Tailors Message at Iowa GOP Dinner," *New York Times/The Caucus*, November 5, 2011, http://thecaucus.blogs.nytimes.com/2011/11/05 /gingrich-tailors-message-and-unites-with-opponents-in-iowa/.

64. Philip Rucker, "For Gingrich and Cain, It's a Friendship and a Contest," *Washington Post*, November 5, 2011, http://www.washingtonpost.com/politics/for-gingrich-and -cain-its-a-friendship-and-a-contest/2011/11/05/gIQAvWTBqM_story.html.

65. In the PEJ data, Gingrich's news coverage increased to 15% of stories from November 7 to 13 and then to 37% and 44% in the subsequent two weeks. The shift in tone was also evident: only 19% of Gingrich stories were positive in the first week of November (versus 25% that were negative). This ratio was 26–25 in the second week of November, however.

66. Trip Gabriel, "As Foes Flounder, Gingrich Gets Bump in Poll," *New York Times/The Caucus*, November 11, 2011, http://www.nytimes.com/2011/11/12/us/politics/newt -gingrich-gets-bump-in-poll-as-foes-flounder.html?pagewanted=all.

67. Karen Tumulty, "Newt Gingrich, on the Rise, Says, 'Hopefully, I'm Going to Be More Disciplined,'" *Washington Post*, November 16, 2011, http://www.washingtonpost .com/politics/newt-gingrich-on-the-rise-says-hopefully-im-going-to-be-more -disciplined/2011/11/16/gIQAeSVkSN_story.html.

68. Dan Balz and Amy Gardner, "GOP Candidates Show Sharp Differences on National Security and Terrorism," *Washington Post*, November 22, 2011, http://www

.washingtonpost.com/politics/gop-candidates-debate-security-vs-rights-in-dc-debate
/2011/11/22/gIQANbsemN_story.html.

69. John Harwood, "In Gingrich, Romney Now Sees a Grave Threat," *New York Times/The Caucus*, December 5, 2011, http://thecaucus.blogs.nytimes.com/2011/12/05/in-gingrich-romney-now-sees-a-grave-threat/; Jeff Zeleny and Marjorie Connelly, "In Iowa, Gingrich Is Gaining Favor, New Poll Shows," *New York Times*, December 6, 2011, http://www.nytimes.com/2011/12/07/us/politics/gingrich-leads-gop-rivals-in-iowa-poll-finds.html?_r=4; Michael D. Shear, "New Romney Ad Turns Up Heat on Gingrich," *New York Times*, December 7, 2011, http://www.nytimes.com/2011/12/08/us/politics/new-romney-ad-turns-up-heat-on-gingrich.html; David A. Farenthold and Philip Rucker, "Romney Supporters Slam Gingrich's Leadership Skills, Vanity," *Washington Post*, December 8, 2011, http://www.washingtonpost.com/politics/romney-supporters-ex-colleagues-attack-gingrichs-leadership-vanity/2011/12/08/gIQAfS4YgO_story.html; Amy Gardner, Karen Tumulty, and Philip Rucker, "Mitt Romney Steps Up Attacks on Newt Gingrich," *Washington Post*, December 12, 2011, http://www.washingtonpost.com/politics/mitt-romney-steps-up-attacks-on-newt-gingrich/2011/12/12/gIQADWihqO_story.html.

70. Dan Balz, "Gingrich's Time of Testing Arrives," *Washington Post*, December 17, 2011, http://www.washingtonpost.com/politics/gingrichs-time-of-testing-arrives/2011/12/17/gIQAVpZkoO_story.html.

71. The PEJ data show that news coverage in December was trending negative. During the week of November 28–December 4, 28% of stories about Gingrich were negative and 28% were positive. During the week of December 12–18, the stories were 35% negative and 25% positive.

72. Pew Research Center for the People & the Press, "GOP Voters Still Unenthused about Presidential Field," January 9, 2012, http://www.people-press.org/2012/01/09/gop-voters-still-unenthused-about-presidential-field/?src=prc-twitter.

73. This is from a March 8–11 Gallup poll (http://www.gallup.com/poll/153272/Romney-Santorum-Stir-Less-Enthusiasm-McCain.aspx). In total, 35% said this of Romney, 34% said this of Santorum, and 28% said this of Gingrich.

74. Frank Newport, "Republicans Less Enthusiastic about Voting in 2012," Gallup, December 8, 2011, http://www.gallup.com/poll/151403/Republicans-Less-Enthusiastic-Voting-2012.aspx; Tom Jensen, "Dems Winning on Enthusiasm," Public Policy Polling, April 3, 2012, http://www.publicpolicypolling.com/main/2012/04/dems-winning-on-enthusiasm.html.

75. Mark Halperin, "Rove and Romney on the Republican Party after Bush," *New York Times Sunday Book Review,* April 22, 2010, http://www.nytimes.com/2010/04/25/books/review/Halperin-t.html?_r=1.

76. Frank Rich, "The Molotov Party," *New York*, December 26, 2011, http://nymag.com/news/frank-rich/gop-2012-1/.

77. Of course, respondents' placements of the candidates may not be "accurate" as judged by close observers of politics. Respondents may also tend to assume that candidates they favor share their ideological views, a process known as "projection" in the political science literature. However, neither of these undercuts our basic point: regardless of how they came to this assessment, on average Republican voters did not see Romney as an ideological outlier.

78. These measures weight each issue equally, but the results are very similar if we allow the weights to vary via a factor analysis.

79. Ramesh Ponnuru, "Romney's the One," *National Review Online*, December 2, 2011, http://www.nationalreview.com/articles/284700/romney-s-one-ramesh-ponnuru#.

Chapter 4: All In

1. We originally wrote about these events here: John Sides, "The Santorum Surge," *The Monkey Cage*, January 4, 2012, http://themonkeycage.org/blog/2012/01/04/the-santorum -surge/.

2. *The Guardian*'s Harry Enten also noticed similar patterns: Harry J. Enten, "Decoding the Romney Vote: How Wealth, Religion, and Education Factor In," *The Guardian*, April 6, 2012, http://www.guardian.co.uk/commentisfree/2012/apr/06/decoding-romney -vote-republican-election.

3. The Project for Excellence in Journalism's data also show an increase in coverage in the week of December 26–January 1, with positive coverage outnumbering negative coverage almost 2–1, as one would expect given that the polls were trending in Santorum's favor.

4. Marjorie Connelly, "News Is Good for Santorum and Bad for Gingrich in New Polls," *New York Times*, December 28, 2011.

5. A Public Policy Polling survey conducted during December 26–27 put Santorum at 27%. An American Research Group poll conducted from December 26–28 put him at 11%.

6. Jennifer Jacobs, "As Pro-Santorum Robo-Calls Begin in Iowa, Vander Plaats Says No Rules Broken," *Des Moines Register*, December 22, 2011, http://caucuses.desmoines register.com/2011/12/22/as-pro-santorum-automated-calls-begin-in-iowa-vander-plaats -say-no-rules-broken/. ABC News reported that Vander Plaats attempted to solicit money in exchange for the endorsement, although he denied that charge. Shushannah Walsh and Michael Falcone, "Iowa Conservative Leader Mired in Controversy after Rick Santorum Endorsement," ABC News, December 23, 2011, http://abcnews.go.com/blogs /politics/2011/12/iowa-conservative-leader-mired-in-controversy-after-rick-santorum -endorsement/.

7. David Lightman, "Romney Faces Uphill Climb in Wooing Iowa Voters," *McClatchey*, December 9, 2011, http://www.mcclatchydc.com/2011/12/09/132697/romney -faces-uphill-climb-in-wooing.html.

8. James E. Wilkerson and Craig Johnson, "Candidate Visits to Iowa," *Des Moines Register*, http://caucuses.desmoinesregister.com/data/iowa-caucus/candidate-tracker/.

9. Michael Falcone, "Mitt Romney, an Iowa No-Show, Faces a Backlash from Republicans and Democrats," ABC News, November 20, 2011, http://abcnews.go.com/blogs /politics/2011/11/mitt-romney-an-iowa-no-show-faces-a-backlash-from-republicans-and -democrats/.

10. Sasha Issenberg, "Anatomy of a Narrow Victory," *Slate*, January 4, 2012, http:// www.slate.com/articles/news_and_politics/victory_lab/2012/01/romney_s_iowa_win_it _took_a_lot_more_than_money_.html.

11. See David P. Redlawsk, Caroline J. Tolbert, and Todd Donovan, *Why Iowa?* (Chicago: Chicago University Press, 2011), chap. 7. See also John Sides, "Candidates Who Do Better than Expected Win More Media Attention," FiveThirtyEight/*New York Times*, January 4, 2012, http://fivethirtyeight.blogs.nytimes.com/2012/01/04/candidates-who-do -better-than-expected-win-more-media-attention/.

12. Robert Mackey, "Santorum Insists West Bank Is 'Part of Israel,'" *New York Times*, Lede blog, January 5, 2012.

13. Michael D. Shear, "Spotlight Shines on Santorum, Rough Edges and All," *New York Times*, Caucus blog, January 6, 2012, http://thecaucus.blogs.nytimes.com/2012/01/06 /spotlight-shines-on-santorum-rough-edges-and-all/.

14. Jeff Zeleny, "Romney Is Winner in New Hampshire Blunting Attacks," *New York Times*, January 11, 2012.

15. Jeff Zeleny, "Certainty Fades as Romney Falters," *New York Times*, January 22, 2012.

16. Michael A. Memoli, "Gallup: Mitt Romney Has Widest Lead to Date in GOP Race," *Los Angeles Times*, January 12, 2012, http://articles.latimes.com/2012/jan/12/news /la-pn-romney-gallup-gop-nomination-20120112.

17. The Project for Excellence in Journalism's data do not show this same shift in tone after New Hampshire. Given the decline in Romney's poll numbers and favorability ratings between the New Hampshire and South Carolina primaries—which we document later—we tend to believe that the coverage was likely more negative than positive, especially since there was no highly visible campaign event (such as a primary or caucus) that could have affected public opinion over and above the news coverage.

18. Specifically, they spent $973,930 between January 9 and January 22, according to data gathered by the Campaign Media Analysis Project. This translates into an estimated three thousand airings in various South Carolina media markets. Approximately 80% of these were negative, suggesting their focus on Romney.

19. Tim Mak, "Newt Gingrich: Mitt Romney 'Looted' Companies," *Politico*, January 9, 2012, http://www.politico.com/news/stories/0112/71227.html#ixzz2oopaXyPH.

20. Felicia Sonmez, "Newt Gingrich Accuses Mitt Romney of 'Looting' during Bain Tenure," *Washington Post*, January 10, 2012, http://www.washingtonpost.com/blogs/ election-2012/post/newt-gingrich-accuses-mitt-romney-of-looting-during-bain-tenure/ 2012/01/10/gIQAxrTroP_blog.html.

21. Michael Barbaro and Ashley Parker, "Advisers Work to Put Positive Spin on Romney's Career in Corporate Buyouts," *New York Times*, January 11, 2012.

22. Ron Fournier, "Attacks on His Bain Record Are Making Romney Stronger, Not Killing Him," *The Atlantic*, January 12, 2012, http://www.theatlantic.com/politics/archive/2012 /01/attacks-on-his-bain-record-are-making-romney-stronger-not-killing-him/251355/#.

23. A separate YouGov poll among likely Republican voters in South Carolina showed the same thing. When asked whether they approved or disapproved of "the job Romney did at Bain Capital," many were not sure (48%), but approval outweighed disapproval (39% to 13%). See also Lynn Vavreck, "Are the Attacks on Romney's Time at Bain Capital Working?" *The Monkey Cage*, January 21, 2012, http://themonkeycage.org/blog/2012/01/21 /are-the-attacks-on-romneys-time-bain-capital-working/.

24. To generate this estimate, we regressed Romney's share of national polls of GOP voters on a time trend for January 10–21. Even with only nine polls during this period, Romney's share is estimated to have declined by 0.75 points each day (*t*-statistic = −1.92).

25. Here are all the polls taken during this time period: January 11–12 CNN poll (43% favorable, 42% unfavorable); January 12–14 Fox poll (45–38%), January 11–16 Pew poll (31–44%), January 13–16 Public Policy Polling poll (35–53%); and January 18–22 *Washington Post*/ABC News poll (31–49%).

26. Jordan Weissman, "Newt Gingrich Thinks School Children Should Work as Janitors," *The Atlantic*, November 21, 2011, http://www.theatlantic.com/business/archive/2011 /11/newt-gingrich-thinks-school-children-should-work-as-janitors/248837/.

27. Philip Rucker and Rosalind S. Helderman, "Four Survivors Mix It Up; Gingrich Adds Host to Fray," *Washington Post*, January 20, 2012.

28. In the Project for Excellence in Journalism data, Gingrich's share of news coverage also increased—from 18% during the week of January 2–8 to 57% during January 16–22. The ratio of positive to negative coverage increased from 17–38% the day after the New Hampshire primary to 29–38% the day after the first debate to 41–34% the day after the second debate.

29. The four polls conducted before the debate (with Gingrich's share) were: January 11–13 Opinion Research Corporation (18%); January 12–14 Shaw Research Associates (14%); January 12–15 *Washington Post* (17%); and January 11–16 Pew Research Center (16%). The final four polls were: January 12–17 CBS News (21%); January 13–17 Gallup (16%); January 17 Rasmussen (27%); and January 18–22 Gallup (28%). Note that the first two of these final four polls were in the field during the first debate, and thus do not fully capture any effect of that debate and subsequent news coverage. The final Gallup poll does include a day of fielding after the South Carolina primary itself, and thus its number may reflect an increase driven by Gingrich's primary victory.

30. On the day of the second debate, January 19, Rick Perry dropped out of the race and endorsed Gingrich. However, this likely provided little boost for Gingrich. He was already in the lead at this point and, moreover, South Carolina polls showed that only about 3% supported Perry.

31. These advertising data were originally collected by the Campaign Media Analysis Group and were provided to us by the *Washington Post*. They do not include any advertising aired on local cable networks.

32. It is important to note that the ads may have mattered in ways that we cannot fully account for with the data at hand. For example, we cannot observe what would have happened if Gingrich had aired no ads. Perhaps Gingrich's advertising helped blunt the effects of Romney's ads in certain markets.

33. Karen Tumulty, "Newt Gingrich Wins South Carolina Primary," *Washington Post*, January 21, 2012, http://www.washingtonpost.com/politics/newt-gingrich-wins-south -carolina-primary/2012/01/21/gIQAKTxBHQ_story.html.

34. Nicholas Confessore, David Kocieniewski, and Ashley Parker, "Pressed, Romney Shares Tax Data; A Rate Near 15%," *New York Times*, January 18, 2012.

35. Between January 1 and 24, the day after the debate, there had been 659 news stories that featured the subject of Romney and tax returns in the headline and leading paragraph, according to a search of Lexis-Nexis. Between January 25 and February 15— the day before Santorum released his tax returns—there were only 275 stories.

36. Dan Balz and Rosalind S. Helderman, "Front-runners Go Toe to Toe in Tampa Debate," *Washington Post*, January 24, 2012.

37. Dan Balz and Amy Gardner, "Romney, Gingrich Face Off in Florida," *Washington Post*, January 27, 2012.

38. Richard W. Stevenson, "Gingrich Insurgency Tests Party's Old Guard," *New York Times*, Caucus blog, January 26, 2012, http://thecaucus.blogs.nytimes.com/2012/01/26 /gingrich-insurgency-tests-partys-old-guard/?hp.

39. Gerry Mullany and Richard A. Oppel Jr., "Dole Releases Stinging Critique of Gingrich," *New York Times*, Caucus blog, January 26, 2012. http://thecaucus.blogs.nytimes .com/2012/01/26/dole-releases-stinging-critique-of-gingrich/.

40. Although the Project for Excellence in Journalism data do not show a steady increase in the favorability of Romney's news coverage, they do show that Romney received distinctly more favorable coverage on several days during this period, especially around the time of the debates (January 16–19).

41. In Figure 4.3, the tone-weighted measure of Romney's news share increased from about 4 on January 21, the day of the South Carolina primary, to 10 on January 25. The first polls that showed Romney pulling away from Gingrich were in the field through January 25 and not released until January 26. This may be why Balz and Gardner's summary of the January 26 debate said that "the polls show the contest is extremely tight heading into the weekend."

42. In South Carolina, Romney and his super-PAC aired 8,976 ads, and Gingrich and his super-PAC aired 4,946; the ratio of Romney ads to Gingrich ads was 1.8 to 1. In Florida, the comparable numbers were 20,304 Romney ads and 4,610 Gingrich ads, or a ratio of 4.4 to 1. In the last week before each primary, the ratio of Romney to Gingrich ads was 1.6 to 1 in South Carolina but 2.4 to 1 in Florida.

43. An earlier version of this analysis with less complete advertising data appeared here: John Sides, "Did Romney's Ad Advantage in Florida Help in Florida?" FiveThirtyEight/*New York Times*, February 1, 2012, http://fivethirtyeight.blogs.nytimes.com/2012/02/01/did-romneys-ad-advantage-help-in-florida/.

44. "GOP Primary Dynamics: The Impact of Advertising on Candidate Support," *Evolving Strategies*, http://evolving-strategies.com/projects/gop-primary-dynamics/.

45. In the Florida Republican primary, 1,672,634 people voted, and about 632,000 were estimated to have voted early. Paul Steinhauser, "Final Poll: Early Voting Gives Romney a Leg Up in Florida," CNN, Political Ticker blog, January 31, 2012, http://politicalticker.blogs.cnn.com/2012/01/31/final-poll-early-voting-gives-romney-a-leg-up-in-florida/. Romney's efforts to contact voters with absentee ballots is discussed here: Sasha Issenberg, "Early Bird Gets the Delegates," *Slate*, March 12, 2012, http://www.slate.com/articles/news_and_politics/victory_lab/2012/03/mitt_romney_s_early_voting_mastery_his_rivals_never_stood_a_chance_.html.

46. Paul Gronke, "Miami-Dade by Mode of Balloting," *Early Voting*, January 31, 2012, http://www.earlyvoting.net/commentary/miami-dade-by-mode-of-balloting/. "Florida Presidential Primary Preference," American Research Group, Inc., January 29-30, 2012. http://americanresearchgroup.com/pres2012/primary/rep/fl/. The problem, of course, is that absentee voters may already have been likely to support Romney. Absentee voters are generally older (see Matt Barreto, Matthew J. Streb, Mara Marks, and Fernando Guerra, "Do Absentee Voters Differ from Polling Place Voters? New Evidence from California," *Public Opinion Quarterly* 70, no. 2 [2006]: 224–34, as well as cites therein). And older voters in Florida tended to vote for Romney at higher rates than did younger voters. For example, among exit poll respondents, Romney did better among senior citizens (51% of whom voted for him) than among young people (41% of eighteen- to twenty-nine-year-olds voted for him).

47. Amy Gardner, "Pro-Gingrich Super PAC Builds Shadow Campaign," *Washington Post*, January 24, 2012, http://www.washingtonpost.com/politics/pro-gingrich-super-pac-builds-shadow-campaign/2012/01/23/gIQApLsoNQ_story_1.html.

48. Sasha Issenberg, "How Newt Lost," *Slate*, February 1, 2012, http://www.slate.com/articles/news_and_politics/victory_lab/2012/02/gingrich_florida_defeat_why_newt_lost_.html.

49. Richard W. Stevenson, "Political Memo: G.O.P. Establishment Tries to Exert What Influence It Has against Gingrich," *New York Times*, Caucus blog, January 27, 2012, http://query.nytimes.com/gst/fullpage.html?res=9F04E6DB1338F934A15752C0A9649D8B63.

50. Issenberg, "How Newt Lost."

51. Aaron Blake, "Mitt Romney's Nevada Caucus Win: What It Means," *Washington Post*, The Fix blog, February 4, 2012, http://www.washingtonpost.com/blogs/the-fix/post /mitt-romneys-nevada-caucus-win-what-it-means/2012/02/04/gIQAZZwaqQ_blog.html.

52. Jon Ward, "Rick Santorum Sweeps Colorado, Missouri, Minnesota, Embarrassing Romney," *Huffington Post*, February 8, 2012, http://www.huffingtonpost.com/2012/02/08 /rick-santorum-colorado-caucus-_n_1261734.html.

53. Manny Fernandez, "Santorum Adjusting to Star Treatment on Trail," *New York Times*, February 10, 2012, http://www.nytimes.com/2012/02/10/us/politics/rick-santorum -adjusting-to-star-treatment-on-trail.html?_r=2.

54. Tom Jensen, "Big Day for Santorum?" Public Policy Polling, February 7, 2012, http://www.publicpolicypolling.com/main/2012/02/big-day-for-santorum.html.

55. Michael D. Shear, "As Campaign Heads to Midwest, Romney Turns His Focus to Santorum," *New York Times*, February 6, 2012, http://www.nytimes.com/2012/02/07/us /politics/heading-midwest-romney-takes-aim-at-santorum.html; Dan Balz, "Mitt Romney and the Enthusiasm Gap," *Washington Post*, February 8, 2012, http://www.washington post.com/politics/mitt-romney-and-the-enthusiasm-gap/2012/02/08/gIQAvoRLzQ_story .html.

56. Tom Jensen, "Big Day Possible for Santorum," Public Policy Polling, February 6, 2012, http://www.publicpolicypolling.com/pdf/2011/PPP_Release_COMNMO_206.pdf. Santorum did better in Colorado counties that had larger numbers of conservatives and evangelicals: Seth Masket, "The Secret of Santorum's Success," *Enik Rising*, February 8, 2012, http://enikrising.blogspot.com/2012/02/secret-of-santorums-success.html, "Scatter-plot Dump: Colorado Caucus Edition," *Enik Rising*, February 10, 2012, http://enikrising .blogspot.com/2012/02/scatterplot-dump-colorado-caucus.html.

57. Balz, "Mitt Romney and the Enthusiasm Gap."

58. Julie Bykowicz, "Gingrich Seeks to Ease Fundraising Woes as Big Donations Slow," Bloomberg, February 10, 2012, http://www.bloomberg.com/news/2012-02-10/gingrich -seeks-to-ease-fundraising-woes-as-big-donations-slow.html.

59. The RWBF spent about $7.5 million during the primary campaign. Doré gave $2.25 million and Friess gave $2.1 million. "Red, White, and Blue Outside Spending," http:// www.opensecrets.org/outsidespending/detail.php?cmte=C00503417&cycle=2012.

60. These were the ads aired in any media market reaching these three states during the weeks ending January 29, February 5, and February 12.

61. Jim Rutenberg and Nicholas Confessore, "A Wealthy Backer Likes the Odds on Santorum," *New York Times*, February 8, 2012, http://www.nytimes.com/2012/02/09/us /politics/foster-friess-a-deep-pocketed-santorum-super-pac-backer.html.

62. These figures are from *Politico*'s record of the candidates' campaign events: "2012 Live Candidate Tracker," *Politico*, http://www.politico.com/2012-election/candidate-map/.

63. Michael Tesler, "Moral Conservatives Spark the Santorum Surge," YouGov, February 21, 2012, http://today.yougov.com/news/2012/02/21/moral-conservatives-spark -santorum-surge/.

64. Because Santorum was to suspend his campaign in April, he never reaped the potential rewards from his victories. Ron Paul ended up claiming many delegates at the Minnesota and Colorado conventions. In Missouri, Romney actually won the most delegates, 41, while Santorum won only 9.

65. This is somewhat evident in the trend in tone-weighted share of the news in Figure 4.3. The tone of coverage by itself shows the trend even more clearly. The tone of coverage can range from +1 (very positive) to –1 (very negative) in our data. The tone of

Santorum's coverage on the day after the Colorado, Minnesota, and Missouri primaries was 0.60, and in the first week after those primaries it averaged 0.55. By the week before the Arizona and Michigan primaries, it had declined to 0.32.

66. Katharine Q. Seelye, "Santorum Clarifies Remarks on Women in Combat," *New York Times*, Caucus blog, February 10, 2012, http://thecaucus.blogs.nytimes.com/2012/02 /10/santorum-clarifies-remarks-on-women-in-combat/.

67. Brian Knowlton, "Santorum Defends Comments on Obama and Education," *New York Times*, Caucus blog, February 19, 2012, http://thecaucus.blogs.nytimes.com/2012/02 /19/santorum-defends-comments-on-obama-and-education/.

68. Michael D. Shear, "Debate Looms as a Critical Moment for Santorum," *New York Times*, Caucus blog, February 19, 2012, http://thecaucus.blogs.nytimes.com/2012/02/19 /debate-looms-as-a-critical-moment-for-santorum/.

69. BuzzFeed Staff, "Governors Look to Santorum with Dread," *BuzzFeed Politics*, February 27, 2012, http://www.buzzfeed.com/buzzfeedpolitics/governors-look-to -santorum-with-dread.

70. Ross Douthat, "Can Santorum Win in November?" *New York Times*, Campaign Stops blog, February 21, 2012, http://campaignstops.blogs.nytimes.com/2012/02/21/can -santorum-win-in-november/.

71. Naureen Khan, "Santorum's Mystery Kitchen Cabinet: Who Advises Him Besides Himself?" *National Journal*, March 19, 2012, http://nationaljournal.com/2012-presidential -campaign/santorum-s-mystery-kitchen-cabinet-who-advises-him-besides-himself--2012 0319?mrefid=freehplead_1.

72. Peter Hamby, "Santorum Adviser on Michigan: 'We Have Already Won,'" CNN, Political Ticker blog, February 27, 2012, http://politicalticker.blogs.cnn.com/2012/02/27 /santorum-adviser-on-michigan-we-have-already-won/.

73. Zeke Miller, "Romney Vastly Outspends His Rivals in the South," *BuzzFeed Politics*, March 12, 2012, http://www.buzzfeed.com/zekejmiller/romney-vastly-outspends-his -rivals-in-the-south.

74. Notably, neither Santorum nor Gingrich was able to meet the requirements to get on the ballot in Virginia, another Super Tuesday state. This is further evidence of how a shoestring campaign hurt their chances.

75. Michael D. Shear, "Before Illinois Primary, Santorum Talks of Brokered Convention," *New York Times*, Caucus blog, March 19, 2012, http://thecaucus.blogs.nytimes .com/2012/03/19/before-illinois-primary-santorum-talks-of-brokered-convention/.

76. Jeff Zeleny and Sarah Wheaton, "Santorum Ignores Pressure to Bow Out to Romney," *New York Times*, March 25, 2012, http://www.nytimes.com/2012/03/26/us/politics/ santorum-ignores-party-pressure-to-quit-race.html.

77. Walter Shapiro, "Who Got the Fox News Vote?" *Columbia Journalism Review*, April 3, 2012, http://www.cjr.org/swing_states_project/who_got_the_fox_news_vote.php. One sample quote, from Bill O'Reilly on April 2: "If the governor [Romney] does win in Wisconsin, it's pretty much all over. And the Republican Party can shift into beating President Obama."

78. The last two Pennsylvania polls before Santorum suspended his campaign were conducted on April 4. One, by Rasmussen, showed Santorum with a 4-point lead over Romney. The other, by Public Policy Polling, showed Romney with a 4-point lead. With the Pennsylvania primary still twenty days away and with the trends in news coverage and national polling working against Santorum, it was a reasonable bet that he would not have won Pennsylvania—to say nothing of the Connecticut, Delaware, New York, and

Rhode Island primaries, which were scheduled for the same day and were arguably very favorable turf for Romney.

79. Some commentators recognized this, of course. One was the *Huffington Post*'s Mark Blumenthal: "Newt Gingrich Surges in South Carolina, But Expect the Unexpected," *Huffington Post*, January 20, 2012, http://www.huffingtonpost.com/2012/01/20 /newt-gingrich-mitt-romney-polls_n_1219928.html.

80. John Sides, "Deep Dissatisfaction with Romney?" *The Monkey Cage*, January 19, 2012, http://themonkeycage.org/blog/2012/01/19/deep-dissatisfaction-with-romney/.

81. We examined several public polls from January where the pollster reported candidate favorability broken down by party. These polls were of registered voters, not likely primary voters, but they showed the same pattern: Republicans perceived Romney and Santorum similarly, with a slightly larger fraction perceiving Santorum favorably. Republicans viewed Gingrich somewhat less favorably than the other two candidates.

82. These data are also from likely Republican primary voters interviewed in YouGov polls from February through May 2012.

83. These results are based on our calculations from the Pew poll, focusing only on respondents who identified with or leaned toward the Republican Party and also said they were "somewhat" or "very likely" to vote in a primary. Romney was more popular among Giuliani's and Thompson's supporters (68% and 67%, respectively, of whom had a favorable view of him), but of course their supporters were less numerous than supporters of McCain and Huckabee, who were the most competitive candidates in the 2008 primary.

84. About 7–8% of Republican primary voters could not place the candidates on the liberal-conservative spectrum. They were excluded from this figure.

85. In a January 2008 YouGov poll of registered voters, fielded as part of the 2008 Cooperative Campaign Analysis Project, voters placed candidates on this same 5-point scaling range from very liberal (1) to very conservative (5). On average, likely Republican primary voters placed themselves at 4.2 and Romney at 3.8. The other candidates were perceived as less conservative: McCain (3.0), Giuliani (3.0), and Huckabee (3.6). A similar finding emerged in a January 2008 Pew survey of registered Republicans: Romney and Huckabee were seen as more conservative than McCain and Giuliani, although Huckabee was seen as slightly more conservative than Romney. Pew Research Center for the People & the Press, "In GOP Primaries: Three Victors, Three Constituencies," January 16, 2008, http://www .people-press.org/2008/01/16/in-gop-primaries-three-victors-three-constituencies/.

86. "Rush Limbaugh Endorses Mitt Romney," *Hot Air blog*, February 5, 2008, http:// hotair.com/archives/2008/02/05/rush-limbaugh-endorses-mitt-romney/; The Editors, "Romney for President," *National Review*, December 11, 2007, http://www.nationalreview .com/articles/223076/romney-president/editors.

87. Sam Stein, "Ann Coulter CPAC Speech: In Support of Romney, 'Let's Try Square for a While,'" *Huffington Post*, February 10, 2012, http://www.huffingtonpost.com/2012/02 /10/ann-coulter-cpac-speech-i_n_1268852.html.

88. Lynn Vavreck, "Perry's Exit Mainly a Non-Event," YouGov, January 20, 2012, http://today.yougov.com/news/2012/01/20/perrys-exit-mainly-non-event/; Jeffrey M. Jones, "Romney, Santorum Tie, as Gingrich Voters' Second Choice," Gallup, March 16, 2012, http://www.gallup.com/poll/153308/Romney-Santorum-Tie-Gingrich-Voters -Second-Choice.aspx.

89. Romney's own supporters were more loyal than Gingrich's or Santorum's. Between the December interview and the later interview, 76% of Romney's supporters stuck with him, while 61% of Gingrich's continued to support Gingrich and 68% of Santorum's supporters continued to support Santorum.

90. For example, support for a candidate affects perceptions of "viability," or whether a candidate will become the nominee—although the reverse can simultaneously be true, suggesting reciprocal causation. See Larry M. Bartels, "Expectations and Preferences in Presidential Nominating Campaigns," *American Political Science Review* 79, no. 3 (1985): 804–15. Similarly, both support for a candidate and perceptions of viability affect perceptions of electability, or whether the candidate can win in the general election. Political scientist Alan Abramowitz calls this "clear evidence of wishful thinking among . . . primary voters: voters tended to perceive the candidate they liked best as having the best chance of being nominated and elected." "Viability, Electability, and Candidate Choice in a Presidential Primary Election: A Test of Competing Models," *Journal of Politics* 51, no. 4 (1989): 977–92.

91. John Sides and Alex Lundry, "You Don't Have to Love Mitt to Vote for Him," You-Gov, January 9, 2012, http://today.yougov.com/news/2012/01/09/you-dont-have-love -mitt-vote-him/. Alex Lundry helped with the design of the experiment but not with the analysis or conclusions. He later became a Romney campaign staff member.

92. The same thing happened in an earlier experiment, except at that point Gingrich was favored to win the nomination and showing people this information increased his vote share among Republicans: John Sides and Alex Lundry, "Do GOP Voters Care About Electability?" YouGov, December 13, 2011, http://today.yougov.com/news/2011/12/13/do -gop-voters-care-about-electability/.

93. Frank Newport, "Romney, Santorum Stir Less Enthusiasm than McCain Did," Gallup, March 15, 2012, http://www.gallup.com/poll/153272/Romney-Santorum-Stir-Less -Enthusiasm-McCain.aspx.

94. Joshua Green, "The Secret Gingrich-Santorum 'Unity Ticket' That Nearly Toppled Romney," *Bloomberg Businessweek*, March 22, 2013, http://www.businessweek.com/ articles/2013-03-22/the-secret-gingrich-santorum-unity-ticket-that-nearly-toppled-romney.

95. Martin Cohen, David Karol, Hans Noel, and John Zaller, *The Party Decides: Presidential Nomination Before and After Reform* (Chicago: Chicago University Press, 2008).

96. Frank Rich, "The Molotov Party," *New York*, December 26, 2011, http://nymag .com/news/frank-rich/gop-2012-1/.

97. Ibid.

98. Some commentators and even Republican Party leaders blamed the longer primary on the alleged shift toward the proportional allocation of delegates in the Republican contests. In fact, this was something of a myth. The change in the rules between 2008 and 2012 was not between a "winner-take-all" rule and a proportional rule but between two somewhat different hybrids of those rules. In fact, Romney likely would have won delegates at a slower pace had the 2012 contest been conducted under the 2008 rules. See Josh Putnam and John Sides, "Republican Rules Are Not to Blame for Primary War," Bloomberg, March 22, 2012, http://www.bloomberg.com/news/2012-03-22/republican -rules-are-not-to-blame-for-primary-war.html.

99. Michael Schwartz, "After Texas Vote, Romney Secures G.O.P. Nomination," *New York Times*, Caucus blog, May 29, 2012, http://thecaucus.blogs.nytimes.com/2012/05/29 /after-texas-vote-romney-secures-g-o-p-nomination/.

Chapter 5: High Rollers

1. Jann S. Wenner, "Ready for the Fight: Rolling Stone Interview with Barack Obama," *Rolling Stone*, April 12, 2012, http://www.rollingstone.com/politics/news/ready-for-the -fight-rolling-stone-interview-with-barack-obama-20120425?print=true.

2. Catherine Rampell, "Reasons Abound for Ebb in Job Growth," *New York Times*, May 4, 2012, http://www.nytimes.com/2012/05/05/business/economy/us-added-only -115000-jobs-in-april-rate-is-8-1.html?pagewanted=all&_r=0.

3. Jill Schlesinger, "Rotten May Jobs Report Underscores Weak Recovery," June 1, 2012, http://www.cbsnews.com/8301-505123_162-57444442/rotten-may-jobs-report-under scores-weak-recovery/; Paul Wiseman, "Jobs Report May 2012: U.S. Employers Added 69,000 Jobs in May as the Unemployment Rate Rose to 8.2 Percent," *Huffington Post*, June 1, 2012, http://www.huffingtonpost.com/2012/06/01/jobs-report-may-2012_n _1561927.html.

4. "Another Month of Devastating Economic News for American Workers, Families," June 1, 2012, http://www.mittromney.com/news/press/2012/06/another-month -devastating-economic-news-america-workers-families.

5. The forecast is here: "Survey of Professional Forecasters," Federal Reserve Bank of Philadelphia Research Department, November 14, 2011, http://www.philadelphiafed.org /research-and-data/real-time-center/survey-of-professional-forecasters/2011/spfq411.pdf. The estimate of Obama's margin derived from a regression of the incumbent party's share of the two-party vote on election-year change in GDP for the presidential elections between 1948 and 2008. Any such prediction has substantial uncertainty, so it is best not to consider the predicted margin of victory sacrosanct but instead as indicating that Obama was favored to win (see also our discussion of forecasting models in chapter 2).

6. "Gross Domestic Product: Second Quarter 2012 (Third Estimate), Corporate Profits: Second Quarter 2012 (Revised Estimate)," Bureau of Economic Analysis, U.S. Department of Commerce, September 27, 2012, http://www.bea.gov/newsreleases/national /gdp/2012/pdf/gdp2q12_3rd.pdf.

7. Larry Bartels, *Unequal Democracy* (Princeton: Princeton University Press, 2008), 104–10. Bartels's analysis covered the years 1952–2004 and used real disposable income as the measure of economic growth. We found the same pattern with GDP: for Republican incumbents, growth was larger in election years than non-election years, but the opposite was true for Democratic incumbents. Like Bartels, we considered economic growth as occurring during a president's tenure beginning one year after his inauguration and continuing until a year after the subsequent inauguration.

8. Douglas A. Hibbs, "Obama's Reelection Prospects under 'Bread and Peace' Voting in the 2012 US Presidential Election," *PS: Political Science and Politics* 45, no. 4 (2012): 635–39.

9. The Index of Consumer Sentiment, which we depicted in chapter 2, stood at about 76 in the first two quarters of 2012, comparable to its value (75) when George H. W. Bush was running. This was better than when Jimmy Carter ran for reelection, when the value was 59, but worse than when Ronald Reagan or Bill Clinton won reelection (values of 98 and 91, respectively).

10. See Robert Erikson and Christopher Wlezien, "The Objective and Subjective Economy and the Presidential Vote," *PS: Political Science and Politics* 45, no. 4 (2012): 620–24. They describe how they constructed the index as well as the weighting procedure. The Conference Board's index includes these factors: average weekly hours, manufacturing; average weekly initial claims for unemployment insurance; manufacturers' new orders, consumer goods, and materials; ISM Index of New Orders; manufacturers' new orders, nondefense capital goods excluding aircraft orders; building permits, new private housing units; stock prices, 500 common stocks; Leading Credit Index; interest rate spread, ten-year Treasury bonds less federal funds; and average consumer expectations for business conditions. See "Global Business Cycle Indicators," Conference Board, December 20, 2012, http://www.conference-board.org/data/bcicountry.cfm?cid=1.

11. David Brooks, "The ESPN Man," *New York Times*, May 14, 2012, http://www.ny times.com/2012/05/15/opinion/brooks-the-espn-man.html?_r=1&hp.

12. The Cook Report, "It Shouldn't Be Close," National Journal, August 23, 2012, http://www.nationaljournal.com/columns/cook-report/the-cook-report-the-presidential -race-shouldn-t-be-close-20120823.

13. Jonathan Martin, "Why Barack Obama Is Winning," *Politico*, September 18, 2012, http://dyn.politico.com/printstory.cfm?uuid=978F5153-3BFA-42E3-83CA-54E1A0C143DF.

14. Jacob M. Montgomery, Florian M. Hollenbach, and Michael D. Ward, "Ensemble Predictions of the 2012 US Presidential Election," *PS: Political Science and Politics* 45, no. 4 (2012): 651–54.

15. Carl M. Cannon and Tom Bevan, *Election 2012: A Time for Choosing* (ebook; New York: Crown, 2012).

16. Zachary A. Goldfarb and Peter Wallsten, "Obama Risks Losing Liberals with Talk of Cutting Budget," *Washington Post*, April 12, 2011, http://www.washingtonpost.com/ business/economy/obamas-speech-on-debt-reduction-a-first-step-in-broader-effort -white-house-says/2011/04/12/AFitkvRD_story.html?hpid=z1.

17. David Brooks and Gail Collins, "Specter Survives, at Least for Now," *New York Times*, April 28, 2009, http://opinionator.blogs.nytimes.com/2009/04/28/specter-survives -at-least-for-now/; Gail Collins, "United We Rant," *New York Times*, January 28, 2010, http://www.nytimes.com/2010/01/28/opinion/28collins.html; Gail Collins, "The Most Unhappy Fellow," *New York Times*, June 30, 2010, http://www.nytimes.com/2010/07/01 /opinion/01collins.html.

18. Matt Bai, "Voter Insurrection Turns Mainstream, Creating New Rules," *New York Times*, May 19, 2010, http://www.nytimes.com/2010/05/20/us/politics/20assess.html?emc =eta1.

19. Fareed Zakaria, "Obama Should Act More Like a President than a Prime Minister," *Washington Post*, January 25, 2010, http://www.washingtonpost.com/wp-dyn/content /article/2010/01/24/AR2010012402300.html?hpid=opinionsbox1; Matt Bai, "The Great Unalignment," *New York Times*, January 20, 2010, http://www.nytimes.com/2010/01/24 /magazine/24fob-wwln-t.html?ref=magazine.

20. See "Party Identification 7-Point Scale (revised in 2008) 1952–2008," ANES Guide to Public Opinion and Electoral Behavior, August 5, 2010, http://www.electionstudies.org /nesguide/toptable/tab2a_1.htm.

21. Studies that illustrate these points include Larry M. Bartels, "Partisanship and Voting Behavior, 1952–1996," *American Journal of Political Science* 44, no. 1 (2000): 35– 50; Marc Hetherington, "Resurgent Mass Partisanship: The Role of Elite Polarization," *American Political Science Review* 95, no. 3 (2001): 619–31; and Matthew Levendusky, *The Partisan Sort: How Liberals Became Democrats and Conservatives Became Republicans* (Chicago: University of Chicago Press, 2009).

22. Paul F. Lazarsfeld, Bernard Berelson, and Hazel Gaudet, *The People's Choice: How the Voter Makes Up His Mind in a Presidential Campaign* (New York: Columbia University Press, 1948), 73.

23. Lonna Rae Atkeson, "Divisive Primaries and General Election Outcomes: Another Look at Presidential Campaigns," *American Journal of Political Science* 42, no. 1 (1998): 256–71.

24. Amber Wichowsky and Sarah E. Niebler, "Narrow Victories and Hard Games: Re- visiting the Primary Divisiveness Hypothesis," *American Politics Research* 38, no. 6 (2010): 1052–71.

25. Michael Henderson, D. Sunshine Hillygus, and Trevor Thompson, " 'Sour Grapes' or Rational Voting? Voter Decision Making among Thwarted Primary Voters in 2008,"

Public Opinion Quarterly 74, no. 3 (2010): 499–529. See also Lynn Vavreck, "Where Will the Anti-Romney Vote Go?" YouGov, January 6, 2012, http://today.yougov.com/news /2012/01/06/will-gop-skeptics-support-romney-general-election/.

26. Frank Newport, "Romney, Obama in Tight Race as Gallup Daily Tracking Begins," Gallup, April 16, 2012, http://www.gallup.com/poll/153902/Romney-Obama-Tight -Race-Gallup-Daily-Tracking-Begins.aspx.

27. Frank Newport, "Dems Happier with Obama than Republicans Are with Romney," Gallup, May 14, 2012, http://www.gallup.com/poll/154655/Dems-Happier-Obama -Republicans-Romney.aspx.

28. Philip Rucker, "Mitt Romney Receives Newfound Enthusiasm from Republicans," *Washington Post*, June 18, 2012, http://www.washingtonpost.com/politics/mitt-romney -receives-newfound-enthusiasm-from-republicans/2012/06/18/gJQAkUuXmV_story.html.

29. Lazarsfeld, Berelson, and Gaudet, *The People's Choice*, 87.

30. Steven E. Finkel, "Reexamining the 'Minimal Effects' Model in Recent Presidential Campaigns," *Journal of Politics* 55, no. 1 (1993): 1–21.

31. Chris Cillizza, "Who Are the 'Undecided' Voters? And What the Heck Are They Waiting for?" *Washington Post*, October 9, 2012, http://www.washingtonpost.com/blogs /the-fix/wp/2012/10/09/who-are-the-undecided-voters-and-what-are-the-heck-are-they -waiting-for/.

32. Noah Rothman, "Chris Matthews Goes Off on 'Bonehead' Undecided Voters: 'What's Your Problem?'" October 16, 2012, http://www.mediaite.com/tv/chris-matthews -goes-off-on-bonehead-undecided-voters-whats-your-problem/.

33. An earlier version of this analysis appeared here: Larry Bartels and Lynn Vavreck, "Meet the Undecided," *New York Times*, July 30, 2012, http://campaignstops.blogs.nytimes .com/2012/07/30/meet-the-undecided/.

34. For one of the earliest discussions of cross-pressures and presidential elections, see Lazarsfeld, Berelson, and Gaudet, *The People's Choice*.

35. John Dickerson, "The Undecided Voter Revealed," *Slate*, October 31, 2012, http:// www.slate.com/articles/news_and_politics/politics/2012/10/undecided_voters_readers _explain_why_they_can_t_decide_to_vote_for_barack.single.html.

36. D. Sunshine Hillygus and Todd Shields, *The Persuadable Voter* (Princeton: Princeton University Press, 2009).

37. See John Sides, "The Origins of Campaign Agendas," *British Journal of Political Science* 36 (2006): 407–36.

38. Lynn Vavreck, *The Message Matters* (Princeton: Princeton University Press, 2009).

39. Vavreck, *The Message Matters*, 80.

40. These CMAG data were originally provided to the *Washington Post*. They were based on monitoring media markets in the United States for ads aired on broadcast stations and national cable networks (but not local cable systems). These data included estimates of the total number of ads aired (by sponsor, market, and week), the total dollars spent airing those ads, and the total dollars spent on a list of issues or themes. We calculated the proportion of total spending on each issue and then multiplied that by the number of airings to get the estimated percent of airings about that issue. In two cases, we combined categories under a broader heading: "Jobs and the economy" includes these categories: economy, jobs, manufacturing, transportation, food and agriculture, technology, and unions. In this time period, the vast majority of these ads were about jobs. "National security" includes: defense, human rights, international affairs, Iraq and Afghanistan wars, national security, and veterans. The vast majority of these ads were

Obama ads about the Iraq and Afghanistan wars. The number of ads aired corresponds closely to other metrics that attempt to directly measure the actual audience for the ads, such as gross rating points.

41. See Danny Hayes, "Difference in Degree: Issue Agendas in a Polarized Media Environment," in James A. Thurber and Candice J. Nelson, eds., *Campaigns and Elections American Style*, 4th ed. (Boulder, CO: Westview, forthcoming).

42. "Reverse—Obama for America 2012 Television Ad," YouTube, May 10, 2012, http://www.youtube.com/watch?feature=player_embedded&v=wnspxInJxHs.

43. "Obama for America TV Ad: 'Jobs,'" YouTube, June 7, 2012, http://www.youtube .com/watch?v=7otav9QveOM.

44. "A Better Day," YouTube, June 1, 2012, http://www.youtube.com/watch?v=yR6JM6 eUOvw.

45. "Jolt," YouTube, June 11, 2012, http://www.youtube.com/watch?v=JwsHRHPcSSU.

46. "Broken Promises: Spending," YouTube, April 30, 2012, http://www.youtube.com /watch?v=KOZJHUZgX1M.

47. Emily Friedman, "Romney Warns of Obama's Debt, Spending 'Inferno,' " ABC News, May 15, 2012, http://abcnews.go.com/blogs/politics/2012/05/romney-warns-of -obamas-debt-spending-inferno/.

48. "Who Will Do More," YouTube, October 28, 2012, http://youtube/VQ8Po4q6jqE.

49. The May–July YouGov surveys included 13,000 respondents, 1,982 of whom were pure independents and 1,193 of whom reported being registered voters but undecided about which candidate they preferred.

50. "Washington Post/ABC News Poll," *Washington Post*, poll conducted August 22–25, 2012, http://www.washingtonpost.com/wp-srv/politics/polls/postabcpoll_20120825 .html; Frank Newport, "Americans Still Blame Bush More than Obama for Bad Economy," Gallup, June 14, 2012, http://www.gallup.com/poll/155177/Americans-Blame-Bush -Obama-Bad-Economy.aspx.

51. Vavreck, *The Message Matters*.

52. Byron York, "Heeding Critics, Mitt Sharpens Pitch for Long Run," *The Examiner*, August 2, 2012, http://washingtonexaminer.com/byron-york-heeding-critics-mitt -sharpens-pitch-for-long-run/article/2503885.

53. John Sides, "What Really Happened in the 1980 Presidential Campaign," *The Monkey Cage*, August 9, 2012, http://themonkeycage.org/blog/2012/08/09/what-really -happened-in-the-1980-presidential-campaign/.

54. Respondents were randomly assigned to see Romney or Obama first. The order of the phrases was randomized, though keeping the order the same for both Romney and Obama. The phrases also included "Takes positions on issues and sticks by them." We first discussed the results of this survey here: John Sides, "Does Mitt Romney Have a Wealth Problem?" *The Monkey Cage*, January 13, 2012, http://themonkeycage.org/blog /2012/01/13/does-mitt-romney-have-a-wealth-problem/.

55. The correlation between these two items was .60 for Romney but only .18 for Obama. Both correlations were statistically significant.

56. For example, the correlation between believing Romney cares about the wealthy and cares about "people like me" was –.14 vs. .19 for Obama. These correlations were statistically significant as well.

57. Donald P. Green, Bradley Palmquist, and Eric Schickler, *Partisan Hearts and Minds: Political Parties and the Social Identities of Voters* (New Haven: Yale University Press, 2002), 9.

58. These data are from a May 26–28 YouGov poll. In this sample, 51% said that Democrats were better for the poor versus 22% who said that of Republicans (the rest said that the parties were about the same or that they were not sure). And 39% said that Democrats were better for the middle class versus 31% who said that of Republicans. By contrast, most (54%) said that the Republicans were better for Wall Street; only 13% said this of Democrats. The parties were evenly matched (32%–35%) in which was better for small businesses.

59. Danny Hayes, "Candidate Qualities through a Partisan Lens: A Theory of Trait Ownership," *American Journal of Political Science* 49, no. 4 (2005): 908–23. Hayes reported to us that his finding in this article applied to the 2008 election.

60. The poll was conducted by YouGov during February 18–21. We originally reported these results here: John Sides and Lynn Vavreck, "Does Romney's Wealth Pay Dividends for Santorum?" YouGov, February 28, 2012, http://today.yougov.com/news/2012/02/28/does-romneys-wealth-pay-dividends-santorum/.

61. For more on these points, see John Sides, "Romney's 'Empathy Gap,' " FiveThirtyEight/*New York Times*, April 11, 2012, http://fivethirtyeight.blogs.nytimes.com/2012/04/11/romneys-empathy-gap/.

62. Chris Cillizza, "Obama's Political Gaffe Will Be Fodder in General Election," *Washington Post*, June 10, 2012, http://www.washingtonpost.com/politics/obamas-political-gaffe-will-be-fodder-in-general-election/2012/06/10/gJQAwZaSSV_story.html.

63. "Remarks by the President at a Campaign Event in Roanoke, Virginia," Office of the Press Secretary, The White House, July 13, 2012, http://www.whitehouse.gov/the-press-office/2012/07/13/remarks-president-campaign-event-roanoke-virginia.

64. Kathleen Hennessey, "Republicans Pouncing on Obama's 'You Didn't Build That' Remark," *Los Angeles Times*, July 18, 2012, http://articles.latimes.com/2012/jul/18/news/la-pn-republicans-pouncing-on-obamas-you-didnt-build-that-remark-20120718.

65. Graeme Wilson, "Mitt the Twit," *The Sun*, July 27, 2012, http://www.thesun.co.uk/sol/homepage/news/politics/4456840/Wannabe-US-President-Mitt-Romney-in-Olympics-insult-but-David-Cameron-insists-Well-show-you.html.

66. Jim Acosta, "Was Romney's Trip 'a Great Success' or a Gaffe-Filled Disaster?" http://www.cnn.com/2012/07/31/politics/romney-trip-success-disaster/index.html.

67. Cillizza, "Obama's Political Gaffe."

68. The reporting about Afghanistan constituted unfavorable coverage because of passages like these: "Less than two hours after Obama left the country, insurgents killed at least seven people in a suicide bombing outside a heavily guarded housing compound for foreigners, news services reported," and "Obama's trip came amid criticism at home that the president is using the anniversary of bin Laden's death to advance his reelection prospects—featuring his decision to launch the mission in campaign videos and other political settings, for example." Kevin Sieff and Scott Wilson, "Obama Makes Surprise Trip to Afghanistan to Sign Key Pact, Mark Bin Laden Raid," *Washington Post*, May 1, 2012, http://www.washingtonpost.com/world/obama-makes-surprise-trip-to-afghanistan-to-sign-key-pact-mark-bin-laden-raid/2012/05/01/gIQAvYHduT_story.html. On the Booker remarks, see Greg Miller, "Newark Mayor Cory Booker Slams Obama Campaign Attack on Romney's Work for Bain Capital," *Washington Post*, May 20, 2012, http://www.washingtonpost.com/world/national-security/newark-mayor-cory-booker-slams-obama-campaign-attack-on-romneys-work-for-bain-capital/2012/05/20/gIQAPVJudU_story.html. On Clinton's remarks, see Aaron Blake, "Bill Clinton Sticks Another Fork in Obama's Bain Strategy, Says Romney Had 'Sterling' Business Career," *Washington Post*,

June 1, 2012, http://www.washingtonpost.com/blogs/the-fix/post/bill-clinton-sticks
-another-fork-in-obamas-bain-strategy/2012/06/01/gJQAt87r6U_blog.html.

69. Holly Bailey, "Romney Gets Aggressive against Obama: 'He Wants Americans to
Be Ashamed of Success,' " http://news.yahoo.com/blogs/ticket/romney-gets-aggressive
-against-obama-wants-americans-ashamed-190113055.html.

70. This story contains some of the plaudits Romney's speech earned: Ashley Parker,
"Romney Tells Evangelicals Their Values Are His, Too," *New York Times*, May 12, 2012,
http://www.nytimes.com/2012/05/13/us/politics/romney-woos-evangelicals-treading
-lightly-on-gay-marriage.html?pagewanted=all&_r=0.

71. Michael Tesler, "Do Presidential Gaffes Matter for People Paying Attention," You-
Gov, June 26, 2012, http://today.yougov.com/news/2012/06/26/do-presidential-gaffes
-matter-people-paying-attent/.

72. Gaffes are more likely to matter in down-ballot races where the candidates are less
well-known and where many people's opinions about these candidates are not solidified.
This is especially likely when the gaffes themselves provoke extraordinary controversy.
Thus the controversies caused by the comments on rape and abortion in 2012 by Senate
candidates Todd Akin and Richard Murdock appeared to have a larger impact on their
poll numbers and likely contributed to their respective defeats.

73. http://www.huffingtonpost.com/news/pollster/.

74. Simon Jackman, "Model-Based Poll Averaging: How Do We Do It?" *Huffington
Post*, September 14, 2012, http://www.huffingtonpost.com/simon-jackman/modelbased
-poll-averaging_b_1883525.html. Other polling averages, such as those by Real Clear
Politics, aggregate national and state polls separately and do nothing to account for house
effects.

75. Obama's comment was on July 13. A July 8–13 Gallup poll put Obama's lead at
47%–45%. A July 15–21 Gallup poll put it at 46%–45%. Rasmussen's July 9–11 and July
15–17 polls showed margins of 45%–46% and 46%–47%. YouGov's July 7–9 and July 14–16
showed margins of 43%–44% and 47%–44%. Romney's foreign trip was July 25–31. Rasmussen's polling before, during, and after this trip showed Romney ahead by 1–5 points,
with no clear trend. Gallup's polling was very stable—e.g., a 46%–46% split the week before the trip (July 22–29) and a 46%–45% split the week after (July 30–August 5). YouGov
also showed little change. The RAND data showed a bit more change during Romney's
trip: Obama's lead increased by about 1.5 points between July 24 and August 1, but that
shift did not break the statistical tie between the two candidates and was ultimately
temporary.

76. Vote intention was coded +1 (Obama), 0 (undecided or other candidate), and
−1 (Romney). Favorability of Obama and Romney were measured on 4-point scales.
Romney favorability was then subtracted from Obama favorability and rescaled to run
from −1 to +1. We regressed each of these measures on dummy variables for the individual weekly YouGov surveys. The magnitude and direction of these coefficients provided
some sense of how the views of these persuadable voters were changing week to week. We
then tested the equality of the coefficients for these variables on weeks surrounding these
gaffes to see how confident we could be that any changes were statistically meaningful.

77. The shift in favorability around Obama's speech was statistically significant
($p = .07$), but the shift in vote intentions was not distinguishable from zero ($p = .79$). We
cannot be as confident in the shift in favorability in the two surveys conducted around
Romney's trip (July 21–23 and July 28–30); the difference in favorability was significant at
only $p = .30$. The shift in vote intentions was insignificant ($p = .96$).

78. These were "Obama for America TV Ad: 'Come and Go,'" YouTube, June 20, 2012, http://www.youtube.com/watch?v=bVaw5cTjxmk; "Obama for America TV Ad: 'Reveal—OH,'" YouTube, June 26, 2012, http://www.youtube.com/watch?v=Oi0qLHHW Bbc; "Obama for America TV Ad: 'Revealed—IA,'" YouTube, June 26, 2012, http://www.youtube.com/watch?v=SLyL4N2O_So; "Obama for America TV Ad: 'Revealed—VA,'" YouTube, December 3, 2012, http://www.youtube.com/watch?v=JZNWVj3w3yY; "Obama for America TV Ad—'Believes,' " YouTube, July 3, 2012, http://www.youtube.com/watch?v=I1pPFlcGav4; "Obama for America TV Ad: 'The Problem,' " YouTube, July 7, 2012, http://www.youtube.com/watch?v=o0tZK_qHHCc; and "Obama for America TV Ad: Firms,' " YouTube, July 14, 2012, http://www.youtube.com/watch?v=Ud3mMjoAZZk. Tom Hamburger, "Romney's Bain Capital Invested in Companies That Moved Jobs Overseas," *Washington Post*, June 21, 2012, http://articles.washingtonpost.com/2012-06-21/politics /35460959_1_american-jobs-private-equity-firm-employment.

79. "Were Romney's Companies 'Pioneers in Outsourcing'?" PolitiFact.com, July 3, 2012, http://www.politifact.com/truth-o-meter/statements/2012/jul/13/barack-obama /were-romneys-companies-pioneers-outsourcing/; Dan Amira, "Why Obama's Singing Ad Is More Devastating than Romney's Singing Ad," *New York Magazine*, July 16, 2012, http://nymag.com/daily/intelligencer/2012/07/singing-ads-obama-vs-romney.html.

80. Andy Sullivan and Greg Roumeliotis, "Special Report: Romney's Steel Skeleton in the Bain Closet," Reuters, January 6, 2012, http://www.reuters.com/article/2012/01/06/us -campaign-romney-bailout-idUSTRE8050LL20120106.

81. This was in the ad titled "Donnie," YouTube, June 10, 2012, http://www.youtube .com/watch?v=FgoFW8N_8_Y. However, Box himself did not plan to vote for Obama, saying in July that he "is a jerk, a pantywaist, a lightweight, a blowhard." Box added, "He hasn't done a goddamn thing that he said he would do." Mike Elk, "Laid Off Steelworker in Anti-Romney Ad Says He Is Not Voting for Obama," *In These Times*, July 17, 2012, http://inthesetimes.com/working/entry/13535/laid_off_steelworker_in_anti-romney_ad _says_he_is_not_voting_for_obama/.

82. This was in the ad titled "Understands," YouTube, August 7, 2012, (http://www.you tube.com/watch?v=Nj70XqOxptU). The ad caused some controversy about Soptic's story—his wife actually had had health insurance through her own employer but was not employed when her cancer was diagnosed—and about the Obama campaign's knowledge of Soptic's story before the ad was released. Nia-Malika Henderson, "Beyond the Obama Ads, Joe Soptic's Steelworker Story," *Washington Post*, August 8, 2012, http://articles .washingtonpost.com/2012-08-08/politics/35491924_1_joe-soptic-obama-ads-pac -priorities-usa.

83. The ad was called "Stage," YouTube, June 23, 2012, http://www.youtube.com/watch ?v=oL00Jwj03JU.

84. This was in the ad "Priorities USA Action: Briefcase,' " YouTube, June 28, 2012, http://www.youtube.com/watch?v=6uMlsQ9HiF0.

85. The DNC also tried to emphasize this theme in a video that juxtaposed images of the Ann Romney's horse and a rider performing dressage with clips of Romney "dancing around the issues": "Mitt Dancing around the Issues Volume I," YouTube, July 18, 2012, http://youtu.be/3API5MnicU4. This referred to the fact that Ann Romney rode show-horses as a hobby and that her horse Rafalca was to compete in the London Olympics in dressage. But the attempt to draw attention to the Romneys' upper-class pursuits backfired because Ann Romney used this hobby as therapy for her multiple sclerosis. The DNC apologized. Jonathan Karl, "DNC Regrets Offending Ann Romney, No More Horse

Videos," ABC News, July 18, 2012, http://abcnews.go.com/blogs/politics/2012/07/dnc-regrets-offending-ann-romney-no-more-horse-ads/.

86. See, for example, the discussion in Glenn Thrush, *Obama's Last Stand* (New York: Random House, 2012).

87. Callum Borchers and Christopher Rowland, "Mitt Romney Stayed at Bain 3 Years Longer than He Stated," *Boston Globe*, July 12, 2012, http://bostonglobe.com/news/politics/2012/07/11/government-documents-indicate-mitt-romney-continued-bain-after-date-when-says-left/IpfKYWjnrsel4pvCFbsUTI/story.html.

88. Michael D. Shear, "Campaigns Trade Salvos over a Romney Role at Bain after 1999," *New York Times*, July 12, 2012, http://www.nytimes.com/2012/07/13/us/politics/campaigns-trade-salvos-over-a-romney-role-at-bain-after-1999.html?_r=1&.

89. Emily Friedman, "Romney Accuses Obama of Lying in New Outsourcing Ad," ABC News, July 12, 2012, http://abcnews.go.com/blogs/politics/2012/07/romney-accuses-obama-of-lying-in-new-outsourcing-ad/.

90. Michael D. Shear, "Romney Seeks Obama Apology for Bain Attacks," *New York Times*, July 13, 2012, http://www.nytimes.com/2012/07/14/us/politics/romney-demands-apology-from-obama-on-bain-allegations.html?pagewanted=all.

91. The news coverage of both Romney and Obama was likely affected in part by the Aurora shootings, since news stories would have included their response to the tragedy and since these stories, replete with references to "attack" and "death" and other such similar words, would have been coded as negative in tone by General Sentiment's algorithms. But coverage of Romney was likely negative for other reasons as well. There was continuing coverage of Bain Capital on July 20 itself. See, for example, Beth Healy and Michael Kranish, "Romney Kept Reins, Bargained Hard on Severance," *Boston Globe*, July 20, 2012, http://www.boston.com/news/politics/articles/2012/07/20/romney_kept_reins_bargained_hard_on_severance/?rss_id=Top+Stories and Philip Rucker, "How a Photo Came to Symbolize Bain," *Washington Post*, July 20, 2012.

92. See John Sides, "Were Obama's Early Ads Really the Game Changer?" FiveThirty Eight/*New York Times*, December 29, 2012, http://fivethirtyeight.blogs.nytimes.com/2012/12/29/were-obamas-early-ads-really-the-game-changer/.

93. For example, in the January 7–10 YouGov poll we discussed earlier, the relationship between perceptions that Romney cared about the wealthy and cared about "people like me," expressed as a bivariate regression coefficient, was –06 (s.e. = .03). In the June 9–11 poll, that relationship was larger (b = –.20), but note that this poll was conducted *before* the bulk of the Bain advertising or news coverage. In the July 14–16 and July 28–30 polls, the relationship was actually a bit smaller than in June (b = –.11 and –.15, respectively). Note also that there was virtually no change between the two July polls, which bracketed the extensive news coverage of Romney and Bain Capital.

94. See, for example, the studies cited in Henry E. Brady, Richard Johnston, and John Sides, "The Study of Political Campaigns," in Henry E. Brady and Richard Johnston, eds., *Capturing Campaign Effects* (Ann Arbor: University of Michigan Press, 2006), 1–28.

95. GRPs are defined as "reach" multiplied by frequency. Thus, for example, an ad that runs for 100 GRPs in a media market is expected, on average, to be seen one time by 100 percent of TV households in that market; an ad with 500 GRPs is expected, on average, to be viewed five times in all TV households (or ten times by half the households); and so on.

96. Alan S. Gerber, James G. Gimpel, Donald P. Green, and Daron R. Shaw, "How Large and Long-Lasting Are the Persuasive Effects of Televised Campaign Ads? Results from a Randomized Field Experiment," *American Political Science Review* 105, no. 1

(2011): 135–50; Seth Hill, James Lo, Lynn Vavreck, and John Zaller, "How Quickly We Forget: The Duration of Persuasion Effects from Mass Communication" (*Political Communication,* forthcoming); Kate Kenski, Bruce W. Hardy, and Kathleen Hall Jamieson, *The Obama Victory* (New York: Oxford University Press, 2010).

97. This estimate and the ones that follow were calculated after estimating the model. They represent the changes in predicted vote share that were associated with different values for the ad differences, all else equal. Respondents' characteristics are left as observed in the data.

98. We estimated the separate effects of same-day Obama and Romney ads and then conducted a statistical test of the hypothesis that those two effects were equal. The results of this test—a chi-squared statistic of 0.89 and a p-value of 0.35—meant that we could not reject this hypothesis.

99. https://twitter.com/MittRomney/status/234253751995736064.

100. Mike Allen, Ginger Gibson, and Maggie Haberman, "Behind the Scenes, Mitt Romney Wanted Paul Ryan," *Politico,* August 12, 2012, http://dyn.politico.com/printstory .cfm?uuid=24CB8F96-AAAC-435F-8581-2EAC9A8B4E13.

101. Ben Smith and Zeke Miller, "Romney Picked Ryan over Advisers' Early Doubts," *BuzzFeed,* August 12, 2012, http://www.buzzfeed.com/bensmith/romney-picked-ryan -over-advisors-early-doubts.

102. Lydia Saad, "Reaction to Ryan as V.P. Pick among Least Positive Historically," Gallup, August 13, 2012, http://www.gallup.com/poll/156545/Reaction-Ryan-Pick-Among -Least-Positive-Historically.aspx.

103. These findings were originally presented here: John Sides, "Paul Ryan vs. the What-Might-Have-Beens," *The Monkey Cage,* August 14, 2012, http://themonkeycage.org /blog/2012/08/14/paul-ryan-vs-the-what-might-have-beens/. The data come from You-Gov polls conducted July 21–23, July 28–30, and August 4–6.

104. These findings were originally presented here: John Sides, "Paul Ryan: The Base Mobilization Strategy That Romney Doesn't Need," *The Monkey Cage,* August 11, 2012, http://themonkeycage.org/blog/2012/08/11/paul-ryan-the-base-mobilization-strategy -that-romney-doesnt-need/.

105. Jeffrey M. Jones, "Romney Sees No Immediate Bounce from Ryan V.P. Pick," Gallup, August 15, 2012, http://www.gallup.com/poll/156692/Romney-Sees-No-Immediate -Bounce-Ryan-Pick.aspx; Mark Blumenthal, "Paul Ryan Pick Causes Little Change: Poll," *Huffington Post,* August 15, 2012, http://www.huffingtonpost.com/2012/08/15/paul-ryan -pick_n_1784520.html.

106. Robert L. Dudley and Ronald B. Rapaport, "Vice-Presidential Candidates and the Home State Advantage: Playing Second Banana at Home and on the Road," *American Journal of Political Science* 33, no. 2 (1989): 537–40; David W. Romero, "Requiem for a Lightweight: Vice Presidential Candidate Evaluations and the Presidential Vote," *Presidential Studies Quarterly* 31, no. 3 (2004): 454–63; Carl D. Tubbesing, "Vice Presidential Candidates and the Home State Advantage: Or, 'Tom Who?' Was Tom Eagleton in Missouri," *Western Political Quarterly* 26, no. 4 (1973): 702–16. See also Nate Silver, "The Overrated Vice Presidential Home-State Effect," FiveThirtyEight/*New York Times,* April 23, 2012, http://fivethirtyeight.blogs.nytimes.com/2012/04/23/the-overrated-vice -presidential-home-state-effect/.

107. Tom Defrank and Aliyah Shahid, "GOP Hopefuls Romney, Bachmann, Pawlenty, Huntsman Slam Obama for July 2011 Jobs Report, Economy," *New York Daily News,* August 5, 2011, http://www.nydailynews.com/news/politics/gop-hopefuls-romney

-bachmann-pawlenty-huntsman-slam-obama-july-2011-jobs-report-economy-article-1
.947980.

108. "Transcript: Ryan Makes First Remarks as VP Choice," NPR, August 11, 2012, http://www.npr.org/2012/08/11/158618943/transcript-ryan-makes-first-remarks-as-vp -choice.

109. Gallup polling showed the same thing: Jeffrey M. Jones, "Obama's Character Edge Offsets Romney's Economic Advantage," Gallup, July 24, 2012, http://www.gallup .com/poll/156134/obama-character-edge-offsets-romney-economic-advantage.aspx.

110. Larry Bartels, "The Fiscal Facts of Life: Do Americans Understand Where Budget Deficits Come From?" *The Monkey Cage*, August 11, 2012, http://themonkeycage.org/blog /2012/08/11/the-fiscal-facts-of-life-do-americans-understand-where-budget-deficits-come -from/.

111. Frank Newport, "Majority in U.S. Still Say Government Doing Too Much," Gallup, September 17, 2012, http://www.gallup.com/poll/157481/majority-say-government-doing.aspx.

112. This question was originally fielded by Daron Shaw of Shaw and Associates for the Fox News poll. In an August Fox News poll, 54% chose "leave me alone." Dana Blanton, "Fox News Poll: Voters Want Uncle Sam to 'Leave Me Alone,' " Fox News, August 23, 2012, http://www.foxnews.com/politics/2012/08/23/fox-news-poll-voters-want-uncle-sam -to-leave-me-alone/.

113. Christopher Ellis and James A. Stimson, *Ideology in America* (Cambridge: Cambridge University Press, 2012).

114. John Sides, "Republican Primary Voters Embrace Government. No, Really," YouGov, March 22, 2012, http://today.yougov.com/news/2012/03/22/republican-primary -voters-embrace-government-no-re/.

115. "Medicare Voucher Plan Remains Unpopular," Pew Research Center for the People & the Press, August 21, 2012, http://www.people-press.org/2012/08/21/medicare -voucher-plan-remains-unpopular/.

116. Alex Isenstadt, "Boehner Tries to Calm House GOP," *Politico*, August 15, 2012, http://www.politico.com/news/stories/0812/79744.html#ixzz2IAzln21Y.

117. On the concept of issue ownership, see John Petrocik, "Issue Ownership in Presidential Elections, with a 1980 Case Study," *American Journal of Political Science* 40, no. 3 (1996): 825–50. See also John Sides, "The Origins of Campaign Agendas," *British Journal of Political Science* 36, no. 3 (2006): 407–36. John Sides, "Why It's Hard for Republicans to Campaign on Medicare," *The Monkey Cage*, August 14, 2012, http://themonkeycage.org /blog/2012/08/14/why-its-hard-for-republicans-to-campaign-on-medicare/.

118. John Sides, "Have the Republicans Fought to a Draw on Medicare," *The Monkey Cage*, August 28, 2012, http://themonkeycage.org/blog/2012/08/28/have-the-republicans -fought-to-a-draw-on-medicare-2/.

119. "Swing State Polls," *New York Times*, http://elections.nytimes.com/2012/swing -state-polls?ref=politics. A *Washington Post*/Kaiser Family Foundation poll posed a similar question and elicited similar levels of support for the current Medicare program, http://www.washingtonpost.com/page/2010-2019/WashingtonPost/2012/08/11/National -Politics/Polling/question_6249.xml.

120. One Romney ad making this argument was "Nothing's Free," YouTube, August 22, 2012, http://www.youtube.com/watch?v=4YfWaERDySo. In large part, this argument was true. See Dylan Matthews, "Ad Watch: 'Nothing's Free,'" *Washington Post*, August 22, 2012, http://www.washingtonpost.com/blogs/wonkblog/wp/2012/08/22/ad-watch -nothings-free/.

121. "Voters Favor Medicare Reform in Order to 'Preserve and Protect' Program,"
Resurgent Republic, May 10, 2012, http://www.resurgentrepublic.com/summaries/voters
-favor-medicare-reform-in-order-to-preserve-and-protect-program.

122. Bill McInturff and Peter Hart, NBC News/*Wall Street Journal* Survey, August 16–
20, 2012, http://msnbcmedia.msn.com/i/MSNBC/Sections/A_Politics/_Today_Stories
_Teases/August_NBC-WSJ_Int_Sched.pdf. See also "Democrats Gaining in Battle
ground; Ryan Budget Could Finish the Job," Democracy Corps, April 18, 2012, http://
www.democracycorps.com/attachments/article/876/April-Battleground-Graphs.pdf.

123. "Facts—Obama for America TV Ad," YouTube, August 17, 2012, http://www.you
tube.com/watch?v=LJb6tA1cXT0. A second ad on this theme is here: "Promises—Obama
for America TV Ad," YouTube, August 25, 2012, http://www.youtube.com/watch?v=b9Xk
VonSIxk.

124. See David Niven, *Tilt? The Search for Media Bias* (Westport, CT: Praeger, 2002),
67–68.

125. The Project for Excellence in Journalism coded news coverage from May 29 to
August 5, focusing on prevailing "narratives" about the candidates and using a smaller
sample of news outlets and different method of ascertaining tone. They found that these
narratives largely reflected negative rather than positive coverage, which is somewhat
at odds with our finding that the coverage was largely neutral. However, this study also
found that balance of positive and negative coverage was essentially identical for Romney and Obama—exactly what we found using the General Sentiment data. See "Press
Coverage of the Character of the Candidates Is Highly Negative, and Neither Obama Nor
Romney Has an Edge," Journalism.org, August 23, 2012, http://www.journalism.org
/node/30588.

126. Dave D'Alessio and Mike Allen, "Media Bias in Presidential Elections: A Meta-
Analysis," *Journal of Communication* 50, no. 4 (2000): 133–56.

127. This conclusion is based on data from *Washington Post*/ABC News polls. See "Fa-
vorability #39: Low Favorability Trails Romney up to the Convention Dais," *Washington
Post*/ABC News poll, August 28, 2012, http://www.langerresearch.com/uploads/1127a39
FavorabilityNo39.pdf.

Chapter 6: The Action

1. Jonathan Strong, "John Boehner: Voters Need Not Love Mitt Romney," Roll Call,
July 9, 2012, http://cdn.rollcall.com/issues/58_1/John-Boehner-Voters-Need-Not-Love
-Mitt-Romney-215934-1.html?popular=true&pos=hln.

2. John F. Harris and Alexander Burns, "Mitt Romney RNC: GOP Still Frets about
Candidate's Image," *Politico*, August 28, 2012, http://dyn.politico.com/printstory.cfm?uuid
=F7106C37-E12C-44C8-955A-B739A65518A7

3. Jeff Zeleny and Jim Rutenberg, "Romney Adopts Harder Message for Last Stretch,"
New York Times, August 25, 2012, http://www.nytimes.com/2012/08/26/us/politics/mitt
-romneys-campaign-adopts-a-harder-message.html?_r=3&ref=jeffzeleny&pagewanted
=all&.

4. Mark Halperin, "The Electoral College Cannot Be Bluffed," *Time*, August 27, 2012,
http://thepage.time.com/2012/08/27/the-electoral-college-cannot-be-bluffed/.

5. Dominic Rushe, "Gawker Publishes Audits of Mitt Romney's Offshore Financial
Accounts," *The Guardian*, August 23, 2012, http://www.guardian.co.uk/world/2012/aug
/23/gawker-mitt-romney-offshore-accounts; John Cook, "The Bain Files: Inside Mitt

Romney's Tax-Dodging Cayman Schemes," Gawker, August 23, 2012, http://gawker.com/5936394/the-bain-files-inside-mitt-romneys-tax+dodging-cayman-schemes.

6. Tali Mendelberg, *The Race Card: Campaign Strategy, Implicit Messages, and the Norm of Equality* (Princeton: Princeton University Press, 2001).

7. Sarah Huisenga and Rebecca Kaplan, "Romney Birth Certificate Remark Sets Off Firestorm," CBS News, August 24, 2012, http://www.cbsnews.com/8301-503544_162-57500031-503544/romney-birth-certificate-remark-sets-off-firestorm/.

8. The ideas and research were first discussed here: John Sides, "How Will Party Conventions Affect the Presidential Race?" FiveThirtyEight blog, August 26, 2012, http://fivethirtyeight.blogs.nytimes.com/2012/08/26/how-will-party-conventions-affect-the-presidential-race/.

9. James E. Campbell, *The American Campaign* (College Station: Texas A&M Press, 2000); James E. Campbell, Lynna L. Cherry, and Kenneth A. Wink, "The Convention Bump," *American Politics Quarterly* 20, no. 3 (1992): 287–307; Robert S. Erikson and Christopher Wlezien, *The Timeline of Presidential Campaigns* (Chicago: Chicago University Press, 2012).

10. Costas Panagopoulos, "Follow the Bouncing Ball: Presidential Nominating Conventions and Campaign Dynamics" (Fordham University working paper, 2005).

11. Thomas M. Holbrook, *Do Campaigns Matter?* (Thousand Oaks, CA: Sage, 1996).

12. Ibid.

13. Erikson and Wlezien, *The Timeline of Presidential Campaigns*.

14. A separate analysis by the Project for Excellence in Journalism found a similar pattern: more favorable coverage of the candidate during his party's convention, with the favorable coverage of Obama relative to Romney extending after the Democratic convention. "How Social and Traditional Media Differ in Treatment of the Conventions and Beyond," Journalism.org, September 28, 2012, http://www.journalism.org/commentary_backgrounder/how_social_and_traditional_media_differ_their_treatment_conventions_and_beyo.

15. Among persuadable voters, the shift in candidate favorability after the Republican convention was about 7–8 points in Romney's favor on a hypothetical 100-point scale ($p = .005$), using the same methodology we described in the previous chapter. The shift in vote intention was in the same direction, but we cannot be as confident that this shift was statistically meaningful ($p = .27$). Gallup's weekly tracking poll showed the same overall pattern as did these YouGov polls. In the poll conducted August 20–26, the week before the Republican convention, 46% supported Obama and 47% supported Romney. The following week, August 27–September 2, 47% supported Obama and 46% supported Romney, a negligible change. But the next week, during the Democratic convention, Obama was up 49%–44%.

16. Polling by Gallup and the Pew Center also showed rising enthusiasm or engagement, especially among Democrats. Lydia Saad and Jeffrey M. Jones, "Democratic Enthusiasm Swells in the Swing States, Nationally," Gallup, September 20, 2012, http://www.gallup.com/poll/157547/democratic-enthusiasm-swells-swing-states-nationally.aspx; "Obama Ahead with Stronger Support, Better Image and Lead on Most Issues," Pew Research Center for the People & the Press, September 19, 2012, http://www.people-press.org/2012/09/19/obama-ahead-with-stronger-support-better-image-and-lead-on-most-issues/. The trends among persuadable voters were again more noteworthy in terms of candidate favorability than vote intention: candidate favorability shifted about 9 points in Obama's favor ($p < .001$).

17. Mike Allen and Jim VandeHei, "Inside the Campaign: How Mitt Romney Stumbled," *Politico*, September 16, 2012, http://www.politico.com/news/stories/0912/81280.html.

18. In Gallup's polling, roughly equal percentages of people reported watching a great deal or some of both conventions, evaluated Obama's and Romney's speeches as "excellent" or "good," and said the convention would make them more likely to vote for the candidate being nominated. Jeffrey M. Jones, "Democratic Convention Rated Slightly Better than GOP Convention," Gallup, September 10, 2012, http://www.gallup.com/poll /157322/democratic-convention-rated-slightly-better-gop.aspx.

19. "Study: Media Framed Benghazi in Obama's Terms," Center for Media and Public Affairs, November 2, 2012, http://www.cmpa.com/media_room_press_11_02_12.html.

20. Louis Jacobson, "Did the U.S. Embassy in Cairo Make an Apology?" PolitiFact .com, September 12, 2012, http://www.politifact.com/truth-o-meter/article/2012/sep/12 /romney-says-us-embassy-statement-was-apology-was-i/; Brooks Jackson, Robert Farley, and Eugene Kiely, "Romney Gets It Backward," FactCheck.org, September 12, 2012, http:// www.factcheck.org/2012/09/romney-gets-it-backward/.

21. Philip Rucker, "Romney Repeats Sharp Criticism of Obama after Benghazi, Cairo Attacks," *Washington Post*, September 12, 2012, http://www.washingtonpost.com/politics /decision2012/romney-repeats-sharp-criticism-of-obama-on-libya-egypt-attacks/2012/09 /12/31074af4-fcdf-11e1-b153-218509a954e1_story.html.

22. "Middle East Turmoil Closely Followed; Romney's Comments Viewed Negatively," Pew Research Center for the People & the Press, September 17, 2012, http://www.people -press.org/2012/09/17/middle-east-turmoil-closely-followed-romneys-comments-viewed -negatively/.

23. "On Eve of Foreign Debate, Growing Pessimism about Arab Spring Aftermath," Pew Research Center for the People & the Press, October 18, 2012, http://www.people -press.org/files/legacy-pdf/10-18-12%20Foreign%20Policy%20release.pdf.

24. MoJo News Team, "Full Transcript of the Mitt Romney Secret Video," *Mother Jones*, September 19, 2012, http://www.motherjones.com/politics/2012/09/full-transcript -mitt-romney-secret-video#47percent.

25. Seema Mehta, "Romney Defends 'Off the cuff' Remarks on Obama Backers as Victims," *Los Angeles Times*, September 17, 2012, http://www.latimes.com/news/politics/ la-pn-mitt-romney-victims-remarks-20120917,0,5600535.story.

26. Michael Barbaro, "A Mood of Gloom Afflicts the Romney Campaign," *New York Times*, September 18, 2012, http://thecaucus.blogs.nytimes.com/2012/09/18/a-mood-of -gloom-afflicts-the-romney-campaign/?smid=tw-thecaucus&seid=auto. The article went on to state that a "flustered advisor . . . said the campaign was turning into a vulgar, unprintable phrase"—a phrase many interpreted as "clusterfuck."

27. Peggy Noonan, "Time for an Intervention," *Wall Street Journal*, September 18, 2012, http://blogs.wsj.com/peggynoonan/2012/09/18/time-for-an-intervention/; David Brooks, "Thurston Howell Romney," *New York Times*, September 17, 2012, http://www .nytimes.com/2012/09/18/opinion/brooks-thurston-howell-romney.html?_r=0.

28. Josh Barro, "Today, Mitt Romney Lost the Election," Bloomberg, September 17, 2012, http://www.bloomberg.com/news/2012-09-17/today-mitt-romney-lost-the-election.html.

29. Josh Marshall, "Devastating" Talking Points Memo, September 17, 2012, http:// talkingpointsmemo.com/archives/2012/09/devastating.php.

30. "Romney's Words Say Plenty," *Sun Sentinel*, September 19, 2012, http://articles .sun-sentinel.com/2012-09-19/news/fl-editorial-romneyvideo-cl-20120919_1_mitt -romney-president-obama-rapid-response.

31. "Romney's '47%' Comments Criticized, But Many Also Say Overcovered," Pew Research Center for the People & the Press, October 1, 2012, http://www.people-press .org/2012/10/01/romneys-47-comments-criticized-but-many-also-say-overcovered/.

32. A *Washington Post*/ABC News poll found a similar split in opinion. Jon Cohen, "Most Are Negative about Mitt Romney's '47 Percent' Comments," *Washington Post*, September 26, 2012, http://www.washingtonpost.com/blogs/the-fix/wp/2012/09/26/public -also-critical-of-romneys-campaign-47-comments/.

33. Lee Sigelman, "Helping Hands for George Stephanopoulos," *The Monkey Cage*, May 11, 2008, http://themonkeycage.org/blog/2008/05/11/post_84/.

34. The shift in vote intentions has an associated p-value of .10. The change in candi-date favorability—about 6.5 points in Obama's favor—has an associated p-value of .01.

35. In the RAND American Life Panel—in which the same set of respondents were interviewed on a weekly basis—Obama's lead increased more dramatically, from about 3 points on September 17 to a maximum of 8 points on September 26. One possible reason that the RAND panelists appear to have shifted more is that they were asked not simply who they planned to vote for but the percent chance that they would vote for Obama, Romney, or someone else. The RAND data may therefore capture something about the intensity of people's choices.

36. It is worth noting that the fraction of Americans who have benefited from a gov-ernment program of some kind is actually much higher than 47%—in fact, more like 96%. Suzane Mettler and John Sides, "We Are the 96 Percent," *New York Times*, September 24, 2012, http://campaignstops.blogs.nytimes.com/2012/09/24/we-are-the-96-percent/.

37. *Washington Post*/ABC News poll conducted October 10–13, 2012, http://www .washingtonpost.com/wp-srv/politics/polls/postabcpoll_20121013.html. There was also no change in perceptions of who "seems like the more friendly and likable person."

38. Philip Rucker, "Romney's '47 Percent' Comments Aren't Going Away, and They're Taking a Toll," *Washington Post*, October 1, 2012, http://www.washingtonpost.com /politics/decision2012/romneys-47-percent-comments-arent-going-away/2012/10/01 /17604654-0be5-11e2-a310-2363842b7057_story.html.

39. Erick Erickson, "Before the Rooster Crows," *RedState*, September 25, 2012, http:// www.redstate.com/2012/09/25/before-the-rooster-crows/.

40. Daniel Larison, "Movement Conservatives Conveniently Forget Their Role in Making Romney Viable," *The American Conservative*, September 25, 2012, http://www .theamericanconservative.com/larison/movement-conservatives-conveniently-forget -their-role-in-making-romney-viable-in-the-gop/

41. Mike Allen, Jonathan Martin, and Jim VandeHei, "In the End, It's Mitt," *Politico*, September 28, 2012, http://dyn.politico.com/printstory.cfm?uuid=0665D7E1-13A2-45EC -876F-271DC28CA86A.

42. Alexander Bolton, "Ten Game Changers That Could Decide the Race between Obama and Romney," The Hill, June 3, 2012, http://thehill.com/homenews/campaign /230583-ten-game-changers-that-could-decide-the-presidency.

43. John Sides, "Do Presidential Debates Really Matter?" *Washington Monthly*, Sep-tember/October 2012, http://www.washingtonmonthly.com/magazine/september october_2012/ten_miles_square/do_presidential_debates_really039413.php

44. Erikson and Wlezien, *The Timeline of Presidential Campaigns*, 81.

45. Kim Fridkin, Patrick Kenney, Sarah Gershon, Karen Shafer, and Gina Woodall, "Capturing the Power of a Campaign Event: The 2004 Presidential Debate in Tempe," *Journal of Politics* 69, no. 3 (2007): 770–85. Something similar happened in 1976. In one

of the debates, Gerald Ford said that there was no Soviet domination of Eastern Europe. This "gaffe," now firmly ensconced in the folklore, did not even register with voters until a day later, when the news had discussed his comment. And it did not actually hurt Ford in the polls either. See Sides, "Do Presidential Debates Really Matter?"

46. Brian Stelter, "Presidential Debate Drew More than 70 Million Viewers," *New York Times*, October 4, 2012, http://mediadecoder.blogs.nytimes.com/2012/10/04/presidential -debate-drew-more-than-70-million-viewers/?smid=tw-share.

47. Peter Baker, "A Clash of Philosophies," *New York Times*, October 4, 2012, http:// www.nytimes.com/2012/10/04/us/politics/debate-a-clash-over-governments-role-news -analysis.html.

48. This would later spawn an Obama ad suggesting that Romney was more con- cerned with cutting funds to Sesame Street than fighting Wall Street corruption. "Big Bird—Obama for America TV Ad," YouTube.com, October 9, 2012, http://www.youtube .com/watch?v=bZxs09eV-Vc.

49. Ron Fournier, "Incumbent Debate Curse: Barack Obama Falls to Mitt Romney," *National Journal*, October 3, 2012, http://nationaljournal.com/2012-presidential-campaign /incumbent-debate-curse-barack-obama-falls-to-mitt-romney-20121003.

50. David Nakamura and Philip Rucker, "Behind Debate Scenes, Romney's Team Re- energized by Republican's Performance," *Washington Post*, October 4, 2012, http://articles .washingtonpost.com/2012-10-04/politics/35501405_1_romney-surrogates-mitt-romney -romney-senior-adviser.

51. Andrew Sullivan, "President Obama: The Democrats' Ronald Reagan," *The Daily Beast*, September 21, 2012, http://www.thedailybeast.com/newsweek/2012/09/23/andrew -sullivan-on-the-promise-of-obama-s-second-term.html; "Live-Blogging the First Presi- dential Debate 2012," *The Dish*, October 3, 2012, http://andrewsullivan.thedailybeast .com/2012/10/live-blogging-the-first-presidential-debate-2012.html.

52. "Chris Matthews Flips Over Debate: 'Where Was Obama Tonight?!'" *Huffington Post*, October 3, 2012, http://www.huffingtonpost.com/2012/10/03/chris-matthews-obama -debate_n_1937950.html.

53. Michael D. Shear, "Debate Praise for Romney as Obama Is Faulted as Flat," *New York Times*, October 4, 2012, http://www.nytimes.com/2012/10/05/us/politics/after-debate -a-torrent-of-criticism-for-obama.html. This compendium of battleground state head- lines also conveys the consensus that Romney won: Andrew Kaczynski, "Swing State Newspapers Declare Romney Winner," *BuzzFeed*, October 4, 2012, http://www.buzzfeed .com/andrewkaczynski/swing-state-news-papers-declare-romney-winner#HTWF2. A good analysis of this style of news coverage is Brendan Nyhan, "Understanding the 'Rom- ney Won Big!' Narrative," brendan-nyhan.com, October 4, 2012, http://www.brendan -nyhan.com/blog/2012/10/how-debate-narratives-are-constructed.html.

54. A separate study by the Project for Excellence in Journalism also found that cov- erage of Obama became more negative after the first debate, while coverage of Romney became more positive. "Winning the Media Campaign 2012: Both Candidates Received More Negative than Positive Coverage in Mainstream News, but Social Media Was Even Harsher," Journalism.org, November 2, 2012, http://www.journalism.org/analysis_report /winning_media_campaign_2012.

55. Frank Newport, "Americans Predict Obama Will Do a Better Job in Debates," Gal- lup, October 2, 2012, http://www.gallup.com/poll/157835/americans-predict-obama-better -job-debates.aspx; Nate Silver, "Polls Show a Strong Debate for Romney," FiveThirtyEight blog, *New York Times*, October 4, 2012, http://fivethirtyeight.blogs.nytimes.com/2012/10 /04/polls-show-a-strong-debate-for-romney/.

56. Jeffrey M. Jones, "Romney Narrows Vote Gap after Historic Debate Win," Gallup, October 8, 2012, http://www.gallup.com/poll/157907/romney-narrows-vote-gap-historic -debate-win.aspx.

57. "Romney's Strong Debate Performance Erases Obama's Lead," Pew Research Center for the People & the Press, October 8, 2012, http://www.people-press.org/2012/10/08 /romneys-strong-debate-performance-erases-obamas-lead/.

58. Tom Holbrook, "Debate Expectations," Politics by the Numbers, October 1, 2012, http://politics-by-the-numbers.blogspot.com/2012/10/debate-expectations.html.

59. Andrew Sullivan, "Did Obama Just Throw the Entire Election Away?" *The Dish*, October 8, 2012, http://dish.andrewsullivan.com/2012/10/08/did-obama-just-throw-the -entire-election-away/.

60. "Getting to the Bold Policy Offer Winning Now Requires," Democracy Corps, October 15, 2012, http://www.democracycorps.com/National-Surveys/getting-to-the-bold -policy-offer-winning-now-requires/.

61. Walter Shapiro, "Against Backdrop of Harvard Power Outage, Obama and Romney Power Players Discuss Lessons of 2012 Campaign," Yahoo News, December 3, 2012, http://news.yahoo.com/obama--romney-power-players-discuss-campaign-lessons -despite-harvard-power-outage-215044327.html.

62. Benjy Sarlin and Evan McMorris-Santoro, "Romney Adviser Shakes Up Race with 'Etch-a-Sketch' Quote," Talking Points Memo, March 21, 2012, http://2012.talkingpoints memo.com/2012/03/democrats-flip-after-romney-advisors-compares-campaign-to-etch -a-sketch.php.

63. David Brooks, "Moderate Mitt Returns!" *New York Times*, October 4, 2012, http:// www.nytimes.com/2012/10/05/opinion/brooks-moderate-mitt-returns.html.

64. John Presta, "Video: Bill Clinton Ridicules Romney Debate Performance Dubs Him 'Moderate Mitt,'" Examiner.com, October 10, 2012, http://www.examiner.com/article /video-bill-clinton-ridicules-romney-debate-performance-dubs-him-moderate-mitt.

65. Mark Halperin, "Excerpts from Mark Halperin's Interview with Senior Obama Campaign Officials at the Chicago Headquarters," *Time*, October 9, 2012, http://thepage .time.com/2012/10/09/excerpts-from-mark-halperins-interview-with-senior-obama -campaign-officials-at-the-chicago-headquarters/.

66. John Sides, "Romney's Pivot to the Center Hasn't Worked (But It Didn't Need To)," *The Monkey Cage*, October 11, 2012, http://themonkeycage.org/blog/2012/10/11 /romneys-pivot-to-the-center-hasnt-worked-but-it-didnt-need-to/.

67. John Sides, "Romney's Debate Win Was about Personality More than Policy," *The Monkey Cage*, October 11, 2012, http://themonkeycage.org/blog/2012/10/11/romneys -debate-win-was-about-personality-more-than-policy/.

68. Peter Kellner, "Obama Stays Ahead—Just," YouGov, October 23, 2012, http://today .yougov.com/news/2012/10/23/obama-stays-ahead-just/. A second panel study, albeit of a non-representative sample, also suggested a smaller shift toward Romney. David Rothschild and Doug Rivers, "Xbox/YouGov Panel Quantifies Romney's First Debate Victory and Obama's Subsequent Debate Rebound," *Huffington Post*, October 10, 2012, http:// www.huffingtonpost.com/david-rothschild/xbox-yougov-panel-debates_b_2038328.html.

69. In the weekly YouGov data that we analyze, after the debate there was also a 12-point increase in the percentage of Republicans who said they were "extremely enthusiastic" about voting.

70. Nate Silver, "No Guarantee of Obama Rebound in Second Debate," FiveThirty-Eight blog, October 16, 2012, http://fivethirtyeight.blogs.nytimes.com/2012/10/16/no -guarantee-of-obama-rebound-in-second-debate/.

71. Shaila Dewan and Mark Lander, "Drop in Jobless Figure Gives Jolt to Race for President," *New York Times*, October 5, 2012, http://www.nytimes.com/2012/10/06/business/economy/us-added-114000-jobs-in-september-rate-drops-to-7-8.html.

72. Jon Cohen and Peyton M. Craighill, "Partisans Line Up behind Their Candidates as Election Nears," *Washington Post*, October 9, 2012, http://www.washingtonpost.com/blogs/the-fix/wp/2012/10/09/partisans-line-up-behind-their-candidates-as-election-nears/.

73. The difference in vote intentions among Democrats interviewed between October 6–8 and October 13–15 is statistically significant at $p = .02$. Obama also lost support among persuadable voters between these two polls, but we cannot be as confident that this drop was significant.

74. Peter Baker and Trip Gabriel, "With Biden Up Next to Debate, Obama's Aides Plot Comeback," *New York Times*, October 7, 2012, http://www.nytimes.com/2012/10/08/us/politics/biden-up-next-obamas-aides-plot-comeback.html?ref=politics&_r=1&.

75. Donovan Slack, "Obama: 'I Was Just Too Polite,'" *Politico*, October 10, 2012, http://www.politico.com/politico44/2012/10/obama-i-was-just-too-polite-138029.html?hp=f1.

76. Helene Cooper, "Obama's Prep Session Goal: Don't Repeat Mistakes of Last Debate," *New York Times*, October 14, 2012, http://www.nytimes.com/2012/10/15/us/politics/a-serious-debate-prep-session-for-obama.html.

77. Jeff Zeleny and Jim Rutenberg, "Biden and Ryan Quarrel Aggressively in Debate, Offering Contrasts," *New York Times*, October 11, 2012, http://www.nytimes.com/2012/10/12/us/politics/biden-and-ryan-quarrel-aggressively-in-debate-offering-contrasts.html.

78. Andrew Dugan, "Vice Presidential Debates Rarely Influence Voters," Gallup, October 10, 2012, http://www.gallup.com/poll/157994/vice-presidential-debates-rarely-influence-voters.aspx.

79. Steve Peoples and David Espo, "Presidential Debate 2012: Obama Gets Aggressive in Rematch against Mitt Romney," *Huffington Post*, October 16, 2012, http://www.huffingtonpost.com/2012/10/16/presidential-debate-2012_n_1970698.html?utm_hp_ref=politics.

80. Karen Tumulty and Philip Rucker, "With Stakes High, Obama Hits Back at Romney in a Fiery Second Debate," *Washington Post*, October 17, 2012, http://www.washingtonpost.com/politics/decision2012/president-obama-mitt-romney-arrive-at-hofstra-for-final-debate-preparations/2012/10/16/1b57bffe-17ba-11e2-a55c-39408fbe6a4b_story.html?hpid=z1.

81. Emely Swanson and Mark Blumenthal, "Presidential Debate Instant Polls Show Narrow Win for Obama," *Huffington Post*, October 17, 2012, http://www.huffingtonpost.com/2012/10/17/presidential-debate-polls_n_1972357.html; Jeffrey M. Jones, "Obama Judged Winner of Second Debate," Gallup, October 19, 2012, http://www.gallup.com/poll/158237/obama-judged-winner-second-debate.aspx.

82. This shift in Democratic support was also statistically significant ($p = .06$). Polling by Ipsos and Reuters showed a similar trend among Democrats during this period. Between their October 5–9 poll and the October 22–26 poll, Democratic support for Obama increased by 4 points.

83. Dan Balz and David Nakamura, "Obama Keeps Romney on His Heels in Last Debate," *Washington Post*, October 23, 2012, http://www.washingtonpost.com/politics/decision2012/presidential-debate-obama-romney-face-off-on-foreign-policy/2012/10/22/ca25b8dc-1c7f-11e2-ad90-ba5920e56eb3_story.html?hpid=z2.

84. Nate Silver, "Obama Unlikely to Get Big Debate Bounce, but a Small One Could Matter," FiveThirtyEight blog, October 23, 2012, http://fivethirtyeight.blogs.nytimes

.com/2012/10/23/obama-unlikely-to-get-big-debate-bounce-but-a-small-one-could
-matter/; Frank Newport, "Viewers Deem Obama Winner of Third Debate, 56% to 33%,"
Gallup, October 25, 2012, http://www.gallup.com/poll/158393/viewers-deem-obama
-winner-third-debate.aspx.

85. Glenn Thrush and Jonathan Martin, "Obama vs. Romney: How They Plan to
Win," *Politico*, October 22, 2012, http://www.politico.com/news/stories/1012/82693.html
#ixzz2HildpZQu.

86. Brendan Nyhan, "The Momentum behind a Misleading Narrative," *Columbia
Journalism Review*, October 26, 2012, http://www.cjr.org/united_states_project/the
_misleading_momentum_narrative.php?page=all.

87. Glenn Thrush and Jennifer Epstein, "Momentum Wars," *Politico*, October 25, 2012,
http://www.politico.com/news/stories/1012/82902.html.

88. Andrew Healy and Neil Malhotra, "Random Events, Economic Losses, and Retrospective Voting: Implications for Democratic Competence," *Quarterly Journal of Political
Science* 5, no. 2 (2010): 193–208.

89. Brad T. Gomez, Thomas G. Hansford, and George A. Krause, "The Republicans
Should Pray for Rain: Weather, Turnout, and Voting in U.S. Presidential Elections," *Journal of Politics* 69 (2007): 649–63, http://journals.cambridge.org/action/displayAbstract
?fromPage=online&aid=1965128; Aaron Blake, "Axelrod Says Hurricane Sandy Could
Hurt Obama by Lowering Turnout," *Washington Post*, October 28, 2012, http://www
.washingtonpost.com/blogs/the-fix/wp/2012/10/28/axelrod-says-hurricane-sandy-could
-hurt-obama-by-lowering-turnout/.

90. John T. Gasper and Andrew Reeves, "Make It Rain? Retrospection and the Attentive
Electorate in the Context of Natural Disasters," *American Journal of Political Science* 55, no. 2
(2011): 340–55, http://andrewreeves.org/sites/default/files/rain.pdf; Andrew Healy and Neil
Malhotra, "Myopic Voters and Natural Disaster Policy," *American Political Science Review*
103 (2009): 387–406, http://journals.cambridge.org/action/displayAbstract?fromPage
=online&aid=6101720; Jowei Chen, "Voter Partisanship and the Effect of Distributive
Spending on Political Participation," *American Journal of Political Science* 57, no. 1 (2013):
200–217, http://onlinelibrary.wiley.com/doi/10.1111/j.1540-5907.2012.00613.x/abstract.

91. Michael Hastings, "Obama, Christie, and a Tweaked-Out Campaign Entourage
Ride the Storm," *BuzzFeed*, October 31, 2012, http://www.buzzfeed.com/mhastings
/obama-christie-and-a-tweaked-out-campaign-entour.

92. Russell Goldman, "Obama and Christie Tour Sandy's Devastation," ABC News,
October 31, 2012, http://abcnews.go.com/Politics/OTUS/president-obama-jersey-gov
-christie-tour-superstorm-sandy/story?id=17606560. Christie's kind words for the
Obama—he said they had a "great working relationship"—angered some Republicans.
One Romney supporter would later refer to him as "Brutus." Ben Smith, "A Bitter Rom-
neyite Emails: 'You Should Identify Governor Christie by His Formal Name, Brutus,'"
Twitter, 9:28 AM, Feburary 6, 2013, https://twitter.com/BuzzFeedBen/status/299208045957
898240.

93. McKay Coppins, "The Making of Romney's Storm Relief Event," *BuzzFeed*, October 31, 2012, http://www.buzzfeed.com/mckaycoppins/the-making-of-romneys-storm
-relief-event. The Romney campaign even bought canned goods, bottled water, and dia-
pers at a local Wal-Mart to ensure that there would be adequate "donations" on hand.

94. "The Final Days of the Media Campaign 2012," Journalism.org, November 19,
2012, http://www.journalism.org/analysis_report/final_days_media_campaign_2012.

95. The reason that poll numbers may have driven news coverage more in the fall
than the summer is that there were sharper trends in the polls as a consequence of the

Democratic convention and the first debate. A careful reader will note that we have also argued news coverage after the conventions and the debates can shape public opinion. If so, why does this not show up in our statistical analysis? We suspect that, as also appeared to be true for some Republican candidates in the primary, the news coverage may drive poll standing for only a brief period after the event. As news coverage of the event fades, however, the reconfigured poll numbers remain and then help drive subsequent horse race–oriented news coverage. We admit this is speculation on our part. Future research may help untangle these dynamics.

96. Harry J. Enten, "Was It Hurricane Sandy That Won It for President Obama?" *The Guardian*, December 4, 2012, http://www.guardian.co.uk/commentisfree/2012/dec/04/hurricane-sandy-won-president-obama.

97. "Stuart Stevens, Republican Strategist," *Charlie Rose*, December 5, 2012. http://www.charlierose.com/view/interview/12682.

98. Quoted in Sasha Issenberg, *The Victory Lab* (New York: Crown, 2012), 264.

99. Cameron Joseph, "Romney Campaign Pins Victory Hopes on Cash Advantage, Late Ad Blitz," The Hill, September 11, 2012, http://thehill.com/homenews/campaign/248643-team-romney-pins-hopes-on-cash-advantage-late-ad-blitz.

100. Dan Eggen, "With More Control over Campaign Cash, Obama Gets More Discounts on Advertising," *Washington Post*, September 26, 2012, http://www.washingtonpost.com/politics/decision2012/obama-has-more-control-of-campaign-cash-and-with-it-an-edge-in-ad-rates/2012/09/26/c85304ea-03f9-11e2-91e7-2962c74e7738_story.html.

101. David B. Caruso, "Obama, Mitt Romney Pulling Ads on September 11," *Huffington Post*, August 16, 2012, http://www.huffingtonpost.com/2012/08/16/obama-romney-ads-september-11_n_1789237.html.

102. Jack Messmer, "Super PACs Pay Up to 4X More for TV," TVNewsCheck, October 10, 2012, http://www.tvnewscheck.com/article/62753/super-pacs-pay-up-to-4x-more-for-tv-spots.

103. T. W. Farnam, "Obama Campaign Took Unorthodox Approach to Ad Buying," *Washington Post*, November 14, 2012, http://www.washingtonpost.com/politics/the-influence-industry-obama-campaign-took-unorthodox-approach-to-ad-buying/2012/11/14/c3477e8c-2e87-11e2-beb2-4b4cf5087636_story.html?wprss=rss_homepage. For a scholarly study of targeting by television program, see Travis N. Ridout, Michael Franz, Kenneth M. Goldstein, and William J. Feltus, "Separation by Television Program: Understanding the Targeting of Political Advertising in Presidential Elections," *Political Communication* 29, no. 1 (2012): 1–23.

104. Maggie Haberman, Alexander Burns, and Emily Schultheis, "Mitt Romney's Unusual In-House Ad Strategy," *Politico*, October 9, 2012, http://www.politico.com/news/stories/1012/82217.html.

105. Michael McDonald, "A Modest Early Voting Rise in 2012," *Huffington Post*, June 12, 2013, http://www.huffington-post.com/michael-p-mcdonald/a-modest-early-voting-ris_b_3430379.html.

106. John Sides, "The Track Record of Pre-Election Polls (in 2 Graphs)," *The Monkey Cage*, October 29, 2012, http://themonkeycage.org/blog/2012/10/29/the-track-record-of-pre-election-polls-in-2-graphs/.

107. John Sides, "How Biased Do the Polls Need to Be for Romney to Win?" *The Monkey Cage*, November 5, 2012, http://themonkeycage.org/blog/2012/11/05/how-biased-do-the-polls-need-to-be-for-romney-to-win/; Simon Jackman, "Converting a Poll Average to a Forecast," *Huffington Post*, October 30, 2012, http://www.huffingtonpost.com/simon-jackman/converting-a-poll-average_b_2044222.html.

108. Andrew Dugan and Frank Newport, "Americans Still Give Obama Better Odds to Win Election," Gallup, October 31, 2012, http://www.gallup.com/poll/158444/americans -give-obama-better-odds-win-election.aspx; David Rothschild and Justin Wolfers, "Forecasting Elections: Voter Intentions versus Expectations" (working paper, 2013), http:// users.nber.org/~jwolfers/Papers/VoterExpectations.pdf.

109. Evan Hughes, "Who Will Be the Wrongest Pundit of Them All?" The Awl, November 5, 2012, http://www.theawl.com/2012/11/wholl-be-the-wrongest-pundits-of-them -all; Brad Plumer, "Pundit Accountability: The Official 2012 Election Prediction Thread," *Washington Post*, November 5, 2012, http://www.washingtonpost.com/blogs/wonkblog /wp/2012/11/05/pundit-accountability-the-official-2012-election-prediction-thread/. Sides predicted an Obama victory but was wrong about Florida. See John Sides, "What About Tomorrow's Election Would Prove Me Wrong? (Plus a Prediction)," *The Monkey Cage*, November 5, 2012, http://themonkeycage.org/blog/2012/11/05/what-about-tomorrows -election-would-prove-me-wrong-plus-a-prediction/. Morris would later suggest that his prediction was motivated in part by partisanship, saying that "The Romney campaign was falling apart, people were not optimistic, nobody thought there was a chance of victory, and I felt that it was my duty at that point to go out and say what I said." Erik Ortiz, "In 'Sean Hannity' Appearance, Pundit Dick Morris Defends Prediction of Romney Landslide as Attempt to Boost Conservatives' Hopes," *New York Daily News*, November 13, 2012, http://www.nydailynews.com/news/election-2012/dick-morris-offers- explanation-predicting-romney-landslide-article-1.1201635.

110. Peggy Noonan, "Monday Morning," *Wall Street Journal*, November 5, 2012, http:// blogs.wsj.com/peggynoonan/2012/11/05/monday-morning/.

111. Joe Klein, "I Don't Know," *Time*, October 29, 2012, http://swampland.time.com/ 2012/10/29/i-dont-know/.

Chapter 7: The Winning Hand

1. These quotes are taken, respectively, from: Stuart Stevens, "Mitt Romney: A Good Man. The Right Fight," *Washington Post*, November 28, 2012, http://www.washingtonpost .com/opinions/a-good-man-the-right-fight/2012/11/28/5338b27a-38e9-11e2-8a97-363b0f9 a0ab3_story.html?; John Dickerson, "How Obama Won Four More Years," *Slate*, November 7, 2012, http://www.slate.com/articles/news_and_politics/politics/2012/11/how _obama_won_he_had_a_better_team_that_ran_a_first_rate_campaign.html; Walter Shapiro, "Against Backdrop of Harvard Power Outage, Obama and Romney Power Players Discuss Lessons of 2012 Campaign," Yahoo News, December 3, 2012, http://news .yahoo.com/obama--romney-power-players-discuss-campaign-lessons-despite-harvard -power-outage-215044327.html; Joel Benenson, "Values, Not Demographics, Won the Election," *New York Times*, November 7, 2012, http://www.nytimes.com/2012/11/08 /opinion/obama-won-on-values-not-demographics.html?_r=0, Charlie Cook, "Obama Can Thank Early Negative Ads for His Advantage," *National Journal*, November 1, 2012; http://www.nationaljournal.com/columns/cook-report/obama-can-thank-early-negative -ads-for-his-advantage-20121101; Ashley Parker, "Romney Blames Loss on Obama's 'Gifts' to Minorities and Young Voters," *New York Times*, November 14, 2012, http://thecaucus .blogs.nytimes.com/2012/11/14/romney-blames-loss-on-obamas-gifts-to-minorities-and -young-voters/.

2. These quotes are taken, respectively, from: Michael Kranish, "The story behind Mitt Romney's loss in the presidential campaign to President Obama," *Boston Globe*, December 22, 2012, http://www.boston.com/news/politics/2012/president/2012/12/23/the-story

-behind-mitt-romney-loss-the-presidential-campaign-president-obama/2QWkUB9pJg
VIi1mAcIhQjL/story.html; Ruby Cramer, "Latino Leaders Say They Gave Obama the
Edge," *BuzzFeed*, November 7, 2012, http://www.buzzfeed.com/rubycramer/latino-leaders
-say-they-gave-obama-the-edge; Benjamin Domenech, "The Election and the Night of
the Long Knives," *The Transom*, n.d., http://us1.campaign-archive1.com/?u=c7c578f94365
a99fb2dd164c1&id=57895aaf14&e=0b9061feb5; Ramesh Ponnuru, "The Party's Problem,"
National Review, November 14, 2012, http://www.nationalreview.com/articles/333344/
party-s-problem-ramesh-ponnuru?pg=1#; Jim Geraghty, "The Nasty GOP?" *National Review*, November 20, 2012, http://www.nationalreview.com/articles/333713/nasty-gop-jim
-geraghty?pg=2; Chuck Todd, Mark Murray, Domenico Montanaro, and Brooke Brower,
"First Thoughts: Obama's Demographic Edge," NBC News, November 7, 2012,
http://firstread.nbcnews.com/_news/2012/11/07/14993875-first-thoughts-obamas
-demographic-edge?lite.

3. Mike Allen, "52 Days to Fiscal Cliff—POSTGAMING WITH AXELROD: What He
Missed in His Election Day Bet; '12 'Grittier' than '08; Obama 'Granular' Debate Prep—
D.C., MILITARY IN SHOCK: Fall of Petraeus," *Politico*, November 10, 2012, http://www
.politico.com/playbook/1112/playbook9440.html.

4. Mark Blumenthal, "Obama Campaign Polls: How the Internal Data Got It Right,"
Huffington Post, November 21, 2012, http://www.huffingtonpost.com/2012/11/21/obama
-campaign-polls-2012_n_2171242.html?ncid=edlinkusaolp00000008.

5. John Dickerson, "The Secrets of the 2012 Campaign," *Slate*, December 5, 2012,
http://www.slate.com/articles/news_and_politics/politics/2012/12/harvard_s_campaign
_decision_makers_conference_barack_obama_and_mitt_romney.html.

6. The 2012 outcome was also in line with the election-year trend in real disposable
income. Seth Masket, "I Spent $6 Billion and All I Got Was This Lousy Economic Retro-
spection Election," Mischiefs of Faction, November 7, 2012, http://mischiefsoffaction.blog
spot.com/2012/11/i-spent-6-billion-and-all-i-got-was.html; Larry Bartels, "Obama Toes
the Line," *The Monkey Cage*, January 8, 2013, http://themonkeycage.org/blog/2013/01/08
/obama-toes-the-line/.

7. The forecasting model that we developed for the *Washington Post*, which was
similar to but somewhat simpler than the model in chapter 2, was also quite accurate—
forecasting that Obama would win 51.3% of the major-party vote.

8. The majority of other forecasts of the national popular vote also predicted that
Obama would win. Various forecasts are listed here: Larry J. Sabato, "Forecasting the
Presidential Election: Other Crystal Balls," Sabato's Crystal Ball, September 13, 2012,
http://www.centerforpolitics.org/crystalball/articles/forecasting-the-presidential-election
-other-crystal-balls/. For postmortems from these scholars, see the January 2013 issue of
PS: Political Science and Politics.

9. Robert S. Erikson and Christopher Wlezien, *The Timeline of Presidential Elections*
(Chicago: Chicago University Press, 2012), 114.

10. That a higher percentage of Obama supporters reported not voting is consistent
with other evidence suggesting that likely nonvoters tended to prefer Obama. "Nonvoters: Who They Are, What They Think," Pew Research Center for the People & the Press,
November 1, 2012, http://www.people-press.org/2012/11/01/nonvoters-who-they-are-what
-they-think/.

11. Gallup polls showed a similar trend among Democrats and an equivalent trend
among independents but Gallup did not separate them into independents who lean
Democratic and "pure" independents, as we did. Lydia Saad, "U.S. Economic Confidence

Surged 11 Points Last Week," Gallup, September 11, 2012, http://www.gallup.com/poll
/157385/economic-confidence-surged-points-last-week.aspx/.

12. Among Obama supporters, the convention appeared to be more important than
the actual objective economy. After matching respondents to the change in real disposable income (RDI) that occurred the month they were interviewed, we found that the
effect of changes in RDI on Democrats' economic perceptions was not statistically significant, but the effect of being interviewed at any point after the convention was significant.
That at least some of the economic improvement occurred after the convention makes it
difficult to separate their respective effects, but the trigger seemed to be the convention.
An open question, however, is whether the convention could have had this effect if the
economy itself had continued to slow down.

13. Republicans' economic perceptions also varied with changes in income—more
because the economic slowdown was associated with increasing pessimism among Republicans than because economic improvement was associated with increasing optimism.
Part of the reason may have been the polarizing effect of the Democratic convention and
its aftermath, which was also associated with increasing pessimism.

14. Harry Bradford, "Jack Welch Tweet: Jobs Numbers an Obama Conspiracy [UP-
DATE]," *Huffington Post*, October 5, 2012, http://www.huffingtonpost.com/2012/10/05
/jack-welch-tweet-jobs-numbers_n_1942270.html.

15. Brendan Nyhan, "Political Knowledge Does Not Guard against Belief in Conspiracy Theories," YouGov, November 5, 2012, http://today.yougov.com/news/2012/11/05
/political-knowledge-does-not-guard-against-belief-/.

16. It may seem odd that we present the nation's economy as a fundamental factor
to election outcomes and then show that people's views of the economy depend on their
partisanship. To be clear, in making predictions or forecasts based on the nation's economic conditions, we have relied on objective statistics, not people's subjective assessments of the economy, which are often skewed by partisanship.

17. Mark Blumenthal, "Incumbent Rule Redux," *Huffington Post*, August 14, 2006,
http://www.pollster.com/blogs/incumbent_rule_redux.php?nr=1; Nate Silver, "Do Presidential Polls Break toward Challengers?" FiveThirtyEight/*New York Times*, July 22, 2012,
http://fivethirtyeight.blogs.nytimes.com/2012/07/22/do-presidential-polls-break-toward
-challengers/.

18. About 72% of persuadable Republicans reported voting in the post-election
YouGov survey, compared to 38% of persuadable independents and 57% of persuadable
Democrats.

19. We categorized Colorado, Florida, Iowa, Michigan, North Carolina, New Hampshire, Nevada, Ohio, Pennsylvania, Virginia, and Wisconsin as battleground states.

20. A statistical model of vote choice among persuadable voters—including dummy
variables for partisanship, battleground state, and the interaction of the two—confirmed
that these differences were statistically significant.

21. James E. Campbell, *The American Campaign: U.S. Presidential Campaigns and
the National Vote* (College Station: Texas A&M Press, 2000); Andrew Gelman and Gary
King, "Why Are American Presidential Election Polls So Variable When Votes Are So
Predictable?" *British Journal of Political Science* 23 (1993): 409–51; Larry M. Bartels, *Pres-
idential Primaries and the Dynamics of Public Choice* (Princeton: Princeton University
Press, 1988).

22. In an analysis of YouGov polls that helped inspire ours, Larry Bartels also finds
that, among only undecided voters, the salience of economic perceptions was greatest in

the summer. Larry Bartels, "The Economy and the Campaign," *The Monkey Cage*, January 14, 2013, http://themonkeycage.org/blog/2013/01/14/the-economy-and-the-campaign/.

23. We estimated the same model undergirding Figure 7.4 but separately for battleground states and other states. As an example, the estimated effect of economic evaluations on October vote intentions was b = .25 (s.e. = .12) in battleground states but actually larger in other states (b = .32; s.e. = .10).

24. Andrew Owen, "The Negativity Effect in Retrospective Voting" (Ph.D. diss., Princeton University, 2011).

25. Sasha Issenberg, "How President Obama's Campaign Used Big Data to Rally Individual Voters, Part 3," *MIT Technology Review*, December 18, 2012, http://www.technology review.com/featuredstory/508856/obamas-data-techniques-will-rule-future-elections/.

26. Ashley Parker, "Romney Blames Loss on Obama's 'Gifts' to Minorities and Young Voters," *New York Times*, November 14, 2012, http://thecaucus.blogs.nytimes.com/2012 /11/14/romney-blames-loss-on-obamas-gifts-to-minorities-and-young-voters/.

27. Jack Citrin and Donald Green, "The Self-Interest Motive in American Public Opinion," *Research in Micropolitics* 3 (1990): 1–28.

28. Dennis Cauchon, "In Ohio: Voters Choose Obama as Auto Bailout Resonates," *USA Today*, November 7, 2012, http://www.usatoday.com/story/news/politics/2012/11/06 /ohio-election-results/1658389/. In Ohio in 2008, Obama won about 56% of the vote among exit poll respondents in union households. In Ohio in 2012, according to the initial exit poll estimates, he won 60% of their vote. There were skeptics of the bailout's effect as well. See Nate Cohn, "The Auto Bailout Didn't Decide Ohio," *New Republic*, November 12, 2012, http://www.newrepublic.com/blog/electionate/109972/the-auto-bailout-didnt -decide-ohio#.

29. Dan Hopkins, "The Auto Bailout Didn't Decide the Election," *Washington Post*, December 9, 2012, http://www.washingtonpost.com/blogs/wonkblog/wp/2012/12/09/the -auto-bailout-didnt-decide-the-election/.

30. "'Women's Choices'—Obama for America TV Ad," YouTube, July 26, 2012, http:// www.youtube.com/watch?v=33NT0_MgsVU.

31. Zeke Miller, "Team Obama Celebrates Romney's 'Binders of Women' Line," *Buzz-Feed*, October 17, 2012, http://www.buzzfeed.com/zekejmiller/team-obama-celebrates -romneys-binders-of-women#HTWF2.

32. Karen Kaufmann and John Petrocik, "The Changing Politics of American Men: Understanding the Sources of the Gender Gap," *American Journal of Political Science* 43, no. 3 (1999): 864–87.

33. These data can be found here: "Party Identification 3-Point Scale (revised in 2008) 1952–2008," ANES Guide to Public Opinion and Electoral Behavior, table generated August 5, 2010, http://www.electionstudies.org/nesguide/2ndtable/t2a_2_1.htm.

34. Katha Pollitt, "Hers: The Smurfette Principle," *New York Times*, April 7, 1991, http://www.nytimes.com/1991/04/07/magazine/hers-the-smurfette-principle.html?page wanted=all&src=pm.

35. For more on these items, see John Sides, "The Contraception Contretemps Continues, But Are Americans Paying Attention?" YouGov, March 14, 2012, http://today .yougov.com/news/2012/03/14/contraception-contretemps-continues-are-americans-/. Gender gaps in knowledge about politics are common. Some of this gap may not reflect knowledge but men's greater willingness to guess at an answer. However, even accounting for this willingness, some gender gap remains. See Jeffery J. Mondak and Mary R.

Anderson, "The Knowledge Gap: A Reexamination of Gender-Based Political Knowledge," *Journal of Politics* 66, no. 2 (2004): 492–512.

36. The figure includes mentions of "contraception," "contraception mandate," "contraception coverage mandate," "birth control," "birth control mandate," "abortion," and "rape." Not all of these will be directly related to the campaign, of course, but the data still convey the spikes in coverage of these topics, which were campaign driven.

37. This comes from a statistical model that includes variables capturing gender and battleground state residence, the interaction of the two, and controls for party identification, race, age, and education. The effect of the interaction term is .03, the standard error is .018, and the associated p-value is .09 (two-tailed). We did not find any difference between women who were age 18–44 or 45 and above.

38. According to *Bloomberg Businessweek* reporter Joshua Green, Obama advisor Jim Messina later expressed some uncertainty about the increase in support among Asians—noting that the sample of Asians was small: https://twitter.com/JoshuaGreen/statuses/316616454139150336.

39. Ronald Brownstein, "His Original Sin," *National Journal*, September 21, 2012, http://www.nationaljournal.com/columns/political-connections/mitt-romney-s-original-sin-20120920.

40. "Hope over Experience," *Wall Street Journal*, November 8, 2012, http://online.wsj.com/article/SB10001424052970204349404578102971575770036.html.

41. Julia Preston, "Republicans Reconsider Positions on Immigration," *New York Times*, November 9, 2012, http://www.nytimes.com/2012/11/10/us/politics/republicans-reconsider-positions-on-immigration.html?ref=juliapreston&_r=1&.

42. Jeff Zeleny, "Romney Campaign Manager Says He Regrets Immigration Stance," *New York Times*, December 3, 2012, http://thecaucus.blogs.nytimes.com/2012/12/03/romney-campaign-manager-says-he-regrets-immigration-stance/.

43. Julia Preston and John H. Cushman Jr., "Obama to Permit Young Migrants to Remain in U.S.," *New York Times*, June 15, 2012, http://www.nytimes.com/2012/06/16/us/us-to-stop-deporting-some-illegal-immigrants.html?pagewanted=all&_r=0.

44. Matt Barreto, "New LD Poll Finds Latinos Favor Obama over Romney, Oppose Rubio DREAM," *Latino Decisions*, August 6, 2012, http://www.latinodecisions.com/blog/2012/06/08/new-ld-poll-finds-latinos-favor-obama-over-romney-oppose-rubio-dream/.

45. David L. Leal, Matt A. Barreto, Jongho Lee, and Rodolfo O. de la Garza, "The Latino Vote in the 2004 Election," *PS: Political Science and Politics* 38, no. 1 (2005): 41–49.

46. Gary Segura and Matt Baretto, "How the National Exit Poll Badly Missed the Latino Vote in 2010," *Latino Decisions*, April 11, 2010, http://www.latinodecisions.com/blog/2010/11/04/how-the-national-exit-poll-badly-missed-the-latino-vote-in-2010/.

47. "Latino Battleground States Poll and Turnout Scenarios," *Latino Decisions*, June 27 2012. http://www.latinodecisions.com/files/4013/4083/4006/LD_AV_Battleground_Webinar.pdf

48. "2012 Weekly Political Tracking Poll Week11: Nov5, 2012," *Latino Decisions*, November 5, 2012, http://www.latinodecisions.com/files/5913/5204/1319/Tracker_-_toplines_week_11.pdf; Lydia Saad, "Hispanic Voters Put Other Issues before Immigration," Gallup, June 25, 2012, http://www.gallup.com/poll/155327/hispanic-voters-put-issues-immigration.aspx.

49. Unfortunately our sample of Asian Americans is small and we are hesitant to make much of the results among Asians. We did find, however, that immigration

attitudes were not associated with the vote decisions of Asians—suggesting that the attitudes we measured were more salient to Latinos. For more on the voting behavior of Asian Americans in 2012, see Karthick Ramakrishnan and Taeku Lee, "Asian Americans Voted Democrat: We Should Not Be Surprised," *The Monkey Cage*, November 29, 2012, http://themonkeycage.org/blog/2012/11/29/asian-americans-voted-democrat-we-should -not-be-surprised/.

50. Similarly, in the 2010 election, House members' support for health care reform appeared to drive down their vote share among independents and Republicans, much more than Democrats. See Brendan Nyhan, Eric McGhee, John Sides, Seth Masket, and Steven Greene, "One Vote Out of Step? The Effects of Salience Roll Call Votes in the 2010 Election," *American Politics Research* 40, no. 5 (2012): 844–79.

51. Jessica Holzer, "Romney Offers Explanation for Loss," *Wall Street Journal*, March 3, 2013, http://online.wsj.com/article/SB10001424127887324539404578338622143476406.html.

52. "June 2011 impreMedia/Latino Decisions Tracking Poll Results," *Latino Decisions*, June 2011, http://www.latinodecisions.com/files/4713/4697/3844/June_2011_Tracking.pdf.

53. John Sides, "The 'Is Obama in Trouble with' Stories," *The Monkey Cage*, April 20, 2012, http://themonkeycage.org/blog/2012/04/20/the-is-obama-in-trouble-with-stories/.

54. Yair Ghitza and Andrew Gelman, "Deep Interactions with MRP: Election Turnout and Voting Patterns Among Small Electoral Subgroups." *American Journal of Political Science*, forthcoming. They find that older whites, especially in the South, swung against Obama in 2008 (relative to their vote for Kerry in 2004) whereas most other groups swung in Obama's favor.

55. For a skeptical view, see Eitan D. Hersh and Brian F. Schaffner, "Targeted Campaign Appeals and the Value of Ambiguity," *Journal of Politics* 75, no.2 (2013): 520–34.

56. Jonathan Martin, "The Looming GOP Civil War—Whether Mitt Wins or Not," *Politico*, May 11, 2012, http://www.politico.com/news/stories/1112/83305.html.

57. Simple regressions of the weekly averages on a time trend show this polarization. For perceptions of Obama: $b = -.005$ (*t*-statistic $= -9.2$). For perceptions of Romney: $b = .011$ (*t*-statistic $= 12.9$). The same trend is evident if we compare the respondents who were interviewed in December 2011 and then reinterviewed right before the election: a small shift in perceptions of Obama toward the liberal end of the scale and a larger shift in perceptions of Romney toward the conservative end of the scale.

58. Stephen A. Jessee, "Partisan Bias, Political Information, and Spatial Voting in the 2008 Presidential Election," *Journal of Politics* 72, no. 2 (2010): 327–40.

59. The analysis includes 2,003 pure independents who reported voting in the post-election survey. We calculated their distance from each candidate as the absolute value of the difference between where they located themselves ideologically and where they perceived each candidate to be. Ideological perceptions were measured whenever respondents were interviewed in the weekly surveys before January and November. Vote choices were measured in the November post-election survey. Thus the model assumes that ideological perceptions did not change between the earlier interview and the post-election interview. (We also examined only independent voters interviewed in the last four weeks of the campaign, who were less likely to have changed their ideological perceptions before they voted, and found similar results.) The dependent variable was coded 1-Obama and 0-Romney. The probit coefficients and standard errors were: distance from Obama ($b = -.05$; s.e. $= .002$) and distance from Romney ($b = .03$; s.e. $= .002$). The pseudo-R^2 was .52.

60. Jacob Weisberg, "Why Mitt Lost," *Slate*, November 7, 2012, http://www.slate.com /articles/news_and_politics/the_big_idea/2012/11/why_romney_lost_he_couldn_t _separate_himself_from_the_republican_party_s.html.

61. Thomas B. Edsall, "Making the Election about Race," *New York Times*, August 27, 2012. http://campaignstops.blogs.nytimes.com/2012/08/27/making-the-election-about -race. The welfare ad was titled "Right Choice" (mittromney, "Right Choice" YouTube, August 7 2012). http://www.youtube.com/watch?v=oF4LtTlktmo). The Medicare ad was "You Paid" (mittromney, "Paid In," YouTube, August 14, 2012, http://www.youtube.com /watch?v=l4gPvToKTWU).

62. Seth K. Goldman, "Effects of the 2008 Obama Presidential Campaign on White Racial Prejudice." *Public Opinion Quarterly* 76, no. 4 (2012): 663–87.

63. Michael Tesler and David O. Sears, *Obama's Race, (Chicago: Chicago University Press, 2010)*; Michael Tesler, "The Spillover of Racialization into Health Care: How President Obama Polarized Public Opinion by Racial Attitudes and Race," *American Journal of Political Science* 56, no. 3 (2012): 690–704; Michael Tesler, "The Spillover of Racialization into Evaluations of Bo Obama," YouGov, April 10, 2012, http://today.yougov.com/news /2012/04/10/spillover-racialization-evaluations-bo-obama/; Michael Tesler, "The Return of Old Fashioned Racism to White Americans' Partisan Preferences in the Early Obama Era," *Journal of Politics*, forthcoming.

64. This was true among all registered voters in both surveys and among white registered voters. Our finding is different than one other that suggested a small increase in racial resentment. See Josh Pasek, Jon A. Krosnick, and Trevor Thompson, "The Impact of Anti-Black Racism on Approval of Barack Obama's Job Performance and on Voting in the 2012 Presidential Election" (working paper, 2012), http://www.stanford.edu/dept /communication/faculty/krosnick/docs/2012/2012%20Voting%20and%20Racism.pdf. However, given that there were differences between the YouGov surveys and these other surveys, including in their exact timing and details of the methodology, these two sets of results are not necessarily diametrically opposed. The upshot in either case is that levels of racial resentment changed very little between 2008 and 2012.

65. The difference in the coefficients for racial resentment in 2008 and 2012 was close to conventional definitions of statistical significance ($p = .07$, two-tailed).

66. These estimates were derived from keeping all other characteristics of individuals that were represented in the model to their observed values for those individuals and changing only racial resentment. These estimates are also similar to those in Pasek, Krosnick, and Tompson, "The Impact of Anti-Black Racism." They found that moving all respondents to the neutral point increased Obama's vote share by 2 points, while moving only respondents with unfavorable attitudes to the neutral point increased his vote share by 4 points.

67. Simon Jackman and Lynn Vavreck, "How Does Obama Match Up? Counterfactuals and the Role of Obama's Race in 2008" (working paper, 2011), http://jackman .stanford.edu/papers/download.php?i=0.

68. David E. Campbell, John C. Green, and J. Quin Monson, "The Stained Glass Ceiling: Social Contact and Mitt Romney's 'Religion Problem,'" *Political Behavior* 34, no. 2 (2012): 277–300.

69. Jeffrey M. Jones, "Atheists, Muslims See Most Bias as Presidential Candidates," Gallup, June 21, 2012, http://www.gallup.com/poll/155285/Atheists-Muslims-Bias -Presidential-Candidates.aspx.

70. David T. Smith, "The Mormon Dilemma: Causes and Consequences of Anti-Mormonism in the 2012 Elections" (working paper, 2012), http://ussc.edu.au/ussc/assets/media/docs/publications/1206_Smith_Mormons.pdf.

71. On news coverage, see Erika Fry, "Romney and the 'Mormon Moment,'" *Columbia Journalism Review*, March 2, 2012, http://www.cjr.org/campaign_desk/romney_and_the_mormon_moment.php?page=all.

72. Ben Smith and Jonathan Martin, "Obama Plan: Destroy Romney," *Politico*, September 8, 2011, http://www.politico.com/news/stories/0811/60921.html#ixzz2Ms4H9e7J.

73. McKay Coppins, "A Mormon Reporter on the Romney Bus," November 14, 2012, http://www.buzzfeed.com/mckaycoppins/a-mormon-reporter-on-the-romney-bus.

74. Franklin Graham, "Can an Evangelical Christian Vote for a Mormon?" *Decision Magazine* (Billy Graham Evangelistic Association), October 22, 2012, http://www.billygraham.org/articlepage.asp?articleid=8998.

75. "Election 2012 Post Mortem: White Evangelicals and Support for Romney," Pew Research Center for the People & the Press, December 7, 2012, http://www.pewforum.org/Politics-and-Elections/Election-2012-Post-Mortem--White-Evangelicals-and-Support-for-Romney.aspx.

76. "Little Voter Discomfort with Romney's Mormon Religion," Pew Research Center for the People & the Press, July 26, 2012, http://www.pewforum.org/uploadedFiles/Topics/Issues/Politics_and_Elections/Little-Voter-Discomfort%20-Full.pdf.

77. See their forthcoming book, *Seeking the Promised Land: Mormons and American Politics* (Cambridge University Press).

78. Campbell, Green, and Monson do find that attitudes toward Mormons have become more polarized by party over time, suggesting that Romney's prominence was helping shift attitudes toward Mormons. See *Seeking the Promised Land*.

79. We examined the relationship between attitudes toward Mormons and voter choice a second way: by considering only those who were undecided or preferred a third-party candidate in December but ended up reporting a vote for Obama or Romney. In essence, we modeled what led them to change their mind and settle on a candidate. Among these voters, the effect of attitudes toward Mormons was not statistically significant.

80. Campbell, Green, and Monson arrive at the same conclusion in their analysis of the 2012 election.

81. Ruth Marcus, "Is Romney Likable Enough to Win?" *Washington Post*, August 28, 2012, http://articles.washingtonpost.com/2012-08-28/opinions/35490818_1_likability-gap-romney-campaign-mitt-romney.

82. Daniel Foster, "The Rehabilitation of Romney," *National Review*, November 16, 2012, http://www.nationalreview.com/articles/333538/rehabilitation-romney-daniel-foster.

83. Jay Cost, "After the Tumult and the Shouting," *Weekly Standard* 8, no. 12 (December 3, 2012), http://www.weeklystandard.com/articles/after-tumult-and-shouting_663841.html?nopager=1. The other traits mentioned in the exit poll question were "shares my values," "strong leader," and "vision for the future." Romney won more votes than Obama among respondents who chose one of these other traits as the most important.

84. This possibility is anticipated by various social science studies. For example, see Wendy M. Rahn, Jon A. Krosnick, and Marijke Breuning, "Rationalization and Derivation Processes in Survey Studies of Political Candidate Evaluation," *American Journal of Political Science* 38, no. 3 (1994): 582–600.

85. In the Pollster averages of the candidate favorability ratings, 47% evaluated Romney favorably and 47% unfavorably. The comparable percentages for Obama were 49%

and 46%. Based on YouGov data, Romney also narrowed the gap in terms of likability and sincerity (whether the candidate believes what he says or says what he thinks people want to hear). Regressions of these indicators on a simple time trend show little to no trend for Obama but a significant positive trend for Romney.

86. Larry Bartels, "The Impact of Candidate Traits in American Presidential Elections," in Anthony King, ed., *Leaders' Personalities and the Outcomes of Democratic Elections* (Oxford: Oxford University Press, 2002).

87. Adam Nagouarney, Jim Rutenberg, and Jeff Zeleny, "Near-Flawless Run Is Credited in Victory," *New York Times*, November 5, 2008, http://www.nytimes.com/2008/11/05/us/politics/05recon.html?pagewanted=print&_r=0.

88. John Dickerson, "How Obama Won Four More Years," *Slate*, November 7, 2012, http://www.slate.com/articles/news_and_politics/politics/2012/11/how_obama_won_he_had_a_better_team_that_ran_a_first_rate_campaign.html.

89. This is spelled out in more detail in Sasha Issenberg, *The Victory Lab* (New York: Crown, 2012). See also Sasha Issenberg, "Obama Does It Better," *Slate*, October 29, 2012, http://www.slate.com/articles/news_and_politics/victory_lab/2012/10/obama_s_secret_weapon_democrats_have_a_massive_advantage_in_targeting_and.single.html.

90. Obama's advantage was also noticed by media outlets. See John Avlon and Michael Keller, "Ground Game: Obama Campaign Opens Up a Big Lead in Field Offices," *The Daily Beast*, October 19, 2012, http://www.thedailybeast.com/articles/2012/10/19/ground-game-obama-campaign-opens-up-a-big-lead-in-field-offices.html

91. For more on the placement of field offices, see Joshua Darr and Matthew Levendusky, "Relying on the Ground Game: The Placement and Effect of Campaign Field Offices" (working paper, 2013).

92. Molly Ball, "Obama's Edge: The Ground Game That Could Put Him over the Top," *The Atlantic*, October 24, 2012, http://www.theatlantic.com/politics/archive/2012/10/obamas-edge-the-ground-game-that-could-put-him-over-the-top/264031/. For a similar portrait from Ohio in particular, see Monica Davey and Michael Wines, "Getting Out the Ohio Vote, Campaigns Are a Study in Contrasts," *New York Times*, November 3, 2012, http://www.nytimes.com/2012/11/04/us/politics/in-ohio-2-campaigns-offer-a-study-in-contrasts.html?hp&_r=0.

93. This is based on the effects of October advertising in all counties in the continental United States. See Michael M. Franz and Travis N. Ridout, "Political Advertising and Persuasion in the 2004 and 2008 Presidential Elections," *American Politics Research* 38, no. 2 (2010): 303–29.

94. Seth E. Masket, "Did Obama's Ground Game Matter? The Influence of Local Field Offices during the 2008 Presidential Election," *Public Opinion Quarterly* 73, no.4 (2009): 1023–39; Darr and Levendusky, "Relying on the Ground Game."

95. John McCormick, "Axelrod Shares His Romney Campaign Surprises," Bloomberg, November 27, 2012, http://go.bloomberg.com/political-capital/2012-11-27/axelrod-shares-his-romney-campaign-surprises/.

96. The apparent effect of placing a single Obama field office in a county is 0.27 points, as reported in the appendix. The apparent effect of a one ad per capita advantage in advertising on the day before the election was 0.09 points. Thus a three-ad advantage is estimated to increase vote share by about 0.27 points.

97. Two other pieces of evidence give us some confidence in our results. First, we found that the change in the presence of Obama field offices between 2008 and 2012 was associated with changes in vote share: in counties that had Obama offices in 2012 but not

in 2008, Obama did better in 2012 than in 2008. Second, the location of Obama's 2012 field offices was not significantly related to his 2008 vote share once other factors were taken into account. Such a relationship would suggest that there were other factors we did not account for, since Obama's 2012 field offices should not predict his vote share four years earlier. Similar evidence is presented in Darr and Levendusky, "Relying on the Ground Game."

98. Darr and Levendusky, "Relying on the Ground Game."

99. Masket, "Did Obama's Ground Game Matter?"

100. Alan Wirzbicki, "Obama Won Ohio with Ground Game," *Boston Globe*, November 9, 2012, http://www.bostonglobe.com/news/politics/2012/11/09/why-president-obama -ground-game-came-through-clutch/857077FGHaCPei6hRfXnbP/story.html.

101. For example, one investigation of voter mobilization by MoveOn.org in the 2004 presidential election found that turnout increased 9 points among those contacted by a MoveOn canvasser. See Joel A. Middleton and Donald P. Green, "Do Community-Based Voter Mobilization Campaigns Work Even in Battleground States? Evaluating the Effectiveness of MoveOn's 2004 Outreach Campaign," *Quarterly Journal of Political Science* 3 (2008): 63–82.

102. Karen Tumulty, "In Battleground Virginia, a Tale of Two Ground Games," *Time*, October 12, 2008, http://www.time.com/time/politics/article/0,8599,1849422,00.html.

103. In the appendix to this chapter, we show that the effect of a 1 ad per capita imbalance was equivalent to an additional 0.09 points of vote share. Thus, a 27 ad per capita advantage would equal 2.4 points of vote share ($27 \times .09 = 2.4$).

104. The effect of a 1 ad per capita imbalance in the previous five days is equivalent to .004 points of vote share. Thus, a 10 ad per capita advantage on each of these five days would translate into a 50 ad per capita advantage, or .2 points of vote share. A 24 ad per capita advantage on the final day would net approximately 2.2 points. The combination—2.2 + .2 = 2.4—would equal the impact of the economy on Obama's vote share.

105. Matthew Dowd, "The Mythic Narrative of the 2012 Election," *National Journal*, November 19, 2012, http://www.nationaljournal.com/politics/the-mythic-narrative-of-the -2012-election-20121119.

106. Michael Gerson and Peter Wehner, "How to Save the Republican Party," *Commentary Magazine*, March 2013, http://www.commentarymagazine.com/article/how-to -save-the-republican-party/.

Chapter 8: Cashing In

1. Molly Ball, "Down and Out with Ted Cruz and the GOP," *Atlantic Monthly*, November 30, 2012, http://www.theatlantic.com/politics/archive/2012/11/down-and-out-with -ted-cruz-and-the-gop/265767/; Elizabeth Mendes, "Republicans' Life Ratings Plunge, Democrats' Improve," *Gallup*, December 19, 2012, http://www.gallup.com/poll/159377 /republicans-life-ratings-plunge-democrats-improve.aspx. The *Politico* articles are collected here: http://www.politico.com/tag/gop-civil-war.

2. Paul Krugman, "The Obama Agenda," *New York Times*, November 8, 2008, http:// www.nytimes.com/2008/11/07/opinion/07krugman.html.

3. John B. Judis, "America the Liberal," *The New Republic*, November 19, 2008, http:// www.tnr.com/article/politics/america-the-liberal; John B. Judis, "The Unnecessary Fall: A Counter-History of the Obama Presidency," *The New Republic*, August 12, 2010, http:// www.tnr.com/article/politics/magazine/76972/obama-failure-polls-populism-recession

-health-care. These pieces are quoted in Larry Bartels, "Political Effects of the Great Recession" (Vanderbilt University working paper, 2013).

4. Paul Krugman, "The Real Referendum," *New York Times*, September 30, 2012, http://www.nytimes.com/2012/10/01/opinion/krugman-the-real-referendum.html .

5. Bob Moser, "Obama Wins the Future," *The American Prospect*, November 7, 2012, http://prospect.org/article/obama-wins-future.

6. Ben Smith and Zeke Miller, "Welcome to Liberal America," *BuzzFeed*, November 7, 2012, http://www.buzzfeed.com/bensmith/welcome-to-liberal-america.

7. Gabriel S. Lenz, "Learning and Opinion Change, Not Priming: Reconsidering the Priming Hypothesis," *American Journal of Political Science* 53, no. 4 (2009): 821–37.

8. This measure was created by political scientist James Stimson. For more details, see his *Public Opinion in America: Moods, Swings, and Cycles* (Boulder, CO: Westview Press, 1991). The data are here: http://www.unc.edu/~cogginse/Policy_Mood.html. On public opinion as a thermostat, see Christopher Wlezien, "The Public as Thermostat: Dynamics of Preferences for Spending," *American Journal of Political Science* 39, no. 4 (1995): 981–1000.

9. Lawrence Grossback, David Peterson, and James Stimson, *Mandate Politics* (New York: Cambridge University Press, 2006).

10. Luke Johnson, "Paul Ryan: No Obama Mandate Because Republicans Control House," *Huffington Post*, November 14, 2012, http://www.huffingtonpost.com/2012/11/13/paul-ryan-obama-mandate-house_n_2125635.html.

11. Michael Lind, "1896 and 2004," Talking Points Memo, August 11, 2005, http://web.archive.org/web/20070102013901/http://www.tpmcafe.com/story/2005/8/11/131457/415.

12. Michael Lind, "Obama and the Dawn of the Fourth Republic," *Salon*, November 7, 2008, http://www.salon.com/2008/11/07/fourth_republic/.

13. John Judis and Ruy Teixeira, *The Emerging Democratic Majority* (New York: Scribner, 2002); Judis, "America the Liberal."

14. John Judis, "The Ecstasy and Agonies of a Permanent Democratic Majority," *The New Republic*, November 16, 2012, http://www.newrepublic.com/article/politics/magazine/110222/the-ecstasy-and-agonies-permanent-democratic-majority. A similar sentiment is expressed by Ruy Teixeira and John Halpin in "The Return of the Obama Coalition," Center for American Progress, November 8, 2012, http://www.americanprogress.org/issues/progressive-movement/news/2012/11/08/44348/the-return-of-the-obama-coalition/.

15. An excellent overview and critique of the concept is David Mayhew, *Electoral Realignments: A Critique of an American Genre* (New Haven: Yale University Press, 2002). His view echoes that of Edward G. Carmines and James A. Stimson, *Issue Evolution: Race and the Transformation of American Politics* (Princeton: Princeton University Press, 1989). See also Sean Trende, *The Lost Majority* (New York: Palgrave Macmillan, 2012).

16. Larry M. Bartels, "Electoral Continuity and Change, 1868–1996," *Electoral Studies* 17, no. 3 (1998): 301–26.

17. Ibid., 319.

18. Judis and Teixeira, *The Emerging Democratic Majority*, 31, 34.

19. Ruy Teixeira, "Public Opinion Watch," Center for American Progress, November 10, 2004, http://www.americanprogress.org/issues/public-opinion/news/2004/11/10/1189/public-opinion-watch/.

20. Judis, "The Ecstasy and Agonies."

21. Ibid. Judis blames gerrymandering for the Republicans' ability to retain the majority in the House in the 2012 election. However, more careful analysis suggests that gerry-

mandering might have won the Republicans a handful of seats at most and likely fewer. See John Sides and Eric McGhee, "Redistricting Didn't Win Republicans the House," Wonkblog, February 17, 2013, http://www.washingtonpost.com/blogs/wonkblog/wp/2013 /02/17/redistricting-didnt-win-republicans-the-house/.

22. Ruy Teixeira, "Is the Obama Majority Here to Stay?" ThinkProgress, April 5, 2013, http://thinkprogress.org/election/2013/04/05/1826221/obama-majority/?mobile=nc.

23. David O. Sears and Carolyn L. Funk, "Evidence of the Long-Term Persistence of Adults' Political Predispositions," *Journal of Politics* 61, no. 1 (1999): 1–28; Jessica Durando, "Poll: College, High Schools Students Favor Obama," American University, November 1, 2012, http://www.american.edu/media/news/20121101_poll_obama_romney.cfm. See also these data from the Pew Research Center for the People & the Press: http://www.people -press.org/2011/11/03/the-generation-gap-and-the-2012-election-3/11-3-11-17/.

24. See slide 18 in this presentation of data from the 2012 NAACP Battleground Poll: http://www.slideshare.net/JamiahAdams/naacp-2012-battleground-poll-15102981.

25. The January 2012 poll is here: http://www.latinodecisions.com/files/1213/4698/9186 /Univision_Florida_2012.pdf. The exit poll is here: http://www.latinodecisions.com/files /9313/5233/8455/Latino_Election_Eve_Poll_-_Crosstabs.pdf.

26. Mayhew, *Electoral Realignments*, 148.

27. One compendium of conflicting advice was compiled by Benjy Sarlin and Evan McMorris-Santoro, "One Month Later: 30 Post-Election Rebuilding Tips from Republicans," Talking Points Memo, December 6, 2012, http://tpmdc.talkingpointsmemo.com /2012/12/republican-post-election-advice-2016-gop-romney.php.

28. Craig Gilbert, "Ryan: 'We're Going to Beat Him,'" *Milwaukee Journal-Sentinel*, September 23, 2012, http://www.jsonline.com/news/statepolitics/ryan-were-going-to-beat -him-il6vfi7-170909701.html.

29. Good examples are found throughout Robert Draper's piece "Can the Republicans Be Saved from Obsolescence?" *New York Times Magazine*, February 14, 2013, http://www. nytimes.com/2013/02/17/magazine/can-the-republicans-be-saved-from-obsolescence.html.

30. John Zaller, "Monica Lewinsky and the Mainsprings of American Politics," in W. Lance Bennett and Robert M. Entman, eds., *Mediated Politics: Communication in the Future of Democracy* (New York: Cambridge University Press, 2001), 252–78; Brandice Canes-Wrone, David W. Brady, and John F. Cogan, "Out of Step, Out of Office: Electoral Accountability and House Members' Voting," *American Political Science Review* 96, no. 1 (2002): 127–40.

31. Martin Cohen, David Karol, Hans Noel, and John Zaller, *The Party Decides: Presidential Nomination Before and After Reform* (Chicago: Chicago University Press, 2008).

32. Zerlina Maxwell, "Bill Burton behind the Super PAC That Succeeded: Priorities USA," The Grio, November 14, 2012, http://thegrio.com/2012/11/14/bill-burton-behind -the-super-pac-that-succeeded-priorities-usa/.

33. Dylan Byers and Mackenzie Weinger, "Media Stumped by 2012 Outcome," *Politico*, October 31, 2012, http://www.politico.com/news/stories/1012/83107.html#ixzz2 OVwMngH6.

34. John Sides, "The Track Record of Pre-election Polls (in 2 Graphs)," *The Monkey Cage*, October 29, 2012, http://themonkeycage.org/blog/2012/10/29/the-track-record-of -pre-election-polls-in-2-graphs/. See also Robert Erikson and Karl Sigman, "How Biased Do the Polls Need to Be for Romney to Win?" *The Monkey Cage*, November 5, 2012, http://themonkeycage.org/blog/2012/11/05/how-biased-do-the-polls-need-to-be-for -romney-to-win/.

35. Andrew Rosenthal, "The First Presidential Debate," *New York Times*, Taking Note blog, October 3, 2012, http://takingnote.blogs.nytimes.com/2012/10/03/the-first -presidential-debate/.

Appendix to Chapter 2

1. "Obama Job Approval," Huffpost Politics, http://elections.huffingtonpost.com /pollster/obama-job-approval.

2. Paul Brace and Barbara Hinckley, "The Structure of Presidential Approval: Constraints within and across Presidencies," *Journal of Politics* 53, no. 4 (1991): 993–1017; Paul Gronke and John Brehm, "History, Heterogeneity, and Presidential Approval: A Modified ARCH Approach," *Electoral Studies* 21 (2002): 425–52; Douglas Kriner and Liam Schwartz, "Partisan Dynamics and the Volatility of Presidential Approval," *British Journal of Political Science* 39 (2009): 609–31.

3. The coding of Watergate and the Vietnam War matched Kriner and Schwartz, "Partisan Dynamics."

4. Stephen P. Nicholson, Gary M. Segura, and Nathan D. Woods, "Presidential Approval and the Mixed Blessing of Divided Government," *Journal of Politics* 64, no. 3 (2002): 701–20. We thank Patrick Kennedy for suggesting the inclusion of this variable and for his other comments on this analysis.

5. Many features of this model are based on D. Roderick Kiewiet and Douglas Rivers, "The Economic Basis of Reagan's Appeal," in John E. Chubb and Paul E. Peterson, eds., *The New Direction in American Politics* (Washington, DC: Brookings Institute Press, 1985).

6. One study that uses this measure is Michael Tesler and David O. Sears, *Obama's Race: The 2008 Election and the Dream of a Post-Racial America* (Chicago: University of Chicago Press, 2010). One recent critique of this measure is provided by Edward G. Carmines, Paul M. Sniderman, and Beth C. Easter, "On the Meaning, Measurement, and Implications of Racial Resentment," *Annals of the American Academy of Political and Social Science* 634 (2011): 98–116.

Appendix to Chapter 3

1. Further information is here: http://www.journalism.org/commentary_back grounder/About+Campaign+2012+in+the+Media+.

2. See Daniel Hopkins and Gary King, "A Method of Automated Nonparametric Content Analysis for Social Science," *American Journal of Political Science* 54, no. 1 (2010): 229–47.

3. In technical terms, we chose a low bandwidth for the lowess smoother (equal to 0.1).

4. We examined the fit statistics provided by the "varsoc" command in the statistical software package Stata.

Appendix to Chapter 4

1. See Seth Hill, James Lo, Lynn Vavreck, and John Zaller, "How Quickly We Forget: The Duration of Persuasion Effects from Mass Communication," *Political Communication*, forthcoming.

2. These results were robust to including some other individual-level characteristics in the model, including gender, age, Tea Party membership, education, identification as an evangelical, and income.

3. It was also possible that Romney's favorability suffered in place with more anti-*Gingrich* ads—through a sort of backlash effect whereby voters punished Romney for airing negative ads. However, we found no such effect, perhaps because so much of the anti-Gingrich advertising came from Restore Our Future and did not have Romney's name attached.

Appendix to Chapter 7

1. This was the case here. Consider a model on the entire January–November sample as a whole, including a control for party identification. When we employed only economic perceptions as measured during the campaign, the association with vote intentions was stronger than when we employed the instrumented version (b = 0.65 vs. b = 0.44).

2. For a similar modeling approach, see Simon Jackman and Lynn Vavreck, "Primary Politics: The Effects of Gender, Age, and Race in the 2008 Democratic Primary," *Journal of Elections, Public Opinion, and Parties*, 20, no. 2 (2010): 153–86.

3. Michael J. Hanmer and Kerem Ozan Kalkan, "Behind the Curve: Clarifying the Best Approach to Calculating Predicted Probabilities and Marginal Effects from Limited Dependent Variable Models," *American Journal of Political Science* 57, no. 1 (2012): 263–77.

4. See Christopher H. Achen, *Interpreting and Using Regression* (Thousand Oaks, CA: Sage, 1982), 71–73.

5. Further details about the 2008 survey can be found in Simon Jackman and Lynn Vavreck, "Primary Politics: Race, Gender and Age in the 2008 Democratic Primary," *Journal of Elections, Public Opinion and Parties* 20, no. 2 (2010): 153–86.

INDEX

Note: Page numbers followed by "f" or "t" indicate figures and tables, respectively.